NEW YORK REVIEW BOOKS
CLASSICS

W9-CSP-987

THE KINDNESS OF STRANGERS

SALKA VIERTEL (1889–1978) was born Salomea Sara Steuermann in Sambor, a city in present-day Ukraine, where her father was the first Jewish mayor. In her youth she had a successful career onstage, marrying the director Berthold Viertel in 1918. The couple had three sons before moving to Los Angeles in 1928, when Berthold was asked to write a screenplay for F. W. Murnau. That winter, Salka met Greta Garbo. The two would become close friends, with Viertel appearing alongside Garbo in *Anna Christie* (1930) and co-writing a number of the actor's 1930s films, including *Queen Christina* (1933) and *Anna Karenina* (1935). Viertel was active in the European Film Fund, which was designed to provide European artists with Hollywood jobs and American visas during the war years, and she and Berthold hosted star-studded salons at their house in Santa Monica. They divorced in 1947, and Berthold returned to Vienna. She remained in California until pressure from the FBI over her associations with alleged communists led her to return to Europe. She died in Switzerland.

LAWRENCE WESCHLER, the grandson of the émigré composer Ernst Toch, is a former staff writer at *The New Yorker* and director emeritus of the New York Institute for the Humanities at NYU. Among his books are *Vermeer in Bosnia*, *Mr. Wilson's Cabinet of Wonder*, and *Seeing Is Forgetting the Name of the Thing One Sees*. His biographical memoir of Oliver Sacks will be published in 2019.

DONNA RIFKIND is a book critic whose reviews appear in *The New York Times*, *The Wall Street Journal*, *The Washington Post*, and other publications. Her biography of Salka Viertel is forthcoming in 2020.

THE KINDNESS OF STRANGERS

SALKA VIERTEL

Introduction by
LAWRENCE WESCHLER

Afterword by
DONNA RIFKIND

NEW YORK REVIEW BOOKS

New York

THIS IS A NEW YORK REVIEW BOOK
PUBLISHED BY THE NEW YORK REVIEW OF BOOKS
435 Hudson Street, New York, NY 10014
www.nyrb.com

Library of Congress Cataloging-in-Publication Data
Names: Viertel, Salka, author.
Title: The kindness of strangers / by Salka Viertel ; introduction by Lawrence Weschler.
Description: New York : New York Review Books, 2019. | Series: New York Review
  Books classics
Identifiers: LCCN 2018019340| ISBN 9781681372747 (paperback) | ISBN
  9781681372754 (epub)
Subjects: LCSH: Viertel, Salka. | Screenwriters—United States—Biography. | BISAC:
  BIOGRAPHY & AUTOBIOGRAPHY / Entertainment & Performing Arts. |
  BIOGRAPHY & AUTOBIOGRAPHY / Personal Memoirs.
Classification: LCC PN2287.V47 A3 2019 | DDC 812/.52 [B] —dc23
LC record available at https://lccn.loc.gov/2018019340

ISBN 978-1-68137-274-7
Available as an electronic book; ISBN 978-1-68137-275-4

Printed in the United States of America on acid-free paper.
10 9 8 7 6 5 4 3 2 1

INTRODUCTION

NOWADAYS THE TITLE reads not only as tepid and banal but as distinctly unrepresentative of the ensuing narrative's principal themes and contours. In fairness, when the onetime Austro-Hungarian actress and subsequently Hollywood scenarist Salka Viertel first began auditioning the phrase "the kindness of strangers" for the title of her memoir in progress, back in the mid-1950s, as her forthcoming biographer Donna Rifkind has pointed out, the words were not nearly as hackneyed as they are today. (The sensational play *A Streetcar Named Desire*, from which they sprang, was only a few years old, having premiered in 1947; the film had only been released in 1951; and the primary chestnut to have emerged from the latter was Stanley's bloodcurdling scream of "Stella! Stelllaaaa!" and not so much Blanche's breathy Southern belle protestations of having always re*lied* on the *kind*ness of *stran*gers.) Salka's husband, the internationally acclaimed theater director Berthold Viertel, had been translating their friend Tennessee Williams's plays for some years already and staging them all over Europe, and perhaps Salka savored the nod in the young playwright's direction. Such selfless generosity, indeed such kindness on her own part, would have been just like her.

But set aside the book's title and turn, instead, to the text, which gleams with a canny freshness from its first mischievous sentences:

Long, long ago, when I was very young, a gypsy woman said to me that I would escape heartbreak and misfortune as long as I lived close to water. I know that it is rather trite to begin a story with prophecies, especially when they are made by gypsies, but luckily this prediction did not come true.

That first sly upending of readerly expectations anticipates all the other upendings that will come to characterize our protagonist's life course, but at this early stage of the narrative, she only goes on to admit that "It was utterly irrelevant as far as the happiness or misery in my life was concerned, how near or how distant I might be to a body of water." Still, she concedes how often her own "inner storms would subside when I looked at the crested waves of the Pacific or listened to the murmur of an Alpine brook," and that in addition the gypsy's mention of water "evoked the landscape of my childhood and the house near the river, where I lived and grew up."

And thus by the end of that first paragraph, we arrive, by way of a gracefully commodious vicus of recirculation, at Sambor, the small town by the banks of the Dniester River (only just emerging "young and wild" from the Carpathian mountains to the immediate west) in Polish, though at the time Austro-Hungarian, Galicia (and, actually, since the Second World War on the far western edge of the Soviet and subsequently independent Ukraine), where Salka was born in 1889, the eldest of the four children of Auguste and Josef Steuermann, a barrister who, following the turn of the twentieth century, began serving as this polyglot and marvelously jumbled town's first Jewish mayor, as he would for decades to come.

The Steuermann progeny would prove prodigiously accomplished in the years ahead. In addition to Salka, there came, in order, Rose, an eminent actress in her own right in pre– and post–First World War Austrian and German theaters, who would marry the immensely successful theater man Josef Gielen, fleeing with him to South America during the Hitler years though returning to Europe for further successes at the end of the Second World War (their son, Michael, going on to prove one of the most prominent Austrian avant-garde composers and conductors during the fifties and sixties); Edward, a pianist and celebrated acolyte of Arnold Schoenberg and his followers, who among many other sterling accomplishments, both in Europe and America, would shepherd and premiere the master's *Pierrot lunaire*; and finally Zygmunt (universally known as "Dusko"), the runt of the litter, who went on, improbably, to interwar stardom as a professional soccer player.

The first third or so of Salka's book unfurls across pre-Hitlerian Europe, from an improbably idyllic evocation of her Galician home and family life (not yet particularly marked by intimations of virulent anti-Semitism), through accounts of her own headstrong determination, in the face of parental resistance, to pursue a career in the theater and her early successes in that regard (under the name Salome Steuermann) across the regional capitals of late-imperial Austro-Hungary before the outbreak of the First World War. She then goes on to vividly render the desolations of the war itself, especially on the home front—a horrific period to some degree leavened for Salka by her courtship and 1918 marriage to the vividly charismatic poet and director Berthold Viertel—and following that, the couple's triumphant sweep through the various centers of postwar Weimar-era Austrian and German cultural ferment.

Salka displays an exceptional talent for conjuring highly visual, almost cinematic scenes in her accounts of those early years—thus, for example, from when she was a young aspiring actress in Vienna:

> Returning from the theater through the brightly lit Kaerntner-strasse with its elegant shopwindows, noisy traffic and hurrying crowds, I would cross the Graben and plunge suddenly into the darkness of a deserted, cobbled *gasse* which had not changed in four hundred years. As in all Viennese houses, doors were locked at night. I had to ring the bell and wait until the *Hausmeister* emerged from his squalid basement lodging, shuffling and coughing, to take his Charon's toll of ten *Kreuzer* and hand me a tiny candle. My weird shadow darkening the walls, I ran as fast as I could up the endless stone steps of the spiral staircase, praying that the candle would last to the fourth floor.*

No less impressive is Salka's flair for rendering character (Berthold's close friend and idol Karl Kraus, her own early mentor Max Reinhardt) and incident (notably, a close call on the casting couch, which, alas, reads

---

*Such passages give one to wonder whether it was precisely this capacity for succinct visu-alization that so excellently fitted Salka for the screenwriting career to come, or whether, conversely, her late-life recollections of those earlier years got recast and colored precisely by way of the scenarist efforts of the intervening decades.

nowadays as disconcertingly pertinent), all of which she feathers into an eventful bohemian narrative that somehow makes room for the charms of early motherhood, with the arrival of the couple's three sons, Hans, Peter, and Thomas.

For many readers, however, it may only be with the couple's arrival in America (and in Hollywood in particular) that the singular fascination of Salka's narrative really ramps up. Strictly speaking, the Viertels were not part of the Hitlerian émigré tide with which they would come to be so distinctively associated. They'd already arrived in Hollywood in 1928, part of an earlier surge of distinguished European theater and film folk that greeted the arrival of sound in the movies. It was thought that such distinguished European theatrical eminences—the likes of Erich von Stroheim, F. W. Murnau, William Dieterle, and, yes, Berthold Viertel himself—might help guide silent actors into the new aural era. For that matter, in those early years, Hollywood studios regularly experimented with making foreign versions of their local successes.

Indeed, it was in the course of one such effort, MGM's German-language remake of their hit rendition of Eugene O'Neill's *Anna Christie*, starring (in both versions) the luminous Greta Garbo in her first spoken roles, that Salka's friendship with the young star really blossomed: Brought on to play the role of the prostitute Marthy opposite the glamorous lead, Salka was in addition assigned the task of coaching the ravishing Swede's German elocution.

Salka's once vital career as a lead theatrical actress wilted precipitously in her transplanted California environs (she was deemed too old and not beautiful enough, and never really took to the chopped-up pace of film acting, which got to feeling, as she writes, "like drinking from an eyedropper"). Nevertheless, she segued effortlessly into a reader, reviewer, scout, and presently developer and co-writer of original scripts for MGM. And she worked especially closely with Garbo, beginning with the 1933 production of *Queen Christina*, the Rouben Mamoulian–directed vehicle in which Garbo starred opposite John Gilbert as the headstrong, tomboyish, somewhat gender-fluid (as we might now characterize matters) new queen of Sweden. In one of Salka's frequently jaw-dropping asides, she notes that she and Garbo had preferred a newly arrived rookie thespian from London, one Laurence Olivier, for the part of the queen's paramour, but his acting chops were not deemed up to snuff by the all-knowing studio brass.

Berthold by contrast had a more difficult time adapting to the Hollywood studio system, especially after the eminence of his Continental career. He and Salka had originally envisioned a professional sojourn of just a few years in California, but owing to the deteriorating political conditions back home, they kept extending their stay, until by 1933, with Hitler's rise to power, they became de facto émigrés after all. Still, although they had established an idyllic if modest new homestead on Mabery Road, overlooking the Pacific in Santa Monica, Berthold grew increasingly restless. He launched out on ever more extended theatrical ventures to New York and Paris and London—the latter being where he teamed up with scenarist Christopher Isherwood for a 1934 film version of *Little Friend*, the story of a young girl's reckoning with her parents' divorce. That production, staffed by all manner of suddenly fleeing émigrés, would years later prove the basis for Isherwood's short memoiristic novel *Prater Violet*, in which the Englishman described the film's director, in his relations with the supervising studio, as "a lion molested by fleas."

As it happens, my own grandfather, the eminent Weimar-era Austrian modernist composer Ernst Toch, provided the score for that London production—a way station on his own eventual progress to Hollywood. There, owing to the perceived spikiness of his compositional style, he was typecast as a specialist in chase scenes (Shirley Temple's sleigh ride in *Heidi*) and horror effects (the Hallelujah Chorus in Charles Laughton's *The Hunchback of Notre Dame*). Only after the war did he manage to wrest himself free of the studio shackles and start composing once again in his own voice (even attaining a Pulitzer Prize for his autobiographical 1955 Third Symphony, with its motto from Goethe's *The Sorrows of Young Werther*, "Indeed I am a wanderer, a pilgrim on this earth, but can you say that you are anything more?"), though the fame and following of his European past would now elude him. And he would often entertain visitors to his home with a melancholy joke about the two dachshunds who meet on the palisade overlooking the ocean in Santa Monica: "Here it's true I'm a dachshund," the one admits to the other, "but in the old country I was a Saint Bernard."

The west side of Los Angeles was rife with erstwhile Saint Bernards in those days,* and Salka regales *her* readers with countless representative tales of fish decidedly out of water, to vary the metaphor slightly—Sergei Eisenstein, for instance (though he had come to Hollywood and signed a yearlong contract at Paramount for reasons somewhat different from those of his German and Austrian counterparts). Salka, who through much of that time served as the Russian master's closest local support and confidant, begins her account of that bollixed year with a typically priceless sentence: "As soon as Eisenstein arrived, Upton Sinclair, who had most impressive friends, gave a picnic lunch for him at the ranch of Mr. Gillette, the razorblade millionaire." From there she goes on to detail the story of how Sinclair's wife mobilized a group of idle Pasadena millionaire wives to sponsor Eisenstein's filming expedition to Mexico, with patrons and director soon falling out catastrophically. Before long the whole project went down in flames, leaving a heartbroken Eisenstein to return to his Stalinist homeland. Salka likewise tells stories of Arnold Schoenberg and Irving Thalberg at ludicrous cross-purposes over a possible score for the latter's production of Pearl Buck's *The Good Earth*, and of Heinrich Mann (brother of Thomas and the author back in Germany of massive historical novels as well as the tale upon which the Emil Jannings–Marlene Dietrich classic *The Blue Angel* had been based) and Bertolt Brecht (arguably the greatest playwright of his era)—all of them utterly squandered by a studio system that had no idea what to do with them.

Most accounts of such calamities characterize them as instances of the philistine provincialism of the coarse American rubes who headed the

---

* I have frequently written on my grandfather's life and on the wider context of the émigré surround in Los Angeles during the thirties, forties, and thereafter, notably in my piece for *The Atlantic*, "My Grandfather's Last Tale," and in "Paradise: The Southern California Idyll of Hitler's Cultural Exiles" (which included a map to all of their homes), my contribution to the catalog for the Los Angeles County Museum of Art's 1997 exhibition *Exiles and Emigrés: The Flight of European Artists from Hitler*—both of which can be found at www.lawrenceweschler.com.

Hollywood studios. (Salka herself does so some of the time.) The reality, though, was somewhat more nuanced and complex, for many of the studio heads were immigrants themselves, Eastern European shtetl Jews from the immediately prior generation who'd been looked down upon (as hugely inconvenient embarrassments) by their haute-bourgeois, high-culture, assimilated Jewish cousins in Vienna and Berlin and Munich and therefore hurried along to Amsterdam and Bremen and Hamburg and onward to New York as quickly as possible. Once in Hollywood, these fiercely ambitious Eastern European Jews set about fashioning and veritably inventing the American Dream. The late arrival of those once supercilious Western and Central European Jews set the stage for a certain degree of class-cultural revenge.

Still, many in Hollywood, with Salka and Berthold among the leading figures, did raise vast sums to bring leading European cultural luminaries, desperate in their flight from Hitler, to Hollywood, going on to help secure many of them at least temporary employ in the studios. And Salka made of her home on Mabery Road the site of weekly Sunday-afternoon salon-like gatherings (featuring her exceptional cooking), where the likes of the Manns (both sets), Lion and Marta Feuchtwanger, the Schoenbergs, the Stravinskys, Franz Werfel and Alma Mahler, Otto Klemperer's clan, the Max Reinhardts, Bertolt Brecht and his women, and countless other such Saint Bernards (including, I suspect, my grandparents) would rub shoulders with the likes of Charlie Chaplin, Johnny Weissmuller, Greta Garbo, Edward G. Robinson, and other Hollywood figures (as well as Aldous Huxley and Christopher Isherwood, the latter of whom had taken up residence in the garage apartment behind the main house). Many of Salka's best yarns revolve around these gatherings on the rim of the Pacific—including one in particular about a seventieth birthday party for Heinrich Mann at which, before the meal could be served, his brother Thomas rose up and pulled a long, many-paged peroration in honor of his brother out of his suit pocket and proceeded somberly to declaim it (as the roast overcooked in the kitchen), whereupon Heinrich responded by rising up in thanks, pulling a similarly hefty peroration in honor of Thomas out of his own suit pocket, and soberly going on to read it in its entirety.

Salka's account of those terrible years—"years of the devil," in the words of her secretary—is hardly limited, however, to the fate of the grand and famous; she is just as attentive to the lives of the more modestly anonymous: onetime doctors and lawyers, for example, who were forced to take up employment as chauffeurs and housemaids (she notes how, what with the sudden transfer of local blacks into the wartime ship- and plane-building industries, these domestic fields had recently opened up), or for that matter, such regular everyday Americans as the sweet lady over at the Santa Monica office of Western Union with whom she became friends in the course of trying to keep tabs on her world-wandering husband and the far-flung members of her own family, some still stranded behind enemy lines.

"The unconcerned sunbathers on the beach, their hairless bodies glistening and brown," she writes at one point,

> the gigantic trucks rumbling on the highway, the supermarkets with their mountains of food, the studio with the oh-so-relaxed employees, the chatting extras pouring out from the stages at lunch time, the pompous executives marching to their "exclusive dining room" or the barbershop, stopping to flirt with the endearing "young talent"—all these familiar scenes were a nerve-wracking contrast to the war horror I constantly imagined.

And indeed, throughout its extraordinary middle half, Salka's memoir shifts back and forth between the grim comedy of life in the studios and the anguish of the war (the terrible reports of the slaughters on the various fronts as her sons, all the while, are coming of age and itching to hurl themselves into the fray; the increasingly desperate rumors of rampaging ethnic carnage as one by one she nevertheless manages to extract her sister and older brother and presently even her mother, the latter by way of an epic sequence of bureaucratic interventions, out of the maelstrom, her mother then coming to live with her, even as the fate of her youngest brother, the soccer player, grows increasingly uncertain).

In the studios, however, Salka seemed to glide from success to success, her friendship with Garbo becoming ever more intimate and inseparable. Salka cobbled together and often coauthored the scripts for films in which the star got cast, variously, as the doctor's adulterous wife in an adaptation of W. Somerset Maugham's *The Painted Veil*, and then as Marie Walewska (Napoleon's adulterous Polish lover), Marie Curie (the adulterous Polish Nobel prize–winning chemist, in a project from which Garbo was subsequently separated), and Anna Karenina (the legendary Russian . . . well, you get the idea). Salka is wonderful at telling stories of the hurdles these projects had to surmount: the meddling of mid-level studio muckymucks, and the countervailing antics in the various writers' rooms. One of her favorite writing partners was Sam Behrman, such that

> When Sam asked me to dictate to the secretary the shots of Anna's suicide, I truly regretted that this was the last scene of the film. Walking up and down I described the night train approaching relentlessly —the lights from the carriage windows on Anna's face— her running down the embankment and throwing herself between the cars, then—a prostrated figure on the rails—the train disappearing in darkness—and last, a woman's handbag on the embankment.
>
> "And that's what's left of a human being," I concluded, almost in tears, and turned to Sam who burst into roars of laughter. For years these words remained our special code. We signed telegrams and letters with: "What's left of a human being. . . ."

Which, come to think of it, would have made a much, much better title for this book: Salka Viertel's *What's Left of a Human Being.*

Because for all her success, the life was exhausting, and as the war came to an end, her own began to fall apart: Her marriage with Berthold was continuing to deteriorate, her own love affairs were ending badly, and the perversities of studio life were becoming less and less endurable. One day Brecht drove up to the house on Mabery Road, with a question: "Why shouldn't we be able to do as well as any Hollywood hack?" To which she replied:

> Because what the producers want is an original but familiar, unusual but popular, moralistic but sexy, true but improbable, tender

but violent, slick but highbrow masterpiece. When they have that, then they can 'work on it' and make it 'commercial,' to justify their high salaries.

In 1947, Salka, now at Warner Brothers, was completing the screenplay for one of her relatively few non-Garbo, non-adulterous films—this one, *Deep Valley*, a vehicle for Ida Lupino and Dane Clark. One day the studio workers went out on strike, and Salka, like most of the writers, honored the picket line. She contributed to the strike fund as well, although her writing partner on the film refused to be intimidated by "communists" and ostentatiously crossed the line.

"It was customary at Warner Brothers," Salka writes, "that when a film was to be previewed, the producers, director, writers and technicians (but not the actors) who had worked on it dined with Mr. Warner." And so, some months later, she reported to the executive dining room, noting her own sense that the enveloping mood doubtless mirrored "the *Gemüt-lichkeit* when Stalin's staff was dining with their boss." There Warner pontificated on the communist menace and how terribly the Soviets had treated the Jews during the war, finally turning to ask Salka's opinion. No sooner did she speak, however, than the unctuous co-writer "interrupted smilingly: 'Salka is a communist, Mr. Warner.' It was supposed to be a joke—but it prompted Blanke [the film's producer] to jump to my defense: 'She is not!' he said. 'One need not be a communist to say that Soviet anti-semitism is not to be compared to the horrors that the Nazis committed.'"

Be that as it may, and notwithstanding the subsequent success of the film's premiere (after which Warner expressed particular satisfaction with the screenplay), that was to be the last time Salka worked in a major studio, "but it took me several years to realize why."

Thus begins the final section, in some ways the saddest and most dis-piriting, of Salka's memoir. Blackballed, her means of livelihood began drying up, she diversified, teaching small acting classes and taking sub rosa writing assignments (notably including consulting on postproduction and then providing, without credit, the voice-over narration for Jean Renoir's first color film, *The River*). To save money, she and her mother rented out the Mabery house, transposing themselves, along with a much loved dog, into the garage apartment out back.

Salka was deeply lonesome, and her pages chronicling these years provide a different sort of illumination from her earlier chronicle of the cultural history of the first half of the twentieth century. Her book becomes instead a deep meditation on the nature of life and love, grace and forgiveness, equally valid and relevant perhaps for people in all places at all times. In this context, hers is a profoundly *adult* book—and I don't mean in any XXX-rated sense, the way that word has come to be degraded over the years. In fact, on the contrary, her hard-won and generously shared insights get proffered in the context of a finely tuned discretion. Marta Feuchtwanger once told me how the really great thing about Salka's book was "the stuff she left out." Hers was no traditional Hollywood tell-all, though she certainly knew a great deal, having become the nexus of a great many people's lives.*

A meditation on life and love, and indeed a profound love story, though one about not any single love but rather all the sorts of love—for parents, siblings, husband, lovers, children—that can fill out an individual life. Berthold and Salka were clearly the great loves of each other's lives, and Salka writes movingly of the end of their marriage:

> It is terrifying how suddenly fate becomes invincible and how unsuspectingly we accept it. "When our marriage breaks up, I shall cease to exist," Berthold once said. But in spite of all the things

---

*And I bracket out here the whole question of whether Salka and Garbo ever became actual lovers, a piece of gossip much speculated upon elsewhere. Indeed, Salka's biographer Rifkind recently commented to me how often she got asked that question. "And who's to say," she continued. "There is evidence for and evidence against, we will likely never know, but what's been fascinating to me is how obsessively fascinated everyone else is by the question, and what does that say about them? I will say this: Salka would have done anything for Greta, been there for her in any way she ever needed, and having lived through the Weimar years, she likely would not have harbored any puritanical misgivings at the prospect."

binding us, all the tenderness and love we had for each other, our marriage was not a marriage anymore. Torn and inconsistent, Odysseus resented bitterly that Penelope had not waited patiently for his return, though he himself had not renounced the Nausicaa's.

And though the two never renounced the love they continued to share, Salka writes with equal grace and verve about what came next for her, how "Much against my wish and my will I did not jump, but slid into a love affair, which to many people appeared quite insane"—this with the much younger son of Max Reinhardt, Gottfried, himself a rising force in studio production.

> "But what did your sons say?" I was asked by a woman, who had herself sacrificed her love, with the result that her children thought her a frustrated and embittered bore. I answered that my two older sons were now adolescents; they understood that I had a right to some happiness. [...] Psychoanalysts are convinced that children want good, simple, conventional moms and dads, preferably sexless; however, I am sure that my sons were not unduly disturbed by the fact that their parents had a complicated relationship.

The "insanity" in question "gave me ten years of happiness and became a very serious commitment," Salka insists, but then "the unavoidable but predictable occurred: Gottfried's falling in love with a young woman he was soon to marry brought an end to our relationship. It is senseless," she went on to note, "to compare one's own grief with the enduring horror suffered by millions, but the consciousness of unspeakable tragedy makes sudden loneliness even more desperate and hopeless."

It was around this time, as the war (and that relationship) ended and the anti-communist hysteria began to take hold, that Salka also learned the probable fate of her brother Dusko. She received a letter from Viktoria, the beloved daughter of family servants, a girl who'd been raised as a virtual member of the Steuermann family. "In 1943," Viktoria now reported, "he came to my house begging me to hide him, but as we were living in a rented place I could not do it, and since the last German *Aktion*

I have not heard from him again." She followed up this news with a request that "Salka, who had always been like a sister to me," send a food parcel to her and the four children she'd had in the meantime. Appalled at the way this virtual member of the family had so "cruelly denied shelter to a hunted Jew," Salka began tearfully to compose an angry letter of recrimination. But then she thought again, "tore up the letter, mailed a CARE package [...] and never told Mama what Viktoria had written."

All of which is to say that this was a woman of preternatural balance, judiciousness, and wisdom.*

"Estuary" is how Salka describes these later years (perhaps with a knowing nod back to the gypsy's prophecy). The deaths continued to mount—Schoenberg ("Hollywood did not recognize his genius and only a few attended his funeral"), Max Reinhardt, Salka's beloved mother, and presently even their dog. Still blacklisted, and no longer able to afford the Mabery Road home, Salka was forced to abandon it for more spare and quotidian lodgings a good deal farther from the sea—and then in 1953, she received word that Berthold, now settled in Vienna alongside the woman with whom he had long been living, was in failing health and longed to see her one last time. She immediately applied for a passport, preparing to travel to Europe, only to receive word, by way of an officious, long-winded, bureaucratic communiqué from the State Department in Washington, that her application had been denied on the grounds that "it has been alleged that you were a Communist."

Desperate, she loaded up a car with her few irreplaceable belongings (notably including a heavy suitcase brimming with the decades of correspondence that would come to constitute the basis for this memoir) and headed back East, intending to appeal her case in person. When she finally arrived, at length, in New York, her brother Edward, his eyes averted, had to inform her that it was too late, they had received word

---

*Such sage and measured sorts of consideration appear to have especially endeared Salka to Isherwood, in whose diaries of the period she repeatedly appears, the two regularly sharing breakfast before the start of their busy days.

that Berthold had died the previous night. (He would be buried next to his friend Karl Kraus.)

She carried on. She appealed her case, eventually achieving surcease, and at long last made her way to Europe, and to Klosters, Switzerland, where her novelist-scenarist son Peter (yet another stellar Steuermann) had recently settled with his wife and young daughter (upon whose birth the couple had decisively separated). And it is there that Salka ends her tale (and an odd place to end at that, given that she would live another decade before she published these memoirs, a decade she chose for some reason to occlude, and beyond which she would live for yet another two decades, only dying, in Klosters, in 1978, at age eighty-nine—for more on which, see her biographer Rifkind's afterword to this volume). Ending it though on a perfect three-word note (and don't spoil things for yourself, don't go peeking ahead, let things come, let them come), the true summation of her essential nature and indeed the words by which the German translation of this memoir would eventually come to be titled.

—LAWRENCE WESCHLER

THE KINDNESS OF STRANGERS

To my sister, Rose
and
to my sons, Hans, Peter, and Thomas

I

LONG, LONG AGO, when I was very young, a gypsy woman said to me that I would escape heartbreak and misfortune as long as I lived close to water. I know that it is rather trite to begin a story with prophecies, especially when they are made by gypsies, but luckily this prediction did not come true. It was utterly irrelevant as far as the happiness or misery in my life was concerned, how near or how distant I might be to a body of water. But I cannot deny that some of my inner storms would subside when I looked at the crested waves of the Pacific or listened to the murmur of an Alpine brook. And so I could never forget the prophecy of the gypsy which also evoked the landscape of my childhood and the house near the river, where I lived and grew up. The name of the river was Dnjester. It was young and wild where we lived, flowing only a short distance from its source in the Carpathian mountains in a pebble-lined bed, shallow in some parts, then suddenly deep and turbulent in others, following an irregular and unregulated course to the Black Sea.

The country of my birth was Galicia. It was that part of Poland which belonged to Austria after the division of 1775. Now it is called Carpatho-Ukraine and belongs to the Soviet Union. The town Sambor had a population of twenty-five thousand. There were approximately four thousand Poles, eighteen thousand Ukrainians and about three thousand five hundred Jews. It also had a garrison which was very important to the younger female population, regardless of creed or nationality.

The town Sambor was two kilometers east of the river and of our place which was called "Wychylowka." "*Wychylac*" in Polish means to lean out.

My father's law office was in town. After he had been elected mayor, the first Jew to achieve this honor, Wychylowka became a suburb of the city, because the mayor could not live outside its boundaries. It remained untouched by the new status, and for us children it made no difference whether it was called town or village. Between the house and the river were our fields and a meadow; beyond the river was the wide, gently rolling country, practically uninhabited, with potato and wheatfields, pastures and forests. The sunsets were blue and golden in summer, and purple-red in winter.

Just across the road from our house was a wood. The "little forest" we called it. Old gnarled trees stood in sparse groups, and the cattle grazed on the grass which grew in between. Beyond them was a wide space of cultivated land, then the long, bluish chain of the Carpathian mountains loomed, distant and hazy on sunny days, and dark, gray-green, terribly close when rain and snowstorms were threatening.

A large, empty lot on the east side separated our property from the only industrial establishment in the area: a liquor refinery, which had once belonged to my father's family but was now (as was also the empty lot) in the possession of the wealthy Pan (Mr.) Tiger, with whom periodically my father was not on speaking terms.

Farther down the road, leaning close to the little forest was old Lamet's Kartschma, an ancient, wooden roadside inn where the peasants stopped on their way home from the market for a drink of vodka.

Old Lamet was a strikingly handsome patriarch, very tall, erect, his beautiful, noble face framed by a long, snow-white beard. He wore the kaftan and skullcap of the Orthodox Jew. On the Sabbath the kaftan was of silk and his hat trimmed with mink. I still remember his extremely pleasant voice and the clear, unaccented Polish he spoke. On Friday evenings, sneaking through the little forest to the back window of the inn, I could see old Lamet sitting at the white-covered table, surrounded by sons and daughters and innumerable grandchildren, waiting for his wife, a small withered woman in a brown wig, to light the candles. Then he would say the blessing. As my parents never cared about any kind of religion and did not practice their own, all this was to me very mysterious and fascinating.

Our house was not an architectural masterpiece. It was large and rambling and sat squarely in a huge garden, the steps of the front terrace descending into the driveway which rounded a large rosebed. Under the windows were lilac and jasmine bushes, and farther away, near the iron fence, clusters of pine trees sheltered us from the road dust and the merciless November winds.

In the back was a long, covered veranda facing the orchard and the vegetable garden, planted in rectangular plots separated from each other by wide gravel pathways bordered with raspberries, gooseberries and red and white currant bushes. There were hundreds of fruit trees in the orchard, which in springtime was a white and pink promise of paradise and in the autumn a stomach-wrecking fulfillment.

Beyond the far end of the garden ran the railroad track. Climbing on the fence, we children waved to the passing trains. They made our world seem narrow and confined. However, the garden and the little forest were large and dense enough to hide us from the tutor and governess. I would disappear there for hours to dream of my glorious future as a world-famous actress.

We were four children: I, the oldest, my sister Rose (Ruzia), my brother Edward, each only one year apart from the other. The youngest, my brother Zygmunt, called Dusko, was born when I was nine, and was not included in our world. We three, each different in temperament and character, were an extremely tightly woven entity, sticking together through thick and thin. And that's how we remained all through our lives. From his earliest childhood Edward was destined to be a musician. He was my mother's reward for her own abandoned career. Rose and I conceded to him without a trace of envy the first place in her heart.

As we lived far out in the country we were not sent to school. We had governesses, and a Polish student-tutor came every day to teach us all the required subjects.

Once a year we were taken to town for our examinations. Later, when I was ten, I was sent to a boarding school in Lwow, while my sister and brother continued to be tutored at home, passing their examinations at the Gymnasium in Sambor, a high school equal to the American Junior College, with Latin, Greek and German as compulsory subjects. As we had German and French nurses and governesses, we spoke both languages fluently from our earliest childhood. When I was five I learned from an older playmate to read and write the Polish (Latin) alphabet. At six I knew the Russian. The Ukrainian language was taught in the second grade (a concession to the otherwise badly treated part of the population) and in the third I wrote German sentences in pointed Gothic letters. We read avidly and with passion. Music and books were the constant topics of our conversation. I will never forget my feverish excitement after I finished Schiller's *Mary Stuart*. I learned it by heart and recited it all day long.

I built a small stage in a corner of our room, using chairs, books and shawls. The performers were the lovely ladies I cut out from Mama's fashion magazines and pasted on cardboard. I spoke their parts, varying my voice from deep to high. The plays went on for days, like those in the Chinese theater. Rose, Edward, Niania and the other servants, even our French governess, were an attentive audience. Still, I had trouble with my casting: there were no men in the fashion magazines.

As a young girl my mother had studied singing, preparing for an operatic career; her unfulfilled hopes, which she conveyed to us, stimulated and fed my obsession with the theater. I wanted to be an actress but was told that I was not pretty enough for the Imperial Burgtheater. Any other alternative was out of the question. My sister Rose, gold-haired, delicate and lovely, would have encountered much less objection from my parents, had she expressed the desire to act. But wisely she suppressed it, while I stubbornly persisted.

To be an opera singer would have been quite a different matter —it was a more "respectable" profession. Mama's clear, lovely soprano voice and great musical talent—she was also an excellent pianist—had justified her ambition. She would have been an ideal Elsa, Gretchen, Sieglinde and Senta. Also her red-gold hair, blue eyes and rosy complexion would have fooled the keenest expert on the Aryan race. But this Nordic beauty came from a Russian Jewish family.

Strange as it may sound to many to whom a Russian Jew suggests a rabbi or a merchant or a violin virtuoso, my mother's ancestors were landowners. My great-grandfather, Solomon Rafalovicz, had inherited from his father large country estates in Podolia and in Bessarabia. He had a beautiful wife, Rachel, and three daughters: my grandmother Deborah, slim, dark and perpetually engrossed in French novels, but surprisingly courageous in adversity; Sophie, a voluptuous redhead; and Nadine, who never married because a childhood injury to her spine left her a hunchback. She was the most vain and frivolous of the sisters but died quite young.

My grandmother Deborah married an attractive young land-owner, Simon Amster. It was a most incompatible match. Still, they had four children and when my grandfather was at home—which he rarely was—they played duets on the piano. Both my grandparents and also my great-grandparents were very musical.

My great-grandfather Rafalovicz must have been an extraordinary man. He had traveled a great deal, spoke fourteen languages and had acquired an encyclopedic education. He was born after Napoleon's victorious armies had marched through Europe, leaving in their wake innumerable corpses, but also the enlightenment and the ideals of the French Revolution. First 1812, and later the uprisings of 1830 and 1863, which Russia brutally crushed, ended the hopes for a united Poland. Hundreds of men and women were sent to Siberia. My great-grandfather had the opportunity to save many from deportation and death and to obtain clemency for political crimes, because the Governor of Poland, General Muraviev ("The Bloody Muraviev"), had taken it into his head to study Hebrew with him. My mother never mentioned what progress he made or how it influenced his attitude to the Jews.

Even in her old age Mama remembered the sprawling, one-story, country house in which her grandparents lived. I had seen similar ones on the estates near Sambor. In the center was a porch, which led into the reception room, the "salon." To the left and the right of it flights of rooms ran through the house. She remembered that there were two kitchens: a kosher one, where a Jewish cook prepared meals for the Orthodox guests, and a second, where a French chef ruled with an iron rod over petrified peasant girls. The two kitchens were always working full blast. Some of the guests came for a day, others for a week. Some stayed a month or two, others a year or more. A pianist, Mr. Horr, remained as long as my great-grandparents lived. Then he moved to the house of my great-grandaunt Sophie, a widow with eight children, where he stayed until he died. Everyone spoke of him with the greatest affection. My grandmother pronounced his name the Russian way: "Gorr." He was one of Liszt's favorite pupils, and could have had a great concert career if it had not been for his attachment to the Rafalovicz family.

In the eighties an edict forbidding Jews to own land forced my grandfather Simon to sell his property and settle in the Austrian Bukovina, where he leased a large estate to farm and raise cattle. My grandmother and the children—besides my mother there were two other daughters, Wilhelmina and Arabella, and a son Emil—moved to the capital Czernovitz, which was a loyal outpost of the Hapsburg monarchy and Austrian culture. But everything went wrong. The cattle my grandfather had imported succumbed to foot-and-mouth disease, the crops failed, all his investments turned out to be disastrous and my mother, who was studying singing in Vienna, was called back home from lack of money. As life in the family had become unbearable, she was determined to marry the first man who came along. It never occurred to her, nor to anybody else, that she could have tried to work. At that same time, in faraway Sambor, my father had decided to look for a bride.

Although almost forty years old, he was a desirable husband. Tall, well-built, handsome and wealthy, he had an excellent reputation and his law practice was flourishing. He commanded respect and confidence. The matchmakers got busy. As he was hard to please they searched in vain for many months until they showed him my mother's photo, which prompted him to travel to Czernovitz. My mother found him quite bald, "not unattractive" and "too serious." After three days he proposed, adding that he had "no objections" to her singing and playing the piano, as long as it did not disturb him, and he insisted that she learn Polish. He was accepted and went back to Sambor. During their six months' engagement they saw each other a few times, always briefly, then they had a June wedding.

My father generously helped my grandfather to arrange his complicated affairs; however, they never could be untangled until after my grandfather's death. He was only fifty-two when he suddenly died of a heart attack after his nineteen-year-old son committed suicide.

My youngest aunt, Bella, told me the story: She was fourteen years old and doing her homework, while my grandparents were in the living room playing an arrangement for four hands of a Mendelssohn symphony. It was their accepted form of communication, as they rarely talked to each other. Emil crossed the room. He was serving a compulsory one-year term in the Austrian army and was wearing his uniform. He pulled Arabella's hair as he passed her, continued to the living room, stopped in front of a large mirror, took out a revolver, said: "Well, good-bye . . . I'm leaving now," and shot himself through the heart.

I was much too young to remember him. But I can still see my mother dressed in black with a long, crepe veil trailing from her hat as she left for his funeral.

2

I DO NOT BELIEVE that any of us knew our father really well. There was an aura of loneliness and aloofness around him which we did not dare to penetrate, not as children and not after we had grown up. I remember rushing toward him in an outburst of tenderness, then stopping taken aback by his tense, absent expression. My mother and my nurse, Niania, often claimed my father had spoiled me in the first years of my life. According to them he carried me around, held me on his lap during mealtimes, and even if I insisted on sitting on the potty right in the middle of the living room, my orders had to be obeyed. All that is completely extinct in my memory, and as I did not remember the time of my glory I cannot say that I felt rejected or unhappy after my father's passion for me subsided. My youngest brother became the absolute ruler over Papa's heart, and Rose, Edward, and I were often outraged about his privileged position, but we agreed that there was an indisputable advantage in not getting too much paternal attention.

Dr. Josef Steuermann—Papa as we called him and always in the third person, for example: "Would Papa permit," or "If Papa wishes—" was born and raised in Sambor, a town to which, unlike my mother who hated it, he was deeply attached. I cannot recall his leaving it for any longer than four or five weeks, and then only twice: once when he had to take a cure in Bad Kissingen, the other time when he had to go for the same reason to a Viennese sanatorium. During the First World War, the Russians invaded Sambor and my father spent the most miserable ten months as an exile in Vienna, reproaching himself, and of course my mother, for having left his occupied town. This did not mean that he considered Sambor such a pleasant or beautiful place, or would not have longed to see the world. There were evenings, when he was in a good mood that he would sit down with us at the table, spread out a map and, consulting the Baedeker, plan a voyage. He would tell us exactly what train we were to take, where we were to spend the night and have breakfast and dinner, and which historical places he would show us. For a few minutes my mother would listen, then shrug and with an ironical or bitter remark leave the room. She knew that we would not budge from Sambor. For me these rare, delightful moments of communication with my father were sheer happiness, and the imaginary trips we took together in our living room were more important than some of my real ones in later years. I could never feel a stranger, or in an alien country, when I traveled with Papa.

We lived on a grand scale and he was a generous provider. The son of a prosperous merchant, he had studied law and having passed his exams brilliantly, he joined the firm of a highly respected lawyer. After the death of his partner, my father was generally regarded as his spiritual heir. His clients were mostly Polish aristocrats, neighboring landowners and Jewish businessmen. He treated them all with impartial severity. Feuding litigants usually followed his advice and made peace out of court. He was elected President of the Bar and was feared but revered by his younger and not always scrupulous colleagues.

I never heard Papa talk about his childhood. He lost his mother when he was quite young and was estranged from his father, who, at the age of sixty-four, suddenly married a middle-aged widow. She bore him a daughter named Natalie, and as he disapproved of his stepmother, Papa was not overly fond of Natalie. We visited them very seldom, much to my regret, because my step-grandmother always made delicious cakes for us and Aunt Natalie was pretty and only ten years older than I. They lived in the midst of town, their house surrounded by a large orchard, where, half hidden by raspberry bushes, was grandfather's prayer house. On High Holidays ten select Jewish citizens gathered there for religious services. My flippant mother used to say that grandfather had this "private chapel" because the presence of poor Jews embarrassed him when he addressed the Almighty.

On Yom Kippur Papa used to attend the memorial services in the synagogue. Although completely assimilated into Polish-Austrian society, he had refused the directorship of a major bank in Vienna because it would have meant having himself and his family baptized. My mother paraphrased regretfully: "*Vienne vaut une messe.*"

When I was older I asked my mother why Papa had married so late. She told me that for many years he had had a love affair with a very beautiful woman. She was Catholic, the wife of a judge, and loved my father desperately. Not only did they see each other every day, they also wrote daily letters, which were delivered by Jendrzej, my father's valet. According to my mother, the letters were read by the whole town before they reached their destination. Then suddenly the judge was transferred to another district and they left. Soon afterward my father married.

My mother went on with the story: Several years later, after Edward was born, the whole family, with Niania and the cook, was spending a few weeks at a watering place in the Carpathian mountains. Rose and I were pretty little girls and people used to stop and smile at us when, holding hands, we danced in front of the bandstand. One day our parents passed by and sat down on a bench to watch us. Suddenly Mama noticed a lady staring at Papa. He jumped up and took his hat off—she acknowledged the greeting, and unable to control her emotion turned and walked away. An hour later Papa was summoned to her hotel. She had had a heart attack and wanted to see him. She died while he was at her bedside.

All this may sound like a Turgenev novel; I only know it made me terribly sad. I was pained by the ironical inflection in Mama's voice and in spite of her lightness and frivolity I could detect that she resented the dead woman. For, in point of fact, Mama was most unsentimental, probably instinctively protesting the thoughtless romanticism of her own mother, who, as my father used to say, never got over the execution of Marie Antoinette.

3

I DO NOT KNOW what kind of childhood I would have had without my Niania; I adored her and she loved me as if I had been her own flesh and blood. From her I have my addiction to country life and animals. From her I have my superstitions, which I am still trying to discard, my "barbarisms" as Berthold, my husband, was to call them many years later.

She was a small woman whose dark, somewhat Mongolian eyes looked at people with a humorous interest not free from suspicion. She was pretty and neat, in her embroidered peasant shirt and voluminous skirts. When she took me for a walk she put on the elaborate, turban-like headdress of the married women of her village. Only a fringe of her shining black hair showed over her brow. She was always busy, always in action. I still see her, the bare feet hardly touching the ground, skirts billowing, and the erect, straight body moving swiftly like a figure in a puppet show; rushing from the stables to the poultry yard, from the vegetable garden to the meadow, and over the fields. She was never idle. When she sat down it was to peel fruit or vegetables, pluck a chicken, mend a tear in my dress, or beat the egg whites for a cake. Then, she would jump up again and run to the cellar or into the garden, or climb a tree to pick the ripest fruit for the table. The poultry yard came to ecstatic life as soon as she approached. A bedlam of crowing, cackling, cooing, screeching, chirping, and flapping of wings would start at the mere sound of her voice.

Later Rose, Edward, and I were entrusted to a French *bonne*, but I still clung to Niania, who was to replace the cook and "studied" for a while in town at the restaurant of Pan Wierczak. He had once been the renowned chef of a Count Potocki. Soon she was able to compete with him and she took charge not only of our kitchen, but also of the whole household.

When I was five I could read and tried to share my knowledge with Niania, but to no avail. Letters somehow "did not make sense" to her. However, she knew numbers, and her extraordinary memory and intelligence made up for her illiteracy.

Our mademoiselles refused to take walks in the country, or let us roam around in our garden. They insisted on dressing up and marching us to town, where they were admired by the officers loafing in the sidewalk cafés of the Promenade. The Promenade was part of the large square around the City Hall. The shops and the pharmacy were on its main sidewalk, which was called Linia A-B. At each end was a *cukiernia*, a combination of a café and *confiserie*. Old acacia trees shaded the sidewalks. In summer Sambor's "society" gathered in the kiosk in front of the *cukiernia* to sip lemonade and consume excellent ice cream and cakes. There were two kiosks, one occupied by the cavalry, the other, at the opposite end of the A-B, by the infantry. They hardly ever mixed, as members of the Austrian and Hungarian aristocracy served in the cavalry, while the infantry was mostly middle class. Some officers, though, belonged to the newly created military nobility, like the infantry colonel whose name "Brenner von Flammenberg" (The Burner from the Flaming Mountain) delighted us. Other names also sounded martial and sonorous.

On Sundays after Mass the "gentry" from the surrounding estates, the wives of the officers and higher government employees, appeared on the Promenade and in the cafés. Gossip flourished, deadly antagonisms and illicit romances were conceived.

Every morning for an hour and a half we strolled back and forth on the Promenade, only turning into a side street when an officer detached himself from his group and followed us. No one would ever dare to address our mademoiselle on the Promenade.

One of our governesses, Mlle. Berthe Fleuty, had soft, dreamy eyes and very thick, long, blond hair which we adored to comb and braid. Edward was madly in love with her. She took us to more interesting places, such as the military training grounds. Our walks were also changed to the afternoons, when the grounds were deserted. We found it great fun to run around and play as we pleased. It was also more fun for Berthe. A handsome infantry lieutenant appeared regularly and they huddled together, hiding from us behind a large mound used for target practice. Then flushed and excited, Berthe would appear at the top of the mound and run down into the open arms of the lieutenant, her loose golden hair flying behind her like a pennant.

In the autumn as the days grew shorter, we would come home almost in the dark, and someone advised Mama to keep an eye on Mlle. Berthe. It turned out that our lovely afternoons on the training ground were not the only reason for her dismissal! Berthe had been seen "half naked" in the window of the lieutenant's quarters. From then on our governesses were unattractive and in their late forties.

I must have been six years old then. Niania had taught me the Lord's Prayer and I said it fervently every night. So did Edward and Rose, but softly and with less dramatic passion; they prayed politely, while I was attacking God with all my violent soul. I pleaded and bargained with Him. I implored Him to let me die before anyone else in my family, because I could not bear the thought of losing them. Rose was indignant about such selfishness. As death was inevitable it certainly was more decent, and showed truer concern, to die last and spare others the sorrow and the mourning; it was very unfair to inflict upon them a pain one did not want to bear oneself. I was furious as I realized that there was some truth in what she said, but I loathed to admit it, and pulled her hair.

The other thing I prayed for, but secretly, was that my father and mother would not quarrel. It always started at the dinner table, making us so miserable, we dared not look up from our plates. Instinctively I was on my father's side, perhaps because my mother was always so much louder and more violent than he. It always seemed to me that Papa, this aloof, immaculate man, was being brutally dragged down from the pedestal upon which he justly belonged.

Once I woke up at night and heard Mama's voice. She was saying that she was sick of it, and would leave. In panic I ran into their room. My father was in bed while Mama, in her nightgown, was walking up and down. "What do you want?" she screamed at me. I wanted to plead with her to stay, but lost my courage and lied that I had had a bad dream. She ordered me back to bed, but I clung to her, sobbing and quite beside myself. Grabbing me by my shoulders, she led me to the door. I resisted violently; Mama turned me around and gave me a few hard slaps on my behind. Just then Niania appeared, scooped me into her arms and carried me to bed, where, outraged at Mama's injustice, I cried myself to sleep.

All this happened before Mlle. Juliette arrived. She was thin, with deep-set black eyes, a sallow complexion and fanatically Catholic.

Having discovered that I prayed more intensely and did not fall asleep as fast as Edward and Rose, she decided to take advantage of my piousness and to convert me to the Catholic faith. Sitting at my bedside she whispered gruesome stories of the martyrdom of Saint Denis, walking with his head under his arm, Santa Barbara having her breast pinched with red-hot irons, Saint Sebastian pierced by arrows, and others. The Crucifixion, in her fanatic version, was the most terrifying of all. She told it with such passionate hatred for the Jews that I was crushed with guilt. I knew that we were Jewish, but we certainly did not belong to those strange people in long black kaftans, with beards and sidelocks, and we did not understand their harsh idiom. Still, we were not Christians either, although we had a Christmas tree and sang Christmas carols. Our parents never went to church—but also they never went to the synagogue. Sometimes Niania or one of our French governesses had taken us to church, and afterward, to their great amusement, we reenacted the chanting and genuflections, Edward officiating with a bath towel tied around his shoulders.

Until Juliette's arrival no one in our house had been serious about religion. Niania was not a churchgoer; she turned to God quietly without the intervention of priests. She distrusted them, as she distrusted all men, my father being the only exception. One evening she overheard Juliette's whispering and my sobbing, and called my mother. They must have listened for a while and then my mother stormed into the room. "Pack your things and leave," she said to Juliette. I was so terrified that I would not have dared to defend Juliette for anything in the world. After Juliette left the room, my mother kissed and comforted me, but I pushed her away. I did not want to belong to those who had killed and tortured Jesus.

In the adjoining room I heard Juliette pulling out her suitcases. She left next morning with a cold good-bye to us children and some very un-Christian remarks about Niania. Mama told us a more objective version of the Crucifixion, dividing the blame equally between Jews and Romans and revealing the astonishing fact, which Juliette had suppressed, that Jesus himself was a Jew.

The weeks "between governesses" were always like a holiday. I spent them mostly in the stable, as I was in love with our coach-man, Michal. He was a stately, middle-aged man with a huge blond mustache. I helped him polish the carriage and groom the horses, and drove with him to town. I intended to marry him, as soon as Michalova, his wife, died. Otherwise, I was very good-hearted. I would give away toys, clothes and candy not only to beggars but, much to Niania's annoyance, also to the gypsies. When they appeared she watched me like a hawk.

There were many beggars in the community. Twice a week they came to the house to receive alms. The Christians on Thursday, which was also market day, the Jews on Friday. The gypsies came and went as they pleased, at irregular intervals.

On Thursdays and Fridays copper coins were piled on the kitchen windowsill and handed out to the beggars. Some got one cent, some two, others only food. Those Niania disliked received a piece of bread, and a severe scolding when they stank of vodka. They were a nightmarish procession of misery: crippled, whining old men and women, young paralytics and drooling imbeciles, some so severely maimed and afflicted that they crawled on all fours like animals. Their knees were padded with dirty rags, many were blind. Most pitiful were the children they dragged along, whom they cursed and beat with sticks.

In summer, after the harvest, when the pilgrimages to the shrines of the Saints and the Virgin started, thousands of beggars followed the processions of singing and praying priests, nuns, townspeople and peasants. The fetid smell of filth, rotting sores and decay hung over the landscape long after they had vanished in clouds of dust.

On such days we stood behind our closed gates and watched the procession. We were told that the beggars stole little children and broke their limbs, so that they might arouse greater pity in people and collect more alms. Also the gypsies stole children and dipped them into a black liquid, to make them look dark. Listening to these tales I was convinced that all over the world there was a gigantic conspiracy against children and that we were in constant terrible danger.

Fräulein Marie's appearance in our household changed my life considerably. This did not happen suddenly: at first I was quite ready to accept her as an indubitable improvement over the governesses we had had. Then, after several major collisions, we became enemies. The excitement which the appearance of a new personality invariably created had subsided and we, Rose, Edward and I, decided that she was a terrific bore. The daily walks on the Promenade were resumed immediately after she took charge of us. She was no less flirtatious than our beloved Berthe, but she was much more of a "lady."

Our lessons took place in her room, which was at the top of the house. Its windows and balcony looked out on the road, where an infantry company marched by every morning. The bugles sounded and we ran to wave to the soldiers; Marie smiled and nodded graciously to the saluting officers. Then we returned to our books and she to her dressing table, with her back to us, but she could see us in the mirror. I sat at the far end of the table, Rose and Edward as a protective rampart between me and Fräulein Marie. Luckily she rarely turned around, as she was too busy experimenting with different hairdos, plucking her eyebrows and putting on all kinds of rouge.

That was the last year of the nineteenth century and extraordinary happenings were anticipated. The assassination of the Empress Elisabeth the year before had made us greatly apprehensive. It left a much deeper impression upon me than the Dreyfus case.

My father subscribed to two daily newspapers, a Polish one which arrived with the evening train from Lwow, and the *Neue Freie Presse* which took a day or two to come from Vienna. He considered the latter the best newspaper in the world. My mother read it as well, but more critically, and I often heard her make ironical remarks about Papa's "Bible." Both newspapers were most conservative. The Polish paper was anti-semitic and nationalistic, while the *Neue Freie Presse*, owned and published by a Jew, was monarchistic and loyally Austro-Hungarian. I was too young to be interested in the reopening of the Dreyfus case, and the mention of names like Clemenceau, Labori and Esterhazy during meals only signaled that dinner would last forever. I don't remember whether my parents believed in Dreyfus's innocence or whether they differed in this also, but I owe an important, enlightening discovery to the Dreyfus case.

Having read Zola's *J'accuse*, Mama ordered the whole Rougon-Maquard series. The yellow-bound volumes were kept under lock and key in the bookcases of my father's study. But, forgetful and careless, Mama would leave the book she was just reading, wherever she happened to be. I used to find them in the garden, the dining room, even in the kitchen, and read surreptitiously and in great excitement while Fräulein Marie created her complicated hairdos. It was *Une Page d'Amour* which affected me most deeply. I identified myself with its heroine, a sick little girl whose mother has an illicit love affair with her doctor.

The birth of my youngest brother had not opened my eyes to the facts of life. Rose, Edward and I were sent to Grandmother, and when we came back Mama was in bed "with flu"—and the stork had brought us a baby brother. However, Kasia, Niania's daughter, with whom I used to play, told me in direct, simple words about the sexual act. She described it drastically, destroying the wistful, poetic notions with which I had superseded the stork.

I don't think that Sambor's society differed from that of any other garrison town. Its morals were, if not exactly austere, not too depraved either. Adultery was the favorite remedy against boredom. The wife of Captain X. had an affair with Major Y., while Mrs. Y. loved Captain X. If it had not been for anonymous letters, denunciations and occasional illegal abortions, this fair exchange would have remained among those concerned only.

After a few months of promenading on the A-B, Fräulein Marie acquired a beau. He was an Infantry officer, a Mohammedan from Bosnia, and his first name was Murad. Fräulein Marie told us that she was secretly engaged to him, but Niania found out that Murad had another girl. We were not surprised—wasn't he entitled to have a harem? Soon Marie became very irritable, losing her temper at the slightest provocation. When, at last, she discovered that I had a novel under my French conjugations, all hell broke loose. I was so engrossed in my reading—this time it was *Nana*—that I didn't even notice her standing beside me. She was furious and slapped my face. I decided at once to murder her and spent hours imagining how to make her death most painful. I planned to trip her when she came into my room, hit her head against the protruding edge of our tiled stove, and then jump with both feet on her hideous face and trample it to a pulp. It was a great relief to conceive this plan.

One day, after we returned home, Marie made a big scene. Lieutenant Murad had told her that I was a shameless flirt (I was not yet eleven). He said that I looked provocatively at the officers, half closing my eyes. "But I have to screw up my eyes, otherwise I can't see!" I screamed. I was so indignant that, howling, I ran to Mama. But my mother didn't believe me. Marie had told her previously that I was just imitating her own short-sightedness— Mama wore glasses when she read music but in public used a lorgnette. Marie assured her that I too wanted to have a lorgnette. My tears and the support of Rose and Edward finally made my mother take me to the doctor, and I was vindicated. Not only was I near-sighted but also threatened with curvature of the spine from hunching over my books and exercise pages. Immediately the hunchbacked ghost of my great-aunt Nadine began to haunt my mother and she traveled with me to Lwow to have an orthopedist examine my back.

A new chapter in my life began. I had just read Sienkiewicz's *Quo Vadis* and Dr. G., handsome, blasé, and forty-five, was for me the reincarnation of Petronius.

4

My PARENTS DECIDED that I should be sent to a boarding school in Lwow. I was entering at midterm and the pupils in my class were well ahead of me. In reading, writing and history I was more advanced than they, but I had never been subjected to school discipline. My father and mother welcomed this change, although, for the moment, my education was a secondary consideration; the most important thing was my back.

Luckily Dr. G. gave a comforting verdict. The slight curvature of my spine would soon be straightened out by the exercises in his Orthopedic Institute. He assured my mother that I would never reach the hopeless stage of great-aunt Nadine's deformity. I was to come every afternoon for two hours of stretching, exercising and massage. I should consider myself lucky not to be put into a plaster cast like the girl I had seen in the waiting room. He spoke softly and kindly; his blue, smiling eyes never left mine.

The boarding school was run by two sisters, political refugees from the Russian part of Poland. They took only a limited number of boarders and the other children were day pupils.

Sophie Czarnowska was a short woman of undetermined age, plump and most unattractive. Her cheeks and part of her forehead were covered with a purplish rash, her mousey hair was carelessly pulled back, and when speaking she revealed long yellow teeth. Yet as soon as her probing eyes met mine, a smile appeared on her poor, blotchy face, and my heart leaped toward her. A few minutes later her sister Wanda Dalecka came in, a strikingly beautiful woman. She was cool and reserved, not like Sophie, who had her arm around me.

The sisters informed my mother that though they took only girls as boarders, the school itself was coeducational—an unheard-of thing in those days—and that religious instruction was only for those who desired it, which impressed Mama most favorably. There was no free bed for me and I was to sleep on the couch in one of the very informal classrooms. I had my cupboard and desk there and, as a matter of fact, with the exception of school hours, it was like having a room to myself.

My mother left and I sat down on my couch, fighting back tears. Sophie Czarnowska came in and asked me if I would not like to have a glass of tea and meet some of her friends. She did not say "other children," she said "my friends."

In the dining room, behind a large copper samovar, old Pani Czarnowska, Sophie's and Wanda's mother, was pouring tea. I had never seen anyone as thin and wrinkled. She told me that she was a Lithuanian, from Wilno, the town in which the great Polish poet Adam Mickiewicz was born. Next to her sat a huge man with a long, gray beard and a booming voice. I was told that he was Bronislaw Schwartze, a survivor of the Battle of Praga* in the 1863 uprising. A citizen of France, but of Polish descent, he had par-

* Praga is the name of a suburb in Warsaw.

ticipated prominently in the ill-fated insurrection against Russia, was captured and sentenced to death. The personal intervention of the Empress Eugenie saved him from execution at the last minute. The death sentence was commuted to life imprisonment in an island fortress on the Ladoga Lake. I was told all that while we were having tea and everyone seemed to watch my reaction. I was almost in tears.

For seven years Schwartze had been held in solitary confinement without books, without papers and without news. The only thing supplied to him were cigarettes, and with incredible ingenuity he wrote poems and his political testament on their paper tips with burned-out matches. Death was always with him. The prisoners knew that their cells could be flooded with lake water. After seven years he was released from the prison and deported to a remote village in Siberia. He lived there, married, had children and waited for an amnesty which never came.

At the time I met him, a few years after he had managed to escape, taking his three children with him, he was sixty-eight. Hiding them in a sledge under fur skins, he drove and walked across the Asian continent, the Near East and Europe until at last they reached the Austrian part of Poland. I met the children that same afternoon—two girls, one fifteen, the other about my age, and a boy of thirteen. The younger girl attended Miss Czarnowska's school. Judging by their slanting eyes and high cheekbones their mother must have belonged to a Mongolian tribe. I never asked what had happened to her.

To cheer me up Mr. Schwartze asked if I knew how to dance the mazurka and, as I happily said yes, he jumped up, singing in his loud bass, and taking my hand danced with me around the room. The samovar and glasses shook and clattered and everybody laughed when the huge, bearded man swung me around, gallantly bowing and even kneeling down before me at the end. Then, to disperse whatever was left of my homesickness, he lifted me high up and almost hit my head on the ceiling.

The other people in the room were an elderly Polish couple, also political exiles, Mr. and Mrs. Poznanski. He taught literature at the University of Lwow; his wife, a lovely, sad woman, helped Sophie to run the school. What struck me most about her were the wide, black velvet ribbons tied around her wrists. I found out that they hid ugly scars made by the chains she had worn marching in a prison convoy to Siberia.

Pani Wanda, as we called Madame Dalecka, taught history and Polish literature. She was overbearing and impatient, but the subjects themselves aroused "creativeness." I started to write stories and poems, all extremely sad and very patriotic. My heroines bore a striking resemblance to the girl in Zola's *Une Page d'Amour*.

Sophie Czarnowska was a biologist. She had the marvelous gift of making "boring" subjects exciting and interesting. For a short while she even succeeded in improving my marks in mathematics, but not for long. I fell in love with Dr. G. and my idiotic inability to concentrate on numbers returned.

In the afternoons I went to the Orthopedic Institute. It was only a few blocks away from the school and I was allowed to walk there by myself. I don't suppose that Dr. G. was as single-mindedly attracted to "nymphets" as Lolita's Mr. H.H., but he certainly did not hesitate to experiment with my emotions. In his presence I invariably had palpitations and dizzy spells.

One day Papa arrived in Lwow and took me to the theater to see a performance of *Warszawianka*—a play by the Polish poet Stanislaw Wyspianski. The leading role was played by Helena Modrzejewska, who, a very old lady then, had returned to Poland after many triumphant years in America. Papa had admired her in his youth, not only as an actress and famous beauty, but also as a great lady. She was a countess by marriage.

I sat beside my father in my best dress and I had never seen him as friendly. He even ventured into a halting, self-conscious conversation with me. But neither then nor later did I admit to him that the performance of Modjevska (as her name was spelt in the States) had left me ice-cold.

The unforgettable moment of the afternoon for me was the appearance of Ludwig Solski, the great Polish actor, who died not so long ago at the age of one hundred. He was celebrated in Communist Poland just as much as in the old divided one and during Pilsudski's regime.

To honor Modjevska, the prominent actors of the Polish theater took supporting parts in the play. Solski's was a walk-on. He was a soldier, returning from the battlefield—the play dealt with the 1830 Warsaw uprising—and all he had to do was to give Modjevska a token of love from her fiancé, killed in battle. Covered with mud he crossed the stage, saluted, handed her the blood-stained handkerchief or hair ribbon, I don't know which; then turned and stumbled into the wings. For a moment all one could hear was the sobbing and sniffling of the audience. Papa wiped his eyes, while I dissolved in tears. At the end of the play Modjevska was showered with roses and had to come out again and again, but I screamed "Solski, Solski," until Papa told me to be quiet and to behave.

In summer I returned to Wychylowka. Fräulein Marie was on vacation and we had many guests. We bathed in the Dnjester, had lunch on the shady veranda and in the afternoons took long walks to the forest. On our way through the wheatfields we picked bunches of cornflowers and poppies and gathered mushrooms and berries. I also went horseback riding with the officers of our cavalry regiment, who began to show an interest in me.

In the evening Mama, Rose and I clustered around Edward when he sat at the piano and, dividing the parts among us, we performed chorales and oratorios, operas by Mozart, Verdi, Wagner, Puccini, Donizetti and the new sensation: Richard Strauss. Edward would accompany Mama when she sang Schumann, Schubert and Brahms *Lieder*. That summer we also discovered Gustav Mahler.

I returned to Miss Czarnowska, sunburnt and healthy.

More and more the theater became my obsession. In class I recited Shakespeare, and poems by Slowacki, Mickiewicz, Schiller and Goethe, and the fervor and the intensity of my interpretations made up for my other scholastic deficiencies. On my way to the Orthopedic Institute I would pass by the theater and gape at the actors loafing around the stage door. I lost my head completely after I saw *Macbeth*. Daydreaming became my main preoccupation. I was waiting breathlessly, anxiously, furiously, to grow up. I had had enough of childhood, enough of frustration, of puberty, enough of grammar and mathematics! In June I would be fourteen. When I put up my red hair I was Mary Stuart. When I wrapped a black shawl tightly around me, uncovering my breasts, I was Cleopatra. I was not a child anymore. My parents were not pleased with me.

As my treatments at the Orthopedic Institute were no longer necessary I had returned home. My father hardly acknowledged my melancholy "good mornings" and delegated Mama to bring me back to my senses. Fräulein Marie did her best to deflate my ego, but nothing could shake my conviction that I was a great actress. There were still a few people who believed in me: Sophie Czarnowska—I missed her quiet humor and warm encouragement so much—my sister and my brother, and our friends Zdzislaw and Wanda. They, however expressed realistic doubts about how I would feel if, not lucky enough to find a job in Lwow, Krakow or Warsaw, I would have to join a wandering troupe and play before crude audiences in the dirty halls of small Galician towns.

Many Polish and Ukrainian companies came to Sambor. The Ukrainians had a good reputation and performed operas by

Glinka, comedies, and folk musicals and dances. They had good orchestras, lovely costumes, and were enthusiastically supported by their co-nationals; but the Polish intelligentsia, always contemptuous of everything Ukrainian, never went to see them. The higher bracket of Imperial and District employees, the big landowners, also the lawyers, Jewish and non-Jewish, were Polish, but they were not interested in supporting the shabby, wandering Polish troupers, and preferred to travel two hours by train and see better performances in Lwow. I have retained a feeling of deep gratitude for those poor, wretched actors, among whom were some with real talent. Their nomadic life fascinated me, and no warning could dispel its attraction.

And so I went on dreaming and reciting Schiller, which drove Fräulein Marie crazy: "Hoer auf, Salomé, sei nicht so exaltiert," she would scream at me. By "exaltiert" she meant being an extrovert, which was a deadly sin in the eyes of my father and mother also. Fräulein Marie referred to me as "exaltiert" at least twenty times a day. As we spoke mostly either German or French, I was always addressed by my full name: "Salomé," with the accent on é; only when we spoke Polish was I called "Salka." Mama's younger sister, Aunt Bella, had joined the antagonistic chorus, and addressed me as "Sarah der Narr"—Sarah was my middle name and "Narr" means "fool" in German—mocking my decision to be a second Sarah Bernhardt. Things would have been different if I had had a vocation for music. Edward had all the support of my parents. But he only needed a piano and a sheet of lined paper to prove his talent. Mine was bound to a bigger and more complicated apparatus.

Mama told me firmly that I didn't have the remotest chance of being sent to a dramatic school. Papa refused even to listen to such an absurdity. I might as well forget all that nonsense and marry a decent man. "But don't you remember," I cried, "how bitter you were because your parents did not let you finish your studies?"

"Oh, well," said my mother lightly, "I was bitter, but now I am glad."

A young university student was hired to tutor Rose and Edward for their exams, and his was also the ungrateful task of giving me lessons in history, literature and science, as required in the higher grades of the public schools. History and literature interested me, but I was an absolute failure in science. Marie continued to devote as little effort as possible to instructing us in French grammar and German.

During the two years I had spent in boarding school, my father had succeeded in "electrifying" the city; even telephones had been installed. Our house had its own power generator in the cellar, which pumped water into the bathroom and toilet. Before this miraculous improvement, the servants had had to carry tubs and huge jugs of hot water into the various bedrooms.

The electric streetlights on the Promenade made night life much livelier. The square around the city hall had been transformed into a garden, the old cobblestones taken out, a well-kept lawn laid, and shrubs planted. The acacia trees looked trim and rejuvenated. Undoubtedly, the town was embellished, and even the bored cavalry officers admitted that Sambor was by no means the worst garrison. This was no comfort to me; I felt trapped and locked out from life. Perched on the garden fence I watched the passing trains with an increasing melancholy.

Otherwise, to be truthful, I didn't have a bad time. I owned a horse and, as my father disapproved of women riding astride, I got a sidesaddle and a riding habit. Young officers, habitués of my mother's afternoon teas, escorted me on my rides. And though still faithful to Dr. G., I was flirting with three lieutenants. In the mornings I infuriated our tutor by my inattention. By silent agreement, Marie and I had decided to avoid each other.

In summer we always had houseguests. One of these was Professor Balasicz from the University of Lwow, whose platonic love for Mama did not interfere with his friendship and respect for my father. He was the only one to take up the issue of my future profession with my parents. Papa, of course, stopped him short, but after a long talk with my mother, the Professor suggested that an actor-director he knew should judge if I had any talent. Then all other decisions should be based on that. He offered to arrange an audition and I went to Lwow with Mama and Edward, who was studying there with the Czech pianist, Vilem Kurz. While Edward was having his lesson, Mama and I rang the doorbell of a shabby apartment in the vicinity of the theater. An elderly man opened the door, motioned us into a dark, poorly furnished room and without letting me take a breath after the four flights of stairs, grumpily ordered me to start with whatever I had prepared. Of course I began with Schiller's *Mary Stuart*, my performance, although appalling, must have been rather touching. After I had finished, the director turned to my mother and said sharply: "I'm sorry, I can't help you, dear lady. The girl has talent. She's not beautiful; girls with talent rarely are. Still it's your problem, not mine, to stop her from becoming an actress. All I can do is warn her that it's not an easy or pleasant life." Then he added: "But there are wonderful women in our profession."

I was beaming, but Mama's reaction, after we had left, was characteristic: "Well, didn't I tell you. It is not a profession for a decent girl."

"But he said that I had talent!" I cried. "Real talent! And you wanted him to tell me the opposite."

As always when she was wrong, my mother got angry and told me to shut up and that from then on all debates about my stage career were finished, once and for all.

An hour later, though, she discussed it at length with Dr. G., to whom she took me for a final consultation. Dr. G. looked at me and in his tired, silky voice said that from his own personal observation the Polish theater was nothing but intrigues and misery. One had to be very strong not to succumb to a dissolute life.

I stared at him and wondered how I could ever have been in love with him.

After this, my life went on tepidly and aimlessly. I was pale and apathetic. The doctor in Sambor stuffed me with iron pills and liver tonics, but nothing seemed to help. Finally he advised a cure in Franzensbad in Bohemia. It was decided that I should go there with my mother's best friend, Esther Mandl, who was married to a Viennese lawyer. The prospect of this trip lifted my spirits immediately. At last I was to visit the place of my dreams: Vienna. But by the time we got ready and everything was arranged, the Burgtheater had closed for the summer and my days in Vienna were confined to sightseeing, of which the Prater left the most vivid memory. The huge Ferris wheel, the carousel and the puppet shows, and then the elegant ladies and gentlemen in the famous *fiacres*, or riding horseback along the Hauptallee with its century-old chestnut trees, enchanted me. The Mandls were delighted with my lack of sophistication. They had no children and their lives were overshadowed by Esther's domineering mother, Mrs. Koffler, a bitter, disappointed woman who lived with them.

In summer Dr. Mandl, an enthusiastic mountain climber, used to take a few weeks off to go to his beloved Dolomites, but Esther had to accompany her mother for her annual cure in Franzensbad. It was impossible to escape this filial sacrifice.

Esther and her maid Poldi were packing, putting mothballs in the cupboards and dusters on the furniture, rolling up the rugs, harassed beyond description by Mrs. Koffler. When everything was done, the two ladies and I took the train to Franzensbad, while Dr. Mandl went hiking.

The famous spa was a huge disappointment. Mrs. Koffler would not even let me order for myself in the restaurant, reducing my standing with the waiters to that of a mere child. There were no young people in the dismal place and morosely I drank the hideous waters and took the revolting mud baths.

I have forgotten what brought Zdzislaw, my childhood friend, to Vienna, but he called on me after we had returned from Franzensbad. As a farewell present Dr. Mandl gave us two tickets to the matinee of *La Dame aux Camélias*, played by Sarah Bernhardt. She was giving a series of guest performances with her ensemble in the Theater an der Wien.

Zdzislaw (he was sixteen) in his best suit and an *Einspaenner* (one-horse cab) took me to the theater. My hands in the new white gloves were icy with excitement.

After the solemn three knocks the audience became silent and the curtain rose. The first scenes left us cold. We found the French troupe no better than the Polish theater in Lwow. Then came the crushing disappointment: the "divine Sarah's" entrance. All we saw was an old, frightfully old woman, holding on to armchairs and leaning against the fireplace, draped like a mummy in costly silks, pushing a mop of brick red hair over her forehead, the big vermilion mouth revealing protruding teeth. Everything about her was artificial; Zdzislaw and I giggled disrespectfully, while our neighbors indignantly hushed us. The curtain fell amid great applause from which we arrogantly refrained. We wondered if we should not leave the theater and take a long stroll through the city, but we did not have the courage and did not dare to hurt Dr. Mandl's feelings.

In the second act Marguerite asks her old lover, Count Something-or-Other, to give her the money for a country house in which she can spend a happy summer with Armand. At that moment a letter from Armand is delivered to her. He has seen the Count's carriage in front of her door and, believing her unfaithful, never wants to see her again.

Sitting by the fireplace, Sarah Bernhardt read the letter, tore it up and said something like: "Cher ami—this letter saves you thirty thousand francs." Suddenly her voice moved me so deeply that tears poured down my face and I could not stop them, much as I tried.

During the next intermission Zdzislaw and I remained silent and did not leave our seats. We were awed by a miracle.

It is now more than half a century since I heard Sarah's famous cry, her thrice-repeated "Armand!" I shall never forget it.

There were dances and garden parties at Wychylowka, and in winter skating and sleigh rides. Rose and I had many admirers and flirted a lot. Rose was courted romantically, as she was delicate and beautiful. As a prospective actress I provoked a less respectful approach. But neither Rose nor I took our conquests seriously. The best times were still when we were alone with Edward, sitting around the piano. Our younger brother, Dusko, led a life quite separate from ours. He spent his time outdoors, bullying the peasant boys who were tending the cows, riding his pony like a circus acrobat, swimming and playing games. He was strong and beautiful. With his copper-colored hair he looked like the child Siegfried. He had our parents completely enslaved. Papa never came home without bringing him a present and knowing his power, Dusko took unheard of liberties with him. We three older children were amazed that it was Papa, the severe, unapproachable Papa, who spoiled him most.

At that time Amalia Kanarienvogel (Canary bird) frequently appeared at Wychylowka. She had a shop on the Promenade, where she sold silks, linen, imported perfume, stockings and haberdashery. Short, stout and very ugly, she had remained unmarried, and grudgingly supported a large family—mother, stepfather, brothers and stepsisters, the latter much younger than herself. They worked in the shop as salesgirls and when Amalia addressed them it was in striking contrast to the drooling sweetness she showed toward her customers (only to curse them in Yiddish when they had left). But she adored my mother and had a strange hold over her, which can only be explained by the fact that at some time my mother had confided too much in Amalia.

I was fifteen when Amalia persuaded Mama that it was time to get busy on my trousseau. Shrewdly she suggested that when I saw all the lovely things I would own as a married woman, I would give up my crazy ideas about becoming an actress. She also got busy finding me a husband.

My father did not like her. He was not feeling well and withdrew to his bedroom as soon as "the canary bird" appeared and had his supper served on a tray.

His illness—or rather discomfort—was diagnosed by the doctors in Vienna and Bad Kissingen as a nervous stomach. Later they found that he had ulcers in the duodenum, and prescribed a rigid, bland diet. My father hated it and became more irascible and ill-humored than ever. Still, he fulfilled all his duties with the utmost discipline. His law practice suffered only because of his administrative tasks as Mayor, but he had two associates to carry on in his office. Needless to say, Amalia Kanarienvogel had her eye on these young men, and soon they were escorting me on the Promenade. But my father's frowns put a quick stop to that. The young men braved only two Sunday afternoons in our house; then they did not show up anymore. Amalia was elated when a new cavalry lieutenant was transferred to our garrison. His name was "Schoen" (Beautiful). He was tall, blue-eyed, dark-haired and pink-cheeked. He looked magnificently manly with his well-groomed mustache and exaggerated cavalry swagger. For Amalia he also had the great advantage of being Jewish. Edward, Rose and I found him a bore, and ludicrous; nevertheless, he came not only to tea, but quite often stayed for supper.

The exquisitely embroidered linen sheets and pillow cases, the table damask with huge monogrammed "SS," arrived and were put away in a special closet. A seamstress sat in one of the children's rooms, sewing yards and yards of batiste. My mother enjoyed herself like a little girl with a new doll's clothes.

That summer our doctor persuaded my father to take a cure in Kissingen, which had been successful some years before. My mother went with him and as the cavalry regiment left for maneuvers, I got rid of Lieutenant Schoen for at least a whole month.

My mother's sister, Aunt Wilhelmina, arrived with her three children to spend the summer with us. She was as dark as my mother was fair, and a great beauty. Three years younger than my mother, she came between her and the unfortunate Emil, and was about seven years older than Aunt Bella. She was witty, her sharp tongue not altogether kind. The one to suffer its sting was her husband, our handsome Uncle Fritz, an Army officer, who had resigned in order to marry her as she did not have the required dowry. Aunt Mina vowed that her daughters would never repeat her terrible mistake of marrying for love. She thought that my mother, with her prearranged marriage, had fared much better.

My cousins, Alice and Olga, were strikingly beautiful, especially Alice. On the street people turned around to look at them. Their arrival reopened the discussion of my acting career. Aunt Mina, though not optimistic about my chances, said that she would talk to Mama, as she herself wanted Alice to be an actress. The Viennese theater offered the right opportunity, because if she failed in her stage career a beautiful, young actress had many other chances: an Archduke might fall in love with her and make her his Pompadour or Lavallière. Aunt Mina was dead set against legality and matrimony. But I soon found out that she despised the bourgeoisie only as long as my father was away. The moment he and my mother returned she reversed her opinions completely—at least as far as I was concerned.

My father was feeling much better—Mama gay and radiantly

happy. She had had a wonderful time, made many friends, among them an English lady she had invited to spend a few weeks with us. My father shrugged and said that my mother was insane to believe that Mrs. Annesley would take the invitation seriously and come to Sambor. How wrong he was.

Mrs. Annesley arrived after Aunt Mina and her children had taken leave, and created a sensation not only on the Promenade, but also among the Orthodox Jews and the rural population, with her eccentric elegance and lavish use of make-up. She was not young but she must have been very lovely once.

She was the first Anglo-Saxon I had ever met. Now I am aware of how typical she was of a certain social set. She spoke German and French with an abominable accent and a limited vocabulary, but as none of us spoke English, we all began to imitate her and invent a new language by mispronouncing French and German. But she was sweet and droll and we liked her at once. By that time Marie was not with us anymore, and Mrs. Annesley stayed in her room. The rituals of her baths, breakfasts and lunches appeared hilarious to our servants. And she always expected to find snakes in the garden, probably because she had lived in India and South America for many years.

Wychylowka provided all kinds of excitement, which made Mrs. Annesley lose her self-control. "Wherever I look I see red," she would cry out. "I have scarlet fever. I keep seeing red pants."

The red pants were part of an officer's uniform and were worn by Lieutenant Schoen. Mrs. Annesley fell madly in love with the pants, with the cavalry and with Lieutenant Schoen. One evening she came into my room, her face thickly covered with cream, her hair in pincurls, and implored me to give him up because he was her last and only love. It took me more than an hour to convince her that it would make me very happy if she would marry Lieutenant Schoen, as soon as possible. She left me, saying that she had spoken to Mama and had already written to her brother in England. Apparently the only person not informed about her plan was Lieutenant Schoen himself.

My mother immediately forgot that Schoen was a prospective son-in-law and was delighted to get him for her friend. Such a match was certainly more amusing than having to have the dull man in her own family. Still, she felt obliged to warn Mrs. Annesley that Schoen was Jewish and from a different background than hers. Rose Annesley was willing to be converted to the Mosaic religion—"It's not as painful for women as for men, is it?"—and she did not give two hoots about Lieutenant Schoen's background. She knew he was not rich, but she had enough money for both of them. Tactfully, my mother mentioned the difference in their ages (he was twenty-six), but Mrs. Annesley had a friend who had married a Frenchman, twenty years younger and she was blissfully happy. All she demanded from my mother was that she tell Schoen that he was completely free to give his attention to her. My mother promised her support. As things moved too slowly for Mrs. Annesley, she asked me to suggest to Schoen that he had a great chance to marry into the British aristocracy.

That same afternoon as I was out riding with two cadets and one sublieutenant, we were joined by Lieutenant Schoen. He maneuvered me into a forest lane and we lost the others. I assume they had their orders. Reaching for the reins of my horse, he brought it to a halt and put his arm around me. I burst out: "Mrs. Annesley is in love with you!"

"What, who?" He looked at me, flabbergasted.

I repeated: "Mrs. Annesley, my mother's friend, you know her, the English lady. . . ."

Schoen bent over to kiss me. I moved away and said firmly: "No. I don't want to be kissed by you. It is Mrs. Annesley who is in love with you. She is very nice and also rich." And I trotted away to find the others.

I was pleased to see that at the picnic to which the officers had invited us, Schoen and Mrs. Annesley were inseparable. She was talking in her silly German, mixing it with upper-class English and he was listening, flattered, and smiling sheepishly. She stayed with us until they got engaged, and a few months later they were married in her brother's castle.

Just before the First World War my mother received a letter from Mrs. Schoen saying: "Alas, my Austrian husband is like a beautifully plumed parrot, who sits on a tree and repeats 'Gib Geld, gib Geld'" ("Give money, give money"). She divorced him shortly afterward.

Amalia Kanarienvogel gave up looking among the armed forces for my future husband. There was nobody as eligible as a twenty-seven-year-old lawyer who had arrived in town and joined the office of one of my father's colleagues. His name was Stanislav Hoeniger.

5

EVERYBODY WAS PUSHING us toward each other: his aunt and uncle, my mother and Amalia Kanarienvogel. I don't think he was aware of it. He was a stranger, rather out of place in such a provincial garrison town. I remember his eyes, large, dark blue, looking at me with tender amusement, but I cannot recall his voice, although I know that it was his voice which attracted me when I first met him. He had gone to the University in Vienna, then lived in Krakow, where life was less lethargic than in Sambor. Later he told me that if he had not fallen in love with me, he would not have stayed a week.

It was by pure coincidence that he came into my life. An army physician, Dr. Eisenstein, had been transferred to Sambor, and Mrs. Eisenstein, who was Stanislav's aunt and had a deep affection for the son of her dead sister, persuaded him to spend a year in a Sambor law office before opening his own.

As soon as they were settled, the Eisensteins called on my parents. I was surprised when my mother invited them to her Sunday afternoons, because they were rather stuffy and not the kind of people with whom she would usually make friends. Then, after I had met Stas, and seen the speed-up on my trousseau, her motive became transparent.

I hardly ever was alone with him, but one day we ran into each other on the A-B and together we headed toward Wychylowka, making a long detour across the fields. Suddenly he held me back and kissed me. I was numbed and could only say: "I don't love you!"

He turned pale and murmured that he was sorry. He had had the impression I was fond of him. Yes, I was, but love must be quite different. Yes, of course, and he would not impose himself upon me again. Immediately I was horrified at the thought of not seeing him anymore.

"Why can't everything be as it was?"

He smiled: "This is a philistine town—I asked your mother. . . ."

"You *are* conventional, aren't you?" I interrupted indignantly.

Just then two dark figures appeared, walking in our direction. It was old Lamet with one of his sons. They were wearing their holiday kaftans and fur-trimmed hats. It was their field on which we were standing. Only a few days before I had seen them plowing it. To pass us they had to step into the wet, black earth. The old man, who usually greeted me with a smile, looked severe and disapproving. As they went on I could see clumps of earth sticking to their polished boots.

"They can't be going to the synagogue?" I said to Stas.

"They are. It's Yom Kippur. Didn't you know?"

I had forgotten. I had always been awed by this day; it made me uncomfortable with all the Jewish men and women fasting and going to the temple, looking reproachfully at us apostates.

I was terribly unhappy. Stas said he would take me home.

My mother was waiting for us and immediately knew that something had happened. I excused myself. She asked Stas to stay and they talked for a long time. After he left she burst into my room. She was very angry. "You'll never meet anyone like him again." Not only was he handsome and brilliant but in love with me, something she could not understand. Who did I think I was? A stage-struck idiot! "You'll end up an old maid or even worse, a streetwalker." I wondered if an old maid wouldn't be worse than a streetwalker.

Mama was through and left, slamming the door.

I undressed and went to bed without supper. Rose had eaten with the family and when she came into our room we talked while she brushed her hair. I wanted to know how Papa had reacted to the whole thing. But apparently all he had said was: "Doesn't that Hoeniger know better than to propose on Yom Kippur?"

For a week I avoided going to town, so that I would not run into Stas or his relations. Then one afternoon my mother went shopping and returned, gay as a lark, with him carrying her packages. He acted as if nothing had happened.

He resumed his visits, and in a short time I would be disappointed when he was busy and could not come. We saw each other alone now. This "amitié amoureuse," of course, appealed to me very much. I poured out my frustrations to him. I loathed my idle, meaningless life; I wanted to work in a profession I loved.

He listened with humorous tenderness, often suppressing a smile and often moved. After a while I ceased being preoccupied with myself and became concerned about him and his feelings. Once this concern was aroused, and I realized what a wonderful person he was, all my resistance broke down.

My parents gave a party to announce our engagement and Niania cooked a fabulous dinner; but what enchanted me most was my first trailing dress and the champagne. This provoked Papa to observe that I was rather childish and that he did not wish me to marry before I was seventeen. But he offered Stas a partnership in his law firm. This put an end to my secret dream of moving to a big city, but by then I was so much in love that I was willing to stay in Sambor for the rest of my life.

As Papa and Stas were in daily contact now, their conflicting political views caused the inevitable friction. Papa's favorite bête noire was a man named Diamant, a socialist member of the Sejm.* Extremely overweight, he annoyed his opponents by getting up in the House and opening his speeches with: "We starving proletarians . . ." which infuriated Papa. Such a fat man had no business to call himself the champion of the starving. Stas supported Diamant, and I was torn between my love and loyalty to my father. No one could deny that during his "paternalistic" government the city had been cleaned, the roads repaired, wages raised and electricity installed. I opposed Papa's contempt for socialism ("mob rule!"), but I admired his integrity and, paternalistic or not, his concern for the underprivileged. He could not stomach Stas's sympathy for the overfed Mr. Diamant. But, whatever his appearance, Mr. Diamant told the truth: the workers *were* starving. Little industry as Poland had, the conditions in it were medieval, and he was one of the first to arouse and organize the apathetic proletariat.

A general strike was called in the district of Sanok, not too far from us. There were bloody clashes with the gendarmerie, and the cavalry charged into the crowds. The dead and wounded lay on the streets, and hundreds of strikers were arrested and had to stand trial in the District Court. Only a few lawyers volunteered to defend them; Stas was one of the first. My father put before him the alternative of either withdrawing from the defense or severing their partnership. Stas chose the latter and decided to open his own office in Sanok. Papa retired to his room, and let me know through Mama that he expected me to break off my engagement immediately. Of course I refused. Mama was on my side. She was sure that once the trial was over my father would change his mind. Perhaps I should stay for a while with my Aunt Wilhelmina in Czernowitz. Stas and I thought it a very good suggestion and

* Polish parliament in Lwow.

that same evening we parted: he to Sanok and I to visit my relatives.

Aunt Mina and her two lovely daughters and even the usually indifferent Uncle Fritz, were most sympathetic. They tried to amuse me, showing me the pretty town with its mixed population of Moldavians, Rumanians, Austrians, Ukrainians and German-speaking Jewish intelligentsia. Czernowitz appeared like a metropolis to me. Stas arrived for a brief visit; he looked haggard and pale and said that he was exhausted by his work. Hundreds of people were in jail; among the strike leaders were many Jews, a fact which was being exploited by the anti-semitic press. Innumerable witnesses were to be heard and, as usual, the Court took its time, while the families of the defendants were starving. Although Stas joked about his health, I worried and insisted that he see a doctor, which he promised to do.

My aunt and cousins were considerate and left us alone. Stas rested most of the time, stretched out on the couch, his head in my lap. We were happy and peaceful together and it was unbearable to part. I told him that I did not care whether Papa disowned me, that I wanted to live with him in Sanok, without the blessing of a rabbi. He was moved but his reaction disappointed me. He said we were not in a position to brave convention. The scandal would jeopardize his case and make it impossible for him to defend his clients. And what a blow to my parents—they did not deserve that! We had to wait. But he wanted to see me more often and asked me to return to Sambor, which was much nearer to Sanok and where we could meet on Sundays at the Eisensteins. Obediently I went back home, where life went on as usual: Papa aloof and withdrawn, but not unkind.

The preparations for the trial continued, and from Sunday to Sunday Stas looked worse than when I had seen him last. But he was sure that he would win an acquittal for the group he was defending.

One dark Sunday evening we walked arm in arm to the station. The train arrived and, seized by an inexplicable anguish, I broke into tears. I stood there crying until Stas's white face in the compartment window disappeared in darkness.

There was another temporary postponement of the trial, but he did not come to Sambor. He wrote me that the doctor suspected he had an ulcer and had advised him to go to Vienna and consult a surgeon. He could not bear the thought of a long-drawn-out treatment and would rather submit to an operation. He did not tell me he had had a hemorrhage.

It was November 28 and the weather was awful—at three in the afternoon it was so dark that the lights had to be switched on. For three days I had had no news from Stas and, disregarding a snowstorm, I went to town to see if any mail had been delivered at Papa's office. I had almost reached City Hall, when our coachman caught up with me, saying that my mother wanted me to come home. We stopped at the office, but there was no letter.

Niania was standing in the open front door, but when she saw the carriage she disappeared inside. I got out and ran after her. My heart was pounding.

I crossed the dining room; the door to the drawing room was open and I could see Papa walking up and down, holding a handkerchief to his face. I had never seen Papa crying and I was petrified and could not take a step toward him . . . I was aware that Niania was holding me and that my mother was kissing my hands. She too was crying. I wanted to ask her why she was kissing my hands, but could not speak. She was sobbing: "A telegram arrived while you were gone . . . my darling child, a telegram. . . ."

She did not have to say it. I knew.

Stas's stepmother had wired that he died two hours after the apparently successful operation.

I had no desire to live; I wanted to die. My parents took me to the Adriatic coast, to Abbazia. For hours I walked along the shore or sat staring at the sea dotted with the ochre sails of the Chioggia boats. But the gypsy who had told me to live near the water proved right. I began to recover.

Esther Mandl invited me to stay with her in Vienna and my parents agreed. Wychylowka was too full of memories of Stas.

The hugeness of the Zentral Friedhof and the thought of Stas buried among all these thousands of dead, was another shock. But Esther found his grave quite easily and turned away as I knelt down and kissed the brown earth. I still had Niania's simple faith that the dead feel the presence of those who loved them.

Whenever I could escape I visited Stas's grave. One day a strange thing happened. Returning from the cemetery in an almost empty streetcar, I noticed a young girl on the opposite bench staring at me with Stas's eyes. She leaned forward and asked: "Aren't you Salka?"

She moved next to me and took my hand. "I'm Stas's cousin Erna. He must have told you about me."

Yes, Stas had often spoken of his Viennese uncle and aunt and their three daughters. Erna, the eldest, a medical student, was his favorite. Dark-haired and blue-eyed, she resembled Stas, though her eyes seemed lighter in color. She had recognized me from a photo Stas had at his bedside. The black dress, and my presence on the streetcar coming from the direction of the cemetery had confirmed my identity.

Erna's friendship and warmth put an end to my disconsolate brooding. She also insisted that I "return to the living" and start to study. As she knew from Stas that I wanted to be an actress, she arranged an audition for me with Alexander Roempler, the distinguished actor-director of the Burgtheater.

Roempler's villa was in a very exclusive district of Vienna. A butler admitted us—again I went with Mama—and a white-aproned maid led the way to a large study, where a short, stout man with an imposing Roman head greeted us. After some sympathetic questions about my age and my being in mourning, Roempler said that he would like to hear the Eboli monologue from Schiller's *Don Carlos*. It was very dramatic and, thank heaven, not too long. When I had finished he remained silent for a moment, then said: "Come closer—let me take a good look at you."

Pulling me down on a low taboret next to him, he lifted my chin. "Yes, you have a rare dramatic temperament, but. . . . That accent!" Tears came into my eyes. "Don't cry—are you really determined to work hard?" Then he would send me to an ogre of a teacher, a very severe lady whose speciality was correcting speech defects and foreign accents. "If you survive two months of her training, I'll see you again and work with you." He turned to Mama: "The girl is exceptionally gifted—exceptionally," he repeated. I grabbed his hand and kissed it.

My mother asked what the financial arrangement would be and he laughed. He was not a professional teacher, but he was interested in talented young people.

6

THERE WAS NO SNOW that February, and it seemed like spring when I moved into the room Esther had found for me. It was rented by a "highly respectable family," the Froelichs. They were a friendly old couple, looking more like identical twins than husband and wife. Both were short, plump, white-haired, with pink cheeks and bright blue eyes, and smiled apologetically as they explained that they only took a "paying guest" because two of their four daughters were married and they had an empty room. Their eldest and youngest lived at home. Camilla was the name of the youngest; she was pretty, very lively and studied the piano at the Academy. We became good friends.

The apartment was on the fourth and top floor of an old house in a narrow street at the back of St. Peter's Church, right off the Graben. Returning from the theater through the brightly lit Kaerntnerstrasse with its elegant shopwindows, noisy traffic and hurrying crowds, I would cross the Graben and plunge suddenly into the darkness of a deserted, cobbled *gasse* which had not changed in four hundred years. As in all Viennese houses, doors were locked at night. I had to ring the bell and wait until the *Hausmeister* emerged from his squalid basement lodging, shuffling and coughing, to take his Charon's toll of ten *Kreuzer* and hand me a tiny candle. My weird shadow darkening the walls, I ran as fast as I could up the endless stone steps of the spiral staircase, praying that the candle would last to the fourth floor. When I finally reached my room it took all my will power not to telephone Esther Mandl and tell her that I wanted to change lodgings.

Imperial Vienna exuded an intense erotic atmosphere. It was impossible for a young woman to walk alone without being followed. Alternating between the sentimental and the rudely obscene approach, men pursued one with undaunted persistence. On my way home from the theater I had to take the Kaerntnerstrasse, which at night was the domain of the prostitutes. Sometimes they chased me, sure that I was a novice intruding on their hunting grounds. In panic I would race down the street, hoping in vain for the appearance of a policeman. There were several other streets leading to the Graben but they were dark and deserted, and Camilla had warned me not to take them because the pimps used to wait there for the girls. Camilla was well informed and not afraid of the streetwalkers. She even knew some by name. "How is business tonight?" she would ask them in her brittle, high-pitched voice and look at them with impudent blue eyes. They laughed and called her "*herziger Fratz.*" * With me it was different, I was full-bosomed and red-haired and distracted the customers.

Three times a week I went to my diction teacher, Miss P., an exceptionally ugly woman. The worst feature in her face was her mouth on which she insisted I concentrate all my attention, so that I would know how to "project" properly the *a, e, i, o, u* and all the *Umlaute.* I also dreaded her consonants; when her tongue clicked against her old, yellow, protruding teeth, she gathered bubbles of spit in the corners of her mouth, which was garlanded with long, stiff, gray bristles. She had a big, soft belly, which heaved up and down and she would press my hands to her sides so I could feel her "correct" breathing. I could not imagine anything more revolting. Still, my German diction was improving: the Slavic *r*'s softened, the lazy consonants became clear.

In my room I walked up and down, learning by heart idiotic combinations of words, sentences devoid of any meaning, practicing for hours until one day I thought I was losing my mind. I phoned Roempler that I could not stand it any longer. There was a silence at the other end; then he said he would see me in the afternoon. I arrived trembling at his villa, but still had enough strength left for a violent outburst against Miss P. Roempler listened and laughed: "Congratulations! Miss P. is an excellent teacher! I never thought you'd lose your accent." Of course Miss P. became less repulsive at once, especially after Roempler said that he would study a role with me. How about Mary Stuart? But he insisted that I continue my diction lessons.

Before going home my mother had introduced me to her former singing teacher, Fanny Muetter. I suppose Fanny was in her sixties at that time. Her round, very black eyes gave her wrinkled doll's face a constantly startled expression; the small mouth with regular white teeth was still young and attractive, the black curls were

* "cute brat."

firmly plastered to her forehead. The ample bosom and short, thin legs gave her the appearance of an overstuffed pigeon. Her pupils adored her and seemed never to leave her studio. I was invited to come as often as I felt like it, and sit around with the others. Listening to the lessons I learned a lot, as Fanny was a master not only of the *bel canto* but also of clear enunciation of the text. I was fascinated by her technique and her great musicianship.

Two of her pupils, the sensitive, delicate Emmy Heim, an outstanding *Lieder* singer, and Ilka von Orsbach, who had a beautiful soprano voice which gave promise of a great operatic career, befriended me. Both were older than I, in their middle twenties, but they admitted me to the "inner circle."

Several months went by and Roempler became very ill. He sat in his armchair wrapped in blankets, his eyelids drooping. I hardly had the heart to go on with my scenes, but he said that the lessons distracted him. Soon I received a note, apparently from a secretary, saying that I should not count on further coaching; Mr. Roempler's condition had become very serious. Two weeks later he died.

I think that it was upon the advice of some of Esther's theater-addicted friends that my dramatic training was entrusted to the "bon vivant" of the Burgtheater, Mr. N. He was younger than Roempler and very handsome. The main advantage of my studying with him was that on his frequent guest performances in the Austrian summer resorts, he took me along as his leading lady. Neither he nor the producers paid me a salary, because I was his pupil. As a matter of fact, one of my provincial directors suggested that I should pay *him* for my appearance, but this was too much even for Mr. N. And so at the end of June and during most of July we played Suderman's *Heimat* (I was Magda) and Ohnet's *Huettenbesitzer* (*Le Maitre des Forges*) in Baden, St. Poelten, Pressburg, Ischl, etc., where Mr. N. was acclaimed and admired in roles he did not have the chance to play at the Burgtheater.

I cannot remember having ever suffered stage fright when I first stood before an audience. My attention was concentrated on my teacher with whom I had most of my scenes. The whole thing seemed more like a game of tennis and he was pleased when I returned the ball correctly. He also arranged my official debut as *Medea* at the Stadttheater in Pressburg. For this important event my mother came from Sambor, but I think she would have preferred to see me play a younger and gentler role. All she had to say was that my make-up was too dark, and that I was much too young and not at all like the famous Frau Bleibtreu. Esther was noncommittal. But my friend Ilka von Orsbach was terribly moved, shedding buckets of tears and declaring that I was a genius.

The *Medea* performance brought me an offer in Teplitz-Schoenau, a health resort and quite a large city in the Bohemian Sudetenland. The director, Mr. Frank, had signed Ilka as his leading soprano and wanted me for the classic and modern young "heroines" of his dramatic repertory. It was terribly tempting to join Ilka, and Teplitz was not too far from Dresden, Berlin and many other renowned and well-subsidized German theaters.

Because I was a minor Papa was obliged to sign my contract. A painstakingly correct lawyer—the briefs he drew up were famous for their clarity and fairness—he was astounded by an actor's agreement. "In a brothel, at least, they don't sign contracts," he burst out.

Until 1919, German theatrical contracts were documents of sheer slavery. They contained no guarantee of employment, no provision for accidents or illness; tuberculosis or venereal disease justified immediate dismissal. Beginners had to present a list of classic parts, studied thoroughly, so that they could appear in them if a change in repertory demanded it. Actresses had to supply their own period costumes and also a "complete wardrobe in good condition" for contemporary plays. Of course, stars and prominent members of the Imperial and Royal theaters had special rights and privileges, but the provincial actors, and especially beginners, had to sign standard commitments. I succeeded in convincing my mother that these medieval clauses existed only on paper. She was also comforted by the hope that, if harshly treated, I would break my contract and this would put an end to my career. Nevertheless, she ordered lovely brocades, silks and velvets at Amalia Kanarien-vogel's shop and her talented dressmaker copied historical costumes from reproductions of well-known paintings. I am convinced that in her imagination Mama was wistfully transforming them into fashionable evening gowns and peignoirs, in case I would return home and get married after all.

As usual, the whole family was spending the summer at Wychylowka. Grandmother and Aunt Bella had arrived, but Bella, in love with a young man, stayed only a few days. Rose had returned from Lwow, where she had not only been studying at the university but participating in semi-amateur theatricals. Like a cautious swimmer, she was sticking her toes into the water first to see how cold it was, while watching me plunge head-on into the deep. Edward had been in Basel, where Ferrucio Busoni was conducting a "master class" and accepted him as a pupil. In the autumn he was to continue his studies in Berlin. My mother gloomily mused about the time when the three of us would be gone. My father was aloof and irritable but Dusko, our youngest brother, got more than his usual share of adoration. He was ten years old now and there was some vague talk of sending him to a boarding school, as his various tutors and governesses had given up their efforts to break his resistance to education. He was wild, unruly, disobedient, but he played marvelous tennis, rode his two ponies standing upright, with one foot on the back of each galloping animal, and had the habit of vanishing for hours and remaining undetected, even in the limited surroundings of Wychylowka. Papa reprimanded him with incredible mildness when dirty, smelly, his copper-colored hair disheveled, he would show up for dinner. Dusko sneered at us "artists." None of us could ever beat him at tennis and we did not play soccer. But though our parents considered soccer a game for rowdies and had a very limited understanding of sport in general, they were strangely captivated by the physical prowess of their youngest son.

My mother and other charitable ladies had opened a free kitchen for the poor, and Rose and I helped to serve meals. There was also a new library started by the younger Jewish generation—the sons and daughters of merchants and craftsmen. Emancipated from their Orthodox upbringing they were in full intellectual revolt against their elders and attracted to Zionism and socialism.

Otherwise, Sambor had not changed. There were new cavalry officers to ride with. Colonel Brenner von Flammenberg in his impeccable uniform and snow-white gloves still came to tea and the usual gossip flourished. Now that I was an actress the attitude of the officers and other male friends who used to visit our house had changed. The colonel departed from his "nice uncle" role and acquired a surprising penchant for touching my breasts and pinching my buttocks. I realized that this was the penalty I had to pay for having chosen a "disreputable" profession.

However my mother had ceased to worry about me: Ilka wrote that her sister Mia had arrived from St. Petersburg with her husband Alja and their little daughter, and they would stay with us in Teplitz-Schonau. The thermal baths there were the very thing Alja needed for his rheumatism. It was not family life I yearned for but my parents were delighted, as was Grandmother, who knew Alja's family. They were rich and almost as refined and distinguished as the Rafaelowicz—but not quite.

7

I HAVE LIVED IN MANY PLACES and I am sure that even after all these years if I went back, I would recognize in most of them some landmark, street corner or building. But all I remember of Teplitz, or Teplice-Sanov as it is now called, are the hotels and *Familien-Pensions*, their shutters closed after the summer season, a fountain wrapped in a huge straw cape and dark tree trunks soaked in rain, their brown, decaying leaves covering the ground.

We lived in a large, badly heated villa which, except for our lodgings, had closed for the winter. Ilka and I each had a room on the first floor. Mia, with husband and baby was right above us. They also had a maid. Alja, tall, heavy, with a beard cut exactly like Czar Nicolas', was a dedicated Oblomov type. Stretched out on the sofa, melancholy and complaining all day long, he was waited on by his devoted wife. He was not really ailing, at least not seriously, but just sorry for himself. Mia was a miniature Ilka, prettier and more delicate, but lacking Ilka's humor and vitality. She spent her days nervously stuffing tobacco, with a special little tool, into the thin long Russian cigarettes which they smoked incessantly, drinking their pale tea and discussing Alja's rich relatives in St. Petersburg.

Ilka was unhappy because she was separated from her Béla, a dazzlingly handsome Hungarian nobleman, young and poor, whom she loved madly and wanted to marry. Béla was slowly climbing the bureaucratic ladder in the *Kaiser-Koeniglich* * government service until he would reach the rung from which he could afford to plunge into matrimony. If it had not been for the necessity of making money, Ilka would have said good-bye to the opera and gone back to Vienna. It was Béla who wanted her to

* Imperial and Royal.

have a career, speculating that sooner or later she would land in the *Hofoper*.

In Teplitz I lived under the impression that there was no town around me, no streets, no shops, no apartment houses, no markets, no churches, nothing but the tree-lined promenade and the café-restaurant where unshaven actors sprawled yawning and shivering, staring gloomily into their coffee cups. When at last I stood on the stage and the curtain went up, I was amazed to see that there really were people in the theater. The women in the boxes wore jewels and furs just as splendid as in Vienna. Teplitz was a rich town.

My first role was Schiller's *Mary Stuart*, put on for the *Salondame*,* the protégé of a wealthy industrialist, who insisted on playing Queen Elizabeth. In Schiller's drama Mary and Elizabeth meet only once, in the third act. It is a famous scene and has been parodied by Bertolt Brecht as an exercise in alienation. Instead of the two Queens fighting for the throne he has two fishwives passionately fighting for their market stand.

Having coldly acknowledged my presence, the *Salondame* announced that she did not see any reason for going over the scene, as we had only two rehearsals of the whole play. The director nodded at this suggestion. In the evening she surprised me by punctuating my impassioned speeches with contemptuous "poohs" and "ohs" and practically drove me into the wings. But somehow I managed to hold my own and received applause.

Mr. Frank, the director, was known to express only negative criticism, and my colleagues warned me not to expect that I would be any exception. Upon leaving my dressing room I saw him on the stage talking to Klaus Moss, the opera conductor, and I tried to sneak out quickly, unnoticed. But Moss called to me: "Wait! Ilka asked me to fetch you. We are going out together."

Klaus Moss was tall and very thin, with a cheerful, boyish face and curly black hair, which was always disheveled. He was in his early thirties, had wasted too much time in provincial theaters and was getting panicky about his career. He spoke a broad Saxon dialect, which made the most serious things he said sound hilarious. Thousands of German jokes are told in this dialect, just as many as in Yiddish. I often wondered how it was possible for a man with a fine ear for music to speak like that and still to be so attractive.

Director Frank stared at me gloomily. "You are from the Baltic, aren't you?" he said. "In your last scene you made me think you were from Riga." He made Riga sound as if it were the most

* An actress usually employed in drawing room comedies.

disreputable place on earth. I did not dare to say where I was from, knowing that would be even more disastrous.

Moss came to my rescue: "Nonsense! I was in Riga for two years, so I would have noticed it." He began to imitate the Baltic accent, which, mixed with his original Saxon would have made me laugh if the director's red-rimmed, alcoholic eyes had not been focused on me. Ignoring Moss's clowning, he said: "Come to my office tomorrow afternoon." And he waddled away, crossing the stage on his flat feet.

"He is furious that I caught him as he was going to your dressing room," said Moss. I froze. The thought of being alone in my dressing room with Director Frank and my Baltic accent was terrifying. "I warn you," Moss went on, "he wants to sleep with you."

"I won't go to his office," I said.

"I think you'll have to."

Ilka, Mia and Alja were waiting for us in a restaurant. A young married couple who had played in *Mary Stuart* and the lovely Helen R., our *Sentimentale*, joined us.

Moss was in a lyrical mood. He had appropriated one of my gloves and was kissing it and talking to it endearingly in his Saxon dialect, pronouncing *p* for *b* and *d* for *t*, which made the "Parons," as he called Ilka and Mia, laugh till they cried. But soon Alja, with all his majestic dignity, announced that he was going to bed. Mia and Ilka followed obediently. I stayed with the others until Moss offered to see me home. His arm around me, we walked slowly under the dripping trees, my much fondled glove in his breastpocket. He said that he did not want to fall in love with me as he did not intend to get married. Indignantly I assured him that I had not the slightest intention of marrying him. When we reached my door he embraced me and said, "Good luck for your rendezvous with Director Frank. Be smart!" And he walked away, his coat flapping around his long thin body, while he sang "*Steuermann halt die Wacht*" from *The Flying Dutchman*, at the top of his voice, waving my glove like a flag.

At breakfast Alja read us the reviews, which pointed out my lack of experience and maturity, but admitted that I had "great assets" qualifying me to play tragic roles. Ilka and Mia were pleased. The general impression of my debut was favorable, they said, and I should be happy about my notices.

But I did not care about notices. In a few hours I was to see Director Frank and I was sick with fear. Everyone in the theater was talking about his drunkenness and brutality, and if my mother thought that living with the "Barons" would shield me from unpleasant experiences, she was evidently mistaken. Some of my colleagues were determined to scare me out of the theatrical profession, which in their opinion did not need "well-bred young ladies." After *Mary Stuart* several of them showed me more cordiality, but I knew that to be accepted one had to be tough and cynical. Another great disadvantage was my nationality. Most of the ensemble were German or Austrian and hated the Poles and Czechs. A favorite pastime was trying to shock me. The comedian, a deceptively gentle, soft-voiced man, with the long, loose neck and head of a turtle, never failed to tear open his trousers and expose himself as soon as he caught sight of me. The elderly character actor, to the roaring amusement of the stagehands, would chase me all over the place, trying to force me into a dark corner. Fortunately I was stronger than he and could defend myself. But sometimes the snide remarks and dirty jokes were so funny that I laughed with the others. I was afraid of them but they fascinated me.

In the evening the ghost of their talent hovered over them, and in their exaggerated make-up, they acquired a mysterious dignity. Wandering amongst piled-up scenery they resembled strange, barbaric priests. They despised the audience and they despised Teplitz.

Both my enemies were in Director Frank's waiting room, talking to the baldheaded secretary, when I came in. The comedian immediately put his hand to his fly, then changed his mind and told a very dirty but funny joke. I had to laugh. The secretary looked at me and said: "Tomorrow at ten, on the stage. *Manon* rehearsal."

"That does not concern me."

"It does. You are one of the young whores in the gambling scene and in the last act."

I could not believe it. *I* should be a walk-on in an opera? It surely was a joke. I asked the secretary to announce me to the director.

"The director is busy."

"He wanted to see me."

"Well, there's someone else in there, and he does not want to be disturbed. You better be at the rehearsal tomorrow. Ten sharp."

I was outraged and humiliated, but at least I had escaped the dreaded interview with Frank. I decided to find out if Moss knew anything about my demotion.

He was rehearsing with Ilka and the tenor. My glove, now very dirty, was prominently displayed on the piano, right next to the score. As soon as he saw me, he kissed it, but did not interrupt his work with the singers. I waited; Ilka kept making the same mistakes and could not concentrate, and the tenor, who had a little more experience, was in a bad temper. At last they finished. Moss knew immediately why I had come.

"Now, don't you make a scene," he said, taking my arm. "I don't want this performance ruined by the mugging of our ancient, fat chorus ladies. Can you see them as Parisian cocottes? I *must* have lovely girls in that act. Actresses! You must do it for my sake. Helene R. said she'd do it if you would."

He implored me not to be selfish. The director from the Royal Opera in Stuttgart would see the performance, also a well-known impresario, etc., etc. Moss could be irresistible and anyway, there was nothing I would not have done for him and Ilka. But he was mistaken in thinking that Helene R. and the other actresses would cooperate. Helene promptly caught a bad cold; the others had long sessions with the director and got excused. Only I, two dancers, the ingenue and four extras, the youngest and thinnest, showed up for the rehearsal.

The première was much too soon, as the cast needed more rehearsals, but it seemed to go well. In the gambling scene we "courtesans"—on the program Moss had promoted us to this higher rank—looked glamorous and won his praise. Later, in ugly, gray prison garb, we stood on the stage, waiting to be deported to the distant shores of Louisiana. The protruding bow, mast and ladder of our ship could be seen in the opposite wing; the deportees were being jeered at by the chorus of citizens, while in the foreground Manon and de Grieux, eyes glued to Moss's baton, were singing their farewells. Miraculously, Moss was holding everything together, except for the young singer who had to call the names of the "courtesans" as they boarded the ship. He forgot his cue, and petrified, he stared at Moss without uttering a sound. Finally I decided to take the matter in hand and get the courtesans aboard myself. I tugged the young man by his coattail and prompted him to call "Suzette," the first one on his list. Then, trying to follow Moss's beat, I nudged and winked to signal each name, but the young man was now so confused that I could only chose my own timing, disregarding Puccini's music. As the last one to board the ship, I showed such eagerness that my hurried exit caused a ripple of laughter.

A note from Frank's secretary waited for me in the dressing room, which I shared with the ingenue. The director wanted to see me *immediately* in his office.

"He'll give you hell," said the ingenue. "You should have let that damned scene go to pieces."

"I'll pretend I did not get the note."

"Frank can fire you."

I went, my heart pounding so wildly that I thought I could hear it echo in the deserted corridors. The waiting room was empty, the door to the office open. I saw him, in his shirt-sleeves, sitting on the couch. I knocked and he motioned me to come in, then staggered from the couch and closed the door.

There was not much dialogue in the ensuing scene. Director Frank was not what one would call an articulate man, but by grunts and by transferring the weight of his massive self to me, he drunkenly managed to convey that the time had come for us to know each other more intimately. Once I was able to extricate myself from his grip, it was easy to win the wrestling match. He lost his balance, fell, and cursed me. In a second I was at the door. Luckily he had not taken the key out, though he had remembered to turn it.

Bruised, disheveled and breathless, I raced back to the dressing room. The ingenue was still in front of the mirror, taking off her make-up. "That was fast work," she said appreciatively, but then she looked at me and shut up.

For a few days Frank was invisible. Moss was in excellent humor and full of tenderness; I had told him and Ilka about my scene with Frank and both worried about the consequences. *Manon* was a great success. Moss's agent promised to get him a better position; Ilka was offered a contract with a small German Hoftheater. She refused, because she did not want to be separated from Béla. After the second performance of *Manon* I had waited for Ilka and together we went home. As we were passing the blackboard we saw a group of actors whispering and laughing about a pompous announcement: "The next great event of our theatrical season will be Schiller's *Wallenstein* Trilogy. The parts have to be picked up from the stagedoor porter. Upon urgent public demand Director Frank has consented to appear as Max Piccolomini." The character actor was Wallenstein, Helene R. his daughter Thekla, the "*Salondame*" had the important part of the Countess Terzky. Other names followed in the lengthy cast, and at the very bottom I discovered my own: Thekla's lady-in-waiting: Miss Steuermann.

My role consisted of one single sentence. I was to enter and announce: "The gentleman from Sweden" (in German: *Der Schwed'sche Herr*), and that was all. On the dreaded day, when the scene was rehearsed, Frank dominated the stage. To look the part of the dashing, romantic young hero, Thekla's lover, he had squeezed his stomach into a wide, tight sash, which cut him into two huge bulges. He mumbled Schiller's noble verse, interrupting himself to direct the other actors. The whole ensemble was in the wings watching with suppressed amusement. My cue came, the stage manager gave me a nod and opened the door. I stepped forward and said: "*Der Schwed'sche Herr.*" The next second Frank was shouting: "Once more." I went back, repeated my entrance and immediately Frank said: "Once more." Again I announced the Swede and again I heard "Once more."

"What am I doing wrong?" I asked.

"I said 'once more,' didn't I?"

I went back for the cue, then said my three words. Again Frank made me go back. This he repeated at least thirty times. The people in the wings began to show concern. "Keep calm," they advised; even my dreaded enemy the comedian approached and patted my shoulder: "Never mind him, do it again." Helene R. passed by and stroked my hair. By then I was trembling and almost losing my mind.

"This is the last time," I said to the stage manager.

"Don't be a fool. He'll tire first," he whispered, opening the door for my entrance.

Again came the now quite hoarse: "Once more." But this time I walked to a table, grabbed a heavy, bronze candlestick and threw it at Frank's head, which I missed. All I remember is that I heard a scream; then I was taken to a dressing room, where Helene gave me a brandy.

This could have meant the end of my theatrical career, but Frank feared a scandal. He preferred to pay me one month's salary and fire me.

As all this happened in the midst of the season it was impossible to get another job. Ilka tried to persuade me to go to Vienna, and look for work there, but I did not have enough money and would have had to ask my father for help. Of course, Esther Mandl would always welcome me with open arms, and urge me to give up my ill-fated career. I knew she would say: "Thank heavens, you are not like the others!"

Moss approved of my "courage." He had written to his agent, but was not sure if the man could do anything for me, as he only handled opera singers.

Time was running short when I received a telegram from the Schauspielhaus in Zurich, offering a three year contract. It called for guest performances as Graefin Terzky in *Wallenstein's Death*, and *Hedda Gabler*. My traveling expenses were to be paid, and the salary, with yearly increases, appeared dazzling. The Schauspielhaus had an excellent reputation and I accepted enthusiastically, disregarding the fact that both parts demanded more maturity, experience and technique than my few months in the Teplitz ensemble could have provided.

It was my last evening and Moss was free. Ruthlessly I dodged the farewell supper planned by Ilka, to spend the evening with him. The weather was at its worst: snow and rain and a beastly, cold wind. There was no question of taking our nightly walk after the melancholy meal in a deserted restaurant and, for the first time since we had known each other, Moss suggested that we go to his place.

Had I only loved him as I had loved Stas! But in the sadness of the early morning I knew that the memory of my first night of love would be forever associated with his dreadful Saxonian accent. Besides it was late, I had not packed, and I dreaded running into the janitor.

At the entrance to my house Moss held me in his arms and I promised to be patient and faithful and to come back after my *Gastspiel*. A few hours later Ilka and Mia took me to the station. As the train was moving the unshaven Moss appeared on the platform with a bunch of violets in his hand.

8

As far as Munich I shared my compartment with an attractive gentleman in gray tweeds, gray suede gloves and shoes, and with chic Vuitton baggage in the rack above his seat. He had watched me memorizing Graefin Terzky, and introduced himself as Baron von M., attached to the German Embassy in Paris. He said he knew many young actresses and was an expert in cueing. I accepted his help and by evening, as we approached Munich, I knew my part so well that he leaned back with a big sigh of relief, and assured me the part fitted me like a glove.

Next morning I arrived in Zurich. The town and the lake were wrapped in one huge gray cloud. The fog was so dense that it was impossible to distinguish the buildings from the water; nevertheless, my cabdriver brought me safely to the Baur au Lac, the charming hotel my traveling companion had recommended.

After my experience in Teplitz, the politeness of the Zurich ensemble was overwhelming. Everyone was well-mannered, some of the actors wore gloves to avoid the stage grime, some addressed each other as "Herr" and "Frau."

The director, a potbellied young man with long hair and eyeglasses, contented himself with telling me where I had to stand, where to sit, where to enter or exit. Now and then he would whisper with one of my partners, then come back and say: "Fräulein C. is used to playing this scene in a lower key." Or: "Herr K. would suggest you stay on his right." "Frau B. would be grateful if you would not block her from the prompter." We rehearsed all my scenes and I did not fluff a line.

At two-thirty in the afternoon the *Herr Intendant* (General manager and producer) appeared, a gray-haired, distinguished-looking gentleman. The director introduced me. He looked surprised: "Aren't you a little young for the part?" "And you have never played it?" He turned to the director and took him backstage, where they walked up and down. The director must have calmed his apprehensions, because he shrugged, wished me *"Hals und Beinbruch"* * and left.

Meanwhile the actress playing Wallenstein's daughter asked me cautiously about my family, then invited me for lunch. Pleased that my father was a lawyer (hers was an industrialist), she took me to a vegetarian restaurant, crowded with middle-aged females.

When I told her that I was staying at the Baur au Lac she almost fainted. "What an insane thing to do! How much do they charge you?" I confessed that I had not asked for the price of my room. Her opinion of me greatly reduced, she insisted that I move immediately to another hotel, only a block from the theater and much less expensive. I anticipated that it would be as dreary as the restaurant, but did not dare to protest. As I had not unpacked, the moving went very swiftly and my suspicion proved wrong: the new room was clean, pleasant and warm. My helpful colleague went home—she had an evening performance, which I promised to see

---

* A superstition in the German theater forbids saying "good luck." Instead one wishes you to "break your neck and legs."

—and I fell on my bed for a short rest but, worn out by the long journey and nerve-racking rehearsal, I did not wake up until the next morning.

Again the day was dark and foggy and the rehearsal very long. Although very tired I felt confident; perhaps I was not quite the commanding and deliberate matron I had to portray, but it did not seem to bother my partners nor the director. I always felt secure as soon as I had stageboards under my feet, and it was in my nature to be blind to danger. I took a hot bath and went to bed for a short rest, convinced I could not fail. For a long while I was wide awake but must have dropped off to sleep suddenly, because I was aroused by the maid knocking at my door: they had been phoning from the theater. I dressed in a second and ran downstairs. The sedate concierge firmly refused to call a cab. It was ridiculous: the theater was right there, a block away.

I stepped out and was lost. Wherever I turned in the impenetrable fog I could hear the splashing of water against the embankment. Shapeless shadows emerged and disappeared, answering my desperate pleas to show me the way to the theater with guttural sounds. Finally something which looked like an igloo but turned out to be a kind woman, took my hand and led me to the stage door.

In the theater everybody was frantic. The stage manager was just about to call the police. The wardrobe woman and the hairdresser raced me to my dressing room and while the one was changing me into my costume, the other pulled on my wig. It was all in curls and made me look like a stylized, black lion. They were still sticking hairpins into my scalp when the bell rang and I ran toward the stage, the wardrobe woman holding up the mirror for the hairdresser. Then I was pushed out, for better or for worse.

The first scene was short and went quite well, though the nightmare of wandering in the fog was still in my bones. Afterward I had enough time to repair my make-up. "If you only had been here an hour earlier," moaned the hairdresser, "I could have used your own hair." It was too late. The wig robbed me of a very important asset: confidence in my appearance. But Countess Terzky could not turn into a red-head in the middle of the play.

The performance dragged on. Finally the fourth act, in which not long ago I had so unfortunately announced the Swedish gentleman, started. I was waiting in the greenroom for my call. While I was trying to pin back my annoying curls, I saw the director standing behind me. In the next second he was covering my face and neck with moist kisses, murmuring that he *had* to spend the night with me. My call interrupted him and I went on stage. In a long scene before Thekla's lady-in-waiting announced the "gentleman from Sweden," I had to refer to him as the "Swedish envoy," but instead I repeated those fatal three words, which Director Frank's sadism seemed to have forever engraved on my brain, just as "Calais" was engraved on the heart of Bloody Mary. No one would have cared had I not gasped and stopped dead. My colleagues whispered, the prompter shouted, in vain. I could not remember one single word, and heard murmurs and laughter in the audience. At last I pulled myself together and finished the scene. The stage manager asked me what had happened, but I could not speak, and ran to my dressing room. The wardrobe woman gave me a glass of brandy and comforted me. I asked her to make my hairdo as simple as possible, changed into the nightdress I had to wear in the last scene and with my heart pounding waited for the last act.

As soon as I appeared I could hear an ominous giggle in the audience. I could feel their hostility until at last the curtain went down and I saw the manager waiting in the wings. He was very friendly, took my arm and led me to the greenroom. The perspiring director was already there. I burst into tears and did not stop crying until I left Zurich.

The manager was extremely kind and understanding. He advised me to forgo my second guest performance. I was not yet a Hedda Gabler, and certainly not the leading lady they were looking for. This he had known as soon as he saw me. He added that he should not have permitted me to play such a difficult part. Nevertheless, he offered me a contract, not as leading lady, but in a position more suitable to my experience. He assured me that I would play excellent roles, as he and his director were interested in my talent. Sobbing, I answered that the audience would always remember my getting stuck. The director reprimanded me: wasn't the offer the *Herr Intendant* made reassuring? And it was independent of what the critics would say. His mention of the press was decisive. I refused. No, I would not stay in Zurich.

It was long after midnight. The office was closed and I could not get paid, but I had enough money for the hotel bill and a third class train ticket. The director asked where they could forward my salary. Yes, where? A great longing for Edward and Rose overcame me. Rose was in Poland and Edward in Berlin studying with Busoni. I decided to go to Berlin.

Edward was waiting on the platform of Bahnhof Friedrichstrasse with a pile of newspapers under his arm, when I arrived next day. He welcomed me with his usual tenderness and expressed one of his most gentle understatements: "I am afraid the Zurich reviews are not too favorable."

They certainly were ferociously unfavorable. The kindest of the critics was the one who wrote: "Miss Steuermann (my name means "helmsman" in German) should turn her compass to other shores. We here are thoroughly convinced of her lack of talent." Others elaborated on my getting stuck, and on my wig. If Baron von M. of the German Embassy ever read Swiss papers, he must have been disappointed.

Edward had a furnished room in Charlottenburg; I slept on a couch in the landlady's living room. I must have been very depressing company. When he was not practicing or composing, we discussed my dismal future.

One evening, to cheer me up, Edward suggested that we see *Lancelot*, a new play performed in Max Reinhardt's Kammerspiele. It was a smaller house next door to his Deutsches Theater. The play had already started when we arrived, and we hurriedly got our tickets at the box office; then, having entered the dark auditorium, realized that we were in the wrong theater. "Let's leave," I whispered, but at that moment a Negro appeared on the stage and the first words he spoke held us spellbound in our seats. It was Albert Bassermann playing Othello. I had seen *Othello* before, but now, taken out from the mothballs of the declamatory tradition, it was a revelation. I was beside myself and even Edward, always more critical and restrained, shared my enthusiasm.

That same night I mailed a letter to Max Reinhardt. I don't remember what I wrote, but Edward warned me not to expect an answer. However, two days later I received a postcard from a Mr. Keindl, the secretary of the Reinhardt Theaters, notifying me that the "Herr Professor" would see me and I should prepare two scenes from different plays.

Needless to say, long before my ten o'clock appointment on the decisive day I was sitting, feverish with excitement, in the empty anteroom to Max Reinhardt's office. It was a lovely room with antique furniture, most of it baroque. I had not been able to eat breakfast, and as the hours passed I became dizzy with hunger. It was now after one and obviously I was forgotten. At last a red-haired young man stuck his head into the room and seemed very surprised to find me there. It was Mr. Keindl, who had given me the appointment. He immediately remembered my letter and cheerfully announced that Professor Reinhardt would be back in his office soon, *if* he had not decided to go to lunch first. In that case he would come to the office later, though one never knew when. He, Mr. Keindl, would advise me to wait, but if I was hungry (was I! I had black spots before my eyes), then I could run downstairs to the restaurant of the Deutsches Theater and grab a bite. But on second thoughts this would be rather risky, because the Professor might come back just when I was gone, and if I missed him it would be difficult to get me another appointment, as he was leaving in three days. I decided to starve and wait. Mr. Keindl waved to me and said he was going to lunch. Again I was alone in the lovely, quiet room, and exhausted I fell asleep.

It was dark already when I heard voices and steps; somebody turned on the light. Like Napoleon surrounded by his generals and aides-de-camp (I know that this apt comparison has been made before), Max Reinhardt walked through the anteroom and disappeared into his office. His staff filed in after him. For a short second his large blue eyes rested on me, then the door closed. After a few minutes Keindl stuck in his red head and asked: "Is he there?" I nodded.

"Fine," he said. "Now wait." I wondered what I had been doing all day long! I must have looked desperate, because he ceased smiling and went inside. I heard him speak, then another voice answered and then somebody laughed. This was the end of my endurance. I would go back to Edward, lie down and die. Just as I was about to leave, Keindl called my name and holding the door wide open, motioned me to go in.

At that time Max Reinhardt was about forty years old, short, stocky with thick, dark hair and a face one would have called ordinary, if it had not been for the wide, iris-blue eyes. These eyes looked at me rather kindly, but at the same time they penetrated and probed.

He was sitting behind an antique desk; at his right stood a young man, who, although in civilian clothes, appeared every inch the Prussian officer. This was Baron von Gersdorf, Reinhardt's assistant. The others were Felix Hollaender, small, jumpy and nervous, writer and stage director and the second in command, and the *dramaturg* Dr. Kahane, a friendly man with a long, black beard. Keindl and two other men were in the background.

Herr von Gersdorf brought me a chair; then Reinhardt asked a few questions. He sounded just as embarrassed as I. He said he liked my letter. Felix Hollaender reached for it, but hardly gave it a glance. In Berlinese German with a funny lisp, he suggested that as the Professor was tired, we should postpone my audition for another day. My heart stopped. "Professor Reinhardt is leaving,"

Herr von Gersdorf reminded him. There was an awkward silence. Nobody seemed to wish to listen to an audition, until Gersdorf leaned forward and whispered into Reinhardt's ear. I suppose he told him to get it over with and that I had been waiting since ten in the morning. Reinhardt nodded. Immediately the others made room for me and Kahane asked what scenes I wanted to do. I said *Medea*. The next moment I was on my knees, imploring Jason not to desert me. There was a silence at the end; then Reinhardt said he would like to hear more.

Hollaender had not liked my choice; had I prepared anything else? Hebbel's *Judith* for example? But Dr. Kahane suggested I should do scenes I had chosen myself. I asked if Queen Margaret's cursing scene in *Richard III* would be all right. Yes; Reinhardt said quickly that he would like to hear it. I gathered my remaining strength and cursed with all the steaming hatred I could muster.

Professor Reinhardt said that I was very good. Yes, he would like to have me at the Deutsches Theatre. The others murmured approval, but Hollaender still wanted me to do a scene from a contemporary play. Reinhardt waved aside this suggestion. He got up, shook my hand and said I should see his brother Edmund Reinhardt, the business manager of the theater, and sign a contract. He left, the generals and aides filing out after him. Gersdorf was the only one who stopped to congratulate me.

9

FOR MANY YEARS TO COME this was my only encounter with Max Reinhardt. I was one of those who prayed in vain that his blue eyes might for a split second rest upon them. Whenever I saw him passing me in the vestibule, he was surrounded by such an impenetrable wall of satellites and society women, that to make him notice me I would have had to faint at his feet, as more enterprising actresses frequently did. At that time Reinhardt was traveling with his productions in Europe and the United States, returning only for short intervals to Berlin.

Only once did I participate in a production which he directed. It was the *Orestie* in the huge Circus Schumann, with Moissi as Orestes. I was among the Trojan slaves Agamemnon brings home with Cassandra. We were grouped in the arena on huge, wide steps covered with a black cloth and leading to the brightly lit Greek palace in the background. Baron von Gersdorf and Herr Held were transmitting Reinhardt's instructions to the chorus and the huge masses of extras through a megaphone. Reinhardt himself was invisible in the dark auditorium. Only his voice penetrated it from time to time.

In those first weeks I was doomed to play Trojan slaves. In Goethe's *Faust II*, of which Reinhardt made a much discussed but successful theatrical event, I had several small parts. One of them was *Die Klugheit* (Wisdom), which gave me an impressive entrance. I appeared in floating robes, sitting on the back of an enormous elephant, which looked as if it came straight from the jungle and not from the workshop of the Deutsches Theater. From my lofty seat I recited an allegorical poem, without really understanding its meaning. Then, after a majestic exit, I was transformed quickly into a Siren or a Nereid—I do not remember which—and rushed to the opposite side of the revolving stage. After that, at breakneck speed, I changed successively into several other costumes, to end up as a Trojan slave, this time escorting Helen on her return to her husband in Sparta. While the stage was revolving I groped in darkness for "the shore near Menelaus' palace," where we were to land. *Faust II* had been in the repertory two years, but the new cast had had no stage rehearsals and I am sure I would never have arrived at my destination, had not a firm hand taken my arm and a hoarse voice whispered in my ear: "Don't be frightened. I'll lead you to your place." And, as though I would not have recognized his voice among millions, he introduced himself: "Bassermann is my name." From that day on he never forgot to wait for me during the blackouts and to lead me to my place.

After *Faust II* had at last disappeared from the repertory, Gersdorf suggested to the *Direktion* that I replace the actress who had played Hebbel's Judith. Paul Wegener was the formidable Holofernes in the evening; his understudy, a talented young actor, replaced him at the matinees. Arrogant and humorless, the understudy provoked practical jokes, which Ernst Lubitsch, the future film director, never tired of playing.

During the Easter Sunday matinee, as I was entering Holofernes' tent, veiled and escorted by a maid, I was startled to see her crumple on the floor, while on the proscenium Holofernes was delivering a lengthy soliloquy, with two enormous, grotesquely obscene, white Easter eggs dangling below his buttocks. My face was hidden by the veil, but I was unable to speak. The situation became even more hilarious when Lubitsch, as an attendant, crawling devotedly around Holofernes, snatched the eggs away whenever he turned his back to the audience. Finally I managed to say my first lines, dreading the moment when I had to take off my veil. Holofernes became aware that something was going on and reported me to Edmund Reinhardt. I was fined seventy-five marks, which was a fortune at that time, and Lubitsch's hypocritical sympathy made me very angry.

I do not believe Heinrich Kleist's *Penthesilea* has ever been performed in England or the United States and I doubt whether it would be possible to translate the wild beauty of its language. In its unrestrained ferocity and perversion it is related to Marlowe, and to the *Sturm und Drang* period. I loved the role because of its extravagance. Penthesilea's bacchantic jubilations, her demented despair and maniacal ravings were enough to release any amount of pent-up passions.

When the rehearsals began, Felix Hollaender, the director, gave me a walk-on, a "one-sentence Amazon," one among the many who excitedly report the off-stage happenings on the battlefield "near Troy." The play abounds in belligerent descriptions, but my meager task was to remain half-hidden behind a piece of scenery and shout that the Greeks were coming. The day of our first dress rehearsal changed my fate.

Reinhardt's set builder, Ernst Stern, had transformed the huge, revolving stage into a hilly landscape with valleys, and bridges arching over imaginary gullies. The Amazons wore very short tunics, just reaching to the upper part of the thigh, metal breastplates and helmets with horse tails. Their bare legs and arms were covered with a dark brown make-up and Stern ordered us to the greenroom so that he could check whether the least speck of white skin was visible. There was no question that my legs and those of Mary Dietrich, who played Meroe, the second lead, were the most "Amazon-like." They had to be shown. (These were not the days of bikinis and mini-skirts!) Stern refused to have a pair of good legs hidden by a piece of scenery, and demanded that I trade places and lines with a somewhat hefty actress. He and Hollaender asked me to run across the stage and deliver my excited report, to which a few verses were now added.

After the première Mary Dietrich took over the title role, but her voice could not endure the strain and I was advised to be prepared to step in for her. Of course I knew every word! I played Penthesilea many times with great success, but, alas, the wandering Max Reinhardt never saw me.

Wilhelminian Berlin was cold, Prussian, clean-swept and well-organized. Edward and I liked it because of its utter strangeness, in which we managed to create our own small Wychylowka, especially after Rose joined us. We had a two-room apartment in the west of Berlin, in a so-called *Gartenhaus*, which had no resemblance whatsoever to a garden. We took our meals at a nearby pension run by a kind, Austrian-Jewish lady, Frau Ehrenzweig. In no time most of our colleagues either lived or ate at the pension and we dominated the conversation at the dinner table, often putting to flight the stolid, middle-class guests. Frau Ehrenzweig complained about our "immoral" ideas and bad manners, but she was delighted and amused.

In sharp contrast to the dinners at the pension were the afternoons at Ferrucio Busoni's house, to which he and his blond, Norwegian wife, Gerda, often invited us. Everything was very formal and dignified. International celebrities, Berlin high society and promising young musicians gathered in the large salon. Romantic and beautiful, Busoni moved from group to group, always followed by three small, hunchbacked ladies, all in love with him and jealous of each other. Michael von Zadora, a pupil of Busoni, told us that the ladies were malicious gossips and that their presence at Busoni's receptions was due to the Italian superstition that to touch a hump brings good luck.

It took my reticent brother some time to show Busoni his compositions. Very impressed, Busoni advised him to leave the Berlin Academy, and introduced him to Arnold Schoenberg, who had just arrived in Berlin. It was before the performance of the *Gurre Lieder* and he was practically unknown. He lived with his family in a modest house in Zehlendorf, where Edward went to show him his work. Schoenberg found it very promising, and immediately chose Edward as the interpreter of his own music, which was then hardly understood. Edward became Schoenberg's apostle, sacrificing his promising piano career to propagate the works of the master.

On Sundays we often went to Zehlendorf with Schoenberg's other pupils: Alban Berg, Anton von Webern, Hanns Eisler and a young Englishman, Edward Clark. Berg was very striking looking —slim, dark and delicate; the others appeared to be much younger. There was always excellent coffee and a homemade cake, highly appreciated by all. With his great vitality Schoenberg dominated the conversation, while his awed pupils listened and rarely said anything. An inspired teacher, he was interested in everything, and everything seemed to give him new ideas. From household chores to music and art he asked questions and immediately formulated conclusions. His wife Mathilde, a frail, sick-looking woman, sat silently in the corner of the couch, always wrapped in a warm shawl. Two lovely, uninhibited children ran in and out of the room. In all the years that I knew him Schoenberg hardly changed. He was of medium height, quick in all his movements, a fringe of black hair showing at the back of his remarkable head. His most striking features were the huge, dark, burning eyes, the eyes of a genius. They had a constantly changing expression: wide open, almost bulging when something surprised him, attentive and concentrated when he listened, and often sarcastic or angrily glaring. Sometimes, because of his long upper lip, he looked as if he were sulking.

For many weeks to come, the early morning mail brought a large envelope containing a sheet of lined paper, on which the most controversial music of our century was written. It was Schoenberg's score to the series of short French poems, translated into German by the poet Hartleben, and called "Pierrot Lunaire." As if it were a very simple tune, Edward would sit down at the piano and play it. Then he would rush to the house of an elderly lady, Frau Albertine Zehme. Married to a wealthy man, her children grown up and the boredom of a middle class existence upon her, she had decided to have a fling at an artistic career, and, dressed as Pierrot, she toured Germany reciting the moody, delicate poems. She felt that "incidental music" would increase their effect, and somebody had advised her to get in touch with Arnold Schoenberg. Frau Zehme commissioned Schoenberg to write the score to the Pierrot cycle. Because he needed money, he agreed, but categorically demanded his sponsor's complete artistic surrender. Frau Zehme had to accept not only the score, but also his interpretation of the poems, and to study with Edward the intricate rhythms, the pitch and the inflections of the precisely devised speaking part. She was not very musical and I remember well Edward's despair over the difficulty he had in teaching her the difference between two-part and three-part rhythm. However, her "capacity for taking pains" was infinite, although I do not claim that in her case it was a sign of genius.

The music to "Pierrot Lunaire" demanded a small orchestra. Edward played the piano, the young Dutchman, Hans Kindler (later conductor of the Washington, D.C., Philharmonic Orchestra), the cello; then there were also a flutist and a clarinettist. Schoenberg conducted. The subdued Frau Zehme implored him to make one, single concession: she should be the only performer seen by the audience. Schoenberg invented a special system of screens, which hid him and the instrumentalists, yet made it possible for Frau Zehme to keep her eyes on his baton.

When she appeared in a Pierrot costume, her painted, frightened face framed by a ruff, her aging ankles in white stockings, she was greeted by an ominous murmur from the audience. One could not help admiring her courage, as she went on from poem to poem, disregarding the hissing, booing and insulting invective shouted at her and Schoenberg. There were also fanatical ovations from the young generation, but the majority were outraged. A well-known virtuoso, his face purple with rage, shouted: "Shoot him. Shoot him," meaning Schoenberg, not the poor, undaunted Pierrot.

Fifty years later Edward wrote: "It is usual in artistic events of this kind that when people are confronted with something new, they don't realize how deeply they have been affected. Though the critics were scandalized, it was exceptional that some acknowledgement of Schoenberg's genius was not voiced." We admired Schoenberg's genius, but with the disrespect of youth, I considered that it was damaged by Frau Zehme's dilettantism.

In the summer we went home, where as usual the whole family had gathered. I had a huge success imitating Albertine Zehme and telling about Holofernes' Easter eggs. Mama laughed until she cried, but I never dared to relate the story in front of my father. Niania outdid herself in cooking our favorite dishes and repeated, beaming, that her "Salusia" had not changed at all. My parents agreed that my sister Rose should continue her studies at the university in Berlin, and at the end of the summer we three took a larger apartment in the west, and started housekeeping. With increasing melancholy Rose went to her lectures on German literature until, alarmed by her evident depression, I forced an admission from her: she had only one longing—the theater. She did not have the heart to write our parents. After long discussions, I arranged an audition for her with Mr. Held, who was the director of Reinhardt's dramatic school. He found her talented and was much taken by her blond loveliness. To our great astonishment there was no objection from Papa—Mama had long since reconciled herself to the fact that her daughters were not interested in marriage.

During the performances of *Penthesilea* I had become acquainted with Ellen Geyer, an actress of great warmth—frail, dark, with an inspired semitic face, and married to a theatrical producer.

Having watched my progress from "an Amazon" at the bottom of the program to the title role of *Penthesilea,* Ellen invited me to meet her husband, Dr. Emil Geyer, who was starting his own theater in Vienna. He had seen me on the stage and, deploring Reinhardt's preoccupation with stars and his absentee leadership, made me an offer to join his Neue Wiener Buehne. He intended to create a literary theater, with an ensemble as closely knit as Stanislawski's. He and Ellen believed that I would fit into their enterprise, and also that it would be good for me to depart from classical roles for a while. They wanted me to play Vassilissa in Gorki's *Lower Depths,* as well as Strindberg, Ibsen and the new dramatists Dr. Geyer hoped to discover. Full of enthusiasm, I decided on the spot to ask for a release from my contract, which still had another year to run, and went to see Edmund Reinhardt. He was sitting at his desk, opposite him Arthur Kahane. His calm, steady gaze made me very nervous, when I blurted out my request. He refused promptly and indignantly: a contract was a contract. Why did I want a release? I said that in the two seasons I had been with the Deutsches Theater I had not yet played a première. Would Professor Reinhardt give me Lady Macbeth in the new production I heard he was planning? "Lady Macbeth?" Edmund stared at me as if I were out of my mind. Dr. Kahane shook his head unbelievingly. "I thought you might ask for Lady MacDuff," he reprimanded me. I considered this for a second; then courageously said that I was not interested in playing Lady MacDuff. Both were horrified at such blasphemy. Who did I think I was? Then Edmund said, coldly, that it was against his principles to give in to demands of temperamental actresses, and walked out of the office. Dr. Kahane looked sadly at me. "Don't you think that great, well-established actresses like Lucie Hoeflich or Tilla Durieux have more right to play Lady Macbeth than you, who are just starting?" he said.

"I cannot be starting forever," I cried, and told him about Emil Geyer's offer. Kahane, who was a friend of the Geyers, immediately changed his attitude. He realized how tempting it was for me to take part in their venture and promised to do his utmost to persuade Edmund to let me go. I was free, but now I was no longer sure that I had done the right thing.

My mother's friend Esther was happy to have me back in Vienna—though I had only made the Neue Wiener Buehne and not the Burgtheater. She had rented a pleasant room for me with a separate entrance, in an apartment belonging to an ailing widow. A dear old housekeeper, Agnes, offered to cook my breakfast and any meal I desired. I settled for the breakfast.

The rehearsals of a new Don Juan play by an Austrian-Polish dramatist, Thadeus Rittner, began as soon as I arrived, with Moissi playing Don Juan. Director Geyer had departed from his original program of creating a "closely knit ensemble," and had invited the famous star for guest performances. This was hardly consistent with the aim of the new enterprise, but it helped the box office. To me it did not matter very much, as I had an interesting role.

The play had a limited critical success, but the theater sold out each night. Although Moissi received the lion's share of the critics' attention, I was welcomed as a new "feminine," "charming," "strong," "very moving" personality. I was very happy and so were the Geyers and Esther. I could have looked forward to a busy, successful career had it not been for an undefined feeling of longing and emptiness, which I had not experienced in Berlin.

IO

"The next battle for freedom will be fought against the feudalism of love" (*Feudalismus der Liebe*), wrote Frank Wedekind sixty years ago. "The old barbaric superstitions, which hunt the whore like a wild animal and make virginity a commodity on the marriage market, belong to the era of witch trials and alchemy."

Since then the lot of women has improved enormously. They have acquired the right to toil like men and compete with them in commercial, scientific, communal and artistic professions. Virginity has lost its market value and the whore is not "hunted like a wild animal." Hers is a freely chosen profession, although still denied social security.

My own conflict with the then prevailing "feudalism" took the form of falling in love with a married man, twenty years older than myself. He had that self-confidence which had been so irritating in the cavalry officers I had known at home. But this time I was impressed by it. Ellen Geyer began to call me "Titania"—not because she thought my lover was a donkey-headed Bottom, but because I had become blind and deaf to everything around me.

He was a sculptor, admired by the Viennese bourgeoisie, but without any contact with the new trends in art. His "lonely" position, as he called it, isolated him. Jealous, suspicious and possessive, Andreas resented the freedom of my bohemian life, while he was restricted by family and social considerations. As we could not be seen together we met in the afternoons in my room or in his studio. His wife loyally obeyed the strict orders not to disturb him during his working hours. His evenings belonged to her and their two children.

We never talked about his wife and rarely about my work in the theater. Often I wondered what kind of person she was, that strange, powerful figure looming over his life. I had met them both at a reception given by the Geyers. She was a handsome woman, a little like a Walkyrie, and they looked well together—he, thin, tall, in well-cut clothes, carefully avoiding any identification as an "artist" (which I rather liked). She looked at me with her cold, blue eyes, while he complimented me on my performance in the Rittner play. Her silent, critical scrutiny annoyed me.

Meanwhile, bad attendances had forced Emil Geyer to turn to commercial plays. The first was, oddly enough, Eugene Brieux's drama about syphilis. Ellen Geyer refused to appear in it and Emil insisted that I take her part. I loathed the play too but I wanted to work. Besides I was sure that it would close in a week. However it turned out to be a hit and had a long run.

There was a scene in the second act, in which the family doctor explains the symptoms of syphilis, and the actors used to make bets about how many people in the audience would faint, or leave in a great hurry. It was the end of 1913 and Salvarsan was not generally known.

After the New Year the ensemble was sent on a tour as a patriotic service, sponsored by the government. I enjoyed our traveling, unaware that Austria was preparing for war—I never read the political articles in the papers; they seemed so unimportant, compared to the theatrical news! But we played mostly for garrisons, and seeing only men in uniform in the audience, I began to have an apprehensive feeling. However, war was inconceivable, and it was fascinating to see the Alps for the first time, the old towns like Ljubljana, Klagenfurth, capitals of ancient provinces, and the heterogeneous nationalities of the Hapsburg monarchy. On some days Andreas would appear unexpectedly at one of our stops.

In Vienna, meanwhile, the theater had been rented to a company playing a musical farce. Their success was so great that Director Geyer decided to end the season with a comedy, in which there was no part for me. However, I had to stay in Vienna as the Brieux drama was still in the repertory.

Disappointed with Director Geyer's leadership, preoccupied with my love affair, I was hardly aware that spring had suddenly changed the city into a Riviera resort. Even now, after so many, many years, I remember the carpets of hyacinths, daffodils and narcissuses spread in front of public buildings. The Ring, Volksgarten, Stadtpark and the Prater were steeped in fragrance and color. Andreas would invent excuses, and lie to his wife, to escape with me to the Wienerwald. We went for long hikes, lunched under huge, gnarled trees, and fell asleep in soft green glades. We returned in darkness, through lanes aglow with fireflies.

It was 1914 and my parents decided to spend the summer in the High Tatra. Dusko had a persistent bronchitis and the doctor said that mountain air would hasten his convalescence. The whole household, with Niania and maid, moved into a rented villa in Zakopane. Rose and Edward arrived from Berlin and I joined the family at the end of June. I had promised Andreas to write every day. We were both addressing our letters to post restante because our mail was censored—his by his wife, mine by Mama's irrepressible curiosity. She never hesitated to open a letter when the handwriting or a stamp intrigued her. "You don't have any secrets, do you?" she would ask with a disarming smile.

She was rosy and radiant because "the children have come home." For hours she listened to Edward explaining the intricacies of the twelve-tone system, fascinated though not convinced. She was pleased that Rose was looking hopefully toward the next theatrical season, and that I, for once, did not intend to break my contract. As usual, our father remained on the fringe of our activities, never directly taking part in the conversation. He walked slowly up and down in front of the veranda, where we used to sit and talk, apparently not listening; but alone with Mama, his Minister for Domestic and Foreign Affairs, he would reexamine everything we had discussed.

Dusko, who was the reason for our mass dislocation, was bored stiff with the beauty of the High Tatra. He would have gladly given all the mountains in the world for a good soccer game. The days went by quickly, but the intense well-being which always pervaded me after a Wychylowka summer, the heady suffusion with sun and air, was missing. The forbidding mountains seemed to close in on me and I was cold and depressed. I missed the wide spaces, the fields, the river and my love.

On June 28, the Archduke Franz Ferdinand and his wife were killed in Sarajevo and everything, which appeared built for eternity, began to falter. Uninvited, history entered our lives, and our roots were plowed under by tanks and guns. At the moment we were hoping naïvely that little Serbia "would not dare." Only Niania in her peasant wisdom knew better. "There will be a war," she said, staring at the huge, rocky Tatra peaks in their red, sunset glow, and she crossed herself.

All through July we lived between hope and an unpatriotic gloom. "They can't draft Edward," Mama comforted herself. "He is too near-sighted." Niania was thinking of her son, Vassili, my foster brother, and of her brother Fedja, who had just passed his exams to become a high school teacher. Vassili also was preparing to teach. With great sacrifice, and Papa's help, Niania had put both of them through school.

Then one ultimatum followed another, and we were stunned that all of Europe was against us. Papa returned to Sambor. A few days later war was declared and the whole family left Zakopane. Neither Rose nor I could think of our careers anymore.

Our train was constantly delayed by the troops rolling east towards the Russian frontier. Horses and soldiers packed into freight cars and trucks, decorated with flowers and jingoistic inscriptions, endlessly passed us. Italians, Tyrolians, Czechs, Austrians, Poles, Ukrainians, Slovenians, Croatians, and Hungarians, traditionally disunited under the Hapsburg rule, were now singing together "Ich hat'einen Kameraden." In the evening they would change to their melancholy native songs.

From the first-class compartments the officers waved to laughing and cheering girls serving refreshments at each station. Wailing and sobbing peasant women were kept back by gendarmes from the platforms as they tried to catch a brief glimpse of their men.

In Sambor the station was seething with people and we could hardly push through. The town was packed with troops; our house had become the headquarters of an archduke, who commanded the division east of the Dnjestr. His and the staff's automobiles were parked in the backyard and Dusko could not tear himself away from them. The barn and the stables were filled with soldiers and horses; the orderlies slept on the floor in the hall, bathroom and garret. Our parents and we were crowded into the back rooms.

In the kitchen, the maids giggled and shrieked, having great fun
with the orderlies. Niania, who slept there, had to enforce a curfew.

In general the billeted soldiers behaved well. Only the passing
troops, especially the Tyrolians and Hungarians, were under the
impression that they had already entered enemy land. Our carriage
and horses were "requisitioned" on the road by a Hungarian officer
brandishing his pistol, and the coachman had to walk home.

But Rose and I had no transportation problems. At six every
morning the General's auto drove us to the hospital, where we had
enrolled as volunteer nurses. The Red Cross had rushed us
through a primary course and after two weeks of perfunctory instruction, we took care of the wounded who began to fill the
wards.

According to the war bulletins, the Austrian army, in "planned
retreat," was "adjusting" the front surprisingly close to us. At first
the rumbling guns made only the windowpanes shake, then the
whole house, until the panes broke and fell out. The archduke
disappeared with his staff and the generals only stopped for a few
hours, otherwise "everything was proceeding according to plan."

As there was nobody to drive us to the hospital anymore, we
walked through the strangely empty town. In the first days of
September Grandmother and Aunt Bella arrived with their maid
and were easily accommodated. We lived by sheer nervous tension
as if outside our own selves. Mama and the town ladies had organized a buffet service at the railway station, and saw to it that not
only officers, but also the soldiers got some refreshments. Trains
from the east, Tarnopol, Stanislawow, Brody, etc., arrived crowded
with starved, parched, ill-smelling people, mostly Jews who, with
memories of pogroms still in their bones, were fleeing before the
advancing Russians.

One evening, while waiting on the blacked-out station for a
transport of wounded, I watched the train coming in quietly, then
heard piercing screams break the silence, and a young, white-faced
woman leaned from the window holding out a naked child. The
small body looked like a yellow wax figure. The woman kept up
her sharp, inhuman screaming, to which the waxen immobility of
the child made a horrifying contrast. I tried to take it from her,
but the medic pulled me away. "It's dead. Don't you see?" he said.
Then the woman and the child disappeared inside, and desolate,
half-wailing and half-singing sounds came from the compartment.
An old woman near me pointed to the starless sky where a tiny,
greenish light was moving directly above us. It was an airplane.
The first I had ever seen. Was it Russian or German? The people

were whispering that only the Germans had airplanes and that now we would win the war.

The hospital, a converted school, was crowded, dirty and unprepared for catastrophe. As there was no running water the orderlies lugged heavy jugs from the well in the courtyard all day and heated water on field kitchens. Two of the classrooms were transformed into operating rooms, each equipped with four long tables. Minor and major surgery were simultaneously performed. Putrid sores, gangrened limbs, were operated on right next to "clean" wounds like perforated lungs, stomachs, arms and legs shattered, as some doctors insisted, by dumdum bullets. I don't remember anyone wearing a surgical mask.

My sister and I were nurses' aides. The nurses, mostly nuns, showed us how to wash the wounded, clean the surgery rooms, change the dressings, bring the urine bottles and bedpans, and feed those who were unable to eat by themselves. Very soon they let us attend to more responsible chores. What seemed most important and what we desperately wanted to convey to those dazed, maimed men, was that we were personally concerned, and we tried to draw them out from the horrible anonymity into which they had been thrown. I could not bear the harsh, brutal, drill-sergeant tone in which the Ukrainians especially were addressed by doctors and nurses.

We were told that regiments were deserting en masse to the Russians, that they were shooting their own officers. It was rumored that our friend Colonel Brenner von Flammenberg had been killed by a bullet in the back of his head. Long columns of infantry passed Wychylowka, dirty, dejected, dragging their feet, numb with exhaustion.

The newspapers still claimed that thousands of Russians were surrendering, but we never saw Russian prisoners. A few Mongolians and Kalmucks were brought to the hospital. They had surrendered while on patrol but their wounds were not serious. All the wounded had that same uncomprehending stare. Lying in rows on the lumpy straw mattresses, they did not complain. Their patient, humble suffering was heartbreaking.

In the first weeks of the war aristocratic ladies used to inspect the hospitals. A princess and two pretty Hungarian countesses appeared in the operating room, escorted by the delighted chief surgeon. Lovely and fresh, in spotless white uniforms, the coquettish caps with the red cross emblem on their "marcelled" hair, perfumed handkerchiefs close to their pretty noses, they remained near the open window. The princess lifted her lorgnette to her eyes and looked with remarkable composure at the bloody mess, which was the leg of a dying man. After a few minutes, politely murmuring their great satisfaction that we were doing so well, the ladies hurried out of the room. We could hear the backfire of their automobile as it raced away. The young surgeon, to whom I was handing the swab, said in a loud voice: "*psia krew.*" These were the only Polish words he knew and they mean "bloody bitch."

The Russians had Lwow and were encircling the "unimpregnable fortress," Przemysl, where our High Command intended to annihilate them. While the newspapers were triumphantly announcing: "Przemysl is still in our hands," the population in the eastern parts of Galicia greeted the Russians as liberators. Then the Austrian defense collapsed, and at last the order to evacuate the hospital was issued. The wounded, unable to travel, were transferred to the civilian hospital; for all the others and the medical staff, to which my sister and I belonged, a train was waiting at the station. I went home after the last of the wounded were placed on it.

It was late in the afternoon and the house looked sad and neglected, the broken windowpanes had not been replaced, the autumnal garden was devastated, no one was laughing in the kitchen, and I saw artillery digging in between the rose beds.

Inside, everything was in chaos. My mother and the servants were packing, in a great hurry, Papa's precious Persian rugs, which he had collected with love and expense. Rolled into bales, they were to be taken to the Catholic church and hidden in the vaults. The *Canonicus* had offered to keep them there until our return, but Papa refused to be evacuated. He also protested my mother's decision to bury the silver under the floor of the barn, because "The Geneva Convention protects private property and all belligerents have to abide by it." This made Mama fly into one of her impetuous rages. My father slammed the door of his room, saying that he wouldn't budge and we all could go wherever we chose. Friends who had come to say good-bye, tried in vain to talk to him. Finally a deputy of the city council convinced him that the Russians certainly would take him as a hostage and deport him to some horrible place in the interior of "mother Russia." Papa gave in, and in a frenzy we all began to pack. We were permitted one suitcase each, but there were ten of us, not counting Aunt Bella's two dogs. My Grandmother's maid, Magda, and Niania were going with us. Niania took charge of a problem no one had thought of. In a short time she provided an enormous quantity of roast chicken, loaves of bread and cakes, dozens of hard boiled eggs, tea and cereal for Papa, also an alcohol stove. The foodbasket was the biggest and most important piece of luggage we carried with us. She even remembered to take food for the dogs.

The Russians were very close when we pulled out in the middle of the night. First everyone appeared despondent and frightened, but then, probably as a necessary outlet after the hectic weeks of emotional strain and physical exhaustion, we young people were seized by a sudden gaiety and recklessness. The sick and wounded joined in our mood.

Proceeding at a snail's pace toward Hungary, for days shuffling back and forth, our train was only a few kilometers ahead of the advancing Russian army. After six days of what was normally a trip of two hours, we crossed the Carpathians and the train stood still in a muddy field, under the incessant November drizzle. On both sides of the track there were abandoned wagons loaded with gorgeous grapes, melons, plums, pears and apples, sending a tantalizing fragrance to our freightcars. We were forbidden to touch any fruit as we had suspected cholera cases among our wounded.

Our next stop was at Satoralya-Ujhailly in Hungary and the mayor of the City, notified that a colleague was on the evacuation train, sent my father a large basket of choicest fruit. In spite of all the warnings, we could not resist eating them. In Satoralya the hospital train was dismembered. The wounded and the doctors were divided among different hospitals in the hinterland and our family establishment transferred to a train for Budapest. From there it was only four hours to Vienna.

In those four hours, my thoughts turned from the beastliness and desolation of the present to the brighter aspects of the immediate future. The first thing that had reestablished my *joie-de-vivre* was the hot bath and excellent breakfast in the Budapest hotel. If, as I hoped, the Neue Wiener Buehne had opened (I had been completely out of touch with the Geyers), I would be obliged to continue my contractual obligations. A longing for grease paint and footlights overcame me and a great tenderness for Andreas, who had been very distant during the last months.

II

IN THAT FIRST YEAR of the war I became a member of a family again, and to make it more difficult, a refugee family. Comparing this with the hardship and sorrow war had imposed upon others, I considered it a minor sacrifice. The casualty lists in the morning paper and the anxiety about my brother Edward had subdued my desire for independence for a while. Soon after our exodus from Sambor, Edward had been drafted and, because of his near-sightedness, given an office job. But as the war went on and the physical fitness requirements were constantly lowered, there was always the chance that he could be sent to the front. Meanwhile he was giving concerts for the Red Cross, the bereaved families, and hospitals, which made him more useful to the war effort than his doubtful ability to shoot.

We lived first in a crowded, extremely ugly apartment, which Esther had rented. The atmosphere was unbearably depressing. Then Mama found a pleasant eighteenth century house on the outskirts of Vienna, in Grinzing, and we took the second floor. The large courtyard was enclosed by a vine-covered pergola and the grapes were still hanging from the leafless, twisted branches when we moved in. A graceful staircase led to our apartment and I can still feel the wooden steps sink in like the keys of a piano when I ran down in a hurry.

The Austrian and the German armies were entrenched on the Western Front, and Hindenburg, after his Tannenberg victory, was gathering forces to drive the Russians from Galicia.

Apprehensive about the outcome of the war, my father had nevertheless considered it his duty to invest all his money in war bonds. To him Europe without the Austro-Hungarian monarchy was unthinkable. When he emerged from his room to sit down at the dinner table, the meal invariably turned into a dreaded ordeal, especially for Dusko, who had been running wild in the big city. He had joined the roughest elements in his high school and the attraction was mutual. Excelling in sports, he completely neglected his studies and Papa had visions of him as a soccer-playing hoodlum, while I worried about his constant demands for larger sums of money. This we did not dare to reveal to Papa. Optimistic as ever, my mother said there was no need to despair about Dusko, that she had had a serious talk with him; he had admitted a gambling debt, but promised to reform and avoid bad company. A few days later I noticed that Grandmother was no longer wearing her diamond brooch.

I tried to appeal to my younger brother's reason, but was astounded by his complete lack of emotion, his cold disregard for our parents. His excuse was that in a year or so, he might be in the army—the war would still be on, he might be killed, so at least he intended to have a good time as long as he was alive. He was only concerned with his pleasures and his dominant position among the young toughs. I looked at him as he sat there, strong, stubborn, handsome and extremely antagonistic. He did not understand what the fuss was about; all he wanted was more spending money.

Rose had returned to Germany. She had accepted an engagement with the Görlitz Stadttheater. Aunt Bella had a new profession: she was playing the piano in a movie theater, improvising with great ingenuity the incidental music to slapstick comedy and gaudy melodrama. Her free hours were divided between two lovers, one young, the other middle-aged. She could not decide which one she liked better.

Of course, the first thing I did after my return was to rush to the café where I used to meet Andreas, and telephone him. There was no answer in his studio. A feeling of anguish seized me. I had written to him and he must have read in the newspapers that Sambor had been evacuated. I was walking down the street dejectedly, when I saw him coming toward me . . . Was there a greater proof of love, belonging, telepathy, call it what you may! Neither war, distance, nor time had changed him. He said that every day he had gone to our café to read the papers and wait for me.

The theater had reopened but the actors were paid only half of their former salaries. The war had interrupted Emil Geyer's ambitious program and like most other producers he was concerned with profitable entertainment. We played farces, light comedies and, of course, the Brieux play about syphilis. It was our patriotic contribution to the war.

In the Spring of 1915 a German offensive had thrown the Russians out of Galicia. Sambor was freed, but the prospects for victory were dimmed when the Italians joined the Allies. Hindenburg's victory at Tannenberg and the breakthrough at Gorlice balanced the scale, and made it possible for my father to return to Sambor and resume his duties as mayor. Niania went with him, overjoyed to leave Vienna. She had been so unhappy there that she had even refused to go sightseeing. Once I persuaded her to visit St. Stephen's Cathedral, which I had hoped would impress her, but her only melancholy comment was: "It is big." At night she would bring the tray with my supper, sit down at my bedside and unburden her heart: Vassili was prisoner of war in Russia and it was a relief to know that he was no longer in danger of being killed; but "did they give him anything to eat?" It took ages to get news through the Red Cross.

An officer we knew, who had stopped in the now liberated Sambor, brought us the rugs from the vault of the Catholic church. Mama intended to sell a few particularly valuable pieces, to finance the rebuilding of our dilapidated Wychylowka, but when we opened the wooden crates we saw that the rats had been more destructive than the passing armies. They had eaten holes as huge as wagon wheels, and the damage to the rugs was so great that it was impossible to have them repaired. We were also told that all the furniture in the house had been looted, and only the walls and the roof remained.

Mama, Grandmother and Dusko also went home. Edward had been transferred to the "liberated" Przemysl. Only I remained. Life in Vienna had changed. Although the night clubs and swank restaurants were crowded, the blockade was felt strongly by all those who did not have the money to hoard. I often went hungry.

Toward the end of the season Dr. Geyer gave me a leading role in *Der Graf von Gleichen,* a drama in which Albert Steinrueck, the great German actor, appeared as guest. He must have been in his middle-forties then, a square-set man with a lion's face framed by hair so fair it seemed almost white. Off stage he was one of the most fascinating human beings, without any pose, straightforward and a talented painter. He drank a great deal.

It was difficult for me to concentrate on my acting career during the war. The struggle for roles and success had become meaningless; on the streets one saw more and more women in mourning. My colleagues advised me to break with Andreas and leave Vienna. I had an offer to return to Reinhardt, but paralyzed by my infatuation I refused to move.

It must have been late in July that the theater closed and I was free to return to Wychylowka. The trains, though they took much longer, were more or less on schedule, and terribly crowded and dirty. It was hot and stuffy in the compartment. A late moon broke through the clouds when we were traveling through Galicia. In the cold, gray-green light I could clearly see the landscape: miles and miles of ravaged forestland of which nothing was left but black, broken treetrunks, their charred, skeleton arms desperately reaching up to the sky. Among them were thousands of white crosses. They made the forest an unending, nightmarish cemetery.

The station in Sambor had been bombed and damaged; detachments of Austrian soldiers, hundreds of peasants, and Jews in kaftans were milling around, dragging boxes, suitcases and packages. One did not know whether they were leaving or returning. We drove home in a hired *fiacre*, as we no longer had our horses. Mama, rosy-cheeked and smiling, hugged me, happy that I was back. She had good news: Edward had a furlough and would be coming home. Papa felt much better and was busy at his office. Everything else in the house was going well, thanks to Loginoff, the Russian prisoner of war allotted to Wychylowka for farm work. Presently, as we drove up to the house, I saw a huge, beaming, strikingly handsome Russian standing at the gate, waving happily and announcing at the top of his voice: *"Barynia* Salka," as if we had known each other all our lives. And as usual Niania, Marynia the maid and fourteen-year-old Ivan, who functioned as cowboy, kitchen help and Dusko's personal valet, came running to embrace me, all barefoot.

From outside, the house looked unchanged. The windows and doors had been replaced, but still needed a coat of paint. Asters and carnations were growing in the front garden and the lawn was well cared for; but the rose bushes were gone, having given their lives for Kaiser and *Vaterland.* Inside everything had been destroyed, the furniture stolen or burned, even the tiles in the stoves were missing. The two grand pianos had been disembowelled and used as mangers. They were now a sad pile of disconnected parts. But to Mama's great triumph, the buried silver had been found untouched, and now shone, brightly polished, from the roughly hewn sideboard Loginoff had made for the dining room. The other rooms also had plain wooden furniture: chairs, benches, shelves, beds and tables he had constructed. Only the living room contrasted sharply with the crude primitiveness of the other rooms. Great-grandfather's eighteenth century desk with all its drawers and secret compartments, which had mystified us so much when we were children, was there. Leather armchairs, a sofa, and a rug under the oak table, made the room comfortable and even elegant. The black marble Empire clock stood on the white mantelpiece again. All had been rescued by a kind soul from Papa's office.

It is impossible to imagine how Wychylowka would have withstood the war if it had not been for Loginoff, the carpenter, gardener, farmer and veterinary, who adopted it as his new homeland. In Russia he had a wife, three children and a fertile farm overlooking the Volga, which he had abandoned to fight for the Czar. Luckily for us, he thought it better to stay alive, and on his first patrol went over to an Austrian infantry regiment, whose Ukrainian detachment was just debating whether they themselves should not surrender to the enemy. As the Austrian casualties were extremely severe, more peasants were drafted and the prisoners of war distributed among landowners to ease the labor shortage. Loginoff never ceased to bless his fate that he was assigned to my father; he was received with open arms in our household. He was also very popular in town, where he was permitted to move freely by day and he became very successful in bargaining with black marketeers. He liked to tell us about his family and the rich crops of his farm, but he was not a man to live on memories. It was obvious to everyone except Papa, that he and our attractive maid Marynia were very much in love, although the law made it an offense for the female population to "fraternize" with prisoners of war.

Outside our garden fence was a German ammunition dump. Railroad tracks had been built to connect it with the station, and at the crack of dawn we would be awakened by the freight cars rolling in and the officers and sergeants cursing the prisoners who loaded them. They were Mongolians, Tartars and Kalmucks, all looking like skeletons. Loginoff told me that there had been five hundred of them, but half had died of hunger and typhoid fever. He had dug a hole under the fence separating the dump from our barnyard, and at night the starving men came crawling in with their mess tins to get the cabbage and potato soup Niania cooked for them. Sometimes Niania's relatives illegally slaughtered a pig and brought a slice of fat or a few bones to add to the soup. This meager help was only a drop in the bucket, but if the POWs saw us on the road, something like the shadow of a smile lit up the skull-like faces.

The German officers had a bowling alley and the commander paid us a formal visit and invited us to bowl with them. It was impossible to refuse, and I shall never forget that afternoon. Neither Mama, Rose nor I showed any talent for bowling, especially as the presence of the two skeletons putting up the pins prevented us from appreciating our hosts' humor and indubitable politeness.

It was a bad summer because of the ammunition dump, and the

war bulletins. Later, when Edward arrived and a piano was rented and we all gathered around it, life became more normal, even the weather—until one day Andreas appeared.

It was an unexpected visit as he had not written that he would be transferred to Galicia. I introduced him to my family, which I had not dared to do in Vienna. Mama suspected my involvement and was disturbed.

When I returned to Vienna the rehearsals for *The Lower Depths*, in which I was playing Vassilisa, started. Andreas was in Hungary and we wrote each other every day. Suddenly, before the opening, I received a letter which said that he had proof that I had been unfaithful to him. He was breaking off our relationship, returning to his wife and did not want to see me again. I had not been unfaithful; Andreas's accusation shattered me.

Help came from kind, loving Esther Mandl. She asked me to move to her apartment in the Zedlitzgasse, so that she should have me "at hand," and see more of me. Her mother's room was now empty, as Mrs. Koffler had suffered a mental breakdown and was confined to an institution. I gladly accepted as I feared that alone in my cold, dreary place I also would lose my mind.

Some weeks later Ellen Geyer said that after the performance she would like to meet me at the nearby café. I had a date with Fanny Muetter, but Ellen insisted that I break it because we were to meet a young stage director, Berthold Viertel, now on furlough from the Eastern Front. Her husband intended to sign him for the Neue Wiener Buehne as soon as he could get a release from the army.

I had previously run into his wife, Dr. Grete Viertel, a handsome woman, a little haughty and condescending. She had a chemistry degree, but to my surprise, she told me that she was taking dramatic lessons and wanted to be an actress.

I arrived late at the café, where Ellen and a dark-haired lieutenant were sitting at one of the tables, deeply engrossed in conversation. I went over and she made the introductions. The lieutenant got up. He was rather thin and not exactly a military figure. The very black hair made his face quite pale. It was a strong, attractive face dominated by a broad forehead, thick eyebrows and dark, compelling eyes. He offered me a cigarette, approved heartily that I did not smoke, and lit his and Ellen's rapidly and nervously. I liked his hands.

"Mr. Viertel has only seen the first act," said Ellen apologetically.

I had been distracted in the first act, but he said: "You were very good. When you entered I knew immediately that you owned the place."

His voice had a dark, warm timbre. He continued staring at me with a curious and searching expression, then asked where I came from. "Sambor, Galicia." "Galicia!" That was a new world to him, unknown until the war. It had been a revelation; he never thought he would love it so much. Enthusiastically he described to Ellen the Ukrainian peasants and Chassidic Jews he had met, their wisdom and humor, their hardships and philosophical endurance. He made me quite homesick and in some remote way, rather proud. He wanted me to tell him about my family and Wychylowka and could not hear enough about Loginoff and Niania and Edward. Especially Edward fascinated him. "Twelvetone in Sambor . . ." he kept repeating.

The café closed and we were faced with the difficulties of getting home. No buses nor streetcars were running anymore, and only one lone taxi, which we forced Ellen to take. Lieutenant Viertel insisted on accompanying me, though he lived on the opposite side of the town. And so we walked through the Ring and the inner city, past the Minoriten Church, the Freiung, Am Hof, discovering each other.

He was leaving in a few days, but he hoped to be back as a longer furlough was due to him, after two uninterrupted years at the front. He was certain that the war would last another year and he had told Emil Geyer that it was unrealistic to make any plans whatsoever. It was the end of 1916, the old Emperor had just died and it was as if his death had put a seal to the end of Austria. We both felt it strongly, though the Germans had rescued us on the Eastern Front.

"Still," he said, "I could never have stayed behind and pursued my profession, while others were torn from their existence. I do not mean to sound heroic. I am not exposed to actual danger. I *was* in Serbia, but now I am quite safe."

During the whole evening he had not spoken of his wife and I did not mention that I had met her. We arrived at my apartment building; I rang for the janitor. Berthold said: "You know that I am going to marry you?"

I laughed. "Aren't you married already?"

"We are not living together, my wife and I," he said quietly.

"But I am involved with somebody else."

"It does not matter. I will marry you."

The next day was a Sunday and I slept until the telephone woke me. It was Berthold Viertel, who wanted to know when we could see each other. He said that he had promised to look up the relatives of a comrade and they had asked him to lunch, but afterward he was free and wanted to meet me wherever I chose. I also had a luncheon invitation and gave him the telephone number of my hosts, so he could call me when he was about to leave. We discovered that we were both invited by the same people, a pleasant stage-struck couple I used to visit quite often.

"You see," he said, "it was inevitable. Even if you had not come to the café last night, we would have met."

The lunch was sensational, as our wealthy hosts had exploited their black market connections lavishly. I felt warm, well-fed and exuberant as I had not been for many, many months. Afterward Berthold took me to the Café Central. In the entrance we caught a glimpse of Peter Altenberg, who looked like Verlaine and wrote enchanting short stories. He was wrapped in a dark loden cape, which, as he assured everybody, had the magic quality of lifting him into the air and making him able to fly. We watched his take-off: he unfolded his wings and disappeared around the corner.

This encounter was the cue for Berthold to talk about the time when, at the age of sixteen, he was skipping classes, following Peter Altenberg around and, driving to desperation his very "buergerlich" Jewish parents. A friend showed his poems to Karl Kraus, who published them in *Die Fackel*. Had I ever read *Die Fackel?* Had I an idea who Karl Kraus was? The press never mentioned him. Had I ever heard Kraus read Shakespeare or his own poems? No, I hadn't.

For Berthold, Karl Kraus was a genius, a prophet, the greatest satirical writer since Swift, a lone voice raised against the corrupt values of our time, against social injustice and the general vulgarization of taste by the hideous jargon of publicity; a voice passionately protesting the war and attacking all those who, untouched and unmoved by the slaughter of millions, profited by it.

I had not noticed that Grete, his wife, had come in with some friends. Berthold looked up and waved to her. She stopped at our table and reminded him that a Kraus lecture was taking place that evening and that Kraus would not forgive him if he missed it.

When we arrived, the hall was already packed with people. Kraus appeared on the podium, a fragile, gray-haired man with a stoop, one shoulder higher than the other. When he began to speak I was startled by the strength and sonority of his voice, his superb diction and his incredible vitality. He had a noble, finely chiseled face and very expressive hands. To protest against the war in 1916 took great courage, also to ridicule the warlords, many of whom were members of the Imperial family. He quoted those writers, poets, and lyricists who were glorifying death on the battlefields, while they themselves were safely ensconced behind an editor's desk. The audience shouted, cried, laughed and cheered. I also cried, laughed and applauded and Berthold beamed with satisfaction.

There were only a few people at Karl Kraus's table when we joined him later; next to him sat his friend, a blond lady, pretty but no longer young. He looked at me curiously with his large, pale eyes: I was too awed to say anything. He and Berthold began talking about people I did not know and articles I had not read. Everything Kraus said was extraordinary, and brilliantly formulated; his constant obsession was his cause and himself. Only later, when I knew him well, did I understand his great heart. The evening seemed never to end; nobody thought of going home. I still remember the shocked expression on the blond lady's face when Berthold got up, saying that I was exhausted and that he had to take me home. Next day he went back to the front.

Long, wonderful letters from a place called Kolendziany began to arrive every morning. They were about the Ukrainian country, its people, the war, but most of all they were about us. He became as close to me as Edward. I also wrote every day. Later we discovered that we were writing the same thoughts and the same words at precisely the same moment. Kolendziany, that faraway village, became a symbol.

The Neue Wiener Buehne was preparing Strindberg's *Father*, with Paul Wegener as guest star. I was to play my first Strindberg woman, Laura.

Paul Wegener arrived and the rehearsals were long and intense. The performance was a great success. Encouraged, Emil Geyer decided to produce Ibsen's *John Gabriel Borkman* with Steinrueck and Ellen in the role she had always wanted to play: the tender, loving Ella Rentheim. A young, talented actress, Leontine Sagan, who distinguished herself later directing the film *Maedchen in Uniform*, played Mrs. Wilson and I was Borkman's hard, pitiless wife Gunhild.

We gave guest performances of *Borkman* and *Der Graf von Gleichen* in Linz, Graz and Innsbruck. It was a wonderful experience to be in daily contact with an artist like Steinrueck. Then the season ended and I went home for the summer. A month later Berthold arrived from Kolendziany to visit me and Wychylowka.

12

IN THE SPRING OF 1917 the population of Wychylowka had been increased by a tiny but self-assertive creature named Viktoria. She was the product of Loginoff's and Marynia's love. When I arrived she was already three months old and my father still unaware of her existence—Marynia's voluminous skirts had hidden her pregnancy from his unsuspecting eye. The name "Viktoria" suggested by Mama was to symbolize the victory of love over the "antifraternization law." Like the child Moses, little Viktoria slept in her basket among the shrubs, or was carried by her father to the field whenever he was working there. At night she shared his quarters in the laundry room. Loginoff was a dedicated father, whereas Marynia seemed rather casual about the blessings of motherhood. Very soon she ceased to give the baby her breast, and whoever walked by the basket stuck the milkbottle into the mouth of the happily kicking and gurgling Viktoria, or fed her a spoonful of cereal. On this collective care the baby thrived.

In April America declared war on Germany and Austria, and we knew that we were defeated. We read that there was mutiny in the Russian, French and Italian regiments, but the newspapers never mentioned that the same was happening in our armies.

When, on a lovely summer morning, Berthold arrived at the house, I was at the far end of the garden changing Viktoria's diapers. Our barefooted shepherd-butler Ivan led Berthold straight to me, as nobody else was at home. Mama was shopping, my father in his office, Loginoff and Niania in the field. Marynia, who was to watch over her child while gathering raspberries for dinner, had followed Loginoff. Neither Edward nor Rose had come home that summer. Dusko, though only seventeen, had volunteered and was training with an artillery regiment in a Czech town.

Although he later denied it, Berthold's face took on an odd expression when he surprised me with a baby in my arms. He always insisted, however, that it would not have made the least bit of difference to him had he found me surrounded by four illegitimate children.

The whole household approved of Berthold. Niania liked him at once, Mama found him most interesting, and he also pleased Papa, who only thought it "odd" that my suitors were mostly married men.

Our next meeting was in Vienna and it coincided with the furlough of his friend Ludwig Muenz. The introduction took place in the inevitable Café Central. Ludwig was unusually handsome, immaculate in his officer's uniform, but tense; he concealed his nervousness with loud laughter.

Berthold had warned me not to ask Ludwig about his war experiences. He had been on the Italian Front, commanding an artillery unit. They had been exposed for many days and nights to the fire of a camouflaged Italian battery and had heavy casualties. At last he located the battery and moved his guns to another position. Next morning he saw the Italians below him. They were a bunch of young boys, rinsing their canteens, unaware that they were now a perfect target. He gave the command to fire. The hit was direct and the nightmare never ceased to haunt him.

Grete Viertel joined us and we began to talk about the theater. Determined to show me off, Berthold insisted that I tell them about the Wallenstein performance in Zurich and my audition with Max Reinhardt. These were his favorite stories. They all laughed. Ludwig wondered what auditions were like, and Grete suggested that we go to her place and that I repeat the scenes I had played for Reinhardt. It would be her farewell party as she had signed a contract with a provincial theater in Germany. So we all went. Her room was quite large and, like most rooms in wartime, cold and badly lit. We pushed the furniture toward the wall, leaving space in the center.

I started with *Phaedra,* and after that Berthold asked me in a hushed voice to do *Penthesilea.* Each time I finished a scene he said: "Go on, please," and cued me to the next. Everyone seemed very moved. When they spoke it sounded like the voices in a sickroom. Then they started berating me for my indolence, for wasting my time, for letting myself be pushed around and not demanding release from my contract. I had lacked encouragement and confirmation for so long, that their praise and enthusiasm made me exuberant. Suddenly everyone grew very loud, complained of a terrific appetite and had to eat at once. Ludwig suggested that we go to the Café X., Karl Kraus's headquarters, which would serve us relatively decent food. Anyway, he and Berthold had promised to look up the master. Grete declined to come with us and I said good-bye to her. We never met again.

On the street Ludwig asked Berthold if it was true that he had asked Grete for a divorce. "Yes, I have," was Berthold's curt reply.

If there was any bitterness Grete had not shown it.

Kraus was alone at his usual table, piles of newspapers around him. He looked thin and pale. "Worn out," as Berthold said, "by his daily polemics against every single word printed in the newspapers."

At the sight of Berthold and Ludwig, he brightened, though reproaching them for being late.

"You must forgive us," said Ludwig. "Something very important happened." He liked to use the word "important."

Kraus looked puzzled and they told him about my "audition." I felt embarrassed, but Kraus was interested and wanted to know more about me. Theater was his obsession; he had memories of the old Burgtheater actors and, as he described them, they must have been volcanoes of passion and masters of characterization. He loathed the now fashionable "naturalness" and mumbling on the stage. He considered Reinhardt the greatest offender against *Wortregie*, despised his publicity and the international ballyhoo around him. I summoned my courage and defended Reinhardt.

"He liked you a lot. You really got away with murder," laughed Berthold when we were both walking toward my house. We had left Ludwig with Kraus, who never went home before dawn. A taxi passed and we hailed it. That night we stayed together, and all the other days and nights of Berthold's furlough.

The Russian Revolution and the collapse of the Eastern Front precipitated our next meeting. After three years at the front Berthold had the right to be recalled for a civilian job. The *Prager Tageblatt* engaged him as theatrical critic and columnist.

Berthold's parents were business people and belonged to that same middle class their son so strongly disliked and which his whole being so violently opposed. His father was a manufacturer of furniture, on a small scale, which he exported to Russia. The war had ruined his business and he complained a lot, though the family seemed quite well-off. A wiry, nervous man in his fifties, he was restless and mercurial, the expression of his gray eyes constantly changing from mischief to melancholy. He had lost his left hand trying to retrieve his hat from under a train which was beginning to move, but I have never seen anybody tie a parcel, slice bread, peel an apple or orange as neatly and efficiently as he did with his one hand. We were on excellent terms, but Berthold's mother was not pleased that he wanted to marry an actress. Even after I had presented her with three grandsons she did not get over it.

Immediately after Berthold's return from the army he and Grete were divorced, and our wedding date was set for April 30, 1918. Mama promised to attend but Papa only sent his best wishes; he was too harassed in his office. Rose was in a play in Berlin, Dusko on the Western Front. But Edward had been transferred to Vienna, where the "Schoenbergianers" were gathering around the master, who had been drafted and was patriotically fulfilling some dreary barrack duties. I remember an afternoon at his house in Moedling, with Edward, Anton von Webern and Erwin Stein, all in baggy, soldier uniforms.

As soon as Berthold started his job in Prague he got an unexpected offer to direct at the Royal Theater in Dresden. Its head, Count von Seebach, invited him to come to Dresden to discuss a contract. Aroused from my lethargy by Berthold's and Ludwig's prodding, I also had begun negotiations with German directors.

In high spirits we decided to have a premarital honeymoon and travel together, first to Berlin where I was to meet a Munich producer and where Berthold was eagerly awaited by Siegfried Jakobsohn, the publisher of the *Schaubuehne,* to which he was contributor. Years later *Die Schaubuehne* changed to the *Weltbuehne,* and its new publisher, Carl von Ossiectzki, was to become the only recipient of the Nobel Prize given to an inmate of a Nazi concentration camp.

Drab, cold and hungry as it was, Berlin seemed much more alive than Vienna. The atmosphere was more invigorating, the plays more interesting, the audiences more responsive, though just as peaked and gray-faced as the Viennese.

We had forgotten our ration cards and the only nourishment we could get was oysters and liquor. We had oysters and Moselle wine for breakfast, oysters and wine for lunch, hot brandy or rum drinks to warm up in the afternoon. Supper did not matter, because by then we were so tipsy that we did not want to eat.

From Berlin we went on to Dresden, then returned to Vienna, both of us with a contract. Berthold had signed for three years with the Royal Saxonian Theater, provided he could be reclaimed by September 1918. (How unperturbed the monarchies still were and how unaware of the approaching debacle!) My contract was with the Kammerspiele in Munich. From the career point of view nothing better could have happened to us, but alas, Munich and Dresden were quite a distance apart.

My mother arrived in April, happy and excited. She had brought the complete wedding dinner from Wychylowka: ham cured and cooked by Niania, roast turkey, bread, butter and a small wedding cake. She was staying at Esther Mandl's and the "reception" was to take place there. We all looked forward to the dinner which in itself made the marriage worthwhile.

A cab drawn by a white horse took us to the Seitenstaedter Temple. I sat between Mama and Edward, holding both their hands. "It's lucky," said Mama. "A white horse is very lucky." We passed a chimney sweep with a ladder on his shoulder; this again meant good luck.

At the entrance to the synagogue, Berthold, his parents, his sister Paula, Dr. Mandl and Esther waited for us, with Poldi, Esther's faithful housekeeper. Dissolving in tears she gave me good advice: "Step first on the rug in front of the altar" (she was a Catholic), "then you will always have the upperhand."

Berthold and I stepped together on the rug. We were both awed and moved. The rabbi told Berthold to slip the ring on my finger and repeat the vows after him, which Berthold solemnly did. The Jewish bride is only permitted to say "yes."

13

THE WINDOW WAS OPEN and the sweet fragrance of lilies of the valley filled our room. They stood in huge bunches on the table, the cabinets and even the floor. The room had a pale green ceiling and green walls and it was like waking up in a flower bed. Close to me Berthold was sound asleep. I was overcome by an enormous tenderness. I wanted a son who would have his dark eyes and the same thick, black lashes.

In Prague we moved into a room his sister Helene rented for us in the same house where she and her husband Willi Bruekner lived. From there our existence in furnished rooms, furnished apartments and furnished houses was launched. For many years to come, we would have to cope with other people's ugly furniture, pretentious, middle class and mostly covered with dust sheets by the cautious owners. It depended on our financial condition whether I would muster up the courage to remove the dust sheets. The room in Prague had the advantage of proletarian simplicity, and was easy to keep clean, but to live in it with Berthold was like being in a place hit by a cyclone. I cooked breakfast on a small alcohol burner, the other meals we shared with Helene and Willi, who had a maid. Willi was a tenor under contract to the *Stadtopera*.

Helene was in the last months of pregnancy and her daily campaign to feed us was truly heroic. As the debacle of the Hapsburg monarchy became inevitable, the Czech antagonism against the German-speaking population of Prague was openly displayed. Their fertile country provided the Czechs with more produce than other lands of the monarchy, but they refused to sell to German-speaking people. Sometimes by addressing them in Polish, I succeeded in being waited on in the foodshops.

In June cherries appeared on the market in great abundance and though they did not appease our hunger, they enhanced the charm of the beautiful city. When I think of Prague, which I have not seen since, I see the stands bulging with baskets of cherries, their rich red against the old, gray, stone palaces and the green of the Hradchin.

As Berthold had to review the premières at the Stadt Theater all the actors were extremely friendly to us. But our greatest pleasure was in going to the opera, which under Alexander von Zemlinsky (Schoenberg's brother-in-law) was of a remarkable excellence. The second conductor and the choir director were Dr. Heinrich Jalowetz and Anton von Webern, both Schoenberg's pupils and close friends of Edward's. We spent many evenings with them and their wives, talking about the war, the Russian Revolution and the disintegration of the Austro-Hungarian Empire. But the constant, most absorbing topic was where and how to get food. We were always hungry. The Weberns and Jalowetzes had small children and I remember Webern staring at sausages and a single can of sardines in the window of a foodstore, inaccessible to him because of the price and his ignorance of the Czech language.

Max Brod, Franz Kafka and a witty Viennese journalist, Anton Kuh, came sometimes for supper. I remember that once the main dish was spinach and that I could not grasp the witticisms of

Anton Kuh, who made political jokes about it. Kafka was tall, dark and handsome. Although we saw him quite often, mostly at Max Brod's house, I was too awed and too shy to talk to him. He was very quiet. It was hard to believe that he had tuberculosis, he looked so brown and healthy.

In July we traveled to Wychylowka. It had been a rainy summer and the meadows near the Dnjester were flooded. A gypsy camp was marooned very close to our field and the caravans stuck deeply in the muddy water. Berthold and I went to take a look at the gypsies and see if we could help. There was a mother with a sick child who aroused our sympathy and we spent more time than was good near her wagon. A few days later Berthold had a high temperature and the doctor said he had caught scarlet fever from the gypsy. He was quarantined in our room and I took care of him. I have never known anybody as indifferent to physical pain. It was in direct contradiction to his extraordinary sensitiveness, his acuteness to the slightest nuances in people's attitudes. Even though running a high temperature, he would dictate essays and articles and poems to me. I loved our total seclusion, although when the quarantine was over the greater part of our vacation was gone.

The weather had improved and we watched little Viktoria, now eighteen months old, toddling around in the garden when my father was in his office. Her incognito presence in the laundry room continued. Loginoff was still taking loving care of her, but was restless and worried about his legitimate family in Russia. Marynia knew that he would leave as soon as war prisoners were exchanged. He said he would come back after he had reassured himself about his wife and children. But while the fighting continued he could not think of going, and I am sure Marynia wished that the war with Russia would go on for ever.

Shortly before our departure, Papa came home after an unpleasant session with the magistrate and, worn out, ordered his supper brought to his bed. Niania asked me to take it to him. The simple meal contained the first corn on the cob from our garden. The door to the bedroom stood open and Papa was in bed, reading. When I came in with the tray, he looked over his glasses, his eyes fixed on something behind me. I turned my head and saw Viktoria standing in the door, her thumb in her mouth, staring attentively at my father. They had both the same scrutinizing expression. I put the tray down and waited for the thunderstorm.

Silently my father beckoned to the child and, sucking her thumb, she approached fearlessly. He motioned her to come closer and immediately she took the thumb out of her mouth and climbed on the bed, encouragingly pointing to his tray. My father began to loosen the kernels from the corncob and offered them to her on his palm. Like a bird she picked them up with her mouth; then both smiled at each other. I left them alone, not wanting to intrude upon the beginning of a great love. It lasted until my father's death.

None of us ever found out whether Papa had known the truth all the time. Loginoff went back to Russia, Marynia married a widower, but Viktoria remained a member of our family, spoiled by Papa as he had spoiled Dusko and later his grandchildren. Nothing could melt this severe, aloof man as easily as a child's hand reaching out for his.

Berthold accompanied me to Munich and after a few lovely, but much too short days, he left for Dresden. The season started with rehearsals for an Andreyev play of which I only remember that I was a Russian student and had to play a guitar and sing.

The war seemed endless; the cold and hunger had become unbearable, and I wondered how long people would stand it.

In the first week of November my sister Rose, who was in a play in Nuremberg, had a few days free and came to visit me. In the evening the "extras" appeared with headlines that the sailors in Luebeck, Bremen and Cuxhaven had revolted. They were converging on Berlin in crowded trains to overthrow the Kaiser's government.

Rose and I wanted to see what was happening in the streets. We were nearing the Heldenplatz when we met thousands of people marching, among them soldiers and sailors, obviously just back from the front. They were singing the *Internationale*. Detachments of police appeared, and everybody was running and shouting. There were some shots and people ducked into side streets and doorways. We started to run. A man called to us to go home, as there would be more shooting.

The theater had closed, the telephone was cut off, I could not call Berthold, and my sister and I sat hungry and desperate in my cold room. Next day, after some street fighting, all the public buildings were occupied by the revolutionaries. The Regent had abdicated and Kurt Eisner proclaimed the Republic of Bavaria. He had been put in prison for his pacifism and had broken with his party, the Social Democrats, when they voted the war funds. He became Prime Minister three days later when the Armistice was declared. In defeated Germany the bells did not ring and though relieved, people did not rejoice.

At last I had a letter from Berthold. The revolution had taken place more sedately in the Saxonian capital than in Berlin and Munich. The King made his famous pronouncement: "*Macht*

Euch Euren Dreck alleene" (something like: "Now you take care of your own filth"), and left. Count Seebach resigned and a collective of five: three actors, one director (Berthold) and the *dramaturg*, Dr. Karl Wolff, took over the Schauspielhaus. The three actors were old, prominent *Hofschauspieler*, much bewildered to say the least, at having to head a revolutionary regime. But Berthold and Dr. Wolff steered the theater on an artistic course, for which it was soon to become renowned.

Meanwhile in Munich the *Räte* (soviets) of soldiers, workers and artists were formed. In all the theaters the actors organized, to fight for the long overdue reforms of their standard contract, and the *Genossenschaft* (Actors' Equity) came into existence. Each theater sent its representative to discuss the new constitution at a general meeting. The ensemble of the Kammerspiele elected the young, fiery Erwin Faber, me, and another actor, whose name I don't remember. Besides playing Paulina in *Winter's Tale* and rehearsing the evil Queen in Strindberg's *Snow-white*, I attended meetings and reported everything in long letters to Berthold.

I was busy and hungry and expected to be cold and lonely at Christmas, but Berthold surprised me by suddenly arriving and I was beside myself with joy. For two months we had not even been able to telephone—it was incredible to be together again! However our happiness was dampened by my falling ill with the Spanish flu. I almost died, as starvation had weakened my resistance. Desperate, Berthold went to look for some food which would sustain my failing strength. A colleague told him that one could still buy a piece of meat at the truckdrivers' canteens. He returned home triumphantly with a big chunk of roast goose wrapped in greasy newspaper. We ate it with our fingers, right out of the paper, and I am sure it saved my life.

One morning the bell rang and opening the door I recognized Rainer Maria Rilke, who silently handed me a letter, then quickly turned and ran away. The letter, on blue stationery, expressed the hope that Berthold and I would be able to come for tea the next afternoon. I was baffled by why he was so mysterious about handing it to me. Berthold thought that Rilke had not expected me to open the door myself. I never found out, as I did not mention it when we went to see him. He was extremely correct in his manners, charming and gentlemanly, showing great warmth toward Berthold. He talked a great deal about his visit to Tolstoy. He had been so awed by the old giant, that he did not dare to lift his eyes to his face, and when they took a long walk together, he looked only at the big hand with the bluish veins, which Tolstoy kept stuck into his belt.

The separations from Berthold were now harder to bear. I could not visit him in Dresden, because I was playing every night. Meanwhile Kurt Eisner's government was fighting for its existence. The general misery and starvation had increased. In Berlin the "Spartakists," Karl Liebknecht's and Rosa Luxemburg's socialist party, were gaining power. The returning soldiers multiplied the ranks of the unemployed. A letter from Mama, which took months to reach me, said that Dusko had come back from the Italian Front and was now in the Polish army. Loginoff had left; masses of people were dying from the Spanish flu and the war in Poland went on endlessly.

In Munich the actors' meetings were bitter and acrimonious. I participated in the discussion about a new Equity contract. The old one had, among other obsolete articles, an atrocious paragraph granting the director the right to dismiss immediately, without financial compensation, any actor who had tuberculosis or syphilis. In the case of tuberculosis all my colleagues agreed that it should be treated like any other affliction, with a paid leave for so-and-so many weeks, etc., etc., but syphilis was a disgraceful sickness, acquired from an immoral life and therefore not deserving any benefits. I had so far refrained from making any speeches, but this time I got up. It was the first and only speech I ever made at a public gathering, but it made an impression and immediately labeled me a Bolshevik, although I only said that syphilis was a sickness like any other, that the war had increased its danger of spreading, that it happened in the best families (the Brieux play had made me an expert on that topic). There were interruptions and heckling. Faber tried to support me but the chairman closed the meeting before the vote.

The New Year began with the threat of civil war and Friedrich Ebert, the President of the new German Republic, appointed Gustav Noske, a Social Democrat, as minister of the *Reichswehr*. Noske recruited his soldiers from the hungry, jobless masses and put them under the command of the former officers of the Imperial Army. They did not hesitate to shoot at the demonstrating workers.

Karl Liebknecht and Rosa Luxemburg were murdered in the Hotel Eden by officers of the Guards. Shortly afterward Kurt Eisner was assassinated. As I feared to be cut off from Berthold by political events, and was expecting a child, I begged Director Falkenberg to release me from my commitment. He admitted a *force majeure* and kindly let me go.

14

In Dresden I felt as though we were among a hostile tribe, in the alien world of *Hoftheater* employees, who mourned the disappearance of their king and the representatives of the Saxonian society, who sat in their boxes, the men with their Iron Crosses, the ladies with bird's nest chignons, fans and long fur pieces around their necks.

We lived in a hotel near the theater, expensive and uncomfortable and full of demobilized officers, aggressively and noisily expressing their anti-revolutionary sentiments. At night, when they were passing our door, they woke us by their drunken shouting and anti-semitic remarks, and I was in constant fear that Berthold would rush out and get into a fight.

But the theater was marvelous, equipped with the most modern devices. The lighting had been installed by a technical genius who could realize the most capricious directorial dreams. Berthold's staging of A *Midsummer Night's Dream* and Walter Hasenclever's *Jenseits* (*The Beyond*) achieved sensational effects. Many expressionistic plays, which had flopped elsewhere, had a surprising success in Dresden. Berthold was accused of propagating the "expressionistic style," but his style was his own and his great contribution to contemporary theater was to strengthen the play dramaturgically and to make it lucid where the author seemed vague. The Dresden Schauspielhaus became as vital and interesting as the best Berlin theaters, and critics from all the big German cities came to see performances of the new plays. The impact of Berthold's personality was undeniable and the new leadership was proud of their "revolutionary" achievements.

We lived quite alone and had only a few friends: a young actress, Olga Fuchs, whose kindness, warmth and practical advice helped me in the difficulties of daily life and Paul Wiecke, who regretted that he could not keep me in Dresden, as the constitution of the State Theaters forbade the employment of husband and wife. I had signed with the Volksbuehne in Leipzig, one of the new "People's Theaters" which had mushroomed after the revolution. They were financed by the Workers' Union and subscriptions. The Volksbuehne in Leipzig was an enormous theater, seating two thousand people. It also had a smaller auditorium for intimate plays and there I had played Strindberg's *Father* with Paul Wegener. Although my child was due in two months I had joined him in a short, very successful tour.

One day Berthold and I ran into Oscar Kokoschka, who invited us to lunch. Entering his studio I noticed a blond woman reclining on the couch, which in my short-sightedness I believed to be another guest, but which was a life-sized doll, the replica of a lady he had been in love with, and which always traveled with him. We ignored her presence and had a wonderful meal with a fascinating host.

The summer came and we were anxious to leave the city. I was at the beginning of my seventh month and before then we had to find a place to live. But at the very sight of me the landladies slammed the door with a horrified: "Oh, no, we don't want any babies here." The writer Camil Hoffmann and his family lived in Hellerau—an artist colony on the outskirts of Dresden—and suggested that we move there. The Greek buildings, which the wealthy brothers Wolf and Harold Dohrn had built for Jacques Dalcroze—father of eurhythmics, whom the war had forced to leave Germany—stood empty. There was a theater in which Dalcroze dancing and Paul Claudel plays had been staged, and spacious houses for Dalcroze's numerous pupils.

The Dohrns offered us shelter and the Hoffmanns provided us with furniture for a bedroom, and a living room with eight windows and two glass doors leading to a large terrace. It was a princely room but the central heating did not function. As we would not stay for the winter I thought I could rely on the fireplace to keep us warm on rainy days.

There were only a few people living in the large house, all refreshingly disconnected from any bourgeois reality, all reassuringly eccentric, kind and helpful. There was a small kitchen at the end of the hall, but I cannot remember anybody's using it except me and the painter Walter Spiess, a blond, strikingly beautiful, nineteen-year-old giant.

Life in Hellerau, in spite of the severe scarcity of food, was much more friendly and congenial than in Dresden. The Hoffmanns were not too far from us. Camil and Irma attracted to their house many intellectuals. Later, in Berlin, when Camil became head of the press bureau of the Czechoslovakian Legation, their house was to remain the gathering place for liberal politicians, writers, conscientious objectors now out of jail, theatrical people, and journalists. Bianca Segantini, the daughter of the well-known Swiss painter, who enhanced her resemblance to Dante by a medieval headdress lived in our house. Then there was Herr von Luecken, an emaciated Estonian nobleman, who never washed, but was the kindest soul in the world. He often came to see us and insisted on giving me his weekly meat ration, because I was "carrying life" and he was "not distant from death."

Berthold was using the summer to work on a new book of poems. His publisher Jakob Hegner and his young wife also lived in Hellerau. Then we had to get a piano, because Edward arrived, to stay with us until the child was born. Rose was appearing in a play in Berlin and had no vacation.

We were always hungry, the world looked grim, the victors in Paris were betraying the peace—but I had Berthold, and Edward, and the child in me, and would have been absolutely happy if it had not been for the war in Poland. Dusko was still in the Polish army fighting the Bolsheviks. This was the scanty news which reached us through Esther, but she had not heard from my mother directly.

It was August and my child was due any day. All I could provide for it was a big straw basket where it would sleep, and a few shirts and diapers made from an old linen sheet. One day I was sitting on the steps of our Greek mansion and Walter Spiess, blond, sunburned, wearing only his white shorts, was telling me that in the north of Siberia mothers never dressed their babies—they smeared grease on their bodies and wrapped them in furs. The children were strong and healthy, and all the fuss European mothers made was nonsense. But I did not have even a tiny bit of fur and remained unimpressed by Siberian childcare. Then the mailman appeared with two large boxes for me from Munich. Right there on the steps I opened them and discovered the loveliest, complete baby layette. On top was a letter from a woman, an utter stranger. She had seen me play Paulina in *Winter's Tale*— "at least five times"—and was deeply disappointed that my name had disappeared from the billboards. She had inquired about me, heard I was pregnant and knowing how impossible it was to get baby things was sending me the layette of her own children, all born before the war.

I was so moved that I wept. Walter looked at me, disgusted, and said: "I would never have thought you'd be so conventional."

On the first of September my doctor advised me to go to the hospital. Hellerau was too distant for an emergency. The clinic was small and old-fashioned, but immaculately clean and cheerful. My room had red wallpaper and except for the white furniture and hospital bed, it was like a hotel room.

The birth was difficult. The endless hours of agony were interrupted by an unexpected joy. Walking up and down in the room, timing my pains, I approached the window and was sure I had a hallucination: wasn't that my mother on the other side of the street, walking with Edward toward the hospital? Screaming "Mama!" I ran out of the room, down the stairs and onto the street, with the midwife and nurse after me. And indeed it was Mama, who, braving the war in Poland and disputed frontiers, had traveled two long weeks under appalling hardships to be with me when my child was born. Miraculously she had arrived on time. After forty-six hours of torture, they took me into the operating room and I shall never forget the blissful moment of oblivion when they put the mask on my face.

My mother's voice, calling from a great distance, woke me. First I saw a sky full of red clouds, it must have been the wallpaper of my room, then I felt Berthold's hand touching my forehead and then my mother saying in Polish: "Open your eyes, look, you have a son." Before my eyes could pierce through the red clouds I heard him cry. It sounded like a cello, a deep and soft "aa." They put him in my arms. He was long, skinny, had Berthold's forehead and dark eyelashes, and seemed a little mangled after his difficult entry into the world.

The ensemble of the Schauspielhaus showered the most gorgeous flowers upon me. Nurses and patients flocked into the room to admire my little John Jacob.

It is commonly assumed that to give birth is the happiest moment in a woman's life. Why then was I possessed by such an abysmal sadness, such black depression? I was exhausted and had the feeling that something in me had died and that I would never be my old self again.

They kept me in the hospital for three weeks. When I finally recovered, Edward had returned to Vienna and Mama had gone with him. Sambor was now Polish. The dual monarchy had fallen apart and with it my father's entire fortune. My mother never complained: "I am lucky to have you all," she said. "My sons are alive after the holocaust, my daughters have the profession they love and Papa is well and still active." After twenty-five years as mayor, my father had resigned to devote himself to his law office, which had suffered through his political activity.

It was a cold and wet autumn, when I returned with my son to the Grecian mansion, and we froze in our large room. Everyone crowded around the fireplace: my bed and the baby's crib stood close to it; Berthold's table was pushed near it; our guests sat around it; and Emma our new maid insisted upon drying the diapers on the mantel. Like gypsies we lived around the fire. Walter Spiess was displaying a remarkable talent for baby care. It was he who with great patience explained to Emma the importance of modern hygiene.

Olga Fuchs, the young actress, who had become our guardian angel, was trying to get an apartment for me in Leipzig. There was nothing to be had except rooms in a pension, which ordinarily would not tolerate a woman with a newborn child; but the landlady was mad about the theater and relented, at a higher price of course. Hans, as John Jacob was called, was six weeks old when, with Emma, we moved in. He astonished the guests in the pension by never crying. My schedule was rigorous: I nursed him every four hours, from six in the morning until after the evening performance. During rehearsal Emma would bring him to my dressing room and my colleagues gathered around me when I gave him his "lunch." He was a most admired baby.

My first role was once more Laura in Strindberg's *Father*; the second, Medea in the big house. Berthold came every second weekend, often nervous and harassed.

Medea was a great success. The critics compared me to every wild beast they could think of: a lioness, tigress, panther, leopard, even a she-wolf. Soon I became a very haggard one. The play was staged on steps with platforms in between, and during each performance I climbed and ran down the forty steps more than a hundred times. We played night after night with matinees twice a week.

After four months I had to stop nursing. Owing to the blessed activities of the Quakers, the milk supply for small children was well organized and with a doctor's prescription one could buy the ready-made formulas at the pharmacy. My son remained strong and healthy.

One Sunday, in March, 1920, I took the streetcar to go to friends, who had invited me for lunch, and saw thousands of workers, men and women, marching toward town. They were quiet and orderly, keeping their distance from the streetcar, a huge gray stream moving in the middle of the street. I asked the conductor what was happening and where these people were going.

"It's a demonstration," he said uneasily. "Some damned *Putschists* or something again."

At my friends' I learned that an anti-government *Putsch* had been staged by a man called Kapp, who had proclaimed himself Chancellor of Germany, and was joined by the Kaiser's ex-chief of police, Herr von Jagow, and General Ludendorff. The socialists were expected to declare a general strike. "Then I'd better go home," I said to my hosts, "the streetcars may stop running." I was right; within an hour all public transportation had come to a standstill. Two ladies, who had succeeded in getting a cab, saw me at the tramstop; they had recognized me and offered me a ride. They told me that there had been considerable shooting on the Augustusplatz; "Of course, the unions started it! It is high time that all those Bolshevik agitators should be hanged." I did not share their joy about the *Putsch*, and hurriedly got out of the cab.

Next morning there were barricades on our street and the shooting went on for a week, with many killed and wounded. The windows in my room were shattered by bullets which lodged in the wall, just above my bed. Emma and I had moved Hans's crib into the windowless hall, where other guests of the pension also camped. They all were hoping that the *Putsch* would bring back the Kaiser. My son was indiscriminately bestowing his most radiant smiles upon the bloodthirsty monarchists.

The workers had notified all householders that every day at noon shooting would stop to give mothers a chance to buy food. Each noon I hurried to the pharmacy for the baby's milk, but I often had to take shelter in doorways to dodge bullets. Some *Putschists* did not observe the cease-fire.

After the Ebert Government regained control of the situation and the fighting ceased, the theater reopened, and on the surface life returned to normal.

During the whole *Putsch* Berthold and I had not been able to communicate with each other. The sympathetic leaders of the Dresden Theater, Paul Wiecke and Lothar Mehnert, tried to find a way to reunite us. As the lady who had played Medea in Dresden was now in her sixties, everyone agreed that the ensemble needed a younger actress for tragic roles. They also knew that to hold Berthold in Dresden it was necessary that we be together, especially at such a turbulent time. Of course, I could not become a member of the Schauspielhaus, but I could appear as a guest. They offered me three roles with fifty performances during the season. There was a valid reason which made me accept: I was expecting a second child.

15

My son Peter, blond and fair, arrived feet first into this world. We were both battered and exhausted, but Peter, determined to take a firm hold on what life offered him in adoration and nourishment, recovered in a few days, while I needed more time.

After six weeks of exercise and dieting I began to rehearse Donna Isabella in Schiller's *The Bride of Messina*. The director was Paul Wiecke. He was afraid that my vitality might "dynamite" the traditional staging. Berthold was not permitted to watch the rehearsals, and I was glad because they were tiring and uninspired. The première was well received by the audience, but the morning press was divided between bewildered praise and hostility. The critic of the most important paper wrote only that he saw no reason to impose an "alien" personality upon the public. Other reviewers were more appreciative, and as a whole I had fared quite well in the opinion of Wiecke, and those colleagues who knew their Dresden.

My second role was Medea and after the reception it had had in Leipzig, nobody had the slightest doubt that it would mean my conquest of Dresden also. Indeed, after the curtain went down the audience applauded wildly, my colleagues, and the directors embraced and congratulated me. But next morning we read surprising notices. The leading critic exploded this time with a blast: only nepotism could explain my playing Medea at the State Theater. Poor Paul Wiecke could not believe his eyes.

Berthold's sense of humor began to deteriorate and he was inclined to overestimate the importance of provincial attitudes. I went through my fifty performances and hoped we would move to Berlin, which offered us both interesting work.

It was true that Berthold's temperament made him exaggerate trivial incidents, and it was not surprising that his insistence on staging controversial plays, casting small roles with important actors and choosing young artists like Walter Spiess to design sets, annoyed the old Hoftheater cliques, which only Count von Seebach could hold in check. Their motto was: "We have done it for so many years, why change now? Mr. Viertel stages the new plays only because he wants to impress Berlin."

Meanwhile the war and unrest in Poland came to an end. I had not seen my father for three years and he did not know his grandsons. We decided to spend the summer at Wychylowka. Rose would also be there and Edward had asked if he could bring a young pupil. Talented but self-centered, moody and difficult, Hilda did not make life easy for any of us—including Edward. I knew immediately that he was in love and would marry her.

My parents were delighted with my two little boys and so was Niania. I was shocked to see how much she had aged, but she still ran the house and was able to give me a hand with the children.

Grandmother was now living permanently with my parents. Deaf but patient and undemanding, she still read her French novels. As she had never taken any exercise, she was heavy and walking was a strain for her. The afflictions of old age were making her lonely. Viktoria was four years old, very intelligent and considered "Panek," * as she called my father, her exclusive property. He had to apologize to her when Peter or Hans sat on his lap, but he impartially distributed his love and attention among the three children.

After Edward arrived there was much music and long political discussions. My father was bitterly disappointed with "that dilettante," Woodrow Wilson, who had no knowledge of Europe. "It's insane to dismember the Austro-Hungarian monarchy. Small nations are like little children and have to be ruled before they learn to rule themselves; otherwise they are the prey to demagogues and corrupt politicians. The Treaty of Versailles is the worst disaster that ever happened to the world." Twenty years later I remembered Papa's prophecy, though I never shared his faith in the Hapsburg monarchy.

Sambor was dirty and neglected. The walls of the buildings were peeling, the streets either dusty or muddy after the rains, the sidewalks torn up, the electricity failing every few days. But pretty girls still promenaded on the Linia A–B, where the Austrian officers were replaced by students and Polish government employees, loafing in front of the two cafés. Amelia Kanarienvogel was disconsolate about the fall of the Hapsburgs and mourned the disappearance of the Hungarian cavalrymen, who had lavished

* Diminutive of Pan (Sir).

perfumes and silk stockings on their girlfriends. Now everybody was poor, even the Steuermanns.

Many of my parents' friends were dead or had left during the war. Others had expressed nationalistic and anti-semitic opinions and my parents did not see them anymore. Mama was joined in her charity work by several young Jewish women. They were a dedicated generation, with intellectual interests, trying to alleviate the misery surrounding them. The majority were Zionists.

That summer Rose was more silent than usual. She was in love. Having lost patience with her slow progress in Berlin, she had signed a contract with the Stadttheater in Koenigsberg, which offered her all the roles she desired. There she met the young actor and director, Josef Gielen, just demobilized after four years in the trenches. Dusko was his old self again, the champion of the soccer team. It was quite a sight to see him playing, in his white shorts, his golden hair gleaming, and the girls among the spectators chanting: "Dusko! Dusko!" He received worshipful admiration from everybody but Papa. "Who can make a living playing football?" Dusko did not help in the fields or garden; he did not study and had no intention of looking for a job.

No, Wychylowka was not what it had been. The "patriarchal feudalism" was gone. Everything had become less noble, less comfortable and much less clean. Cobwebs and dust gathered in all corners; weeds grew in the flowerbeds. Niania and young Ivan could not cope with house, garden and field. Papa walked around in his beige silk duster and cap, suspiciously inspecting his immaculate hands after he had touched a piece of furniture or when he wanted to sit down on a garden bench. Viktoria, always at his side, would wipe it with her petticoat. When later I saw Kachalov play Gayev in *The Cherry Orchard*, I thought of Papa. Mama's vitality made her rise above the dust and difficulties, but her hair was white now.

In August, rested and full of new ideas, Berthold went back to Dresden, promising to find us a new apartment. The summer days were so glorious that I did not have the heart to take my healthy children back to the city.

In the fields and orchard the harvest was in full swing. Niania was busy supervising the hired farmhands, when one morning the postman brought a Red Cross card and Niania asked me apprehensively if it was not from her son Vassili. I read the card and must have turned white, because she grabbed my hand and said: "Read it." We were both standing on the steps to the veranda. I read it to her and like a felled tree she dropped to the ground. Vassili had died of typhus.

I sat down on the steps, cradling her in my arms. Her eyes were closed, the face drained of blood. Mama came and helped me lift her up. There was nothing one could say. I knew what hopes she had had and how she had waited for him. Her brother Fedja had come back, so Vassili would come back too. Now he was buried somewhere in Siberia.

After a while she got up, took the bucket she had left on the steps and turning her haggard face to me said: "I have to feed the animals." I followed her while like an automaton she went about her chores.

Because of Niania I was glad I had stayed longer, but a telegram from the Schauspielhaus in Hamburg, inviting me to play Medea, precipitated our departure. From the professional and financial point of view the invitation was very welcome, and with my two sons I set off on the long journey. I had first to leave the children in Dresden with Berthold, who was still looking for the apartment and a children's nurse. Peter was ten months old and I had to carry him—a sweet but not a light burden. We had to change trains first in Przemysl, then on the Czechoslovakian frontier, then again in Prague, from where, at last, we had a direct connection to Dresden. Because of the inflation with its changing prices and currencies, I had to buy tickets at each transfer. I had with me a few Polish zloty; the rest of my money was in German marks. The provisions Niania gave us dwindled. In Krakow I had to buy milk and was staggered at how expensive it was; all my zloty were gone.

In the evening we arrived at the Czechoslovakian border and my luggage underwent endless, infuriating inspection. Even Peter's soiled diapers appeared suspicious to the surly customs officer. After he had finished I joined the long line at the ticket window, Peter sound asleep in my arms, Hans sitting on top of the highly piled suitcases on the luggage trolley, amusing the porter with his serious remarks. When I reached the window the irascible, hungry-looking employee took a look at the banknotes in my hand and said that they were not enough to pay my way to Prague. The inflation, several paces ahead of me, had deteriorated the value of currency to such an extent that I could not even reach Brno.

"Then what should I do?" I asked, desperately aggressive.

The man, who had heard that question many times during the day, shrugged and motioned me to move on. With Peter sleeping unperturbed on my shoulder I sat down in the hall. The porter hesitated for a while, then slowly began to unload Hans and the suitcases. I wanted to tip him but he waved it aside: my situation was too pitiful and my marks worthless. I was ready to cry and

Hans, sensing difficulties, looked anxiously at me with his golden eyes. A young, well-dressed woman passed by, stared at me, turned, approached again and asked: "Excuse me, are you Frau Steuermann?" I said that indeed I was.

"I recognized you immediately. I am so glad to have the opportunity to tell you how much I admired you in . . ."

I interrupted her: "Then could you do me a great favor and send a telegram for me—provided I have enough money for it."

"Of course I will," she said eagerly. "I suppose you are caught short by the devaluation of the mark?" I told her that I did not have enough to continue my trip.

"But I have enough for a third-class ticket to Dresden. Please let me buy it for you."

I did not want to accept but she insisted. "In a sense I am a colleague of yours. I sing in a cabaret." She told me her name, which was vaguely familiar.

This kind stranger attended to the telegram and bought me the ticket. There was no time to thank her properly as we were leaving immediately. I could not even buy a warm breakfast for the children.

We were squeezed into a crowded third-class compartment among Transylvanian peasants. They were large, heavily built people, the women taking up a great deal of space as they wore at least six petticoats. Four centuries ago their German ancestors had settled in Transylvania, which, after the war, was given to Roumania, and they had to leave their farms to resettle in Germany. They spoke a strange-sounding dialect, but we could understand each other. Hans and Peter stared at them wide-eyed. The old woman opposite laboriously extracted from the luggage rack, a huge loaf of bread and an earthenware pot of raspberry jam. The smell of home baking and country kitchen filled the compartment. The loaf was as big as a cartwheel and Hans said: "Oh!" pointing to it expectantly. The woman unpacked a knife and passed it to her husband, who began to cut thick slices on which she spread jam, and distributed them among her companions. Their slow, deliberate chewing made Peter's mouth water and he stretched out his hand, making demanding sounds. Hans, more restrained, swallowed hard. The woman laughed and asked me if she could give them a piece of bread.

"It would be very kind of you. They have not eaten since yesterday evening." And I told her about our difficulties. She could not stop commiserating with me, and put so much jam on the slices that the boys were smeared all over with raspberries. They held onto the bread with both their hands, refusing to let me break it into smaller pieces. Not for a second would they part with it. The old woman had not offered me a piece of bread, and pride prevented me from asking her.

A Transylvanian from another compartment opened the door and announced that we were approaching the German frontier. They all got up, crossed themselves, knelt down facing the window and prayed aloud that the new earth would receive them with friendliness. I often thought of them during the Hitler years.

In Dresden I had just enough time to give the children their bath, feed them and put them to bed in Olga Fuchs's apartment. The place Berthold had rented was not yet free, the nurse had taken another job, and so far he had not found anyone to replace her. Hans and Peter could stay one night with Olga; then another friend of ours insisted on taking care of them. I dreaded the prospect. The children were so young and so used to being with me, and though Berthold assured me that he would spend all his free time with them, it was terrible for me to leave under such circumstances. If only we didn't need the money! More than ever everyone's existence had become endangered by the inflation. No, that was not true; some people were making millions. Only the threat of the penalty I would be obliged to pay, if I did not appear next morning at the rehearsal, made me tear myself away.

This time I traveled in a sleeping car, for which the Schauspielhaus was paying, and I could have rested, had I not been worrying all night.

The *Medea* rehearsal was merely a run-through, to adjust to the guest performer. The actors, with the exception of a new young girl who played Kreusa and needed more direction, had been in Hamburg many years, and their mannerisms had that same dignified pomposity as that of their colleagues at the Hoftheater. But they were cordial and cooperative.

The audience that night was most receptive: they clapped and shouted until the safety curtain came down. The manager, Dr. Paul Eger, who looked like an old style diplomat, came to my dressing room and said that he would like to discuss a contract. I was gratified but worn out. It is very depressing to be alone after a success—almost as bad as after a failure. Not even a telephone call to Berthold was possible at that hour.

Next day was a Sunday. I played a matinee and again in the evening. Monday was free, so that if I could make the night train to Dresden, I would be able to spend twenty-four hours with Berthold and the boys. Then, leaving early on Tuesday morning, I would return just in time for the evening performance. I asked Dr. Eger if he would let me go. He made a face. And what if the train was late? No, he could only give me his permission if I promised to be back in the morning, but that would mean two nights in the train! I said that it did not matter.

The curtain calls never seemed to end that evening, but as the theater was right next to the station I caught my train. I shared the compartment with an old lady, who, fascinated, watched me remove my make-up. After a while she said enigmatically: "Well— I suppose we are all human beings—aren't we?"

Berthold was waiting at the station. Those two days in Hamburg had been so long that I felt I had not seen him for ages. In the taxi he told me what I had sensed all the time. The night I had left, Hans woke up and called me. Olga explained to him that I had gone away for a few days but would be back. Desperate, he had run through the apartment, searching in every corner, and crying for me. His grief was so great that Olga and Mrs. Waldheim were helpless. They called Berthold and when he arrived Hans clung to him, until he fell asleep exhausted.

Since then many years have passed and greater tragedies have occurred. Hans has long forgotten his tears, but I am still haunted by them.

They were eating breakfast when I came into their room. Peter stood up in his highchair, stretching out his arms to me, but Hans looked away. The next second he was crying and clinging to me for dear life. The new nurse, Fräulein Thea, red-haired and spinster-ish, was a friendly Saxonian and I was told the children had taken to her at once.

The remainder of my visit was spent explaining to Hans why I had to leave again, but I could not convince him of the necessity of our parting. In the evening I put them to bed and stayed with them until they fell asleep. Then, again with a heavy heart, I boarded the train.

This became the pattern of my life for months. Sometimes I stayed two or three days, but often I could not leave Hamburg for a whole week. This brought me another kind of suffering: Hans and Peter, now used to my sporadic appearances became very attached to the more permanent Thea.

I had hardly seen anything of Hamburg. I had no time to stroll around, but I liked the few streets I knew and the *Alster*. It was a big city with a harbor. One breathed the salt in the air; this alone was exhilarating. I signed a contract for the next season and re-turned to Dresden for Christmas. In February Berthold went to Berlin to direct for the Reinhardt theaters.

Soon after the war a young man by the name of Moritz Seeler, fanatically dedicated to the theater, had founded the Junge

Buehne (Young Stage) and put on plays by unknown dramatists which the leading theaters, for one reason or another, did not have the courage to produce. The authors Seeler presented were Bertolt Brecht, Annemarie Fleissner, Carl Zuckmayer and Arnolt Bronnen. The first of the plays, Bronnen's *Vatermord*, was to be directed by Brecht. But some of the actors refused to submit to the authority of the young man. Brecht resigned and Seeler asked Berthold to take over. As Brecht had no ill feelings, Berthold agreed. Elizabeth Bergner, Agnes Straub and Alexander Granach played the main roles. *Vatermord*, Bronnen's one and only flash of talent, helped by a remarkable performance, had a tremendous success, and for a long time was considered an important, revolutionizing theatrical event.

In April of that year the management of the Reinhardt theaters asked me to play in Hebbel's *Judith* in the Grosses Schauspielhaus, the rebuilt Circus Schumann. Heinrich George, a new star, was to play Holofernes; Berthold would direct. As Berlin was not Dresden, I welcomed the opportunity to work with Berthold.

16

"YOU CANNOT SLAUGHTER A COW and milk it," was one of Niania's frequently expressed wisdoms. Berlin in 1922 made me often think of this. The war profiteers sat in cafés, restaurants and nightclubs, gorging themselves on black-market food, while the gray-faced jobless and the war veterans on crutches stared hungrily through the plate glass windows. The most heartbreaking were the emaciated children, who looked as if they had stepped out of Kaethe Kollwitz drawings. There were demonstrations, pacifists and workers carrying signs with *Nie Wieder Krieg*; but chauvinistic organizations like *Feme* and the *Ehrhard Brigade* and Noske's regiments put a bloody end to marches and meetings, and they disappeared from the streets. The estimated number of political assassinations in the first four years of the Republic was more than five hundred. Among the victims were men like the Foreign Minister Rathenau and Matthias Erzberger, who had signed the Armistice in 1918.

The Government seemed ineffectual against the Rightist terror, and Hitler, first unknown, then ridiculed and shrugged off, was making speeches and gaining ground. Though politics were infuriating there was no question but that Berlin was much more stimulating and interesting than Dresden. First of all it had become international as never before, and in spite of hunger and inflation, artistic life was flourishing. There were exhibitions of Feininger, Kandinsky, Klee and Barlach. The music of Arnold Schoenberg, Alban Berg and Anton von Webern was gaining recognition. There were exciting performances at the Reinhardt theaters; Jessner, Fehling and Piscator were presenting Shakespeare, Brecht, Toller, Georg Kaiser, and thousands were nightly falling in love with Fritzi Messary, the enchanting star of the Metropol theater. Influenced by the Russians, Piscator was the first to originate the political theater.

In the Romanisches Café we met Bertolt Brecht, Fritz Kortner, Alexander Granach and the young actress Gerda Mueller. Very often Egon Erwin Kisch and a young communist, Otto Katz, would join us. Many years later, when he was known as André Simon, Katz was executed by the Stalinists in Czechoslovakia, where he had been Minister of State.

Brecht was thin and dark, with narrow eyes and a sharp nose, his hair combed down over his forehead. He could have been painted on a silk scroll as an Oriental sage, had it not been for his eternal leather coat and cap, which made him seem dressed for an automobile race.

I had known Kortner since our early days at Reinhardt; meanwhile, he had become one of the great stage and film stars. At the Berlin State Theater, under the direction of Leopold Jessner, he had sensational success in *Wilhelm Tell*, *Richard III*, and *Othello*. Kortner's roots, like Berthold's, were in Vienna. They both had the same *Fackel*-inspired, ironically negative attitude toward their hometown, and the same inherited longing for the *Wiener Kueche*. Fritz Kortner, who is now a distinguished-looking, gray-haired, much honored artist, was at that time a tall, broad-shouldered young man, with glowing dark eyes and short black hair. He was one of those ugly but attractive males women worship. When we saw him again in Berlin he had already fallen in love with Johanna Hofer, his Desdemona, a radiantly beautiful, shy woman and a very gifted actress.

Berthold knew Kortner from before the war, when, impressed

by his talent, he had given the then unknown actor the leading part in a play he was directing. In their long "on and off" relationship the two attracted and repelled, fascinated, irritated, fought with and ardently admired each other. Both were violently egocentric, Kortner several degrees more so than Berthold. Falling in love with people, Berthold would enthusiastically "create" an idol, put it on a pedestal, persuade himself of its unsurpassed qualities. When the cruel moment of truth came, a crisis not uncommon in the theater, worship unavoidably turned to animosity. I would say that rifts were rarely caused by Berthold, who merely became disappointingly "objective," something the dethroned idol could not bear.

At the time they were rehearsing *John Gabriel Borkman*, Kortner and Berthold, both firmly established on their separate pedestals, not only enjoyed working together, but began planning a common artistic enterprise.

The Moscow Art Theater and Tairoff's *Kamernyj* were touring Germany. Not since that first evening in Berlin, when I had seen Reinhardt's *Othello*, had I been so aroused and so in love with my profession. What we admired most were not only the great actors, Stanislawski's direction, Chekhov's plays and Tairoff's magic expressionism, but the discipline and dedication of both ensembles. Like everything else, after the war the ensemble idea had deteriorated in the Berlin theater and the star system prevailed. A new element precipitated the decline: the great temptations of the film. Not only for financial reasons, but also for the enormous popularity it gave them, actors preferred to make films than to come to rehearsals. Although most of the films were cheap and vulgar, a few remarkable ones had emerged. They were *The Cabinet of Dr. Caligari*, Paul Wegener's *Golem*, Lubitsch's *Anne Boleyn*, with Jennings as Henry VIII, and the first films of Fritz Lang and F. W. Murnau. The latter had a great deal of calculated sadism, and for myself I preferred Mauritz Stiller's wonderful Swedish tales. But most of all we were all admiring the Little Tramp: Charlie Chaplin.

For a director, the possibilities the new medium offered were so fascinating that when UFA asked Berthold to write the scenario and direct Ibsen's *Nora*, he decided to accept, though the subject was rather problematic for a film. Berthold wanted me to stay in Berlin while he was working on the script, but it was summer and I intended to take the children to the country. Of course, the country could only be Wychylowka.

Grandmother had died that winter. She was eighty-two years old and deafness had made her withdraw into such loneliness that she could hardly be reached. I missed her absent-minded remarks and now I could no longer brush her long, lovely, silver hair. Sadly I realized that this had been the only attention I had given her in the last years of her life.

Rose was married and had come with her husband. Although Papa strongly disapproved of our profession, he approved of the men we married. Josef Gielen was lovingly received into our family. He was handsome, well-educated and warm-hearted. His sense of humor and simplicity were refreshing and endearing. He had given up acting and become a successful director. The State Theater in Dresden engaged him to replace Berthold. Edward arrived after a strenuous season of concerts and teaching, bringing new twelve-tone compositions.

At the end of August I returned to Hamburg, taking the children with me. For some time Ludwig Muenz had been living there, doing research at one of Hamburg's private collections.

I have often been asked, usually by young women: "When and where have you been happiest in your life?" It was impossible to answer. Happiness demands a special kind of selfishness, never lasting, seldom approved, and you have to pay for each minute of it, usually too dearly. There are people of such harmonious, Apollonian disposition, of such well-balanced desires and temperament, that they never abandon the prudent domain of self-control. I belonged to a more reckless race.

That year in Hamburg was a wonderful year. Hans and Peter were growing, they were intelligent, healthy and happy. I played interesting roles, not only the obligatory, classic heroines. I had Ludwig's affection and friendship. But Berthold was the heart of my heart, the root of my being.

17

Fritz Kortner arrived in Hamburg to play Othello at the Stadt-theater; he had great news for me. He and Berthold had decided to have their own theater; they had found a businessman, a millionaire, who would finance it. Of course I had to join them.

To have our own ensemble had been our cherished dream. Berthold and I had planned it from the day we met. Now I was surprised that things had advanced so rapidly. By the sheer force of his personality, Kortner's partnership changed the whole idea of what we originally had in mind: no stars, an ensemble where all the actors would participate in a common cause.

We were to share the profits (nobody had the slightest doubt that we would rake in the money), bring back great but neglected plays of the past, and introduce meaningful ones of the present. We hoped that if we succeeded we would attract courageous young people unafraid of experiment. I was moved by Kortner's decision to be part of such a group. His enthusiasm silenced my doubts, though I was aware of his idiosyncrasies, and *Die Truppe* came into existence.

As a student I had met, in Fanny Muetter's circle, Franz Singer, and his girlfriend, Friedl Dicker, both talented artists who stretched their aims far beyond painting. They believed fanatically in new mediums of expression which, had they presented them forty years later, would have been a great success. They were planning workshops to make a new kind of furniture, looms to weave new materials, bookbinding, printing and even publishing. They invented new shapes for pottery and an ultrarevolutionary puppet theater. Their workshop would only accept orders from customers who respected the creative freedom of artists and artisans. Naturally, they were interested in designing sets and costumes for our theater.

Long before we knew each other, Berthold, Ludwig and I had been good friends of Franz Singer and admired his stubborn integrity. I was not always in agreement with his purism, especially when we discussed theater and dramatic productions and, to be honest, I would have gladly dispensed with the preponderance of distracting sets. Often I would have preferred an empty stage with all attention centered on the performance. The most impressive sets could not help, when the actors spoke badly and were inadequate. When I said this to Franz and Friedl I rarely encountered opposition. With a shrewd smile Franz would put his hand on mine and ask: "But you admit that a set, lighting and costume can help you to act?" Of course I agreed. Then Friedl continued ambiguously: "Then why shouldn't the sets reflect or symbolize the context of the play?" Berthold and Kortner trusted their theories and let them make the set and costumes for the first offering of *Die Truppe: The Merchant of Venice.*

I did not think that it was a play for *Die Truppe.* The reason for producing it was not to pay homage to Shakespeare, but Kortner's

understandable desire to play Shylock. Antonio was Rudolf Forster, who accepted the part only after much persuasion. Forster
was then one of the most interesting and talented actors on the
German stage.

In 1923 when we founded *Die Truppe*, the dollar was worth
more than nine thousand marks, and the French had occupied the
Ruhr. Our sponsor, the millionaire, was not only married to an
heiress, but was also increasing his fortune by currency speculations. For a modest amount of dollars *Die Truppe* gave him cultural and social importance. Our business manager, Dr. Bruck, had
leased a theater in far off East Berlin, the only one he could get.
The actors' contracts were for a year; salaries were based on the
Index of December 1922, and regulated according to the standing
of the mark. The stars were to receive at first between seven and
nine million marks a year, plus a percentage of the net profit. They
soon became billionaires.

Die Truppe was to present a new play each month, with which
one part of the ensemble would travel, while the other played it in
Berlin. In the building of a repertory and the choice of plays,
Berthold was helped by a literary advisor (*Dramaturg*), Mr. Heinrich Fischer. When I had played Judith in the Grosses Schauspielhaus a young man came backstage one evening to express his
enthusiasm. It turned out that he was an ardent adherent of *Die
Fackel*, and had appreciated greatly Berthold's articles about Karl
Kraus. There was no doubt that Heinrich Fischer was "one of us."
He shared our idealism, our artistic convictions, but most of all,
our lack of experience. His literary taste was incorruptible and
unbiased.

That year Berthold did not go with me and the children to
Wychylowka, but stayed in Berlin to audition actors and prepare
the opening. The rehearsals began in August. The summer in
Poland was wonderful and I enjoyed my family, the bathing in the
Dnjester and the great musical feasts Edward offered us. But Berthold's ominous letters forced me to cut short our vacation and
return to Berlin.

As it was impossible to find a furnished apartment, I remembered that a friend had spoken highly of a pension in the west. Its
owner was Fräulein Luise Wenzel. Tall, almost haggard, nearing
fifty, she resembled the portraits of England's Elizabeth I. Her
clear and penetrating eyes were blue-green, which was appropriate,
as she was the daughter of a sea captain. Having always lived on
boats she walked with a sailor's rolling gait, and had the fresh,
breezy outspokenness of people who don't waste words and never
evade a direct *yes* or *no*. And so not only did we find shelter but

also a friend. Elizabeth, as we called her, gave me and Berthold two quiet rooms which she used to keep for herself, while the children and Fräulein Thea had theirs close by on the same corridor.

Immediately after the children were installed I took the subway to the theater and arrived to find a divided ensemble, holding back Kortner on one side of the stage and Berthold on the other. The reasons for the flare-up, besides disagreements about interpretation, were the sets Friedl and Franz had made. My appearance calmed the belligerents. Berthold resumed the rehearsal and Kortner asked me to lunch. In the Bristol Bar he unburdened his grievances. I remember that we were both very hungry and I devoured an excellent Beef Stroganoff while listening to an impassioned and eloquent indictment of my husband. I was not surprised. Years later, after he returned from his Nazi-imposed exile, Kortner became one of Germany's most successful stage directors. He had never been the man to take direction himself or even to amalgamate his own ideas with those of another. Worse than that, he could not bear anyone else to direct Johanna Hofer. Then there were always sycophants flattering either Kortner or Berthold, reporting and distorting every word said in anger. Anyway, the rising animosity exceeded all reason and could only be explained by the tensions, insecurity and extraordinary pressures imposed upon everyone.

Summoned from Hamburg, Ludwig conducted the negotiations with Franz and Friedl, persuading them to change the costumes, as his was the only authority on art they respected. They compromised in order to make the performance possible.

The première was an enormous success for Kortner. The reviewers' opinions about Berthold's direction varied, but all were unanimous in their condemnation of the sets. Today, as our eyes have become accustomed to surrealism, expressionism and abstract art, Franz Singer and Friedl would be greatly admired. They had made serious mistakes in the costumes, which were too symbolic and stiff, but the sets, at least those I remember, had beautiful colors and shapes. However Berlin had seen the "real" Venice of Max Reinhardt and did not like it in triangles and cubes.

Berthold and Kortner stopped speaking to each other. Kortner asked for the annulment of his and Johanna Hofer's contracts, which was granted. *The Merchant of Venice* ran for a month, after which the divorce became final—Kortner and his wife left *Die Truppe*, which nevertheless continued to exist.

As our second play we had planned Eugene O'Neill's *Emperor Jones* with Kortner. Deprived of our main actor we had to find a replacement. Bertolt Brecht, who was in Munich, recommended a young, unknown actor, Oskar Homolka, and Karl Kraus supported this recommendation. Homolka was to play at the Kammerspiele in Brecht's adaptation of Marlowe's *Edward II*, but the production had run into difficulties and he was free. Berthold sent me to Munich to report if Homolka could carry the O'Neill play.

We met in the house of Lion and Martha Feuchtwanger. Brecht had shaved and was vigorously "selling" Homolka. At a glance I knew that he was right for the part. We telephoned Berthold; he and Homolka agreed quickly about the terms, and a few days later rehearsals began. The sets this time were made by the painter, F. Kiesler, and although the jungle was just as geometric as Franz Singer's Venetian streets, Homolka was able to convey the necessary horror. He got rave notices. *Emperor Jones* could have had a long run, but it was a play that kept only one actor busy, and our ensemble became restless. Also we had to stick to our program.

Knut Hamsun's *Vom Teufel geholt* (*Driven by the Devil*) had been selected as our third play, with me being "driven." My role was that of a nymphomaniac, a once glorious cabaret singer, desperately frightened of losing her grasp on men, and falling from one degradation to another, until the end when she welcomes with open arms the Negro butler of her former lover. Why we all liked this play seems incomprehensible now, but Hamsun had the same attraction for our generation that Hemingway had for the "lost" one.

It was a cold and wet winter and the dollar now stood at between two and three billion marks. The Government notes were covered with zeros. We got paid every day; at noon we would appear at the cashiers, our billions and trillions stuffed into large paper bags or suitcases, and those of us who lived in boarding houses would rush home to deliver cash to our distraught landladies, who hastened to the stores and bought food before the Stock Exchange closed and another deluge of marks swept away the value of the old ones. Only the heroism of our Elizabeth and a kind of *Galgenhumor* made it possible to live, love and go on stage.

I was amazed that there were still people who would buy tickets, but they did; and tottering but determined, *Die Truppe* continued its frail existence. We played Georg Kaiser's *Nebeneinander*, with sets by George Grosz, and it was the only unanimous success we had. Even the most reactionary press praised the excellent performances. Night after night we were sold out, only to see in the morning paper that we were just as broke as ever. And in the audience sat foreigners who lived like kings on ten dollars a week.

Vincent, a delicate, sophisticated comedy by Robert Musil, was much too intellectual for the audiences, and I don't remember much about it, because Peter had pneumonia. He was very ill. But even at his bedside I could not stay out of the stormy affairs of *Die Truppe*. An organization like ours could not satisfy all its members, and there were always some who coveted the part another played, or were at odds with the one they had. My job was to comfort and explain and also to coach.

Karl Kraus arrived in Berlin and to celebrate the twenty-fifth anniversary of *Die Fackel*, Berthold planned to stage his two one-act plays: *Das Traumstueck* and *Traumtheater*. It was to be the last act of faith of the dying *Truppe*.

Those days of despair, inflation, and worry about a sick child are irresistibly connected in my memory with the sight of Ketchup. Among other blessings from America, that red sauce had appeared in Berlin, and the famous Kempinsky had several, in all shades of pink but all tasting alike. Kraus was addicted to it and every day an attractive actress, Caecilie L., Kraus, Berthold, Ludwig and I lunched at Kempinsky's. Kraus's irritation with the waiters, impervious to his sarcastic remarks, and the sending back of dishes Caecilie tasted and did not like, were most trying. Caecilie was overacting the role of a capricious female, and our great Karl was enslaved.

For twenty-five years *Die Fackel* had been attacking and accusing the bourgeois press of lying, war-mongering, scandal-snooping, servility to those in power, hypocrisy and corruption of the language. It did not spare theatrical critics. Kraus's favorite target among many others was the mighty Alfred Kerr from the *Berliner Tageblatt*. To celebrate *Die Fackel* was to challenge the power of the press.

When, at the première, Berthold stepped before the curtain to tell the audience what *Die Fackel* had stood for, for over a quarter of a century, actors and stagehands gathered in the wings in expectation of a scandal. The house was packed. The people Karl Kraus had so mercilessly castigated occupied the front rows.

The evening has been called by those who witnessed it a memorable one, but a sponge, soaked in blood has wiped over the slate on which it might have been recorded. The moral courage displayed by the troupe and its director has vanished from German intellectual life, and also the courage of the audience, who stood up at the end and cheered. The repercussion was inevitable. Our sponsor withdrew his financial support, then the stabilization of the mark sealed our financial debacle.

Many of our ensemble had a ten-month contract. As we had closed after seven months they were entitled to three more months' salary. We had no further financing, and the lawyers advised *Die*

Truppe to declare bankruptcy. But though he incurred personal debt, Berthold raised the necessary sum (in dollars), so that the actors should receive their salaries.

The only thing which remains of the ensemble spirit is a sheet of paper on which the members of *Die Truppe* signed their names and expressed their appreciation:

> With tonight's performance ends the first season of *Die Truppe*. It has completed as difficult work as could ever be achieved by an experimental theater. It was full of joy and rich in artistic gain. The members of *Die Truppe* feel deep gratitude toward their leader, whose courageous, idealistic drive has led them not only through all the hazards of this year, but given them also invigorating help in their immediate artistic tasks. The good spirit which manifested itself as much among the members of the ensemble as in their relationship to their director, is the most certain evidence of the vitality of an idealistic enterprise.

In *The Fervent Years* Harold Clurman mentions that when The Group Theater encountered financial difficulties, the well-paid members relinquished part of their salaries to help their poorer colleagues. Such comradely spirit was lacking in our ensemble. Berthold and I alone carried the burden of the debts of *Die Truppe*. The bankers charged high interest, and also we owed money to friends: Karl Kraus and Ludwig. Although both were lenient, our obligations to them were most pressing, as neither of them was rich.

Peter's health was still very fragile. The doctor advised mountain air, and I took him and Hans to the Semmering, while Berthold stayed in Berlin to work on a film. Immediately afterward he began rehearsals at the Lessing Theater, of Paul Reynal's anti-war drama *The Tomb of the Unknown Soldier*; a play which Paris had rejected as defeatist. In Berlin it became a hit. The hero could be any young soldier who has to sacrifice his life. He sees at the front what all young men are forced to see, thinks what they all think, suffers what they all suffer. His thoughts are everyone's thoughts, his actions and his death anonymous. "I despise this war," he says, "I fight with contempt." And then in one heartbreaking sentence he expresses his fate and the fate of his comrades: "Some generations have no luck."

With my sunburned sons, I returned to Berlin. We now had an apartment in Charlottenburg, surrounded by parks and gardens, but in spite of Berthold's earnings, our finances were at their lowest ebb. Also his health had suffered. He was sleepless, nervous, and showing symptoms of diabetes—which had to be controlled by diet and insulin.

Strange men appeared regularly in our apartment to seize furniture and silver, refusing to believe that it belonged to the landlady. Our encounters with them began calmly and reasonably, but soon Berthold would spice the dialogue with biting epigrams, which were not appreciated, and it ended in absurd mutual insults. Berthold's dress suit and winter coat would wander from Elizabeth Wenzel's closet to Thea's and back. My possessions were so humble that they were not worthy of legal attention. The engagement ring from Stas and a diamond brooch from Esther had been pawned to finance the hospital bills when Hans and Peter were born, and had never been redeemed.

The harassments of poverty were persistent. I had been offered a part and could have contributed to our income, but had to refuse because I was pregnant. We did not have many friends in those days. Staunch and faithful were the Camil Hoffmanns, our Elizabeth, Ludwig, Karl Kraus and Alfred Polgar, Berthold's old friend, whose subtle prose reflected all his personal charm and deceptive gentleness.

Friedrich Ebert, the first President of the Weimar Republic, died on February 28, 1925. There were new elections and the National Socialists supported General Ludendorff. Karl Jarres, a National candidate, led against the socialist Otto Braun but without a decisive majority. Ludendorff received only a small fraction of votes and was subsequently dropped by Hitler. A second election was called for April 26. On that day the Hoffmanns had asked us and several other people for dinner. An American journalist with a German wife, both anti-Russian, were worried that the communist Thaelmann could be elected. He had two million votes. Long after midnight the returns had not yet come in. Camil grew more and more pessimistic, while Irma, dead tired, was concealing spells of yawning. I finally broke up the vigil, suggesting that we go home and let the morning papers surprise us. We said goodnight to our hosts and waited outside for a taxi. The cool, pleasant scent of spring drifted in from the Tiergarten; a big, black automobile turned into the street and slowed down as it passed us; the head of a German military man popped out of the window, shouting happily: "*Hindenburg ist gewaehlt!* Hindenburg is President! Hurrah!" Waving to us he disappeared around the corner, convinced that he had made us supremely happy.

On the surface little seemed changed: Hindenburg had sworn to maintain the Constitution of the Republic, Stresemann remained in office, the Dawes Plan considerably eased the payments of war reparations, and the French withdrew from the Ruhr.

Berlin had become increasingly international and quite mad, with night clubs for homosexuals, male and female prostitution, drug peddling and drug addiction. The *kinos* and theaters were packed and D. W. Griffith and American Westerns were giving us glimpses of the "new world." A Negro revue with Paul Douglas and Josephine Baker was a sensational success. Her radiant sensuality, humor and wild grace, the impudent charm of her nakedness, were a triumphant contrast to the decadence of most postwar amusement.

The Stanislawski Ensemble returned with *The Cherry Orchard*, *Uncle Vanya* and *The Three Sisters*. Eisenstein's *Potemkin* created an uproar, partly because it was forbidden but more because it was a masterpiece. Another sensation was Mauritz Stiller's *Gösta Berling*. There was a loud gasp from the audience when the extraordinary face of the young Greta Garbo appeared on the screen.

Around that time Berthold was working on a film. I think it was *The Wig (Die Peruecke)*, and his cameraman was Hjalmar Lerski, a wonderful artist. He and his wife came to see us often. It was Lerski who encouraged me to write my first film story, which was based on a novel by Barbey d'Aurevilly. I wrote it in longhand on large sheets of paper, in one big sweep. Lerski read it and showed it uncorrected to Gabriel Pascal, who later became G. B. Shaw's favorite film producer. He was then head of a film company called The Nordisk and bought the story. I felt invincible but The Nordisk soon collapsed and the film was never produced. Miraculously, my check for five thousand rentenmark did not bounce.

I was combining my household chores with assisting Berthold in his work on the screenplay, but as we now had a little more money we decided to engage a young woman "with a pleasant personality," who proved herself much more efficient, though less romantic than Thea. To Fräulein Laue we could safely entrust our two sons when the time came for me to go to hospital. As Peter had to spend another summer on the Semmering I followed the advice of Berthold's sister Paula to have my baby in Vienna.

Babies abounded in our family that year. In July Edward and Hilda had become the parents of a little girl, my own confinement was close, and Rose was expecting her first in the autumn. The days were terribly hot and I did not go out. The evenings were invariably spent with Karl Kraus. The endurance with which he and his friends could sit for hours at the coffee-house table was unequaled. Had I dared to say that I was worn out and wanted to go to bed, he would have been most concerned but also appalled. So, as long as I could carry on in my semi-conscious way, I said that I was fine and prayed that the waiters would turn off the lights.

Kraus's tyranny did not stop me from being extremely fond of him. I felt his great loneliness, which increased the older and more famous he became. In Vienna I heard him read his war drama *The Last Days of Mankind*. "A play meant for a Martian theater. Audiences of this world could not bear it, as it is blood of their blood and its happenings so unreal, unthinkable and inaccessible to a wakeful mind, that they cannot be remembered and will only persist as a bloody nightmare in which vaudeville characters enact the tragedy of mankind."

On August 7 my third son, Thomas, was born. He had red hair, was strong, well-shaped and seemed of such a sweet and gentle disposition that I immediately worried about how he would cope with this harsh, cruel world.

18

GENTHINER STRASSE 19 WAS OUR NEXT ADDRESS, and it was destined to be our last "home" in Berlin. Close to the Tiergarten and only two blocks away from the school where Hans was enrolled in the first grade, it was conveniently situated. The large Wilhelminian rooms were less tasteless than the places we had had before, and provided Berthold with enough space for pacing up and down, without the danger of stepping on the boys' blocks and railroad constructions.

Karl Kraus and Ludwig arrived, the nightly session continued, making it difficult for me to get up in the morning and give Tommy his bottle.

The circle of our friends became larger as impatient youth began to invade Berlin. Thomas Mann's children Klaus and Erika, Pamela Wedekind, Mops Sternheim and Anna Mahler, Gustav Mahler's daughter, briefly married to the composer Ernst Krenek, emerged from their nurseries to join us at our table in the Romanisches café, bringing freshness of outlook and a reckless disrespect for the *status quo*. Some of them soon disappeared from our lives. Among those who remained were Francesco and Eleonora von Mendelssohn, the children of Guilletta and Robert von Mendelssohn, of the renowned banking house. One hundred and fifty years of intermarriage with Italian and Basque women had contributed beauty, talent and eccentricity to the ancient Jewish blood of the eighteenth century philosopher Moses Mendelssohn. From their father and Italian mother, Francesco and Eleonora inherited their musicality and obsession with the theater. As Duse was her godmother, it was obvious that Eleonora was destined to be an actress. Robert von Mendelssohn had died, their mother lived in Florence, and brother and sister had at their disposal the large Grünewald villa with its extensive library and famous collection of paintings.

Beauty, intelligence, money and the background of Italian, German and French culture could have given Francesco and Eleonora a leading role in Berlin society—but they preferred the friendship of actors and bohemians. Now and then Francesco, flamboyant and ostentatious, united the diverse elements: high society, theater and film people, diplomats, prize-fighters and marathon cyclists, at huge receptions.

Eleonora was twenty-four and looked like a blue-eyed Nefertiti. She had a contract with the Schauspielhaus in Duesseldorf, but was quite unprepared for the parts she was to play. The Duesseldorf Schauspielhaus, with its own dramatic school under the leadership of Luise Dumont and Gustav Lindemann, was a renowned and respected theater. The Lindemanns had expressed great sympathy and admiration for the valiant struggle of the *Truppe*. They had always endorsed a theater with cultural responsibility, and through Eleonora they let us know that they would like us to take over their theater.

A few weeks later—I just had given Tommy his bath—the door opened and Berthold motioned two people to enter; they were Luise Dumont and Gustav Lindemann. It was not from gallantry that Luise's name always preceded Gustav's. Decidedly she was the domineering personality. When I met her she must have been sixty, perhaps more. Of middle height, with magnificent, compelling eyes, her well-groomed, black hair streaked with gray, she had, in spite of her square, peasant body, the grandeur of a

Roman empress. Her husband, younger than she, was handsome, inscrutable and had dreamy, velvety eyes. But he was a hard-working, disciplined artist.

They both felt that the time had come for them to sit back, help and advise, and "let a younger leader hold the reins." And instantly they *knew* that Berthold was the one to continue their work. Then having seen me—I was playing with Steinrueck Romain Rolland's *Play of Love and Death*—they had nodded to each other in silent agreement.

"You are real, my dear child," Luise proclaimed. "Every word you say rings true. You and Viertel are out of place in this hellish Berlin."

They knew about our financial plight and were promising us years of security, productive work, and the advantage of their invaluable experience. In return they asked that we give their cherished theater our talent and our idealism. Gustav added that an ensemble meant not only a dedicated group of actors, it also needed organization and a firm hand. Berthold and I sat there like children in front of the Christmas tree. What we had aimed at had failed, but now it was miraculously offered to us on a silver platter.

The Lindemanns told us of their beginnings, their failures and successes, and explained the organization of their theater. Gustav would add funny marginal remarks when Luise was bitter about one or another deception. They were both fascinating and entertaining and it was impossible not to reciprocate their warm and spontaneous affection.

Luise asked me if I had any experience in teaching, and when I told her that the developing of young talent was one of the aims of *Die Truppe*, she suggested I take over her drama classes. At the end of the evening we were deep in projects for the next season, full of new ideas and all madly in love with each other. When we said good-bye, the childless Luise whispered that she had found in me what she had always longed for: a daughter.

After they had left, Berthold said that everything seemed too marvelous to be true. Emotionally we were already committed. Dreading the pressures and inconsistencies of the commercial theater, Berthold, although he loved Berlin, longed for a long-range, artistic program, and I was looking forward to the varied, interesting work the Lindemanns offered me. Of course, Luise was overwhelming, but she was generous and warmhearted. Lastly, neither Berthold nor I had forgotten that during all our married years we had been trying to work together without harassment and intrigues. When our contracts arrived, we both signed with happy anticipation.

The moment the die was cast Berthold began to regret our decision, which, in the end, had been much more his than mine; but by then I was numb about his vacillations. A feverish productivity possessed him. He wanted to make a film, to write a novel, new poems and essays. Words were Berthold's magic and his weapon. He seduced and chastised with them. He would write letters unequaled in tenderness and beauty, and then wound mortally with a sentence. He had completed a short novel *Das Gnadenbrot*, for which the Hegener Verlag had been waiting a whole year, and was finishing a war book he had started in Kolendziany. I always loved this book but as it was autobiographical, he hesitated to have it published. Later, in the Thirties, when I begged him to resume work on it, he thought that it had lost its impact. I always regretted it because it was such a fascinating portrait of Berthold.

When we moved into our apartment we had told our landlady that we would not keep it during the summer, but now that we were leaving she took it as a personal insult. She became most disagreeable, constantly intruding into our rooms and when, at the end of May, Hans came down with scarlet fever, she insisted that we go immediately. As the owner of the apartment she had the right to turn out a person with a contagious disease. Her lawyer confirmed this.

To make everything worse, Fräulein Laue was getting married and could not take Peter and Tommy to Wychylowka, while I was quarantined with Hans.

Through the half-opened bathroom door I interviewed a Fräulein Helene Gnichwitz, a motherly or rather grandmotherly woman. She asked me to call her Nena and confessed that, though a Fräulein, she had a son in the Reichswehr. She was pleased that it did not matter to me and that I admired her courage.

With her clean-cut, strong, German face, Nena was much more commanding in appearance than my old Niania; nevertheless, they had something in common: kindness and firmness. Poor little Peter was unusually quiet without Hans and me, but he liked Nena and I felt confident that once in the country and spoiled by his grandparents he would cheer up. It broke my heart when, looking down from the window, I saw him dejectedly getting into a taxi. Tommy, in Nena's arms, fidgeted happily.

Hans's recovery was progressing and Francesco Mendelssohn

offered us his hospitality. I began to breathe more freely. When I woke in the morning, my eyes would focus on Van Gogh's "Blue Irises" above my bed, then turn to an exquisite pale green Monet on the opposite wall. (Berthold refused to have his coffee and rolls in the awesome presence of masterpieces. "I don't take my meals in a museum.")

Life with Francesco was pleasant and just as bohemian as it had been before. He was enthusiastic, full of insatiable curiosity about new things, and boundlessly hospitable. A heterogeneous crowd converged on the Mendelssohn villa. One never knew who would appear half-naked at breakfast or join us at lunch. Sometimes it was the handsome art historian from Bale, Christoph Bernoulli (he wore pajamas!), with Alice, his charming Russian wife; Erich Engel, who discussed Hegel with Berthold and was soon to stage Brecht's *Dreigroschenoper*. We adored his companion Sonia Okun, a gentle, lovely creature. She perished in Auschwitz.

I don't remember whether it was before Murnau had made his famous *Sunrise* or afterward that he asked Berthold to write his films. He was to be one of the first German motion-picture directors called to Hollywood. His film *The Last Man,* in which Emil Jannings played a lavatory attendant, was such a hit that the William Fox Studios signed him up at a huge salary. Emil Jannings, one of the many European stars to go to Hollywood, was grabbed by Paramount.

A towering, red-haired man, Murnau was so stiff and reserved that at first sight he gave the impression of arrogance. His real name was Plumpe. We had started together at the Reinhardt Theater but when I laughingly reminded him that he had been one of the Greek warriors in *Penthesilea,* and that I was the cheeky Amazon who garlanded him with flowers, it obviously annoyed him. Later I knew that it was not difficult to "defrost" him and see his true value. What brought us together was our great fondness for Walter Spiess, who was leaving Germany, European culture, Western civilization and secret armaments for freedom and adventure in the Tahitian islands, then Bali—never to return.

From the very beginning Berthold's relationship with Murnau was complicated to say the least. He was constantly analysing his reactions, and rebelling against Murnau's authoritative but deeply uncertain personality, and his pose of a grand seigneur. However, the few months spent in America had changed Murnau for the better: he was less Prussian and showed a more relaxed sense of humor.

19

ALL I KNEW ABOUT DUSSELDORF was that it is a city on the Rhine, occupied by French troops during the Napoleonic wars, and that Heinrich Heine had been born there. In his *Das Buch le Grand*, which I dearly loved when I was twelve years old, Heine says that in 1806 Emperor Napoleon had freed the Jews of Dusseldorf, who until then had lived in a ghetto, and had given them equal rights.

We arrived in the afternoon, deposited the boys and Nena in our new lodgings and went with Gustav Lindemann to his and Luise's place. They lived in the theater building. We crossed the dark, empty stage, then a long corridor, halted at a green, padded door which Gustav opened with a key, and found ourselves in a round, delightful room with flowers and plants outside and inside the windows. Luise in a long, red velvet gown welcomed us warmly, then led us through the ingeniously built apartment, which was in a small tower added to the theater.

The next day the Lindemanns introduced Berthold to the Ensemble, while I enrolled Hans and Peter in school. Later with Tommy and Nena we went to look at the Rhine and watched Brueghel-like figures, men and women in thick, padded coats, selling fish and vegetables from anchored barges.

It did not take us long to find out that the Ensemble was not as closely knit as we had been led to believe. It was rather like a large family ruled by a matriarch: instinctively everyone ran to "Mother" to complain, but officially it was Gustav who had greater authority and the emotional Luise "bowed to his decisions," although she strongly influenced them. In that way, balancing *her* power, they had successfully ruled the theater for many years.

All the young actors were waiting impatiently to work with Berthold. Eleonora Mendelssohn's beauty was an indisputable asset, but she was considered a talented amateur, and Luise entrusted to me the task of making her a professional. I had been warned about Luise's moodiness, her deviousness, and her habit of favoring those who flattered her; nevertheless, my personal and professional relationship with her proved the contrary. She respected my often dissenting views and was always generous with encouragement and praise. I began to teach in the dramatic school located on the upper floor of the theater. There were six girls and several young men in my class, among them a girl with fair, almost white hair and delicate skin, whose name was Ruth Greiner, and the small, dark Mia Engels, who was soon to marry Josef Gluecksmann, the young, handsome *Dramaturg* of the Schauspielhaus. Both became close friends.

As I remember, Berthold's first assignment was Marcel Achard's circus comedy: *Voulez-Vous Jouez Avec Moi?* a charming, frail play, which only mildly appealed to the Duesseldorf public. Our "official" introduction was in Schiller's *Mary Stuart*, which had not been played at the Schauspielhaus for many years, with me as Mary Stuart, Lilly Kann as Queen Elizabeth, and Berthold's staging.

It was an undisputed success and we played it three times a week. My understudy, Eleonora, prayed every morning that I might catch cold or get a sore throat, so she would have a chance to substitute for me. But I did better than that!

We were preparing a comedy by Lernet-Holenia and I had great fun playing a voluptuous adultress in trouble. At the dress rehearsal I had fever and spells of dizziness; nevertheless, in the evening I played Mary Stuart as usual. Afterward I went to bed and was so cold that my teeth chattered. Still, I had no pain. The doctor came in the morning and told the Lindemanns they should be prepared for a change in the repertory, because I should stay in bed. Gustav was distressed. The theater was sold out and the comedy promised to become the moneymaker they were hoping for. Berthold went to the theater to suggest a substitute. But Luise exclaimed: "No one can take over the part. I know Salka will not let us down—she'll play and nothing will happen to her. . . ." Luise was a Christian Scientist. I swallowed pills, stayed in bed until evening, then, wrapped in my warmest coat, took a taxi to the theater. The doctor, who had seen me in the afternoon, issued another warning. I pooh-poohed it. I wasn't coughing, or sneezing. Luise was right: nothing would happen to me. Berthold screamed that it was sheer madness and he and Luise had a violent quarrel in my dressing room. Their angry voices reverberated down the corridor while I was on my way to the stage. The doctor stood in the wings, checked my pulse, then shook his head in despair.

The curtain went up. I was not quite conscious of what I was doing, but I could hear the audience laugh. Afterward Luise and Gustav embraced me and thanked me for saving the evening. His face grim, Berthold wrapped me in my coat and took me home.

In the middle of the night I woke, feeling I was going to die. Two men in white coats were putting me on a stretcher; Nena was bending over me, saying: "I'll never leave the boys, I promise you." I remember the sound of the siren, the coolness of Berthold's hand on my forehead and then for a long, long time I remained unconscious.

One night the doctors thought I would not survive the crisis and they tried to reach Berthold. He was not at home and Nena did not know where to find him. Finally they located him in a restaurant, having a late supper with a pretty actress I shall call Therese, who was a good friend of ours. It was early morning when he arrived at the hospital. Luise never forgave him, that while his wife was dying he could eat, drink and "carry on a love affair." Today pneumonia is treated with antibiotics and can be over in six days; but at that time the doctors considered it a miracle that I recovered.

When I returned to our flower-filled apartment, Berthold told me that he and Luise were hardly speaking to each other. The Ensemble was divided into two camps, Gustav remaining in no man's land between. Therese was the main scapegoat and did not get any new parts.

When I looked from our window or went for walks along the Rhine, I could often see young men in steel helmets pushing people off the sidewalks and singing the *Horst Wessel Lied*. From time to time, when we bought a "red" paper, we read that the old powers in Germany were clandestinely resuscitating the army.

But I was still in "shock condition" after my illness and the conflict between Berthold and Luise depressed me greatly. It was obvious that Therese was in love with Berthold and I knew how susceptible he was to melancholy charm, persecuted innocence, loneliness, etc., etc. I begged Luise not to listen to gossip.

I asked her why she took it upon herself to judge the affairs of others. She answered: "Because I know more about people than you." However, a few days later I met Therese on the street and she told me that she had just got a very good part in Shaw's *Back to Methuselah*, which Gustav was directing. I was cast in a very unimportant bit, "to restore discipline and underline the absence of favoritism in the Ensemble."

There was no mention anymore of our succession to the throne, and our "step-parents," as Berthold now called the Lindemanns, had tacitly reclaimed their realm. Only one project remained unchanged: the tragedy *Ignorabimus* by Arno Holz, a strange drama about spiritualism, which since then has been plagiarized, banalized, and mutilated in films, but, as far as I know, never performed again. I had never had the remotest interest in spiritualism and the supernatural, but the part fascinated me. Having fearfully learned how easy it is for an exhausted heart to cease beating helped prepare me for my role: a woman who, from the beginning of the first act to the end of the fifth, stands under her own imaginary death sentence.

The weeks of rehearsals, exciting as they were, seemed to me like a continuation of my illness. I went home limp with fatigue and only the children dispersed my gloom. But at night the uncanny part would take hold of me again, as in my childhood, when Mademoiselle Juliette scared me to death with her stories.

Our tortures were not without reward. They earned Berthold and the actors a great success and the gratitude of the author, who, embittered by the neglect of his contemporaries, had at last seen his major work performed. Lean, tall, with a thick, white mane crowning his fine head, Arno Holz resembled Bertrand Russell. Outstanding among those who initiated a revolution in German drama, he has been forgotten by his country. Critics from Berlin and other German capitals, even those critical of the play, praised the courage of the Schauspielhaus.

Immediately after the première Berthold resigned. Luise again offered me a long-term contract. "If you stay with us you will achieve your highest aims as an artist," she told me. She was hurt that I refused, and our friendship ended.

The season was over, the last performance of *Ignorabimus* happened to be on my birthday. Berthold was in Berlin, discussing film projects. Nena had packed all our belongings as we were going to Austria to stay with Eleonora Mendelssohn, who had invited us to her *Schloss* in Kammer. Later Berthold and I would go together on our first, longed-for holiday in Venice.

My dressing room was filled with roses; they were on the dressing table, around the couch, everywhere. A new elegant suitcase, the gift of my pupils and colleagues, was filled with roses. Garlands of roses adorned the corridor through which I walked toward the stage. Only much later did I realize how final this farewell had been. . . .

I have always remained grateful to the Lindemanns for the artistic opportunities they gave me. Both were extraordinary, courageous people and many new dramatists such as Franz

Werfel, Fritz Unruh, Arno Holz, etc., owed much to them. After the war they were among the first to open their theater to Yvette Guilbert, Anna Pavlova, G. B. Shaw, Paul Reynal, Marcel Achard, Rabindranath Tagore and other foreigners. But the theater with its tawdry sins and grand, dramatic passions contradicted Luise's mystical inclination. She was unable to transform it into a temple.

As the gypsy had told me, my happiness was near the water and in Venice there was plenty of it. We lived on the Lido, had a *cabana* on the beach, swam and lay in the sun. At lunchtime an airplane from the Tirol brought baskets of wild strawberries, and in the afternoon we would dress and take a vaporetto to Venice. After our last lira was spent I picked up the children in Kammer and took them for the rest of the summer to Poland. Berthold returned to Berlin. Murnau had arrived from Hollywood and wanted him to write a screenplay based on Herman Bang's *The Four Devils*.

20

AGAIN WE WERE HAPPILY GATHERED together at Wychylowka on the hospitable veranda overlooking the large, wild garden. If it had not been for the children, growing so fast, it would have seemed that time had stood still. Papa and Mama had not changed and neither had Rose and Edward. Because we were so fundamentally influenced by our childhood we warmed ourselves at its glow in middle age. At Wychylowka all past struggle, achievement, success and failure submerged in a new hope.

Of course, the youngest ones were stealing the show. The Gielens had proudly presented their daughter Carla Stella (Bibi, for short) to her grandparents. Had I had more patience with the camera, that summer would have been thoroughly documented.

But my snapshots have faded and only the few Josef took still show the happy faces of all our children and Viktoria.

Sometimes Edward, Rose and I would think wistfully of the trips we would have liked to take and the places we would like to visit, instead of spending our summers, year in and year out, in Poland. But the mere idea of not seeing our parents appeared sacrilegious. The house, though it had become more and more dilapidated, dirty and worn out, was still dear to us. It was wonderful to see Papa so well, holding himself erect and going every day to his office. Mama's hair was snow-white, otherwise she was the same: lively, energetic, happy that the house was full of children and grandchildren.

The only one who showed wear and tear was Niania. She could hardly walk and her head and hands were shaking with palsy. Dusko was at the peak of his fame as a soccer player, participating with his team in games which took him to different cities and countries. I remembered how on our trip to Sambor I was trapped into a dreary conversation with a fellow passenger. He was a middle-aged, well-fed gentleman, probably a lawyer or a government official, and of insatiable curiosity. After I told him where we were going and why, he asked me what my maiden name was. Collapsing in awe, he repeated: "Steuermann! Are you by any chance related to the famous Steuermann?" I was sure he meant Edward who, after the war, had achieved prominence as a pianist and teacher and had played with great success in Lwow a few months before. The man informed me that he was not speaking of Edward but of Dusko Steuermann, the famous soccer player. I repeated this story to my father, but he only shrugged.

The *dolce far niente* was interrupted by a wire from Berthold: "WOULD YOU GO FOR THREE MONTHS TO AMERICA? HAVE OFFER FROM FOX TO WRITE AND DIRECT FILMS."

For the first time my father displayed interest in Berthold's profession. He seemed also to have revised his attitude toward America: "Economic conditions in Europe are getting worse every day and, sad as it is for us to have you so far away, this is a chance you cannot dismiss lightly." My mother agreed. Three months in America was not bad. She envied us the experience. But my father shook his head. "I don't believe they would pay the trip for only three months."

Although I was hoping to play in Berlin, the desire to go to America was greater and I cabled *yes*. Then I asked my father where Hollywood was. He showed it to me on the map. So far away! On the Pacific!

Berthold's letter was studded with exclamation points:

Salka! My dearest heart!

Have I done the right thing? I have signed! It will now only depend on how soon I can extricate myself from my commitment with the Reinhardt theaters as to when we shall leave. If I can bear Hollywood for *three years* it would make us financially secure for the rest of our lives!

The Americans can drop the option at the end of each year, but in case I want to return to Europe they are obliged to let me go. . . .

Salka, they say Hollywood is a paradise! We will have a bungalow. They have engaged me as a writer but in the course of time I am to direct, which will mean a financial increase and a separate agreement. I will work at home and will have more time to be with you and the children. I am sure it will be wonderful for them!

But, of course, it's a long journey! One week on the boat, four days and four nights on the train!

Salka, I believe that this will be my salvation! I will also have time to write my own stuff, which I must do, to be at peace with myself! But this is only one aspect. What spurs me most is the memory of our days in Venice! Since Venice I have had the compulsive desire to take you and the children and go off somewhere and build a new life for us. I know that you will miss the theater terribly and I would never have signed if you had not agreed. But it will not be for long!

Dearest heart, let me know your thoughts, give me advice, tell me your wishes, and embrace Papa and Mama tenderly from me. Tell them we shall be coming back every year. Dusseldorf also was far away. Kiss the three Americans: Hans, Peter and Tommy for me . . .

So my father was right. The contract was for three years, not for three months. And the next mail brought me the much desired Berlin offer. At once I regretted my emphatic yes. But how could I have thwarted Berthold's enthusiasm by thinking of myself?

Now that Hollywood had become a reality my father began to worry. He had had some dealings with Americans, but only one lawyer in Cincinnati had proven to be a reliable man. Papa thought that if "this Fox company is a hoax," Berthold could turn to him. My father hoped that his colleague was still alive; the last time he had heard from him was before the war.

On my last afternoon at home, while we were having tea on the veranda, Niania appeared in the door and motioned to me. I followed her to her room and she asked me to lift the lid of her trunk, painted dark green and with an iron band around it. As a child I had often sat on it and was always admonished not to bang my feet against it. The trunk contained all Niania's possessions: a few colorful handkerchiefs, three skirts, cotton shirts and in an old discarded candy box a few photos: one of herself in her turban-like headdress and a richly embroidered shirt, holding me, a serious-looking baby; another of her daughter and grandchildren, all very citified, sent from Chicago, where her son-in-law had been working in the slaughterhouses. There was also one of Vassili in his soldier's uniform, and the card notifying her of his death in Siberia.

She took out a neatly folded shirt with faded, red and blue cross-stitch embroidery, the same she wore in the photograph, and gave it to me.

"I wanted to be buried in it," she said, "but it's better you have it, so you remember me in America."

I put my arms around her trembling, emaciated body and held her close. Softly I said: "I'll be back, you will see! Next summer I'll be back. . . ."

But she shook her head and we both cried.

21

"HE WHO HAS BEGUN A THING must go on with it," was the first sentence in Berthold's English Grammar, while I contented myself with *Thousand Words*. A thousand words should be sufficient for our arrival in America; but the difficulty of pronouncing "TH" was insurmountable and so were the baffling vowels.

Regardless of impatient cables from Murnau our departure was delayed: first by the State Department, which took its time in issuing our visas, and second by Berthold's commitment to the Reinhardt theaters, which agreed to release him only after he had staged *Peer Gynt*.

Many of our friends advised Berthold to go alone and see how he liked Hollywood, before moving his whole family westward. Murnau wrote that it would be more sensible to leave the children in Europe until we knew that we would stay.

Alfred Polgar called to say that Ferenc Molnar was in Berlin and wanted to see us. He knew Hollywood and would give us firsthand information. We met for lunch in the Eden Hotel. Molnar, a plumpish, pink-cheeked, white-haired man, drew a very funny and extremely pessimistic picture of the virile Wild West, and of Hollywood. But he had an enormous appreciation of the dollar. "Save money and come back quickly," was his dictum. Worried about the children I asked: "Is the climate really as bad as they say?" He laughed. "Very bad for writers."

Meanwhile there was a great deal of work for Berthold in Berlin, with the rehearsals of *Peer Gynt*, and immediately after the very successful première, he began to write the screenplay for *The Four Devils*, Murnau's second American film.

Social life was at its peak and there were endless parties. Francesco Mendelssohn gave a huge reception for Yvette Guilbert. Diplomats, society people, prominent actors, French and German film stars, all gathered in the white music salon, with its wonderful Corot landscapes, while Yvette sang her chansons and her ballads. She still had the red hair Toulouse-Lautrec had painted, the ravaged face, the expressive hands, and was still an unforgettable artist. After the concert there was a buffet supper and dancing. The famous French film director Jacques Feyder and his wife Françoise Rosay sat at our table. In tails and white tie, with his decadent thin face, Feyder looked tired and blasé. Françoise was tall and looked very Parisian in a red dress and her prematurely gray hair. Feyder told us that he had a contract with Metro Goldwyn Mayer and was also going to Hollywood. They were taking their three sons with them, who were the same ages as ours, and they looked forward to resuming our acquaintance.

After midnight, sturdy young men in striped T-shirts, dirty trousers, woollen sweaters, some whose rolled-up sleeves bared colorful tattoos on their muscular arms, appeared in the drawing room. They came from the six-day bicycle race at the *Sportspalast*. The ambassadors withdrew quietly. Francesco not only had the gift of recalling, in all kinds of situations, identical scenes from a play, musical or film; he also liked to stage them in his house. That evening resembled *A Midsummer Night's Dream*. It was my last impression of Berlin.

The visas had arrived and we booked our passage on the *Albert Ballin*, a Hamburg-America liner sailing from Hamburg on

February 22, 1928. Suddenly the thought of the six thousand miles separating me from my sons made me panicky. If it had not been for Berthold and our determination to start a new life together, I would have stayed in Berlin.

In the icy winter weather I went shopping for summer dresses and swimsuits, ordered light suits for Berthold and a new tuxedo and tails, which we were told were imperative. Hollywood was constantly discussed among our friends; some of them envied us the adventure, others pitied us, as so much was going on in the theater and interesting work had been offered us in Berlin. The Hoffmanns introduced us to Dorothy Thompson, the American columnist, who was about to marry Sinclair Lewis. She spoke German and invited us to dinner. I prepared myself by reading *Arrowsmith*. Sinclair Lewis's French and German were as inadequate as our English, and as I had memorized only fifty of my thousand words, and Berthold had recklessly abandoned his grammar for Shakespeare's Sonnets (insisting that they were easier to remember than "He who has begun a thing . . ."), the burden of the conversation was carried by Dorothy. She looked lovely in a blue dress with a gardenia corsage, the first I had seen since before the war. Sinclair Lewis, tall, gaunt, and in spite of his blotched face, enormously likeable, had no idea who we were. After each martini we smiled at each other.

"You will love America," Dorothy was saying, "it's such a wide, great country and the people are very hospitable, you will see." Sinclair Lewis got up abruptly and left the room. Dorothy went on talking about America and what an exciting time we would have because of the election year, which was a unique experience. Sinclair Lewis returned wearing a black wig and a thin black mustache plastered to his upper lip. He sat down and began to talk with a loud, nasal drawl. Dorothy laughed and explained that he was showing us a Southern gentleman and how they talked in Mississippi. He left again and came back with a short white beard, transformed into a Yankee from Maine or Massachusetts, I don't remember which and would not have known the difference anyway. He changed twice more, appearing with red whiskers and then with a nice soft, droopy, blond mustache—while his food got cold.

We had our last meal at the Pension Wenzel. Hans and Peter, not fooled by our cheerfulness, were clinging to me, bravely promising that they would be good. Tommy, too little to participate in the farewell supper, was already sleeping. Berthold's *Reisefieber* had reached fantastic proportions. He lost and found his passport

ten times, the tickets twenty times, until finally I put all the
traveling documents in my bag and refused to surrender them.

Elisabeth Wenzel and Francesco took us to the *Lehrter
Bahnhof*. Again there were kisses and promises and when the train
pulled out I broke down and cried.

The *Albert Ballin* was smoothly proceeding westward when a
stowaway was found in the hold. I was very much concerned about
what would happen to him, but the Purser assured me that for ten
days he would peel potatoes, then be locked up while the ship was
in New York; then peel potatoes on his way back. In the hold also
was a dead American officer, killed in the war; now a German ship
was taking him home from his grave in France.

Six thousand singing canaries were also traveling with us. If one
of them got sick the Purser took it to his cabin where it would
recuperate. Canaries, we were told, were very much in demand in
the States and could enter without visas. Berthold figured that
there were 7,637 living creatures aboard. My mathematics were too
shaky to check on his calculations. . . .

We approached New York early in the morning. There was a
thick fog and we did not see the famous skyline. A German-
speaking publicity man from Fox and three reporters waited for us
in the salon. The reporters were starting to interview Berthold
when a German girl with bleached hair appeared, loudly announcing that she had been seasick during the crossing. Immediately the
reporters turned their backs on Berthold and clicked their cameras
while she posed on the arm of a sofa, dangling her legs. We were
curious to know who she was and the Fox man told us a name we
had never heard before nor afterward. She was under contract to
Universal Films.

Lack of sleep and the endless landing procedures blurred my
first impressions of New York. I retained only the memory of
smells that reminded me of the ghetto in Przemysl, and of dreary,
straight streets through which we drove to the hotel, a huge red-
brick building near Central Park. The publicity man informed us
that a famous gangster had been shot there. While we were waiting for the elevator, we heard German spoken behind us, and
there was Max Reinhardt, surrounded by his Berlin staff, also
waiting to go up. He was most cordial, regretted that he was
leaving the same day for Hollywood and hoped to meet us there.
He and the ensemble of the Deutsches Theater had been in New
York, playing Schiller's *Kabale und Liebe*, Shakespeare's *Twelfth
Night*, and *Oedipus Rex*. With Reinhardt was his impresario, Dr.
Kommer, "from Gzernowitz," as was printed on his visiting card.
He warned me about Hollywood and prophesied my unavoidable

collapse and return to Berlin. I had not seen Max Reinhardt since the day of my first audition. He had not changed much; only his hair was turning gray and he seemed tired. "*Amerika-müde*," Berthold said.

In our overheated suite on the thirty-second floor we found flowers and, with the compliments of Mr. Sheehan, the boss of Fox, six bottles of Scotch whisky hidden in the coat closet, which suggested the high personal esteem Mr. Sheehan had for Berthold, and the strictness of Prohibition.

Only the next day did we discover the disturbing beauty of New York. Unlike my first impressions of Venice, where everything seemed well-known, beloved and expected, New York was alien, frightening, and extremely unreal. The afternoon sun bursting in slanting rays into the deep crevices between the skyscrapers made them look like a Feininger painting.

We had sent Dorothy Thompson's letter of introduction to Lee Simonson, one of the directors of the Theater Guild, and he invited us to meet Theresa Helburn and Philip Moeller. Mr. and Mrs. Langner also came to greet us. Simonson and Theresa Helburn spoke a little German and were most charming, but as far as ideas about the theater were concerned, each of us had a different religion. What they admired in the German theater was for us conventional and dreary. They had a firm but biased opinion of Max Reinhardt, whom they considered an entrepreneur. It was not surprising that they had not heard of Brecht, but they were also unaware of Sternheim, Georg Kaiser and Wedekind.

The performances we saw were not very exciting and our English, although improving, was not sufficient to make us respond acutely to the potentialities of the American theater. Still Berthold wondered: "Why can I understand the Russian actors so much better although I don't know a word of Russian?"

The easiest to understand were the Negroes. We were carried away by the performance of Porgy, directed by Rouben Mamoulian. We adored Negro musicals of which we saw several, but I do not remember the titles. We could not avoid an evening at the Roxy Theater, because Murnau's *Sunrise* opened there, and we were amazed by the stage show which the theaters, owned by a film company, put on before the film.

We were told that the interest of the American audiences in silent films had declined and people lined up for long stretches in front of the Warner Brothers' Theaters, where an announcement of the *Jazz Singer* blazed from the marquee. Commonplace and of a sticky sentimentality, it had a tremendous impact on the audience. Berthold wondered what influence the "Talkies" would have on his contract. For a stage director and a writer, the "Talkies" could offer greater possibilities than the silent film, although Murnau looked with horror upon them. To compare the *Jazz Singer* with *Sunrise* or with King Vidor's *The Crowd* was sheer blasphemy. *The Crowd* was a fine motion picture about man's frightening beehive existence in big cities. The *Jazz Singer* had in our eyes nothing to recommend it except Al Jolson in blackface.

We tried to pack as many impressions of New York as possible into the few weeks we spent there, but Murnau's impatient telephone calls forced us to leave. A wonderful, fast train took us West. Everything was fabulously exciting and we reported it to our boys, our parents and friends on train stationery with the head of an Indian Chief on it.

We loved our Negro porter and the waiters in the dining car; we were delighted by our drawing room compartment, fascinated by the landscape. New Mexico and Arizona, with the gorgeous reds and browns and the splurge of purple and ochre in the fantastic rock formations, awed us with their beauty. The train was cutting through the desert . . . The sky was higher and the nights very clear and starry, the weird Joshua trees, the pale sagebrush. . . . All day long we stared spellbound through our window, imploring the porter to wipe it clean of dust. He did it reluctantly, contemptuously repeating, "Desert, it's nothing but desert. . . ."

I was learning by heart the names of the places we were passing: Peabody, Joliet, Independence, Topeka, Amarillo, Santa Fe and Emporia (which I thought must be a good city because in German *empor* means "upward.")

Then, on the fifth day, when we woke up we saw endless orange groves. The sweet smell of orange blossoms pervaded our compartment. We were in California. In Pasadena, Herman Bing, Berthold's new secretary, and an unavoidable publicity man waited for us with a big, black, chauffeur-driven automobile.

22

I EXPECTED CALIFORNIA TO BE all sunshine and flowers but, just as
we were robbed of the skyline view when we approached New
York, so we found Los Angeles cold and overcast, with the sun,
against which we had been so emphatically warned, invisible.
While we were driving along Sunset Boulevard I noticed that
there were no sidewalks in front of the uniform, clapboard houses
and bungalows. An extraordinary fantasy was displayed in roof
styling: some roofs were like mushrooms, many imitated Irish
thatch and the shape of others was inspired by Hansel and Gretel's
gingerbread house. Ice cream was sold in the gaping mouth of a
huge frog, or inside a rabbit; a restaurant was called "The Brown
Derby" and looked like one. The buses we passed offered SERVICE
WITH A SMILE, and during our whole ride Berthold was busy writing in his notebook the slogans on stores, buildings and billboards:

"Hillside Homes of Happiness—your servants will enjoy working as you will enjoy living in an Outpost Home."

"Toilet seats shaped to conform to nature's laws."

"How easy it is to shave when you control hydrolysis."

"Less hair in the comb, more hair on your head."

"Don't fool yourself! Halitosis makes you unpopular."

"Teeth may shine like tinted pearls, still pyorrhea attacks four
out of five."

To avoid the downtown traffic, our chauffeur did not drive
through the city, which on the first fleeting glimpse was uninviting
and ugly. JESUS SAVES, read a sign, towering over a large building,
and Mr. Bing explained that this was Aimée Semple McPherson's
Temple. We had never heard of Aimée Semple McPherson and
wanted to know who she was. Our companions perked up and
eagerly told us the gossip, and much of it appeared to be true,

about the lady preacher. Aimée had brought romance and glamor to religion, joy to the poor, and her Temple rivaled the Roxy in showmanship. It sounded fascinating and we were determined to attend her services as soon as possible.

Our suite at the Roosevelt was almost identical with the one in our New York hotel, and just as overheated. There was a big bouquet of red roses for me and a case of whisky for Berthold, this time in the bathtub. The roses were from Murnau, the whisky a welcome from the studio.

"They must think we are alcoholics," I said to Bing.

He sighed: "In our profession one needs a drink rather often." I offered him one immediately.

Quite heavy, quite tall and still quite young, probably in his thirties, the son of German-Jewish immigrants, Bing had come to Hollywood as an actor. "I was a comedian," he said with a resigned smile. "I was not bad . . . not bad at all . . . I could be very funny."

After we were installed in our rooms he said good-bye, asking Berthold to call whenever he needed him and saying that he would report our arrvial to Mr. Murnau. In the car I had already noticed that when he mentioned Murnau he seemed to be terrified by his grandeur. It did not fail to irritate Berthold.

The telephone rang and I answered. It was Murnau, happy that we had arrived at last. I thanked him for the roses and said that Berthold was taking a shower and would call later.

"Just tell him I don't need him today. I am shooting tests," said Murnau. "Only wanted to say hello."

Berthold was furious when I gave him the message. Murnau's "I don't need him" was sheer Prussian arrogance. Although I explained that Murnau did not sound overbearing, the jarring note was a prelude to the many clashes in their odd friendship.

The German journalist Arnold Hoellriegel, who was also staying in the Roosevelt, wanted us to have lunch with him. Coming downstairs we heard a cacophony of shrill voices as if from an enormous, excited poultry yard. The lobby was packed with women of whom the youngest could not have been less than seventy. About a hundred of them tottered around on high heels, in bright, flowered-chiffon dresses, orchid or gardenia corsages pinned to their bosoms. We wanted to know the purpose of the gathering but were told only that the ladies were Republicans. Hoellriegel's traveling companion and photographer, Max Goldschmidt, was not permitted to take pictures. After lunch Hoellriegel suggested that we take a look at the studios, but I pleaded that we drive first to the ocean.

The afternoon was gray and chilly, a mist hanging over Santa Monica. We drove along Pico Boulevard, a long, straight highway leading to the ocean. Again we saw shabby bungalows, occasional palm trees, gasoline stations, nurseries, markets and endless "lots for sale." Then the highway rose to a hilltop and we could see a bright, silvery glimmer, which changed into a wide strip of an iridescent, mother-of-pearl hue. We passed a lovely cemetery shaded by trees, like those in the "old country." It was called Woodland. Turning right we stopped in front of a rambling hotel surrounded by an old, beautiful garden with enormous gum trees, sycamores and cypresses.

Having crossed the street and the well-kept lawn of an esplanade, shaded by eucalyptus trees and tall palms, we found ourselves on the rim of a cliff. Below was a highway, with automobiles flitting by; beach houses and clubs turned their backs to the road and the glassed-in front porches faced the ocean. To our right was the little bay of Santa Monica Canyon, surrounded by hills covered with shrubs, trees, and scattered houses. On our left was a pier, whose wooden pillars reached far out into the ocean. We drove to its entrance. A gaudy, yellow building with a tower-like superstructure harbored a merry-go-round. It had the most magnificent, fierce horses, carved in wood and painted by a real artist. They looked like the steeds on the monuments of great generals. The loud orchestrion was playing old-fashioned music. At each end of the long pier were fishmarkets, between them ice cream stalls and little shops renting fishing rods and selling bait, dusty abalone shells, starfish, coral beads and chewing gum, and a shack where a Filipino lady in a sequined costume was telling fortunes. Men and women in sunbleached jeans, and of all ages, were fishing from the pier. Boats were tied up below and one could go sailing outside the little bay. Everything was so lovely and peaceful: the people on the pier and the merry-go-round and the swaying boats. I begged Berthold to let us live in Santa Monica.

When Berthold mentioned this in the studio, people were horrified: Santa Monica! Everybody who lived there became rheumatic, had chronic bronchitis and gout. "Then why would all the rich people have houses there?" I argued. I was told that those houses were air-conditioned and sound-proofed; their owners had the means to protect themselves from ocean air and the pounding surf. Only Herman Bing's objection made some sense: living in Santa Monica, Berthold would have to get up half an hour earlier to be on time at the studio. My vision of the mad daily rush made me resign myself to a house in Hollywood.

Emil and Gussy Jannings gave a party for us. Emil, a lusty

character-actor, had the gross and expansive sense of humor one calls "Rabelaisian." His wife Gussy, blond and very chic, had once been a cabaret singer, a well-known *diseuse*, and had become a stoical, imperturbable, though sharp-tongued consort. Invited with us were Conrad Veidt, lanky and handsome, and short cigar-smoking Ernst Lubitsch, now a celebrated film maker, but who had not changed since our *Judith* days. Both had uninteresting pretty wives. A successful German director, Ludwig Berger, was also there. Paramount had signed him because of his European fame, but they did not know what to do with him. Max Reinhardt appeared after dinner, with young Raimund von Hoffmansthal, son of the Austrian poet. He said that he had fallen in love with California, which Jannings, who hardly knew it, detested.

All those who had been some time in Hollywood seemed starved for new faces and, as I soon discovered, irritated with the old.

The Jannings lived in a grand-style Hollywood mansion, which they rented from the millionaire Josef Schenk, one of "filmdom's pioneers." Situated in the center of Hollywood Boulevard, it had a large garden, swimming pool, tennis court, and a huge living room with a multitude of lamps. The diversity of lamps and especially the extraordinary shapes of the lampshades, struck me as a speciality of Hollywood interiors.

Throughout the evening the main topic of conversation was the catastrophic impact of the talking films upon the careers of foreign stars, until the exuberant entrance of the precocious "Mann children," Erika and Klaus, brightened the atmosphere. They had just arrived in Hollywood on their journey around the world. Very young and attractive, they were refreshingly irreverent and adventurous. They brought with them the atmosphere of Berlin's night life which electrified the party. It was very late when we left with them, discussing the evening on our way back to the hotel. Berthold was fascinated by Jannings's impersonation of "Jannings in real life," an amalgamation of his monstrous egotism with roles he had played: Harpagon, Henry VIII, with glimpses of the good-natured, straightforward *Deutscher Michel*. We agreed that it was a great performance; that Conny Veidt was most handsome and a darling; Lubitsch inscrutable but worth knowing better; and Ludwig Berger's fate a warning to European directors.

I had rented the least expensive house I could find. It was on Fairfax Avenue, near the hills of Laurel Canyon, unpretentious but pleasant.

As soon as we moved in I asked Bing to help me choose a car and teach me how to drive. Half an hour later we returned in a

Buick. Berthold was doubtful that a good car could be bought so quickly. I sat behind the wheel, death-defying Bing next to me. Nonchalantly I released the brakes, shifted into first gear and drove around the block. At least one of our problems was solved.

Had Berthold had any sense of direction, had he been less absent-minded and more interested in mechanical things, and had he been able to remember the difference between the brake and the accelerator, he also would have learned to drive. Under the circumstances, it was lucky that he stalled the car as soon as he touched the gearshift. After smashing a bumper and tearing off two fenders, he conceded defeat and De Witt Fuller joined our household as chauffeur. Bing could now devote himself entirely to typing, translating Berthold's script and giving him English lessons. We also engaged Emma, a Negro housekeeper, although Jannings threatened never to have a meal in our house. Now we were set, and certain that we would stay for a while in America.

At the end of May, in suffocating heat, I traveled across the continent again, to meet the *Albert Ballin*, which was bringing my sons to New York. Although they found the four days in the train most interesting, the children were glad when the trip came to an end. They admired the house and the garden, and adored Emma and De Witt, who reciprocated with great warmth. Nena was less pleased with *"die Schwarzen,"* but after my strict and firm appeal to her common sense (often so exasperating!) and her Christian principles, she became friendly and polite.

We were settling down. A German-American teacher prepared Hans and Peter for school. I went shopping, had my English lesson and wrote endless letters. On weekends I drove the children to the beach or to the Santa Monica Pier and my beloved merry-go-round.

The Fox executives began to invite us to parties at which the ritual separation of the sexes brought me in closer contact with their ladies. To do them justice, they were often much nicer than their husbands, and more intelligent. I liked the warm-hearted Marion Wurtzel, wife of Berthold's producer, the incredibly boorish Sol Wurtzel. She was born in Poland in a small Jewish community and used to invite me with other studio wives for lunch, always suggesting that we go shopping afterward. In no time she would spend three or four hundred dollars with the disarming explanation: "When I was a little girl I had to share one pair of shoes with my sister. Now I can afford things I don't need."

The Feyders arrived and were going through the stage when everything seemed *"très amusant"* and *"tordant."* But slowly the lunches and parties were getting me down. Françoise suggested that we play golf, but soon she also became convinced that golf did not answer all our needs. We were professional women and to survive in Hollywood we had to work.

Wonderingly I mused about Berthold's "pilgrim's progress." Although regarded as an eccentric, he was liked and respected. The executives asked his opinion on stories and scenarios, and took his advice on films which needed "doctoring." With his extraordinary inventiveness he averted many calamities. For someone to whom the tough, illiterate mentality of his "superiors" was so utterly alien, this was quite a feat, but from the very beginning the originality of his mind and his talent were wasted on Sol Wurtzel. Murnau also was under great strain and had many difficulties. Indecisions in casting, and disagreement about the story *The Daily Bread*, a silent film, had created a delay in shooting an essential part, the wheat harvest, and only in the last days of August were the crew and the cast finally ready to leave for Pendleton, Oregon, where the wheat was still uncut.

Berthold wrote:

> Imagine a Sambor without Jews. There is only one Jewish shopkeeper here, born in Austria, who came to Pendleton in 1878. You cannot believe how idiotic that man has become, but he is happy. An old, grey, smiling "easy-taker." The other inhabitants drive back and forth on the main street, uninterruptedly and relentlessly honking the horns and letting the engines roar and howl to split your ears.

But suddenly he became fascinated with the Indians and visited the Reservation as often as he could.

From Hollywood I reported:

> I have enrolled the boys in school. Masses of children, all with numbers, were waiting to be called. Ours was Number One Hundred and Eleven, and resignedly we sat and waited our turn. The boys were in a fever, worried they would be put into the lowest grade, with "children who don't know the alphabet." Emma, who had come with us, kept her fingers crossed and was as excited as Hans and Peter. Finally we were called and after a few brief questions Hans was assigned to the second grade, Peter to the lower second. But already after lunch, Hans was promoted to the third, having answered the question: "How was your summer vaca-

tion?" with the account of his trip from Europe to California, all in English. The teacher, a woman, was "thrilled" with his description and you can imagine how proud I was. After only three months in America it is very impressive. I don't know whom we have to thank: the teacher, Mr. Schumacher, or Emma and De Witt. Peter also returned very enthusiastic about the school and his teacher: "She speaks very slowly and I understand every word she says."

The harvest in Pendleton was brought in on celluloid, and Berthold and I met in San Francisco for a brief holiday.

One evening Murnau asked us if we wanted to see an extraordinary film he was running in the projection room. When we arrived he introduced Robert Flaherty, explorer and film maker, a stoutish gentleman of indefinite age, with very blue eyes. We were to see *Moana*, a film Flaherty had shot in Samoa. *Moana* was a poetic and touching document about Polynesian life and had a deep effect on Murnau. It strengthened his conviction that a dedicated film maker could not express himself in a Hollywood studio, and he and Flaherty decided to embark on an independent venture in Tahiti. There were long discussions with Berthold about the story Flaherty had suggested and which they intended to do. We supported the whole project enthusiastically; with the collaboration of Flaherty it could not fail.

Walter Spiess, who had run away from Europe and civilization, wrote delirious letters from Bali. He had found his "own heavenly spot on the globe" and had built a house there. He invited us to come to Bali with our boys, live in his house, forget films, theater, Berlin, America, everything.

> There are fifty monkeys in the Waringia tree in front of my house, I feed them raisin bread. Deer and crocodiles, parrots and marten abound and everything reminds you of Adam and Eve. For you, Salka, and Berthold, there are actors and theater, marvelous dancers and music like nowhere in the whole world. The loveliest and most musical music! [And as his strongest persuasion he added:] It would be great if you came. Probably I'll hang myself out of sheer joy. Your loving—Valjka.

A voyage to Bali was to culminate Murnau's South Seas adventure. Of course, he could not travel like an ordinary person; it had to be daring and adventurous. He bought a slim, lovely yacht and named it *Bali*, thus indicating her final destination.

The rainy season started at Christmas; everything became lush and green. Afterward the orange trees blossomed, and in April roses burst out in fantastic profusion. I sat in the garden reading Upton Sinclair's *Boston*. I don't remember where Berthold had met Sinclair, but that evening he brought him for dinner (Mrs. Sinclair was not feeling well and stayed at home in Pasadena). It was a wonderful occasion to express my gratitude for the book, which had deeply moved me.

Sinclair was lean and held himself very erect, with a clean-cut Yankee face. As Prohibition was generally disregarded, I put a bottle of a harmless Chilean riesling on the table. With a disapproving look Sinclair turned his glass upside down and of course none of us dared to drink a drop. But our great respect pleased him. In spite of his egocentricity and puritanism, he had humor and was a very likeable man.

At last I got Berthold's consent to rent a beach house, "but only for the summer," and drove to Santa Monica.

At the corner of Seventh Street and San Vicente Boulevard, a road led down to the beach. It had rained in the morning and small white clouds hung above the ocean, which was covered with whitecaps. The breeze brought the scent of orange blossoms. On my left was a road winding uphill, on my right shacks and adobe huts and lots overgrown with weeds and geraniums. I faced a clapboard schoolhouse, small and rural, on which the roads seemed to converge. Children, mostly Mexicans, played on the slides and swings of the recreation ground. All this was peaceful and quiet: old sycamores and gnarled oaks, a swollen brook which rushed toward the ocean, dividing the road into two lanes, both leading to the Ocean Highway. I remembered having seen somewhere a billboard advertising a real estate office.

I found it next to "Inspiration Point," where Palisades Park ended and Ocean Avenue began to descend toward the canyon. A young man, tall and dark, introduced himself as Mr. Guercio and offered to show me several houses. One, suitable for a large family, was right below, though not directly on the beach.

We drove down a short, winding road overlooking the ocean, and stopped in front of a large, fenced-in house in the so-called English style. Two pine trees grew on each side of the entrance; next to them a magnolia spread its glossy leaves and enormous white blossoms. The fence was overgrown with honeysuckle, entangled with pink Portugal roses. The air was suffused with fragrance.

To get to the beach we had only to walk to the end of the street and descend the steps to a tunnel under the highway.

Mr. Guercio opened the front door and we went in. The first floor consisted of a very vast living room with a fireplace and a dining area. It had eight windows and a glass door which opened into the garden. A staircase between the dining area and living room led to the bedrooms; they also were spacious and had a view of the ocean. There were plenty of bathrooms and showers, and servants' quarters next to the garage. In the garden grew a pitasphorum tree and the inevitable hibiscus bushes, also an apricot and fig tree. At the far end an old incinerator tried to hide behind a lonely, bedraggled lilac bush. Mr. Guercio said that the lilac never bloomed, but this did not shatter my hope that one day it would, and it increased my desire to take the house. The rent was $900 for the three summer months but, if we wanted to take it for a whole year, it would be proportionately less. The house was in receivership, owned by a bank in Santa Monica. The bank was obviously responsible for the atrocious furniture, the armchairs and sofa covered with black velvet which faced the fireplace, and the shabby rattan garden chairs filling the rest of the room. The bedrooms were less offensive as they had only the essential things. From the windows one could see the ocean and the sharp profile of the hills on the other side of the canyon, and I could hear the waves pounding the shore.

I showed Berthold the house. He liked it, and in June, after Hans and Peter had finished school, we cut ourselves off from Hollywood and moved to 165 Mabery Road.

23

BERTHOLD'S FIRST DIRECTORIAL ASSIGNMENT was the last silent film Fox produced, and all I remember is that Françoise Rosay played a veiled Arab woman in it; it was her debut as a film actress. During the shooting, the studio picked up Berthold's option and doubled his salary. It seems strange now that under these advantageous auspices we kept prolonging our Visitors' Permits and did not apply for Immigration Visas. But Camil Hoffmann, Erich Engel, Francesco, Elisabeth, all our friends, were awaiting our return. Our families also did not wish us to settle in America.

We kept the house for another year. The beach had been an unending source of happiness to us; the boys were brown and strong and had become good swimmers. They had made friends with the Mexican children in the Canyon and when we addressed them in German they answered in English. The two older ones had outgrown Nena's authority and, much to my distress, she concentrated her possessiveness on Tommy, making him very dependent on her.

Meanwhile Murnau had been rigging out his *Bali* for the voyage to the South Pacific. He had a crew of seven, which we thought quite a crowd for the small boat. At last he was ready and we went to the harbor to bid him farewell. Bob Flaherty was to leave a few weeks later on a mail steamer. I gave Murnau two pounds of Malosol caviar, which moved him to tears. He stood on deck waving, while we waved back until he disappeared from view. We knew we would miss him. The next to say good-bye to Hollywood were Emil and Gussy Jannings.

Contrary to predictions, moving to Santa Monica did not impair our social life. On the contrary, our Sunday afternoons became very popular. The living room had become more attractive after I had hidden the black velvet under slipcovers and bought shelves for our books, which had arrived from Berlin. A rented piano, plants and flowers accomplished the rest.

Dramatists, novelists and newspapermen were now being summoned to Hollywood to write scenarios for the Talkies, and Berthold hoped for better scripts. However, the main topic discussed among his co-workers was the stock market. We listened wide-eyed to the miraculous rise of A.T.&T. or some other capitalized initials. Someone had assured Berthold that the stock broker at the First National Bank of Beverly Hills was "a wizard" and the wizard advised him to take advantage of the executives' offer and buy shares in the Fox Theater Corporation. They had climbed to twenty-five dollars a share and were sure to double in value. Berthold's determination to become a capitalist astonished me, but the *Truppe* debts had been paid and the Fox theaters seemed solidly built, until I saw the huge headlines, "Fox Theater Shares down to. . . ." I don't remember what, but it was practically nothing.

I comforted Berthold. We still had some money left for the trip back to Europe and our rent was now reduced to a hundred and fifty dollars a month.

A New York actor, Paul Muni, was to star in Berthold's next film. He and Bela, his wife, young and enthusiastically dedicated to the theater, used to reminisce nostalgically about the Yiddish Ensemble with which they grew up and where Muni had his first successes. In the film Berthold was making, *The Seven Faces*, Muni had ample opportunity for chameleon-like changes of characterization—he played a caretaker in a waxworks museum and also seven of the figures which come to life, among them Napoleon and Jack the Ripper. Catherine the Great also appeared in the film and George Middleton, who was supervising the production, suggested that I should play her. The experience did not make me wish to become a movie actress. Acting in fragments is like drinking from an eyedropper when you are parched.

George Middleton, tall, lumbering and fiftyish, had fond memories of the war and the years he had spent in France. He loved Europeans. His charming, ash-blond wife, Fola, was the daughter of the late Senator Robert M. La Follette, founder of the Progressive Republican League who, with Senator Borah, had opposed America's entry into the War. She was most sympathetic to our unwavering pacifism, and she spoke French, which was very helpful when my English faltered. She loved the theater and the many pleasant hours I spent with her helped me to overcome my homesickness. Through Fola I met people outside the film world. One of them was the exotic, delicate Mrs. Francis Bitter. An Englishwoman, she was born and raised in India until she married a young physicist from the California Institute of Technology. She was a musician and as "Ratan Devi" gave recitals, singing classical Indian songs and playing the sitar. Fola and Ratan Devi were the only people who insisted on improving my English. All our other American friends protested indignantly, when I attempted to speak correctly, "Oh, for heaven sakes don't lose that charming accent," or "It doesn't matter that you don't say it right, it sounds cute." I suppose that this American kindness toward foreigners is one of the reasons for their own bad diction and lazy speech. For hours, with a truly oriental patience, Ratan Devi let me read aloud *David Copperfield*, George Moore's *Esther Waters* and other English novels, correcting my pronunciation.

Europeans were descending en masse upon Hollywood—to write, to report or to act in films. Among them were William Dieterle and his wife Charlotte, Charles Boyer, whom we had admired in Berlin in a play by Henri Bernstein (actresses and actors from France and Germany were imported by the studios, which now began to produce films in foreign languages). I had last seen Dieterle as the roaring Danton in Reinhardt's production of the

Büchner play in the great Schauspielhaus. He still looked like a leading man, but had abandoned acting for directing films. Warner Brothers signed him for the German versions of their products.

Professor Albert Einstein came as the guest of Caltech, taking the long route through the Panama Canal, and thousands of school children, in white and carrying flowers, stood on the docks of San Pedro chanting their welcome. Berthold had known Einstein in Berlin and we were very pleased when Mrs. Einstein asked us to a quiet family dinner. Only two other people were present, his assistant, and their son-in-law. It was the most effortless and gayest evening I have ever spent in the presence of a great man. We laughed a lot as anecdote followed anecdote, and I regret that I don't remember even one. We met again on other occasions but never so intimately and informally. When his stay in California came to an end, we drove to Pasadena to see him off. The station was teeming with thousands and thousands of people; it was impossible to get through to the Einsteins. Only under police escort could they board the train. By good luck Mrs. Einstein caught sight of us and asked a policeman to clear the way, so that we could say good-bye. After the train had left and the crowd was dispersing, a tiny, determined old lady stopped us and asked Berthold if he was related to Professor Einstein. "No, not at all," Berthold informed her hurriedly, but she held onto him.

"I thought you were, because you have such a remarkable head."

"Thank you," he said, a little friendlier.

"I want to shake hands with you," she went on, disregarding the jostling and pushing of the people around us, "because I saw you shaking Professor Einstein's hand." Turning to me she added: "And I want to shake yours too!"

We shook hands and then Berthold tried to get away. But I was curious why she had come to see Einstein. My question baffled her: "Well, I don't know. . . ."

"Are you interested in science?" I asked.

"Oh, is he a Christian Scientist?" she exclaimed, delighted.

"No," I said quickly. "He is a physicist, didn't you know?"

Beaming, she said: "Oh, my dear lady, I don't care what he does. He must surely be a wonderful man when so many people turn out to say good-bye to him. . . ."

One day Mrs. Lubitsch called me to say she was giving a "black-tie party" in honor of a visiting German film star. Forty "prominent" people were invited. The film star's husband was a German producer Berthold had known in Berlin, and out of nostalgia he said we should accept.

As was common in Hollywood, beautiful women were clustered in one corner of the room, while the men talked shop in the other. Jacques Feyder remained of course with the ladies; Françoise was not there as she had gone to Paris for a few weeks. He greeted me and led me to a couch, on which, next to the German star, whose billowing skirt was taking practically all the space, sat Greta Garbo. She was the only woman who wore an austere black suit and not evening dress. As the German star refused to subdue her flounces, there was no room for me on the couch, and we went out to the veranda, leaving her enthroned in her splendor. The night was chilly. Only a few hardy characters were sitting outside. Feyder secured a bottle of champagne and the three of us spent the rest of the evening in a highly animated mood.

Books have been written about Garbo's beauty, "mystery" and talent; her films, constantly reissued, confirm her magic. There is something unexpected in the loveliness of this face; it is always as if one were seeing it for the first time. She was then at the peak of her success, the critics comparing her to Duse and Sarah Bernhardt. Fans and reporters pursued her with such persistence that protecting her privacy became an obsession. This of course was exploited by publicity as the saga of her "mystery." Oddly, when I met her I had not seen any of her films, with the exception of *Gösta Berling*. We talked about its première in Berlin; then she asked about my work in the theater. She was intelligent, simple, completely without pose, with a great sense of humor, joking about her inadequate German and English, although she expressed herself very well. Berthold joined us and we talked until late, while Feyder kept refilling our glasses.

The next day we had just finished lunch, when the doorbell rang and in the open window of the entrance appeared the unforgettable face. In the bright daylight she was even more beautiful. She wore no make-up, not even powder, only the famous long eyelashes were thoroughly blackened with mascara. Her fine skin had a childlike smoothness; the slender hands were sunburned, and contrary to her reputation I found her well dressed: the slacks and shirtwaist were beautifully cut and well-fitting. Gaily she announced that she had come to continue the conversation of last night, and stayed all afternoon. We went for a short walk on the beach and then sat in my room. She told me she was pleased that I had only seen her in *Gösta Berling*, as she did not care much for her other films. She was very funny, caricaturing the repetitiousness of the seduction techniques.

She lived not far from us, and in the evening Berthold and I walked her home. After we had said good-night to her, we exchanged our impressions. What had charmed us was her great politeness and attentiveness. She seemed hypersensitive, although of a steely resilience. The observations she made about people were very just, sharp and objective. "Probably all that fame prevents her from living her real life," I said.

"It's a high price to pay," said Berthold.

She came very often early in the morning when the beach was deserted, and we took long walks together.

In those first years in California I don't think I met anyone who had been born or raised there. The actors and writers, especially those from the East, were transitory, having come to make money and to get out as soon as possible. I also was counting the days till our return to Europe. I became aware that we were constantly explaining ourselves to our American friends, trying to convey our identity and what really possessed us, who we were. Berthold's futile efforts to communicate made me unhappy and I hated when he touched upon matters which I knew his new associates would not understand. Of course there were exceptions, but for a man so erudite and creative in his own language, it was torture to confine himself to the primitive vocabulary of Mr. Wurtzel, and escaping to the men's room to read Kant and Kierkegaard was small relief. The only comfort was the sight of the sea and the happiness of our sons, who had become dedicated Californians.

"Why don't you write?" Garbo asked me.

"Because I am not a writer. I am an actress, temporarily unemployed."

Berthold agreed with her. He had always encouraged me: "You would bear Hollywood much better if you worked."

But his own difficulties were increasing, although *The Seven Faces* had been well received. His next assignment was a story with a Russian background. While he was struggling with the screenplay we heard that Sergei M. Eisenstein, the creator of *Potemkin*, had been signed by Paramount for a one-year contract, and suddenly Hollywood seemed less negative.

As soon as Eisenstein arrived, Upton Sinclair, who had most impressive friends, gave a picnic lunch for him at the ranch of Mr. Gillette, the razorblade millionaire. We drove miles and miles over the winding roads of Topanga Canyon to meet the Soviet artists at the mansion of an American tycoon. When we arrived we found that the doors were locked. The owner was absent and the guests had the use of the garden only.

We had met Mrs. Sinclair at a tea party in the house of Mrs. Crane-Gartz, a Pasadena millionairess, daughter of the Chicago plumbing magnate who was a great friend and supporter of Upton. There were also other Pasadena ladies present, all elderly and provincial in appearance, with the exception of Mary Miles-Minter, a retired film star, who outshone us all in elegance. The guests of honor stood apart; they were Eisenstein with his two Russian collaborators, Edward Tisse and Gregory Alexandroff, and a young British couple, Ivor and Hell Montagu, friends and translators for the three Russians. Mrs. Sinclair, with the capricious charm of a Southern belle, ordered us to eat immediately as they had waited long enough for Mr. and Mrs. Viertel. The lunch was spread out on the grass under an olive tree and I sat between Eisenstein and Alexandroff. Eisenstein was of middle height, his reddish mane receding above a high forehead. He must have been in his early thirties. The scenario writer Alexandroff, blond and blue-eyed and strikingly handsome, did not speak anything but Russian, so my rusty Ukrainian was of some help. Edward Tisse, the cameraman, was the oldest of the trio and knew a little French. Eisenstein spoke German, French and very good English. Upton welcomed the Russians with one of his jovial, pleasant speeches and Eisenstein thanked him, also in the name of his friends. Then he and I talked in German about Berlin, where I had first seen his films. Berthold was between Upton and Mrs. Crane-Gartz. Suddenly Miss Miles-Minter tapped her glass, demanding attention. Everybody stopped talking. She made a lengthy, confused speech about communism and the Soviets and asked the Russians why they had permitted the execution of the Tsar and his family. It was quite embarrassing.

Afterward the Eisenstein collective drove to our house and seeing that we lived so near the ocean, they suggested they would pick us up every morning and together we would go for a swim. Tisse took photos of us on the beach and Eisenstein used to say that they were the only film he had made in Hollywood.

Our circle was enlarged by Berthold's new secretary-assistant, Fred Zinnemann, a nineteen-year-old Viennese, totally dedicated to films. He and his friend Gunther von Fritsch, another amiable young Austrian, became our daily guests.

Meanwhile things were not going well in Tahiti. Robert Flaherty withdrew from his collaboration with Murnau and returned to America. Murnau's self-righteous letters had prepared us for the split-up. From the story Flaherty told us, we gathered that at the outset Murnau shared Flaherty's ideas; he admired him, but his "boss complex" was too overwhelming. According to Flaherty, influenced by German expressionism, Murnau insisted on using theatrical effects, while he, Flaherty, an anthropologist and explorer, wanted to tell the epic story of the lives, customs and struggles of the peoples he loved. Murnau's talent, character and background made such patient, prodding work impossible and his and Flaherty's relationship was doomed once they faced each other in the South Seas.

People who did not like Murnau used to say that his "cloven hoof" was his real name: Plumpe. To compensate for "Plumpe" he had to be more authoritative, more rigid and more exacting than was his nature. There are professions, such as orchestra conducting, directing, film producing and even teaching, which spoil one's character, for it is dangerous always to know better.

In her book *Dämonische Leinwand*, Lotte H. Eisner maintains that Murnau was the greatest film director Germany ever had. She adds: "All Murnau films bear the stigma of his inner discord; they give evidence of his conflict with an alien world, forever inaccessible to him. Only in *Tabu* does he find some peace, some happiness, when he lives in the midst of an exuberantly flourishing nature, where European morals and feelings of guilt don't exist."

Eisenstein and his friends wanted to explore the religious and the sinful Los Angeles, and the first stop on our itinerary was Aimée Semple McPherson's Angelus Temple, which promised to combine both. We were lucky in hitting upon one of Aimée's most glamorous productions. With a new permanent wave in her blond hair, in a white silk gown, clutching red roses to her heart, she appeared at her pulpit to receive a frenetic ovation from a packed house. Her sermon appealed to the senses. She assured her audience that the Lord is sweet, and made gourmet sounds, tasting Jesus on her tongue—the congregation drooled and smacked their lips. The Russians were delighted.

The world success of his films did not prevent Eisenstein from suffering the fate of most European directors in Hollywood. The two scenarios he wrote, *The Glass House* and *Sutter's Gold*, are still gathering dust in Paramount's files. After several months it became obvious that Hollywood had no use for him, and we only wondered why he had been called. As they were about to leave, Upton Sinclair offered to raise money among his wealthy friends so that Eisenstein could make an independent picture in Mexico, because "we hated to see a great artist humiliated." "The Pasadena Group," a few elderly ladies, millionairesses, friends of the Sinclairs and Mrs. Crane-Gartz, declared their willingness to invest twenty-five thousand dollars in an Eisenstein film. Berthold tried to convince Eisenstein that this was not enough, but the Russians were sure that, as they would make the film without a studio, they would not need more. What they did not take into account was that Eisenstein's imagination, stimulated by impressions of a strange and extraordinary country, could never produce a simple documentary.

He had asked me to be present at the signing of the agreement, and my heart sank when I met his sponsors. With the exception of Upton and Mrs. Crane-Gartz they had no idea who Eisenstein was. I am sure they would have been horrified had they ever seen one of his films.

The Russians left. In the most optimistic mood we said goodbye to each other; in four months we would meet again.

Having spent all his money, Murnau returned with a completed film. He moved with his German shepherd dog to the Miramar Hotel in Santa Monica, and came every evening to have dinner with us.

My own recollections of *Tabu* are blurred, but although Berthold admired it he found certain parts of it disappointing. It was much improved by Murnau's editing, but as it was a silent film, the question of orchestration became important. We hoped he would use native music, but his agent and other Hollywood people were for a great symphonic score, a last desperate attempt to sell the silent products, which would cost Murnau fifty thousand dollars. However, it was useless to argue, and Berthold not only ceased persuading but loaned him all our savings, to pay an advance to the composer. To make our future more insecure, the situation at Fox had become so unbearable that Berthold had decided to leave. Then one day, when everything and everyone were steeped in gloom, Murnau telephoned me: "Would you and the boys like to take a ride along the coast?"

I knew that he did not have a car and said: "I'll pick you up in half an hour."

"Oh, no you won't. Tell the boys they'll have a ride in a Rolls Royce." His voice sounded triumphant.

"Murr!" I screamed. "You've sold *Tabu*."

He arrived in a gorgeous open car with chauffeur (he had rented it from Tanner's Liveries) and off we went along the ocean highway, toward Ventura. The day was dark, the sky as gray as the ocean, but after the rain the hills along the highway had turned green.

"It won't be long before the desert will bloom," said Murr. "I wish I could show it to you."

"Why can't you?" I asked.

"Because my mother insists that I come home. I have booked a cabin on the *Europa* for the thirty-first of March. It is the last ship I can take to be in time for the opening of *Tabu*." Having bought the film, Paramount also insisted that he see the writer William Morris, who lived in Monterey and had agreed to "novelize" *Tabu* for a magazine serialization. This was absolutely against Murr's grain and he dreaded the "South Sea Quatsch" which would emerge, but he had to compromise. "Still, I could not have made such a film in a studio," he comforted himself.

Next morning, when I came home from shopping, our housekeeper Jessie told me that Mr. Murnau had stopped by on his way to Monterey. He had a young Polynesian boy with him who had been recommended as a butler-chauffeur. Mr. Murnau would see how he worked out on the trip to Monterey.

After dinner, as Berthold and I were finishing our coffee, we got a call from the Santa Barbara *Morning Post*. A reporter said that Murnau had had an automobile accident and was in the Santa Barbara Hospital. His butler had insisted that Mr. and Mrs. Viertel should be notified. Was Murnau badly injured?—Yes—very badly.

We drove to Santa Barbara with the gloomiest forebodings. The fog was so heavy we could only drive very slowly. On the Gaviotta Pass we passed two mangled wrecks.

At last we arrived at the hospital. It must have been one o'clock. The distraught Polynesian, dark, lithe and handsome, met us at the entrance and told us what had happened. They had stopped at a gasoline station to refuel; then Murnau ordered him to take the wheel. The hired chauffeur objected: he was not permitted to relinquish the wheel to anybody. But Murnau got so sharp that finally the man obeyed. They had not gone twenty miles when a truck came at them around the curve and the boy swerved to the right, crashing thirty feet down an embankment. Neither he nor the chauffeur were hurt, but Murnau had suffered a bad head injury.

While Berthold was trying to reach a brain surgeon in Los Angeles, the nurse took me to Murnau. His room was brightly lit and in the center the bed stood, glaring white. His head was bandaged, his eyes closed, and a thin trickle of blood from one nostril drew a red line to the chin. He looked peaceful. At the foot of the bed stood his devoted secretary, Mrs. Kearin. I leaned over and whispered: "Murr . . . can you hear me, Murr?"

Mrs. Kearin sobbed: "He is gone. He stopped breathing a few minutes ago."

I touched his hands. They were still warm and his face had its usual distant expression.

His body was shipped to New York and left on the *Europa* on the same day for which he had made his reservation.

24

LEO SMITH WAS FOUR YEARS OLDER than Hans. He must have been fourteen. His mother, a squat, stout woman, was the housekeeper for Mr. and Mrs. Garrett who lived at the corner of Mabery Road. Mrs. Smith regularly appeared in the window in her white uniform, when I was passing their house on my way to the beach, loudly announcing to somebody inside: "The foreign woman from up the street!"

Leo, a rough, blond, dull-looking boy, backward in school, was a classmate of my Peter. Apprehensive about his influence on the boys, Nena prophesied that he would end up in jail before he finished school. Louise Garrett told me that Leo was a good swimmer and good at sports, and she did not expect him to be an intellectual. Neither did I, although I did not like Hans and Peter coming home with bloody knees and elbows and scratched faces after their excursions with Leo. One evening while the Garretts were out, the toolshed in their backyard caught fire. There was a great commotion because for some inexplicable reason their collie had been locked in the shed. Leo rushed into the flames and rescued the dog. All the inhabitants of Mabery Road, among them Hans and Peter, witnessed his heroism. From then on Leo could do no wrong.

Oliver Garrett was a successful scenario writer at Paramount. Every day he passed our house in a smart convertible, announcing himself by honking the horn, which had a special signal: tateè-tatà, like that of the German ex-Kaiser. "Dashing" was the most suitable adjective for him as he drove by, wearing a French beret. Without the beret he revealed a bald but well-shaped head, which did not diminish his attractiveness. He and his wife were an obviously happy, well-adjusted couple. Both were in their early thirties, intellectually inclined, good tennis players and addicted to parlor games, especially Louise. Coming from respected Boston families, they emphatically tried to adapt their puritanical upbringing to what was still left of the gay and wild Twenties. However, even in the dangerous Truth game, Louise could not bring herself to tell a lie, and truthfully answered the most indiscreet questions. Under my disrupting influence—I loathed parlor games—Oliver became less scrupulous. But all of that happened after Tallulah Bankhead, who introduced the Truth game, arrived in Hollywood and joined our Sunday afternoons.

At first only Hans and Peter became the intimates of the Garrett household, attracted by the magic of Leo's "he-mannishness" and Oliver's sportiness which contrasted strongly with their father's and my own persistent Europeanism.

I began to worry about Tommy. A slow talker before he came to America, he still preferred to express himself in pantomime rather than words. Not able to follow the English of his older brothers, he ceased talking altogether and only pointed to things he wanted. I asked a doctor, who examined him and assured me that the boy was healthy, normal and should be sent to a kindergarten. When I took him there, Thomas stood silently in a corner, not participating in games, quietly waiting until it was time to go home, where Nena always received him as if he had just escaped unspeakable danger.

At that time Professor Alfred Adler, Freud's revisionist pupil whom Berthold had known in Vienna, came to Los Angeles, and we invited him to dinner. The boys were at the table and also Nena. Tommy was sweet and well-mannered and, as usual, spectacularly silent. After the children said good-night Professor Adler asked me how long Nena had been with us. "She came when Tommy was eight months old," I said.

We talked about Nena and I told him how kind and devoted she was. The only thing which worried us was her possessiveness with Tommy, and his slowness in speaking.

"Why should he talk?" laughed Adler. "She anticipates his wishes before he can even express them. Send her away and you will see that he'll speak." I spent a sleepless night, and the next day I had a long talk with Nena, fully aware of the uselessness of it. Stubbornly, she insisted that if Tommy did not chatter like a magpie it was because his brothers always told him to shut up. To her he always said what he wanted. Of course, English bewildered him, but who wouldn't be bewildered by such a hellish language? How could her love harm Tommy? However, she admitted it would be good if Tommy played with children of his age, preferably German-speaking. The desired companions for Tommy were found, little Mucki Spuhler and her brother Julius, children of a German-Swiss couple Nena had met on the beach. The father, a marble cutter, had been a good provider until the depression had made him jobless. Toni, the mother, was an excellent cook and it was easy for her to find work catering at parties. The friendship between the children turned out to be providential for the parents.

European directors and actors were flocking to Hollywood, and as the demand for European servants increased, it suddenly occurred to me to transform the dejected, jobless Mr. Spuhler into a butler-chauffeur. I bought a braided cap and showed him how to open and to hold the door for his employers, when to take off and when to put on his cap and, after he had finally remembered everything, I got him a job with the Viennese composer Mr. Richard Fall, brother of the creator of *The Divorcee* and other successful operettas. A victim of mistaken identity (Fox thought they had signed Leo Fall), Mr. Fall was not happy in Hollywood and so nervous and irritable he could not stand Julius Spuhler's chauffeuring and fired him. At once it occurred to me to recommend Julius to Jacques and Françoise Feyder, who drove themselves. They also hired Toni as housekeeper, and in their spacious house there was even room for the Spuhler children. Much closer now to Mabery Road, they often played with Tommy and the youngest Feyder.

One evening, as I was about to read to him, Tom unexpectedly broke his silence and said that it was *he* who wanted to tell me a story. Slowly he began: "Once upon a time there was a boy and his name was Unhappy. . . ." He said it in German: "*Sein Name war Unglücklich.*" My heart stood still.

"That's not a name, Tommy."

"*Sein Name war Unglücklich,*" he persisted, his dark, serious eyes anxiously looking into mine. "He had two brothers and their names were Hans and Peter."

I was holding back my tears. Did he know what he was saying? Was this the contented, cheerful little boy who adored his nurse, his brothers, his parents, Jessie . . . ate well, slept well, but—

"*Sein Name war Unglücklich. . . .*"

I braced myself for decisive action. Perhaps Adler was right

—we had to part with Nena, at least for a while. Her Visitor's Visa was expiring and she would have had to leave the States anyway. We would see how her absence affected Thomas. Besides we would be back in Berlin in a year. We were quite sure of that.

Tommy was sad after she left, but not for long. Suddenly he surprised us with his abundant English vocabulary and by firmly refusing to speak German. He never mentioned the boy *Unglücklich* again.

I remained in close contact with Nena. She despised the Nazis and was unhappy that her son was in the Reichswehr. I was deeply moved by her lonely resistance to the Third Reich. She died during the war.

Garbo's first talking film *Anna Christie* was an enormous success, and Metro decided to remake it with her in German. The studio imported German actors, and Jacques Feyder, although French, was chosen to direct. I was cast as Marty, a waterfront whore, admirably played by Marie Dressler in the American film. Being twenty-five years younger, I was not too eager for the part, but Feyder persuaded me that Marty could be of any age. Also he wanted me to help him with the German dialogue.

In the theater actors have a chance to improve their interpretation with each performance; the contact with the audience, the immediate response enables them to try out details and nuances. In the films, once a scene has been shot and approved, it is preserved for ever. It is true that one rehearsed it many times, but only in short pieces. An inspired moment is apt to be discarded, because perhaps the shadow of a microphone or a smudge of powder had been overlooked. Playing *Anna Christie* for the second time, Garbo had to conquer the difficulty of still another language. She worked hard, with precision, and her German was almost without accent. She was a most patient, appreciative and considerate colleague.

I was frightened when my first scene had to be shot. I hated my costumes, my make-up seemed all wrong and there was no time to change it. But Feyder made everything easy. He made me play a long scene just as I would have done it in the theater, without interruption and, although blinded by the lights, I forgot that three cameras were shooting it from different angles. The stagehands applauded after he said, "Cut."

I played in two more films, both for Warner Brothers. The first one, *The Flood*, was directed by William Dieterle. For the second, Somerset Maugham's *The Sacred Flame*, Berthold was borrowed from Paramount. However, I was neither beautiful nor young enough for a film career. If I had been sixty and an American, I could have played the so-called "earthy" character parts. Probably I would have had a chance in the theater in New York, but we were tied to Hollywood. It made me miserable that I, who had started to act at the age of seventeen, had to be idle in my best years.

It was during the shooting of *Anna Christie* that I came upon a biography of Queen Christina of Sweden, which had appeared in Germany. Long before that my interest in her had been aroused by Strindberg's misogynistic play. The preposterous child of the heroic Gustav Adolph, she was eccentric, brilliant; and her masculine education and complicated sexuality made her an almost contemporary character. Also her escapism, her longing for a world outside puritanical Protestant Sweden, to which she was chained by her crown, fascinated me. Greta, who knew a lot about Christina, agreed with me that it would be a wonderful role for her and that such a film should be produced in Europe, preferably in Sweden. Her contract was expiring and Metro was moving heaven and earth to make her sign a new one. Other studios made fantastic offers. She was in a position to ask for the best director and the best actors. She had only to choose.

Contrary to all the gossip, I have never been Garbo's "advisor" in her dealings with the film industry. I had no mind whatsoever for business and what I could grasp of it either horrified or bored me. This defect in my character, perhaps the fault of my upbringing, was most detrimental to my own career. Money was something I never valued excessively as long as it was there, and I tried to ignore it as gallantly as possible when it was gone. I had inherited from Mama a touch of "Oblomovism" when financial matters had to be faced.

Garbo urged me to write the film about Christina. After thorough research I began in German to dramatize the first part of Christina's life. Berthold read it and said that it had great possibilities, and that I should have it translated into English.

Meanwhile Berthold's contract with Fox had expired and he signed with Paramount. Ben Schulberg, the head of production, was indisputably an intelligent man and more understanding than Berthold's previous bosses. Mrs. Schulberg was lively and hospitable. She surrounded herself with writers, dramatists and American liberals. The Schulberg children, Budd and Sonya, a few years older than Hans and Peter, were exceptionally intelligent and gifted.

I mentioned my problem to Ad Schulberg and she told me that her friend, Margaret Le Vino, spoke German and could do the job. She invited us together to discuss the project. Mrs. Le Vino was a distinguished-looking, middle-aged woman, very likeable, and she asked what the story was about. When she heard that it was about a seventeenth-century Swedish queen, she shook her head: "It's a waste of time. Historical films are taboo in Hollywood." Had I a special actress in mind? Before I could answer, Ad exclaimed: "Garbo of course! Salka is a friend of hers." Immediately Mrs. Le Vino became interested and said that she would like to read my story, but several weeks went by and many things happened before we met again.

Berthold had finished two films for Paramount: one with Ruth Chatterton, in which Charles Boyer and Françoise Rosay played supporting roles; the second, with Clive Brook and Claudette Colbert, which was a success in England but failed to make any impression in the States.

For his third assignment he was to go to New York and remake a shopworn melodrama, *The Cheat,* with Tallulah Bankhead. As he felt that he had to escape "the Hollywood spell" for a while, he accepted it.

From the Chief carrying him east he wrote:

> I have lost confidence in Schulberg and no matter how things turn out, they will be better than if they had continued in the old way. This time I shall not run with open eyes into a lousy assignment. (He had not read the script of *The Cheat* yet!) . . . As we still have another year in America I am making strategic plans for our future, *OURS* not only mine . . . I am sending this letter and a telegram from Emporia. Dear heart, do you remember Emporia from our first trip west, three and a half years ago? I am looking at the big stone with the name on it, that ridiculous symbolic name . . . Well, Emporia once more, though in the opposite direction.

For three years we had been uninterruptedly together. If it had not been for Berthold's professional dissatisfaction, they would have been very happy years. I could not go to New York because I could not leave the children. Tommy had started first grade and he and his brothers had to be driven to their respective schools. Hans and Peter's junior high was quite a distance from the Canyon.

I engaged a young student teacher and good driver to help me with my chores and look after Thomas. The three boys fell in love with Larry and competed with each other in chivalry. They fought for who would be first to push the chair under her when she sat down at table and to pull it back when she got up. She was pretty, gay, unpretentious and they found her a sensational improvement on Nena. The unfaithful Tommy was making rapid progress in expressing himself. I found my sons' "spring awakening" normal and reassuring, but what disturbed me more than the American custom of sitting with one's feet on the table, was the growing contempt for intellectuals.

One evening Peter insisted that I give him written permission to join the football team of his school, though he was only eleven. I had just read in the paper that a boy had been killed in the rough game, and refused. He pleaded and argued but, for once, I remained adamant. Suddenly, with clenched fists and flashing eyes, he shouted at me: "You . . . you foreigner!" I was deeply shocked. Next time he would call me "you Polack!" Back to Europe, I thought, immediately.

At the end of 1931 the Depression was felt and the beginning of 1932 was sad for us. Again we were separated. Berthold's mother died while he was in New York. Then came the Eisenstein crisis in Mexico and his cries for help.

Berthold's prediction that twenty-five thousand would not be enough for a film had come true. The year had passed quickly and the money was about gone. First the rainy season, which lasted three months, had detained Eisenstein's shooting; then the search for locations and his becoming ill caused further delays. Eisenstein asked me to persuade his Pasadena sponsors to invest more money in the film. Through Upton I succeeded in the difficult task and the millionairesses agreed to increase the financing. But Mrs. Sinclair insisted that the "irrational artist" be put under the strict control of her brother, Mr. Kimbrough. There were telephone calls and letters, and finally Eisenstein agreed, appointing me to be his representative when the rushes were shown in Los Angeles. As he had no facilities in Mexico for developing the film, the negative was sent to the Eastman Laboratory in Los Angeles. The Mexican Consul had to see the rushes to be sure that nothing detrimental to Mexico had been filmed. My job was to explain to the Pasadena ladies why Eisenstein had photographed this or that from different angles (for example the bare breasts of a dark Mexican girl, or two parrots sitting on twin coconuts).

The filmed material was stunning and is still shown and admired in film museums all over the world. The Christian-pagan rites and processions, the peons and Indians, the desert and the forests were breathtakingly beautiful. To photograph all that and not be able to see one foot of the film must have been torture. But the sponsors were indignant that a scene or a place, a coconut palm

or a parrot, was shot so many times. "A waste of film!" they would
exclaim.

It was useless to explain that, even unedited, the film revealed
Eisenstein's intentions and also the passion and concentration
with which he worked. Then suddenly I was no longer told when
the rushes were to be shown, and a letter from Eisenstein informed me of what had happened:

Mexico, January 27, 1932

Dear Zalka! [He always wrote my name with a Z],

It seems to be your fate that I should be heaping my
despair upon you! In my Paramount days and after—
but this time is the most desperate of all! I don't know
how much Sinclair keeps you *au courant* about our
activities and difficulties. If he does I may be as
doomed in your eyes as I am in his. However, this is the
situation:

You know that instead of the four months schedule
and $25,000, which would have merely resulted in a
pitiful travelogue we have worked thirteen months and
have spent $53,000, but we have a great film and
have expanded the original idea. This expansion was
achieved under incredible difficulties inflicted upon us
by the behavior and bad management of Upton Sinclair's brother-in-law, Hunter Kimbrough. I am blamed
for all sin committed and I accept it, under the condition that from now on I myself should be responsible,
but not Mr. Kimbrough. Or we three: I, Alexandrov
and Tisse, should manage the whole thing until its
completion. But I am facing a situation which, so far,
had been completely unknown to me: blood relationship and family ties. Mr. Kimbrough was recalled, but
then sent back with "increased powers" *as my super-
visor*, which means that now he has the right to interfere in everything I do and make all the cuts! He
presented me to Sinclair as a liar, blackmailer and God-
knows-what else. My direct correspondence with Sinclair stopped, our only contact was through Kimbrough
who, an ambitious man, poisons our existence and
creates an atmosphere in which it is impossible to work.
I wrote this to Sinclair, whereupon he abruptly halted
our work of thirteen months. The last part of my film,
containing all the elements of a fifth act, is ruthlessly
ripped out, and *you* know what this means. It's as if

Ophelia were ripped out from *Hamlet*, or King Philip
from *Don Carlos*.

We saved this episode, the best material, story and
effects, which have not been exploited before, as a
climax and the last to be filmed. It tells the story of the
Soldadera, the women who, in hundreds, followed the
Revolutionary army, taking care of their men, bearing
them children, fighting at their side, burying them and
taking care of the survivors. The incomparable drama
and pathos of this sequence shows the birth of the new
country. Exploited and suppressed by the Spaniards, it
emerges as a free Mexico. Without this sequence the
film loses its meaning, unity and its final dramatic
impact: it becomes a display of unintegrated episodes.
Each of these episodes now points toward this end and
this resolution.

Now to our practical achievements: We have 500
soldiers, which the Mexican Army has given us for 30
days, 10,000 guns and 50 cannons, *all for nothing*. We
have discovered an incredible location and have brilliantly solved the whole event in our scenario. We need
only $7,000 or $8,000 to finish it, which we could do in
a month, and then we would have a truly marvelous
film—and when I say it I *mean* it!—a film with such
mass scenes as no studio could attempt to produce now!
Imagine! 500 women in an endless cactus desert, dragging through clouds of dust, household goods, beds,
their children, their wounded, their dead, and the
white-clad peasant soldiers in straw hats following
them. We show their march into Mexico City—the
Spanish Cathedral—the palaces! For the meeting of
Villa and Zapata we will have thousands of sports
organizations—again without pay—with the cathedral
bells ringing the victory of the first revolution. And all
that has to be sacrificed because of $8,000, and quarrels
—by the way, I am absolutely right and have documents to prove it—Sinclair stopped the production and
intends to throw before the people a truncated stump
with the heart ripped out!

I have exhausted my powers of persuasion. I shall do
everything he wants. . . . I accept Kimbrough, everything, anything . . . if only they let me finish this film.
I have worked under most incredible harassment, no,
not worked—fought. When I see you in Hollywood I

will tell you what we had to go through and what probably is still ahead of us.

I myself am incapable of persuading these people. Zalka, you have already helped in this cause. We, all three of us, are convinced that this is our best film and that it must not be destroyed. I beg you, Zalka, go to Sinclair. As you were authorized to see all the rushes, he will certainly use the occasion to pour out to you everything which caused the present situation; or better, you could ask him and I am sure influence him . . . A film is not a sausage which tastes the same if you eat three-quarters of it or the whole *Wurst.* You will hear horrible things about me (first, they are not true, and second, I know you don't care and I beg you to think only about the film). The situation is different now. I have an ironclad plan. I know the locations precisely; General Calles has promised us all the facilities: those are concrete things! And we are now familiar with conditions here and know exactly how to handle the production. Use your Medea flame and convince him (but especially *her*) to let us finish our film.

We were due to leave but Kimbrough postponed our departure for ten days, to clean up odds and ends of what we have shot. Our only hope is that meanwhile a miracle will happen and that the Soldadera episode will be filmed. Help us, Zalka! No, not us, help our work, save it from mutilation! If they have no money, ask for their consent to let us get it elsewhere. It seems incredible that this amount could not be raised as business. Even here the money could be found, not from philanthropists, but from businessmen, but the Sinclairs are so frightened of businessmen that they prefer to destroy all that they now have.

Wire immediately that you have received this letter and that you take our cause to your heart, regardless of what they tell you about me. One does not write such letters often.

Your,
Sergei

I phoned Upton Sinclair and asked if I could come to Pasadena and talk to him. After a brief consultation with his wife, he said that he and Mrs. Sinclair had a luncheon date in Hollywood and they would come to my house afterward. When they arrived

Upton was, as usual, warm and friendly, but, I could feel, uneasy. Mrs. Sinclair, at first gay and charming, launched soon into a ferocious attack on Eisenstein. I was prepared for it and did not interrupt her, until she said that in Hollywood the Russians had been squandering money like mad, giving "wild parties" for Paramount executives. She knew for sure that the cost of one of them was four thousand dollars. (I was curious how she had arrived at that sum.) She said further that Eisenstein was immoral and a megalomaniac. I asked if she seriously believed these fantastic stories. Berthold and I had been at the party Eisenstein and his "collective" had given for the Schulbergs, at which Mrs. Montagu had been the hostess. It had been a simple, utterly "uncapitalistic" dinner, and like Upton, Eisenstein was a teetotaler. Mrs. Sinclair smiled at my guilelessness. But my greatest mistake was in saying that I could not understand what Eisenstein's private life, and the way he entertained, had to do with his art and talent.

"Of course not!" said Mrs. Sinclair. "But why should fine, trusting people spend their good money to support irresponsibility?"

I suggested that perhaps it would be advisable that less "fine and trusting people" should take over the financing of the film. I added that I knew a producer who would buy the existing film material and pay off the Pasadena group. Upton seemed inclined to give in; I sensed that he did not quite approve of his wife's severity toward Eisenstein.

They left and I waited impatiently until I heard Oliver Garrett's tateè-tatà, then went over to ask his advice. He was very amused by my description of the Sinclair visit, but blamed Eisenstein for the debacle. I had had enough for one afternoon of defending and explaining Eisenstein, and I only wanted Oliver's suggestion— whom to approach for the shabby eight thousand dollars Sergei needed. Oliver wanted me to tell him what I *really* thought of the rushes. "They are extraordinary, marvelous, fantastic, the most beautiful and incredible film I have ever seen. . . ."

He did not trust superlatives: " 'Good' is enough for me."

I would not let him bully me and said: "They are marvelous."

Taking his highball with him, he went to call David Selznick.

David O. Selznick was then the production head at RKO. He was young, and it was said in Hollywood that he was brilliant and heading for a great career. Oliver, who did not like producers, told me that Selznick was the only man in the industry he did not mind working for. The telephone conversation was quite long; then Oliver returned saying that Selznick wanted to see me at his office.

My interview was brief but promising. Selznick authorized me to tell Upton Sinclair that he would like to see all the film Eisenstein had shot, as he intended to buy out the Pasadena group and finance the picture himself. Of course, he did not believe that eight thousand would be enough to finish it.

That evening Eisenstein telephoned from Mexico and I told him of Selznick's offer. Afterward I called Upton, repeated what Selznick had said and added that I had talked to Sergei. But Mrs. Sinclair was adamant. She was determined to call an end to the Mexican venture, and that was that. "Mr. Eisenstein was notified days ago that the production would be stopped. The film belongs to the Pasadena group and can neither be sold nor financed by anybody." That was final.

No one, not even Eisenstein himself, ever saw the assembled film in the form he had planned. It remains a magnificent "mutilated stump with the heart ripped out."

He and his companions waited a whole month in Laredo, Texas, for visas to the U.S. which they never got. We talked often over the telephone. Sometimes I could do him a small favor. Before he left America, he wrote:

> I am very sad because I am not going to see you anymore and I have the feeling that all I have to ask you this time is to send me a family photo of all of you. You and Berthold have been our best friends in the stormy and hard times. I hope the great distance will not interrupt our friendship. . . . [Then, recovering his boyish, unsophisticated humor:] Thanks to our guardian angel, Mr. Kimbrough, we are sitting now a month in this lousy hole . . . I remember that when they were shooting the *Faust* film in Berlin the publicity chief of UFA said to me: "Goethe intended Mephisto to be a mixture of filth and fire." Three years later I saw the film and the same publicity man (now with another firm) added: "Unfortunately, we forgot the fire." Mr. Kimbrough is also a mixture, but it is difficult for me to say of what.
>
> [And later:] . . . we are heading now for New York. We hope to cut the film in Moscow. I am really homesick and very glad about it. I have decided to change the plan of the whole film and to use everything I have shot, but in a different continuity. I hope it can be saved.
>
> Once again, Zalka, I thank you deeply for everything. You have helped me in the most difficult years of my

life and this shall never be forgotten. I hope you won't forget me either. Give my best wishes and greetings to Berthold and the whole family. When are you coming to Moscow? Anyhow, I shall see you.

With my love forever . . .

The last letter, in 1936, was from Moscow.

I have just returned from the Caucasus where— strange as it may sound—I have been shooting a new film . . . I am slowly recovering from the blow of my Mexican experience. I have never worked on anything with such enthusiasm and what has happened to it is the greatest crime, even if I have to share the guilt. But there are things which have to be above all personal feelings. Let's not talk about it anymore.

25

THE NEIGHBORLY RELATIONS with the Garretts developed into a friendship. I suppose that the differences in our background, tastes and opinions attracted us to each other, though I appeared to them very often as odd as they to me. Oliver was intelligent, talented, objective, liberal and emphatically unprejudiced, except when he discussed socialism.

He came from a respected New England family, had enlisted in 1917 and loved to talk about the war, understating the dangers and exaggerating his fear; but the balance of both made him look very brave. After the Armistice he took a job with a newspaper in New York—I think it was *The Sun* or *The World*, and soon became a featured reporter. The gangster film *Underworld*, for which he wrote the scenario, brought him a long-term contract with Paramount and a most impressive salary. With their only child Peter, he and Louise lived comfortably on Mabery Road, in the corner house overlooking the Pacific. On Sunday afternoons his former New York colleagues, now also writing films, gathered on the front porch for drinks, shoptalk and nostalgic memories of the war. All were well-known journalists and successful dramatists. Maxwell Anderson and Laurence Stallings had *What Price Glory* playing on Broadway for years; William Faulkner, small, thin, with a dark, drooping mustache, reserved, polite and taciturn, had just published *As I Lay Dying* and *Sanctuary*, and of course Warner Brothers had signed him. The producers never even looked at the scripts he wrote for them. (Many years later, when I was employed by that studio, I was asked to read the previous scenarios based on the novel I was adapting. One of them was unfinished and contained fifty pages written by Faulkner.) Edwin Justice Mayer, author of *Firebrand*, a Broadway success, worked for MGM, Sam N. Behrman made sporadic appearances at Fox, Dudley Nichols, Ralph Block, permanent refugees from journalism, wrote for Paramount, while Ben Hecht, with his Midas touch, commuted between Hollywood and New York.

In his novel *Madame d'Ora*, Johannes V. Jensen writes about a young American passionately in love with a middle-aged primadonna. She tries to ward off his infatuation by saying: "It's not *me* you love—it's Europe . . . For you I am San Marco, the Alps, Rome, Paris, the Italian lakes . . . you are infatuated with Europe."

Something similar must have taken hold of Oliver. For him also, I was part of that ancient, baffling continent of which he had caught a distorted glimpse during the war, and for which, like so many young Americans, he had brought home an unappeased longing. As he deeply distrusted all emotionalism, he rarely admitted it. "That sounds sensible," was his strongest approval. In Louise's sober and determined matter-of-factness, he had found his terra firma. Her lack of imagination irritated him, but it inspired confidence.

They gave the impression of a happy, congenial couple, now and then in need of outside stimulation, but basically loyal to each other. As I had encountered similar American couples, I did not take their flirtations seriously. Toward me Oliver was chivalrous and protective, while other devoted husbands did not hesitate to "make passes" at the "foreign woman up the street." My sons adored Oliver. He played football and baseball with them, and took them to the big games at the Los Angeles stadium.

Meanwhile I had shown Peg Le Vino my outline of *Christina* and, eagerly, she offered to help me. The love story had to be invented; young Christina's sentiments seemed to have been centered on her lady-in-waiting, but there were some indications that she had been ardently interested in Count Pimentelli, the handsome ambassador from Spain. The passionate affair with a Roman cardinal occurred only after her abdication, when she was forty and converted to Catholicism, but this would have been unacceptable in the film. Besides, Garbo was much too young to play a middle-aged woman.

Berthold meanwhile was finding New York more invigorating than the Hollywood atmosphere, or the idyllic isolation of the Santa Monica Canyon.

> Yes, I think this job was a godsend, though I have never felt as lonely in my whole life—so undecided and tormented. What I would like most is to sit in my hotel room, high above the city, secluded like a hermit. I am reading every morning about comparative religions, while in the afternoon I work on my film story. You will say that I am torn between Tallulah and Jeremiah, but without dwelling in the past millenniums I could not bear the present, the "Here" not without the "Days of Yore." I am reading Hindu philosophy and at the same time devouring the daily news— gangster wars, economic crises, etc., etc. If only I could write down in my journal, step by step, the parallel thoughts as they come . . . But then one should not make a film. . . .
>
> I am forty-six and have not much time left. My first book was called *Die Spur* (*The Trace*). This meant that I had perceived the trace of an ideal life, but merely the trace. . . . The second book was *Die Bahn* (*The Road*). I started to write it in Kolendziany, and finished it in Hellerau. *The Road* began when I met you. I became aware of it for the first time in my letters to you, which are now moldering in Prague, and it is named after the last poem in the volume:

The Road

> Night rises over the clearing.
>
> As the sun descends
> The indifferent watchman
> Calls my hour.
>
> What is alien cannot rescue me.

Oh! Where to turn?
Nowhere, but the place of choice. . .
That bare center.

Only a strict *yes* counts,
The trial spins,
The verdict is cast like lead!

Who can hold what leaves him?
Haste will soon flee the runner.
He turns around
And stands along the way
On his crown-point the road.*

No one understood this poem, no one *could* understand this grandiose, frightening feeling, that the Road before me is not stretched out horizontally anymore, but threatens vertically, from the firmament, the top of my head. The Road, which otherwise leads toward the future, points like an exclamation at my head.

This feeling has not left me for ten years. I am still under the sword, the inexorable *Yes*. It is still not fulfilled. The nervous groping, the search, continue. I am perhaps less nervous now, but sad. Berlin, *Die Truppe*, Dusseldorf and Hollywood . . . everything has been merely an experiment. Only you are the absolute *Yes* in my whole life, the only *Yes* I have never revoked.

I was always aware of the conflict between Berthold's vocation as a writer and his obsession with the theater. "*Ein strenges Ja*," but about this strict *Yes* he could not decide! It meant trading the immediate results, the tangible success, the spontaneous applause, for days and nights of lonely struggle with one's own soul.

We had now spent fourteen years together; the many storms in our lives had often forced us to a change of direction, unwanted company and financial insecurity. I rebelled often, but I never felt that I was sacrificing anything. Security was not important to me; I did not believe it existed. As long as we had our work and each other, nothing could happen to us. I was much too adventurous to be seriously disturbed by economics. I knew I could always provide for my children. I felt young and strong; it never occurred to me that forty meant middle-age. That Berthold, at forty-six, could say "I have not much time left" infuriated me. I wrote him that he had become infected with the American age-consciousness! But as the phases of his Rabbinical mysticism, Hinduism and Chassidism

* Translation by Thomas Viertel.

were alternated with excursions to Harlem and Tallulah's parties, I suspected that he was merely escaping the boredom of his film.

I would read his letters, then call the ruinous long distance—and *what* a long distance it was!—and implore him to give up films. I said I would gladly adapt myself to any kind of life, provided it would be good for the children. If he wanted to return to Berlin I was willing to go back. I reminded him of a time in Leipzig when he was spending Christmas with me, and Stefan Zweig suddenly came to see us. I was changing Hans's diapers when I heard him urging Berthold to give up the theater and remain his true self, a poet and a writer. Then Zweig burst into my room and reproached me for dragging Berthold into an underworld, unworthy of his talent and literary mission. I got angry and said that Berthold had been infatuated with the theater before I met him, but that I would be delighted if he gave up directing because then we could always be together. That I should renounce my profession was absurd, for financial reasons also.

Now, in 1931, it was no longer a question of a career, or where I would function best. The world was just as insecure as in 1919, and our responsibilities were staggering. The Nazis, defeated at the polls by a small majority, were nevertheless gaining power in Germany, and anti-semitism and racism were spreading. I did not want to uproot my sons and impair their free and happy childhood.

The Depression was at its worst. Hitler's hideous, demented voice carried across the Atlantic, but I believed in the future. Often on the road I gave a ride to hitchhikers from the East Coast or the Middle West, who had come to California because it was less cold and hungry than back home. Our housekeeper, Jessie, kept a big pot of soup on the stove for them, when they came to the door. It reminded me of Niania feeding the Russian prisoners of war. But I listened to Roosevelt's election speeches and was sure that the misery would not last.

All children in the Western world, even Jewish or half-Jewish, want a Christmas tree. At Wychylowka we held Christmas twice: the regular one on December 24, and two weeks later another for our Ukrainian servants. Both were made unforgettable by my mother's generosity and her agnostic sense of humor. I could not imagine depriving my sons of the joys of my own childhood.

In spite of the Depression, Christmas in Hollywood was more glittering, more exuberant, more alcoholic and more commercial than ever. Along the boulevards the poinsettia fields were glowing red, the Christmas trees were lit outdoors and indoors and each department store had several Santas. During my years in California they multiplied to such an extent that even the youngest children ceased to pay attention to them.

Our boys were showered with gifts, from us, from our friends and from actors who had worked or wanted to work with Berthold. As usual we had a party on Christmas Eve for the "homeless," but I had also asked our American friends, who celebrated on Christmas Day. Before we opened our presents I made a speech to the children, reminding them that Jesus was a Jew and had preached brotherhood and love of mankind. For that he had been persecuted and martyred. I was quite certain that I was the only one who was moved by my half-revolutionary, pan-religious address. My sons, Leo, Peter Garrett and the Spuhler children listened with politely controlled impatience, their eyes wandering to the heaps of beautifully wrapped packages. Much to Oliver's discomfort, the tree was lit by wax candles, as I would not tolerate any electric bulbs. Oliver could not wait for them to burn down, so that he could switch on the safe "American lights."

After dinner Berthold called from New York and we all stood with our glasses around the telephone, singing "Jingle Bells" and wishing him a merry Christmas. Tommy was thrilled that Father was already in bed, while he was still up, playing with his toys.

Right after Christmas the Garretts took their Peter to Yosemite, into the snow. My two big boys went with them but Tommy and I stayed at home. The rainy season had started; the days were short, dark and gloomy. Telegrams from Yosemite urged me to escape from the flooded Canyon to the "glorious, white, snow mountains." I answered through Western Union, dictating into the telephone that I would not come, that the pouring rain fitted my deep depression. I went to bed and slept soundly until the ringing phone woke me. It was seven in the morning.

"This is Western Union," said a female voice. "I only wanted to tell you that the sun is shining. It's such a lovely day! All night I worried about you, honey . . . your telegram sounded so sad."

Very moved, I thanked her. I was sorry—did sad telegrams always upset her so much?

"Not always, honey," she laughed, "but I loved that darling accent of yours."

Such was the beginning of my long friendship with the Santa Monica branch of the Western Union. For many, many years telegrams and cables, coming and going, were read or repeated to me by the gentle, drawling, nasal voice of my invisible friend. At the first sound of it I knew whether they were pleasant or sad. An intimate telegram she would read in a low, discreet voice, then add: "You want me to mail it to you, don't you dear . . . ?" Often hurriedly, afraid to be caught by the superintendent, she wedged in her own troubles or her scarce pleasures. To her, in all those years, I never ceased to be young and persistently romantic. We never saw each other, although sometimes I went to the Western Union office hoping to find her there.

26

MY MOTHER KEPT US WELL INFORMED about all the events which occurred at Wychylowka and about everyone in the family. Her letters reflected her charm, her vitality, her impatient temper and irreverent humor; they informed us about Papa's moods and professional worries in the new Poland, troubled by political dissent and a dismal economic situation. She was proud of Edward's successes, regretting that he persisted in propagating Schoenberg's music, for which she herself had only a limited appreciation. The visits of Rose with her two children (Josef was now director of the Dresden State Theater) were the great summer joys; also Viktoria's first communion and her progress in school. Mama mentioned lightly that a baby had been born to Hania, the pretty housekeeper, and gently indicated that the child was Dusko's son. Dusko was playing for a famous Zionist soccer team, which took him to games all over Central Europe, and he was also winning many silver cups in tennis tournaments.

The Polish Government was unifying the laws of the country which, from 1775 to 1918, had been divided between Russia, Germany and Austria. In spite of the endemic anti-semitism, my father was entrusted with the coordination of the liquor laws. He was eighty-one now.

The nightmare of my childhood—my parents' marital disagreements—had vanished in later years. Both had mellowed, and had acquired a sense of humor about their common failings. Even the difference in their ages seemed to be evenly balanced: Papa had retained his vigor and my mother had calmed down. He now liked to listen to music, especially Edward's concerts, which they could hear on the radio. My mother wrote that he kept all my letters in his desk drawer and read them again and again. But clients were scarce, and finally my parents agreed to accept a monthly check from us. It was merely a feeble expression of our gratitude for their kindness, generosity and hospitality. The summers at Wychylowka had been our moral and physical regeneration.

Without impresarios and publicity, Edward had become a well-known and respected pianist and teacher. His intransigent musicianship was attracting pupils of all nationalities. At that time he was the only outstanding interpreter of Schoenberg's, Alban Berg's and Anton von Webern's piano compositions. His recitals of modern and classical music in Queens Hall, the Albert Hall and on the BBC were, to my parents' delight, broadcast to Poland. Each month he taught a master class in Krakow and Lwow, which Mama rarely missed attending.

How hard and bare all these years would have been for her without the reunions with her adored son! Any kind of small pleasure or luxury had ceased to exist. When my sister sent a little box of oranges and bananas, Polish customs officials refused to forward it, declaring that it was forbidden to import "tropical" fruit. "You lucky people can pick your lemons and oranges from the trees," wrote Mama. But when she read an interview with a Viennese author, who said that the fruit in California tasted like woodshavings, she was alarmed and offered to supply us with apples from the orchard at home.

I remember that on February 18 Berthold had returned from New York, and that it was my father's eighty-second birthday. But the next day a cable told us that my father had died on February 17. I knew that he had been ill at the beginning of the year, and Berthold had promised me that in summer he would stay with the children so that I could visit my parents. Papa had recovered and my mother wrote that he had been well and working. On the 17th after lunch, he went to his room and she heard him fall. She rushed in and found him on the floor. "It's nothing," he said, "just a dizzy spell." An hour later he was dead.

He bequeathed whatever was left of his property to my mother, confident that "in our family there could never be a dispute over money," and he recommended to all of us the care and education of Viktoria.

The Polish press published eulogies and obituaries, which

praised him as an outstanding citizen and a great lawyer. "He had ennobled the profession." It was the last time, in Pilsudski's Poland, that Gentiles and Jews would mourn together.

For my mother, the year abounded in unhappiness. Aunt Bella finally gave up her struggle with cinema owners and lovers, and defeated, dying of cancer, she fled to Wychylowka. For days and nights Dusko took care of her. His compassion was so great that he suppressed his horror of disease.

Berthold's contract with Paramount was not renewed. Ben Schulberg had left the studio and was preparing an independent production. He wanted Berthold to direct some of his films, but the negotiations were conducted half-heartedly.

Our Visitors' Visas had expired and we had to apply for an Immigration Quota: Berthold and Tommy for an Austrian number, Hans and Peter, who were born in Dresden, for a German one, and I for a Polish. After much red tape and hundreds of dollars spent on cables and lawyers, we finally had the necessary documents assembled, and took off in our big, second-hand Cadillac for Ensenada in Baja California, about one hundred miles south of San Diego.

Immediately beyond the Mexican border the landscape changed, the people looked like Ukrainian peasants, in straw hats and long shirts. Even the roads were in the well-remembered condition. But the old Cadillac drove like a jeep. They don't make them like that anymore!

It was late when we arrived in Ensenada, at an ostentatious hotel with a gambling casino, which Jack Dempsey had built for the tycoons of Southern California. It was planned as an American Monte Carlo and an escape from Prohibition. But the Depression had put a damper on the gay life and the establishment went bankrupt. We were the only guests in the hotel. Before our windows a long sickle of soft, silvery sand hugged the bluest, most serene ocean.

We went to the American Consulate and the Consul told us that it would take a few days, perhaps a week, until our various quota numbers arrived. We had books and magazines with us, and our worries and uncertainties to keep us from being bored. However, after three days, in spite of the beautiful beach and all its space, the empty hotel gave us claustrophobia. The gloomy gambling salons with the sheet-covered roulette and baccarat tables reminded us of a morgue.

Finally our quota numbers arrived and we could leave. The roads had dried, the bridges were flimsily repaired and, just as it was getting dark, we presented our passports to a disgruntled immigration officer and were admitted to the United States.

It was not long after our immigration that Garbo signed a new contract with Metro. She surprised me one morning by unexpectedly taking me to a Santa Monica beach house, where a frail-looking, black-haired young man greeted us at the door. With his fine oriental features, his slender delicate hands and soft, dark eyes, he reminded me of Max Reinhardt's brother Edmund. "This is Mr. Thalberg," said Garbo.

"I've heard wonderful things about you," he said to me.

I could not think of anything to say, only that I also had heard a great deal about him.

"Of course you have," Garbo coached me pointedly.

I did not know that she had shown him the manuscript of *Queen Christina*. Although he did not "believe in historical films and the story was far from perfect," Mr. Thalberg was interested. It needed, of course, a great deal of work. He intended to give it his personal attention. When I asked why he "did not believe in historical films," he gave me an evasive answer, and I had the impression that he had not read the manuscript—only skimmed through the first pages.

"There are several things I like. I would not produce it if I did not think it would make a great picture."

How often in the following years did I hear that phrase!

Calmly Greta said that she had great faith in the story.

"I am always open to new ideas and new talent," Thalberg assured her. "I will be in touch with Mrs. Viertel and get her an experienced collaborator."

I replied that I would like to work with Peg Le Vino, but he interrupted me: "I know Mrs. Le Vino. She is a fine woman but not the person I want on the screenplay." All my arguments were cut short. Miss Shearer, his wife, came into the room and asked us to stay for lunch, but Greta excused us and we said good-bye. Thalberg promised again that *Queen Christina* would be a great picture.

All this had happened suddenly and was a complete surprise to me, but also a disappointment. We had always planned that the film would be made in Europe. I had ardently hoped for it, and my first impression of Thalberg was rather negative. Greta tried to comfort me saying that, after all, Metro was the best studio, Thalberg the most capable producer to deal with, and that for technical reasons it would be difficult to make *Christina* in Europe. She was sure that my "talent and enthusiasm" could defeat Metro's commercialism.

Having taken a decision, Garbo was usually in a hurry to get away. My introduction to Thalberg took place only a few days before she left for Sweden. She had not been home for many years, and no one could better understand her impatience than I. She told me that her agent, Mr. Eddington, would help me with my negotiations with MGM.

I had never been able to persuade Garbo to meet Peg Le Vino. Familiar with all stages of the story, she maintained that Peg's contribution had not been important.

In July Berthold decided to go to Europe. Alexander Korda was launching a large-scale British production and wanted to meet him in Paris to discuss future projects. Then Berthold intended to go to Vienna to see his desperately ill father.

We said farewell in Pasadena, promising each other that the separation would not be long. He was sailing on the *Europa*.

The crossing is coming happily to an end. The day after tomorrow at eight o'clock in the morning I'll be in Cherbourg. The boat is marvelous, one hardly feels that it moves! Lots of space, air and light. Deadly boring though. On the deck the dullest assembly of rich mummies stiffly tacked to their chairs, while below in the second class Polish Jews are tearing themselves apart in fanatic discussion. They wrench their hearts out convincing each other; they beg, threaten, despair when the other does not understand quickly enough, does not believe, does not agree. Standing on the upper deck you can see their gestures, but can't hear what they say because the ocean drowns the sound. If you could see them you would forgive me my arguments with Oliver, and understand that one remains what one is, even when one has been "elevated" into the first class.

My dear heart, have you read about the terrible events in Germany? Five Prussian ministers had been thrown out, the last of the so-called Liberals, Braun, dismissed while on leave of absence, the Ministers of Police and of the Interior arrested because they doubted the legality of the procedure. Von Papen is master of Prussia. In Locarno, at the mere sight of his mug, England and France united to form a new European hegemony. This may be our relative salvation.

Salka, you cannot imagine anything more hideous than the metamorphosis of George Grosz. With beastly doggedness he was telling me for hours that he only believes in the most brutal personal self-interest and ruthless egoism; everything else is a fraud, a swindle invented by Jews and foreigners. Millions of poor devils always existed and always will, and they have to obey and nothing else. "Hitler is greater than Lenin because he openly says that the masses have to take orders." And so he ranted. I am sure he has gone through lousy times, terrible disappointments, and in his bitterness he snarled and growled. But the hideousness of his fury, the babbittry, this subservient heel-clicking before those who have power! He wants to immigrate to America with wife and child, and no Jews and idealists will influence him any longer. He is making a clean break with all that, and for good.

I know that he is a hunted man, worn out . . . He kept me for hours, forcing me to listen to him until I could not stand it any longer and spat all my painful disgust, like a hemorrhage, into his face. I couldn't help it. I am not a politician, not a Leninist, not a Bolshevist, but this ultimatum of betrayal, this *determination to recant*, this jump from a "Left-wing European" to Ku Klux Klan was too horrifying. Perhaps it was a necessary prelude to my return. He warned me: "Wait, only wait . . . you will see what you find. About turn! Away from Europe—run—this is all I can advise you to do."

And we, Salka, you and I, have prepared for our return by signing protests and manifestos for Ossietzki, a "condemned traitor." They won't help; everything will remain just a piece of paper. . . .

Perhaps it was wrong to leave Hollywood without a contract, and I will be relieved when you sign yours. I am sceptical about working in Berlin. I suspect there are no possibilities in Vienna, but one should live there or in Switzerland. London would be the best, provided that we can work and earn dollars or pounds. Everyone says it's very expensive.

The only bearable people on the boat are the Americans: sociable, helpful, friendly, child-like, and once you know and understand them you feel at ease. Even my mediocre Ping-Pong makes me one of them. They watch the game; old ladies bend and pick up the balls. My heart stops when I think that Hans, Peter and Tommy, so trusting and open-hearted, should be exposed to the beastliness in Germany. I am afraid that the closer I come to Europe the more I begin to resemble Grosz. Such are life's dialectics working in contrast. Why am I a weaver of thoughts, a *Geistmacher*—and lately an illusion-fixer? Why am I thrown, a Jewish agitator, into the ferment of spiritual values?

My dearest heart, I will soon see your mother, Rose, Edward and their children. I fear for my father and I am not sure if I should go to Berlin. But this will be decided later. Life will decide—the events will decide, everything goes on as it has to. Soon we shall be together. Take care of yourself; live as it is necessary for you, as you feel you *must*. . . .

This letter crossed with mine of August 7, 1932:

. . . Today is Tommy's birthday. I could not fulfill his main wish and give him a baby sister. But yesterday he had a big party with his school friends and, of course, his beloved Mucki and Julius Spuhler. It was a great success. He got a bicycle and a young kitten, so he had what he wanted, except his main wish—but such is life. He was holding the cat in his arms and his voice almost broke. He kept repeating: "My own kitty! My own." Today they are all at the Olympic Stadium watching the water polo and I am alone at home writing to you.

Greta was two days on the high seas when Mr. Thalberg decided to talk to me. I went to the studio with Eddington. I had not seen Thalberg for several weeks and was shocked how thin and pale he looked. At first he was very pleasant; then the following conversation ensued:

Thalberg: "Well, we have to start working. What arrangements would you suggest?"

I (advised by Eddington): "I leave it to you, Mr. Thalberg."

He: "We want very much to have you here with us and I think it best you join MGM on a weekly salary."

I: "As you know, I have collaborated with Mrs. Le Vino. The studio should first make a deal with both of us and buy the story!"

A long pause, then—

He (charmingly, à la Lindemann): "But there is nothing to buy. You have no copyright. Anybody can come and write a story on a historical subject."

I looked at him speechless.

"You told me yourself," he went on, "that you intended to make changes. Still, I want to be fair. We will pay you a thousand dollars now and four thousand when the script is finished."

I: "No, Mr. Thalberg, you know very well that this is not an adequate compensation for a story which demanded a great deal of work and research."

With that I said goodbye and left.

I was really shocked when he said that anybody could write a story about a historical subject.

Next day Eddington called me to say that Thalberg was furious but wanted to talk to me. Coached by Oliver I answered that I could not discuss business, that Mr. Thalberg was a charming and fascinating man and that I would talk to him about everything in the world, but not about money. Besides Mr. Thalberg was mistaken: the story is *not* in public domain; it is an original, based on a historical character, and he himself had said that it was an ideal role for Miss Garbo.

I had asked Beilenson * and he advised me that $10,000 would be a normal price for a 90-page story. Well, we shall see what happens. It would be wonderful if we could leave our pitiful savings intact for a while.

All during that ordeal I was thinking of you, Berthold. My first encounter with the world of film business made me feel very apologetic towards you! But if they don't throw me out, I hope I will learn to cope with it.

I envy you! You'll see your father and sisters, Edward, Rose, Mama, while I have Thalberg weighing

* Laurence Beilenson was a friend of Oliver and also our lawyer.

upon me, even in my dreams! If only I knew how to be
"tough." He had waited until Garbo was gone to tell
me that I did not have a copyright and that he did not
have to buy the story. But why *didn't* I think of a
copyright?! Beilenson says they cannot steal it. Everything will be decided before this letter is in your hands,
in any case you will have my telegram. Now I am waiting. All I do is wait: for your letters—Thalberg's decision. Françoise is here because of some business and we
see each other everyday. She met Tallulah and it was
very funny. I don't think they took to each other. I also
had invited Vicki Baum that evening, but no one could
talk, because Tallulah drowned all conversation with
her torrents of self-glorification. The Lerts live near the
Canyon, and Hans and Peter have become very close
friends with their two sons, who are intelligent and
have excellent manners. Leo's influence is diminish-
ing . . .

After an armistice of a few days, Thalberg offered $7,500 for the
story, and Peg said we should accept. We signed a contract and
each of us got $3,750. Hollywood rumors made it $37,500.

Two days later a story conference took place in Thalberg's office
and he introduced me to Bess Meredyth, a jolly blond, pinkfaced,
"all dimples and curves," whom I had met before at parties. She
was one of the most highly paid writers at Metro, the author of
the much praised screenplay for *Ben Hur*, which I was ashamed to
admit I had never seen. The other person in the room was Mr.
Paul Bern, a short, restless man, obviously devoted to Thalberg,
but arrogant and pretentious with me. He was married to the
famous Jean Harlow.

Now that he had bought *Christina*, Thalberg surprisingly voiced
his liking for historical films, while Bern expressed the identical
criticism and doubts I had heard before from Thalberg. Bess
Meredyth sat there, a pink-and-white buddha, smiling and saying
nothing. I listened to what could almost be called a lecture from
Thalberg, interrupted now and then by Bern's exclamations:
"Marvelous, Irving," "I see! *Now* it certainly makes sense! *Now* it
becomes an important film . . ." etc., etc. Another small, well-
dressed man slipped into the room and sat down quietly, nodding
to what Thalberg was saying: the film had to be "daring" and
"human," not a pageant, the characters, unusual. However, it
should be possible for the audiences to identify with them.

This dogma of "audience identification" was familiar to me from Berthold's days at Fox.

"All the audience wants is a good love story," said the nodding gentleman. I mentioned that Christina was not an ordinary woman and was besieged by many difficult problems. For a moment Thalberg looked pensive. "That's fine, but how will you dramatize that without making it talkative and dull?" I began to describe the incidents. They were in the treatment, but my instinct told me that it would be a serious mistake to mention it. Everything had to be reinvented at the conference, preferably by the producer. My suggestions were pure theater, and as Thalberg was a showman, he listened attentive and amused. Several times Bess Meredyth said: "That sounds interesting."

Finally Thalberg's secretary reminded him that people were waiting for him on the stage. I was leaving with the others when he called me back. He was standing behind his huge desk pondering; then he raised his head and said: "Well, don't you want to sign with us?"

"Very much, Mr. Thalberg, if you don't expect me to say *yes* all the time."

He laughed. "You had a very bad entrée, but if I were not sure that you will be an asset to the studio I would not make you an offer. We need talent, but talent needs us too. You have no experience and I want you to work with Bess Meredyth. She has written great films."

Then abruptly he asked if I had seen the German film *Mädchen im Uniform*, a great success in Europe and New York. It had been directed by a woman, my former colleague at the *Neue Wiener Bühne*, Leontine Sagan, and dealt with a lesbian relationship. Thalberg asked:"Does not Christina's affection for her lady-in-waiting indicate something like that?" He wanted me to "keep it in mind," and perhaps if "handled with taste it would give us very interesting scenes." Pleasantly surprised by his broadmindedness, I began to like him very much and went to the legal department to sign my contract. MGM paid me three hundred and fifty a week on a week-to-week basis. I refused to commit myself for a long term before I knew the result of Berthold's European negotiations.

Now that I was working for Metro I had to get used to the fantastic waste of time and to the endless waiting for conferences with Thalberg. Even when he summoned us to his office he was constantly on the telephone or suddenly called away, until finally he had to go to New York. Bess Meredyth wanted to spend some time reading about Christina and Sweden, and I grasped the opportunity to ask boldly for two weeks leave of absence to go to Mexico. I suggested that my work for Metro should start after my return, but Thalberg decided to keep me on the payroll as a reward for my "contributions" at the conferences. I cabled Berthold. From the steamer *Santa Anna* sailing to Mazatlan, I wrote him:

Dearest Berthold,

What a wonderful tropical night! The Americans play deck games, I feel an utter stranger, longing to be close to you, who are in Paris and very likely not even thinking of me.

After the endless conferences with Thalberg and Bess Meredyth, I felt the urgent necessity to get out of Hollywood. Also I could not resist Oliver's and Louise's persuasions to join them on an excursion to Mexico. The children are well taken care of and MGM continues to pay my salary. In the last week I had lost seven pounds and was a nervous wreck. Now, cut off from Hollywood, I am beginning to find myself, which has some disadvantage. Oliver, always kind, patient and helpful in my struggles, has become one-hundred-percent Yankee on the boat, and I hope that when we land we will get along better. I miss you. If only I could talk to you about this insane chapter in my life!

This ship is taking us to Mazatlan, then we go by train to Guadalajara to see a lake, the name of which I have forgotten, then to Mexico City. I shall stay there only three days, then return to Santa Monica.

This boat is a mail carrier and the food is horrible, but on deck we have a big tank filled with seawater and one can swim and cool off. The passengers are middle-class American families: quiet, polite and pleasant. I am waiting for your letters which will be forwarded to Mexico. I am so anxious to hear how you found my family and what happened to your film project with Korda. Of course, the tragic condition of your father makes everything else unimportant.

[From Guadalajara:] It was so unbearably hot on the boat that I could not finish my letter. The two days in Mazatlan were even worse, but fantastic. Berthold, we have to see Mexico together, it is an incredible experience. It is Spain and the Indians, the South Seas and my fatherland—the Ukraine. A fascinating mixture. I miss you! The name of the lake is Chapala.

[Mexico City:] I have just returned from a stroll in the city. Large piazzas, old streets and on their pavements live, eat and sleep Indians and peons. They squat in the dust playing dice. A ragged, dirty crowd stands around and watches. Others sell or buy mangos, pottery, garlic, bananas, with great noise but terrific *grandezza*. In the cathedral a priest in civilian clothes teaches little orphan girls to sing. Outside on the steps sits an Indian family. The father, a fat Indian papa, quarrels with his wife about a piece of enchillada which she grabbed from him. Impassively she goes on chewing, then he says something which makes her furious and she spits the enchillada into her hand then stuffs it into his mouth. A sweet, brown child with enormous eyes sucks at her breast, staring at them apathetically. If only I could remember everything I see.

It is a shame that I cannot stay longer and see more of Mexico. I share with my whole heart Eisenstein's infatuation, and understand his despair not to have finished the apotheosis of the Mexican revolution. We should have visited him here while he was shooting but you were a prisoner of Paramount.

This letter took two weeks to reach Berthold and by then my effusiveness seemed ill-timed.

27

YOU ASK HOW EUROPE IS, Salka? It is overwhelming. Impoverished, poisoned by politics, which means by hatred; still, you touch earth again and it is holy earth,

and it is your own. The shock of this encounter makes
you lose your mind; then gradually your old life, buried
and forgotten, emerges from it. If only you were here!
You must come, if only for a visit.

I read this with some bitterness and dismissed the temptation
from my thoughts. Mexico had made me hungry for Europe, but
it was out of the question to leave the children and my new job. In
the studio only Bess Meredyth had missed me; under the shock of
a new Hollywood scandal, Thalberg had very likely forgotten that
I existed. Paul Bern's naked body had been found in the living
room of his house, a bullet through his head. A pathetic farewell
note to Jean Harlow, his wife of two months, provoked sordid and
cynical speculations. The press surpassed itself in sensationalism,
while the studio exerted all its influence to protect their invest-
ment in the star. Harlow's new film was about to be released and
women's clubs were voicing moral indignation.

Bess told me that no one had been designated to supervise
Queen Christina. We plodded along, doubtful that the film would
ever be made.

I had become very fond of Bess, a warm-hearted woman. *Queen
Christina* was not exactly her cup of tea, but she was interested,
and raved about me to the front office where I had encountered
distrust and antagonism. Thalberg had emphatically expressed his
satisfaction with my work, but now a great war was going on
between him and L. B. Mayer, and he threatened to resign. Having
finished the first draft of the screenplay we sent it to his office, and
were told that he and Miss Shearer were leaving for Europe. There
were rumors that he had suffered a heart attack. Weeks of waiting
followed. Bess's salary of several thousand dollars a week was
climbing to a majestic figure, which did not bother her conscience;
but I was uneasy, although the studio could easily afford to
waste the money it paid me.

I could not stand the waiting and the idleness and began to
write an orginal story. It was about jobless people but as there
were twelve million unemployed in the country, the story editor
said that "nobody wanted to see such a film." However, remembering the "identification" theory, he did not discourage me and I
continued to inform myself about life in Hooverville—Hoover
suits made out of newspapers, the hunger marchers shot at by the
police, and the veterans demanding their bonus. It was a quixotic
idea, because all that hardly penetrated the airtight atmosphere of
MGM.

The presidential election was forthcoming. L. B. Mayer was a

Republican and had requested that every employee of the studio donate one day's salary to the Hoover campaign. I declined my contribution with the excuse that I was not an American citizen. With little enthusiasm Oliver and Louise endorsed the Democratic ticket. Oliver considered Roosevelt an "aristocrat, a dilettante," though well-intentioned. He quoted to me a political commentator who said: "Roosevelt is a man who thinks that the shortest distance between two points is not a straight line, but a corkscrew." But I was carried away by Roosevelt's speeches, and sorry that I could not vote.

In constant variations Berthold's letters reiterated his chances, offers, aims and ideas, pouring out brilliant thoughts, sharp observation, disappointments and violent invective. Arriving two weeks after they were written, they infected me with his doubts, and revealed his inner resistance to concentrating on any project. After four years in Hollywood he had come back just when most of the European producers and directors would have given their souls for a call to the Paradise on the Pacific, while others were rapidly adjusting themselves to National Socialism.

Berthold was still weighing Korda's offer against a freelance project with a producer whose enterprising spirit and financial backing he greatly overestimated. Also for weeks he had not been able to tear himself away from Paris and suggested we should all move there.

Finally he went to Berlin:

> On every street corner you see youngsters in uniform shaking their collection boxes; opposite them, on the same corner, the Communists. Lately both the young Communists and the Hitler Youth went on strike together. Four dead. The Government reacted with strong measures, but the strike continues.
>
> You read the results of the election. I heard them at Camil Hoffmann's, on the radio. What the Nazis lost in votes was gained by Papen and the German National Party. The losses of the Social Democrats went to the Communists. I am sure that many Jews voted for Papen, trying to keep the present dictatorship (Hindenburg, Papen and General v. Schleicher), which to them means capitalistic order and protection from the extreme Right and Left. . . .
>
> The sadistic prostitutes still gather on the corner of Tauentzien and Kurfürstendamm, complaining aloud to passers-by that the police will not let them wear their

high boots anymore. Despite the new morality their numbers have increased. They look younger, prettier, rather "bürgerlich," and beg more than solicit. The Eden Bar and other night spots are ultra-chic and full of foreigners and film people. There you can see Conny Veidt, Charles Boyer, prominent stage actors and financiers. Berlin is still more elegant than New York. Less traffic and not many automobiles, an enormous amount of beggars in front of luxurious eating places: Kempinski, Mampe, and new Viennese and Hungarian restaurants—does it give you a picture?

In ten days I may know what I am going to do. Perhaps Brecht's *St. Joan of the Stockyards* or Hauptmann's *Hannele*, the latter as a film for UFA. I was offered a marvelous play by a Hungarian dramatist, it's called *Dentist Asks for Dowry*. But what I would like to do most is the Brecht play. Of course, it's picking chestnuts out of the fire, but these are the best chestnuts existing.

Again the slow mail made my letter a monologue:

. . . No I am not disappointed about the chances for *Queen Christina*. I know it could be a wonderful film, but MGM has the power to spoil it. Until now I had lived in the hope that it would be made in Europe, but Greta is coming back and I am stuck here. Dearest Berthold, if you are not making a film or staging a play immediately, you should return as soon as possible. Alas, I am sure that you are discussing a hundred projects, talking to a thousand people and dissipating your energy. Now that I am earning money we should consider it as a great chance for you to settle down and finish your books. The last check I sent you came from my salary and I did not have to draw on the savings account. I have also sent money to Poland.

I am lonesome for you. The only bright moments are the children, the New York Philharmonic concerts, which are broadcast on Sundays, and books, if I have the time to read them. Last night I read to the boys Perutz's *Bontje The Silent*. We were moved to tears. In spite of his he-man pose, Peter is a tender, poetic soul. Hans is unusually intelligent and thinks very logically—but he likes to take it easy. I have not received the report cards yet.

Berthold:

You urge me to stick to my writing. Of course I do. I don't cease to write. Right now I am finishing a long essay about my return to Europe, what I have seen, thought and experienced. I am constantly writing new poems and working on old ones.

No, darling, I am not as diverted and distracted as you think, and you must not envy me this European trip. I was quite disturbed and shaken when I left Paramount, and I'll return to you refreshed and regenerated. I am afraid I have become a legend to the young people here, a historical figure, and I don't relish it at all. But after Hollywood it is extraordinary. They have built a niche for me and expect me to climb on a pedestal and stay there peacefully and quietly. To tell you the truth, I am just as isolated here as you in Hollywood. We are running parallel now, not as one stream. This is the difference. A painful one and hard to bear. . . .

On October 7, 1932:

Korda introduced me to British-Gaumont and, as I wrote you, they are interested. But they also are not starting production before the New Year. Otto Katz * has arrived in Berlin from Moscow, where he is the director of Mesch-Rab-Pom Films. He says we could work there together: I as a director, you as an actress and also directing. The technical and physical conditions are difficult, and he suggests I should go to Moscow and see with my own eyes. Piscator, Egon E. Kisch and many others are already there. It sounds very tempting. After Hollywood I am not afraid of dictatorship, but the language! Having barely learned English I cannot face Russian. For you it would be child's play, but for the boys!! Tommy?! To make a film there would take more than a year.

Meanwhile, I am sitting in my room at Elisabeth's (she takes excellent care of me) and writing poems. I have shown them to Karl Kraus and he considers them extraordinary. Also Erich Engel is very much taken

* Later known as Breda and André Simon. Active in the anti-Nazi underground, a prominent Communist leader in Czechoslovakia, executed in a Stalinist purge.

with my poetry. And so, while Fate weaves her web, I am writing.

My answer:

> . . . You are telling me about all the people as if I had seen them two weeks ago, and you don't mention how they impress you. Not a word about Hitler's increasing power. Not a word about Elisabeth, Jenny,* whose fate worries me. You cannot imagine how I long for Europe. To consider Katz's offer is quite insane. Now really! "Mesch-Rab-Pom."! I would like to see you in Russia, watching every word you say, controlling your temper!
>
> Your agent said that it would be best for you to direct a film in Europe, a successful one. Then he could "sell" you here at a high price. A genius, isn't he?

President Roosevelt had been elected with an overwhelming majority but between the election and his inauguration on March 3, 1933, the economy of the country continued to deteriorate. The studios cut all salaries in half, though, strangely, the stars were not included in the arbitrary measure. The sudden reduction of my income was a shock, but Jessie offered to stay for half her wages. I did not want to accept, but she insisted, saying that she considered herself lucky to work for people she liked. As so often happens, the poor were more generous than the rich.

December came and with it the usual pre-Christmas melancholia. Berthold wrote:

> It's good to know that you are all together in the dear house on Mabery Road, while my path leads over a bedeviled hill. One should not look back as one climbs.

My letter of December 19:

> You know that I love you and that I belong to you. Once, when I was terribly unhappy because you were infatuated with somebody else, you told me: "Imagine it is an illness; you would not love me less were I sick." But you are leaving me alone in *my* illness. I need you. If it's true that your longing "is unbearable," come back! What are you waiting for, my dearest? I also long for our life together. Do you want me not to see Oliver

---

* A Jewish actress living in Elisabeth's pension.

anymore? Forgive me for saying it so bluntly. But I only feel the same fondness for him as for this new, strange country, and neither he nor I have any serious intentions toward each other.

From Berthold, December 31, 1932:

I did not spend Christmas with the Gielens, which would have been the only solace for not being with you. Suddenly my father's condition worsened and I had to go to Vienna. On Friday morning from seven o'clock we all remained with him until he breathed his last. The end was a slow, constant ebb. . . .

Finally the studio appointed a producer for *Queen Christina*. He was Walter Wanger, a handsome man in his early forties, college-educated, with excellent manners, liberal opinions, but evasive and "diplomatic." It was easier to talk to Thalberg, who could be blunt and arrogant, but was seriously involved in film making. Wanger assigned a new writer with "a fresh viewpoint" to tackle the script. Mr. Ernest Vajda was a Hungarian, whose faulty English and preposterous personality were softened by the perfect syntax and great gentleness of an Englishwoman, Mrs. Claudine West. She was the most self-effacing, recalcitrant collaborator an egomaniac could wish. I was promoted to Wanger's "assistant and artistic advisor."

Vajda's screenplay was filled with the so-called "Lubitsch touches," and the drama changed into a comedy. Of course it no longer had the slightest resemblance to the original story. Wanger comforted me by saying that he wanted first to give Vajda a chance to express his viewpoint and that a British writer, Mr. H. M. Harwood, was en route from London to give "class" to the dialogue.

The *Christina* script was shaping into the very Hollywood vehicle Garbo had hoped to escape. The conferences with Vajda provided occasions for constant clashes. He was unbearably arrogant, personal and provoking.

Meanwhile, the confrontations with Europe had affected Berthold's health and he needed a thorough physical check-up. At the Viennese Cottage Sanatorium, Professor Norden confirmed that his diabetes had increased but, thanks to Berthold's basically strong and healthy nature, it was possible to check it with a rigid diet. As soon as he was free of sugar, Berthold recovered. Even his handwriting showed a miraculous change.

But there was also another reason for his soaring optimism. He had met the philosopher and writer Herman Broch, the author of the *Sleepwalkers* and *Virgil's Death*:

> Broch belongs to the intellectuals who function in a narrow circle because they create a formula, an essence, which afterwards hundreds and thousands of others superficially dilute and popularise. I don't say it bitterly nor with antagonism but knowingly.
>
> Broch is a beautiful, dark, melancholy man, a very noble bird. He had read my poems and came to visit me in the Cottage Sanatorium. For three hours we carried on a most intense and concentrated conversation; then he insisted that I let him read the novel I had started to write in Dusseldorf. I did not tell you that I changed the title to *I Love You, Ariadne*. By Ariadne is meant the labyrinth of one's ego, from which neither reality nor spirituality can point the way out. We have chosen our identity and only death can deliver us from it. Dear heart, to you I know this sounds pessimistic, but it is above pessimism or optimism. It is a spiral which leads from the lowest point to the highest. It is lyricism and religion, not sentimental poetry but introspective activity, transformation and trans-substantiation in the process of writing, which continues endlessly as life itself. It's a second life.
>
> I was extremely nervous and anxious about Broch's verdict. After he finished reading he invited me for lunch, which was scrupulously prepared according to my diet. Then he told me what he thought of my manuscript. I am afraid that by repeating it to you I'll make it impossible for myself to finish the book. Bad criticism is dangerous, but great praise also. He said—and I hardly dare to repeat it—"This book belongs to the two or three most important literary works in the German language." He offered me his publishing house, the Rhein Verlag, which also publishes Joyce. In the first moment I was full of superstitious fear, then immediately I wanted to tell it to you. Now I have to overcome my self-consciousness and work on the novel. To finish it is more difficult than to begin. But to complete everything I have started is the gigantic task of my old age.

Old age was still far off and the next letter said:

> When I think that it took me five days to write my essay: "Lindbergh, Garbo and the Press," and I got 120 marks for it, which won't pay my bill in the sanatorium, I am tempted to accept the offer from Europa Film to write and direct *Little Man What Now*. You know Fallada's book about the German jobless? It would make an important, wonderful film. Still there are difficulties with my "contingent status" (working permit), because I am an Austrian and lived the last four years in America. The authorities claim that there is no "cultural necessity" for my working in Germany. In view of my artistic past this aroused great indignation, and many people like Herbert Ihering * and Eric Engel protested.

Apparently the authorities reconsidered, and having finished his cure Berthold went to Berlin. He arrived on January 31 when the headlines were announcing Hitler's ascent to power. Immediately Europa Film assigned the non-Jew, Mr. Wendhausen, as codirector and cut Berthold's salary. A decent man, Wendhausen was embarrassed and sympathetic. For inexplicable reasons the firm was holding Berthold to his commitment, also Kurt Weill, who was to write the music, and the set-designer Kaspar Neher. For Berthold this was a compelling experience, similar to having been in the war. And he enjoyed working with Neher and Weill.

> We are firmly holding together, which is our only salvation, as the producer, a blond, blue-eyed giant, is outdoing himself to please the new regime and wants to impose upon us the corniest, slimiest "kitsch." Perhaps it is sheer madness to do this film in such times. You have read the novel and know its social theme. [I had, and it *was* sheer madness!] Of course, I have made it very clear to the gentlemen of Europa Film that as an unredeemable Jew and Austrian, I am willing to step out, even after they have signed my contract. But although I am sure my name won't appear on the film, they have no intention of letting me go.

I was desperate; I knew that Berthold was in danger, not only as a Jew but also because of his public statements, his contributions

* Herbert Ihering, prominent German theater critic.

to the *Weltbuehne*, his friendship with Karl Kraus, his opposition
to everything the Germans now so overwhelmingly and enthusiastically embraced. I cabled him to break his contract and to leave
immediately.

He answered that Europa Film insisted that he finish the screenplay, otherwise they would not pay him. Finally the Reichstag fire
made him leave Berlin. In Prague, where he stopped on his way to
Vienna, there were other fugitives: Thomas Mann and his brother
Heinrich, Bertolt Brecht, Arnold Zweig, Alfred Polgar, Kurt Weill
. . . all expurgated from the culture of the Third Reich.

April 11, 1933

Dear Berthold,

I hoped that you had decided to finish your novel in
Santa Monica. Instead you went to Berlin to write the
screenplay of *Little Man What Now*. Hitler interfered
and now you feel like abandoning your novel too.
Hitler is the triumph of the German *Spiesser* and we
will live to see his downfall. Russia and America will
destroy him. Your books will appear in English. An
American poet I met, Sam Hoffenstein, wants to translate your poems.

I understand that the film was very important to you.
After years of compromise you had the opportunity to
do something worthwhile. It was not to be. Now I
cannot leave my work here. After fantastic difficulties I
have managed to establish myself and gain respect from
my collaborators, with the exception of Vajda.

You reproach me for not saying more about the
earthquake. Well, the papers exaggerated terribly, but I
admit that it was very frightening. All during the night
the tremors continued at irregular intervals. We had
the radio on and heard of the catastrophe in Long
Beach, with all those dead. Our telephone was out of
order and Oliver, who was at a meeting in Hollywood,
stopped by on his way home to see if we were all right.
In the morning I discovered that the chimney had
moved about three feet from the house, one could walk
in between. Otherwise there is not much damage, a few
cracks in the walls and in the bedroom ceilings. That's
all.

Now other news: because of the fifty percent cut in
their salaries the writers are organizing a Screen

Writers Guild and the producers are furious. But there are many, like Mr. Vajda, who say that we are not laborers to be in a union, and call us all "Bolsheviks." This sounds familiar doesn't it?

Our sons are wonderful. They discuss things openly, are free, uncramped and well-informed. I want them to become Americans and I have taken out my first papers. And if you don't come back to the States within a year your visa becomes invalid. Don't forget it. The boys plead that we should buy a farm. Perhaps they are right. In case our film careers collapse we would have a piece of land and grow our own spinach.

Dearest Berthold, in spite of temporary infatuations which have nothing to do with our belonging to each other, *you* are the love of my life.

The "aristocrat" Roosevelt began his presidency with sweeping "socialistic" legislation, and with an overwhelming majority the Congress voted the radical measures against further economic debacle. The most revolutionary laws were the federal credit to property owners, the right to collective bargaining for organized labor, and the Social Security against unemployment, poverty and old age.

Before the banks closed on March 4, 1933, the First National of Beverly Hills, where we had our savings, had declared bankruptcy. Luckily I had deposited money I got for *Queen Christina* in a downtown bank. It was all we had left. I had been cabling large sums to Berthold. To his ruined family and jobless friends he was the rich uncle from America, and in his absentmindedness he would forget bank notes in hotel rooms or lose them on the streets.

A few weeks after the earthquake, as I was about to renew our lease, Mr. Guercio, the real estate broker, asked me: "Why don't you buy the house? It's a bargain. The bank holding the mortgage of fourteen thousand dollars is under liquidation and, as large houses are almost impossible to sell, you could buy it for seven thousand, five hundred. The down-payment is two thousand dollars." The balance was to be paid in monthly installments of seventy-five dollars. Mr. Guercio talked also about "amortization" and that any amount I spent on improvements would increase the value of the property and be advanced by federal credit to the owner.

I cabled Berthold. He answered that although he loved the house it would be more advisable to buy one in Austria or Lugano, where there were no earthquakes. Nevertheless, Hitler's speeches and my faith in Roosevelt compelled me to hand two thousand dollars to Mr. Guercio and, as I had Berthold's power of attorney, I also signed his name to the deed. I was sure that after all his wanderings Odysseus would be pleased to have a home.

The next thing was to apply for a bank loan and repair the damage caused by the earthquake, and while I was at it I decided to put in central heating, build comfortable servants' quarters, a large guest room above the garage and a terrace leading from the living room to the garden. Though all this sounds forbiddingly extravagant, the sum the Federal Housing allowed covered these improvements. I remember that for the excavation of the basement and installation of the heating system I paid about four hundred and fifty dollars. I enjoyed myself thoroughly hunting for secondhand furniture, and I bought lovely old pieces discarded by the rich of Los Angeles, who used to "redecorate" their homes almost as often as they changed their clothes. But our beds had to be brand new: I had slept long enough on used, sagging mattresses.

28

As far as I remember it took MGM some time to persuade Sam N. Behrman, the distinguished playwright, to tear himself away from New York and come to Hollywood to rewrite Queen Christina. Mr. Wanger liked to keep his writer team divided. I learned from Mr. Harwood that Behrman had arrived but that I was to be kept away from him because of my disparaging remarks about the Vajda script. Nevertheless, the next day I heard short rapid steps in the hall, and Mr. Behrman burst into my office determined to talk to me.

I had met him casually, when Berthold was still working for Fox, through Sol Wurtzel for whom Sam had a special, though incomprehensible affection. He found Mr. Wurtzel's conversation hilarious.

Sam Behrman was about forty, of middle height and weight; his domed forehead was bald, his features distinguished, the brown eyes looked at one with humorous interest and warmth, but they could change rapidly and become absent, when he was bored. Boredom was unbearable to Sam and he blamed it on his "low vitality" and "terrible temperament." In spite of that—although I am not inclined to feel nostalgic about MGM—I will always cherish the hours, days and weeks we spent together. They have cemented a friendship that has endured through many eventful, exasperating, happy and tragic—and so rapidly vanished—years.

Brilliant, witty, with a weightless sense of humor and a rare gift to uplift, stimulate and exhilarate, Sam has never been "temperamental" with his collaborators, but always generous and inspiring.

Queen Christina was directed by Rouben Mamoulian, an Armenian born in Tiflis and influenced by the Russian Art Theater. Like Murnau, he was a man passionately dedicated to his work. Berthold and I had admired his remarkable staging of Porgy on Broadway. I believe New York appreciated him more than Hollywood. Tall, with melancholy eyes behind large, black-rimmed glasses, he used to stick his head through the door of my office and sternly command: "Say 'Elisabeth.'" He had already conquered the difficulty in pronouncing the 'th,' while I was still trying hard not to say "Elithabess." It made him very happy when I slipped.

Disillusioned with Europe, where she had been mainly busy hiding from reporters, Greta was ready to return to California. Until she could find a suitable house I invited her to stay with us. She was sailing under an assumed name on a Swedish freighter through the Panama Canal, and I was to meet her with the car in San Diego. We hoped that she would disembark unnoticed. To my dismay, on the pier I ran into a large gathering of aggressive reporters, demanding an interview with Garbo. They were determined not to leave the pier until she appeared. There was nothing else to do but give in.

"Are you in love? What about the Prince? Are you engaged to him? Why don't you get married?" were the things they wanted to know.

In Hollywood they extended their harassment to Mabery Road. The movie magazines must have bribed even our dogs, because one evening, returning from the studio I found my sons in the living room giving an interview to two strangers, who asked them if Miss Garbo was "romantically linked" with Mr. Mamoulian.

I had seen an English film in which I was impressed by the

unusual charm of the young leading man. He struck me as the ideal actor to play Christina's Spanish lover and I raved about him to Wanger and Mamoulian. They agreed, but after three days shooting, the studio decided that although he had the looks for the part he lacked the necessary acting ability. His name was Laurence Olivier and he was replaced by John Gilbert.

The shooting of *Queen Christina* had started. Sam Behrman went back to New York and I was assigned to the producer Hunt Stromberg, to work on Garbo's next film, Somerset Maugham's *Painted Veil*. Ten well known writers had already worked on it, all trying in vain to make the basic situation, adultery, "palatable" to the producer. The director, Victor Fleming, practiced golf strokes during conferences. From time to time I was recalled for "advisory duties" on *Christina*, which were a pleasant interruption.

Weeks of uncertainty about the future went by, crowded with work in the studio and furtive happiness. I never doubted that Berthold's longing and love was as strong and real as he expressed it in his letters. Still, I was sure that he was not celibate in Paris. When I asked him he said that no one really mattered.

> Having thrown out a whole year of my life, I shall return to Santa Monica, to your heart, to the children and to the house at the other end of the world . . . I will recover from Europe like from a wild dream and, like a ship after it has been through a storm, I'll have all the damage repaired. Slowly and cautiously I will bring order into my thoughts and to my writing. I will still battle with my sins and mistakes and now and then have a sleepless night. . . .

I did not battle with my sins and mistakes. Berthold's emotional conflicts and self-torture were his necessary incitement and inspiration, while I refused to feel guilty when I loved.

Theoretically Berthold agreed with me that directing films in Hollywood could never be artistically satisfactory. He also agreed that the "lost year" was not lost as far as his writing was concerned.

> It is because of the great straight line in your nature, that you want to give me the possibility to devote myself completely to writing. *However*, I am flying on Monday to London, an additional experience, which again will lead back to my writing. So far no other subject to work on has come into my hands, but my own Self; this disagreeable Self, this magic box. A

writer must be damned careful that his whole life does not turn out to be merely material for his work. What a blessing that I have you and the boys! You prevent everything from becoming unreal. Every word you say always strikes me with its immediate directness, an acuteness of feeling so true and right, like nothing I have ever experienced. It is as if one watched the naked heartbeat of the world.

It is late and all I can tell you, until I am with you, are merely words. Where did this year go? How was it possible that a *whole year* has been torn out from our life. . . .

Finally he and British-Gaumont had settled on *Little Friend*, a novel by the Viennese author Ernst Lothar. The future was now more tangible: Berthold was again the breadwinner and contemplated moving us all to London. Of course, I had first to finish *Christina*. Though I was deeply attached to our house above the Pacific and the brilliant sunsets I loved to watch from my window, I was looking forward to a return to Europe.

Exercise was Oliver's religion and he always managed to squeeze an hour of tennis into his day, sometimes even two, depending on the season and his producer's attitude to sport. As his schedule was more leisurely than mine, he usually left the studio earlier than I. After tennis he would drop in at my house, and stay for a drink.

One evening, as we were sitting and chatting, Fred Zinnemann, now directing shorts at MGM phoned me to say that Gottfried Reinhardt, Max's younger son, was living in Santa Monica and would like to meet me. "Could he come by this evening?"

Oliver stayed another half hour, then left. At the gate he passed a young man, who had just emerged from an ancient, dilapidated roadster. He was tall, heavy set and his thick brown hair fell over his forehead. He had his father's eyes and smile, and told me that while in Berlin, Berthold had persuaded his mother to send him to America. He intended to work in films and was in some vague way attached to the Lubitsch unit at Paramount. Lubitsch's idea that one must start a career on the lowest rung of the ladder did not appeal to Gottfried, who preferred to begin if not exactly at the top, at least half way up. He was very funny, his self-assurance made him appear much older than his years, also his big cigar. In the way he tenderly held it, asking my permission to smoke, he reminded me of Ludwig. Oliver phoned to ask who the young man was, stressing that he was prompted merely by curiosity, not jealousy. I laughed and said that my guest could easily be my son.

This first impression changed very quickly. As the evening went on I discovered that Gottfried could be my grandfather. He was very intelligent, passionately political, disillusioned with socialism and saved from being overbearing by his great sense of humor. Trying to arouse my sympathy, Gottfried described how he was roughing it in a cheap apartment, and that he cooked his own breakfast. When I asked what he ate, he said: "Fresh strawberries, but I wash them myself." In all my American years I had not laughed so much as on that evening. It took me back to my youth in Berlin, to the theater and to my old friends.

On leaving, he confessed that he had hesitated to call me for two months, until Fred Zinnemann assured him that I was not the sad, deserted woman with three children he expected me to be.

Berthold returned in July, but only for the summer. Perhaps, had I gone to New York and had we had a few days to ourselves, everything would have been different. But I could not get leave of absence from the studio. The boys were impatient for Berthold to come home and so, as usual, we met in Pasadena and the "lost year," with its anxieties and disappointments, stood between us like a wall. He was as dear to me as ever, but the impulse which had always drawn us to each other, no matter what happened, was no longer there. I felt an enormous tenderness for him but also the sad certainty that never again would we be lovers.

I had to spend long hours in the studio, then many evenings with the indefatigable and painstaking Mamoulian who, after a hard day's work on the set and in the projection room, rushed through dinner to come to my house and go over new problems, prodding, correcting again and again, saying No to every suggestion, sure that only he himself could find the solution. Around midnight Berthold would emerge from his room, where he had been working or talking with his new secretary, a pale, blond young man, one of the first refugees to reach Hollywood. Gottfried, whom Berthold liked very much, came often, to bemoan the hideous events in Germany. Then, exhausted, we all had a nightcap together.

Ironically, just after they had built a large house with a tennis court in Pacific Palisades, Oliver and Louise were drawing apart. Louise went to Hawaii, when she returned she asked for a divorce.

It is the melancholy privilege of age to smile wonderingly upon the "cold embers of former passions." However, for me time could not extinguish their warm glow. The differences which existed between me and Oliver may have been one of the reasons for our mutual attraction. I had been in love with his manliness and his zest for life, his protest against the hero worship of our time, his firm belief in democracy, but I was often carried away with enthusiasms which I later reconsidered. Oliver's sober criticism of my passionate beliefs made me angry. From the beginning his feelings were stronger than mine, because for me my life with Berthold was always predominant. As long as his own marriage appeared secure Oliver accepted this, at least theoretically, but once Louise asked for a divorce he wanted me to marry him. This I could never do.

The days of Berthold's stay in Santa Monica were numbered. Again I packed his suitcases, wrote out his diet, although I knew he would often ignore it. I was glad that in spite of all the inner turmoil, his "home leave" had been beneficial to his health—he looked refreshed and well. Now the wanderer was off again. With a heavy heart and the knowledge that it was a mistake, I had to let him go. And so one evening Hans, Peter, Gottfried and I stood again in front of a Pullman car; all except Tommy, who could not bear to see his father leave. The two big boys envied Berthold. Gottfried tried to be cheerful, and I was in tears.

Leaning out of the window Berthold reached for my hand and held it until the train began to move. I ran beside it as long as I could, then Gottfried caught up with me and led me back. We got into the car, all of us aware of a sudden great emptiness.

From The Chief—eastbound:

> Salka, you will never regret that you have confided in me so completely. Nothing better and more beautiful could have happened between us. I am proud that I have been of some help to you; even if I often appear to be a swaying reed, my roots are strong and firm. And remember, never do anything out of your mad generosity. Don't jump head-on into decisions you might later regret. Cable me, phone me, and never give up loving me. Do you hear, never! As for me, only death can cure my addiction to you.

29

I BEGGED MY MOTHER to come to America and to live with me. After I had become an American citizen I would bring Dusko and Viktoria over. But she refused: "It is difficult at my age to get used to completely new surroundings. I would adore to come for a visit, but to leave Europe forever and renounce seeing my other three children, abandon everything, even the burial place next to Papa's which the city has given me—no, I cannot accept this thought."

In spite of the growing anti-semitism under Pilsudski, the Jews were participating in Poland's cultural life; Edward had his master class in Lwow and gave concerts in Krakow and Warsaw. This was important at a time when many of his Viennese pupils were leaving Austria. "Milimetternich," as they called the little Chancellor Dollfuss, had brutally suppressed the socialist opposition with artillery fire and was holding onto power with the help of Mussolini. Italian troops at the border prevented or rather postponed Hitler's annexation of Austria. "The Last Days of Mankind" were still not its last; they were merely a curtain raiser to a tragedy which soon transcended Karl Kraus's apocalyptic visions.

While it was possible for Jews and opponents of the regime to flee to Prague, Paris, England, Moscow or, like Bertolt Brecht, to the Scandinavian countries, the Gielens were tied to Dresden by Josef's contract and their financial situation. The Dresden State Theater was completely nazified but Josef was an "Aryan," and so successful that the Ministry of Culture did not dare to dismiss him despite his Jewish wife.

Rose withdrew from all social life, and not to hear the "Heil Hitler," she ceased even to go to the theater. We could not correspond directly any longer because the Gestapo searched their apartment from time to time and it was dangerous to receive letters from me.

"Dearest Salomé," wrote Edward, who always addressed me as in the days of our French governesses, "isn't it possible for you to come to Europe before it completely becomes a Fascist wilderness?" From year to year, from month to month, I had been promising to visit them, but the uncertainty of Berthold's future, and concern for the children, did not permit me to ask for a leave of absence. That weekly check—I was now getting five hundred and fifty dollars—had become of utmost importance, as more and more people depended on it. The exodus from Germany had begun; there was not a day that I did not get letters asking for help, and I besieged my American friends for affidavits. Not only individuals, but also causes needed financial support, and Hollywood was leading in generosity and helpfulness.

It is terrifying how suddenly fate becomes invincible and how unsuspectingly we accept it. "When our marriage breaks up, I shall cease to exist," Berthold once said. But in spite of all the things binding us, all the tenderness and love we had for each other, our marriage was not a marriage anymore. Torn and inconsistent, Odysseus resented bitterly that Penelope had not waited patiently for his return, though he himself had not renounced the Nausicaa's.

"Don't jump head-on into anything you may later regret," he warned me before he left. Much against my wish and my will I did not jump, but slid into a love affair, which to many people appeared quite insane. However, this "insanity" gave me ten years of happiness and became a very serious commitment.

He was unusually mature, which made me rely, perhaps too much, on his advice and judgment, and also on his great kindness and protectiveness and on his patience.

"But what did your sons say?" I was asked by a woman, who had herself sacrificed her love, with the result that her children thought her a frustrated and embittered bore. I answered that my two older sons were now adolescents; they understood that I had the right to some happiness. The youngest simply returned Berthold's and my love. I was closer to them than their father, who was so often away, but his visits were always a joyful and happy event. Psychoanalysts are convinced that children want good, simple, conventional moms and dads, preferably sexless; however, I am sure that my sons were not unduly disturbed by the fact that their parents had a complicated relationship.

Hans and Peter were fifteen and fourteen, ages when boys are supposed to be especially obnoxious and rebellious. I would not say that my first-born was a good student. Considering his extraordinary intelligence and the opportunities he had, he could have done much better in school. Peter got his A and B grades without any visible effort. At home they were considerate, amiable and stimulating company. From time to time I would get angry with one or the other but never for serious reasons.

All three had very different personalities. The eldest, thin and tall, was an avid reader, but undisciplined and moody. Peter, a mixture of precociousness and boyish charm, appeared more interested in sports than in literature. His good grades always amazed me, as I had the impression that he spent most of his time on the tennis courts and in stables. Thomas, awed by his brothers, clung to the dream world of childhood, expressing it in sweet poems, and trying bravely to grasp the reality of school.

Queen Christina was finished and previewed with great success. Now, thirty years later, it is still acclaimed by audiences, and strangers write me bemoaning the fact that such films are not made anymore. The success was mainly due to Garbo and her unique personality, talent and beauty, but the film survives also on its own merits.

Meanwhile Berthold's assimilation into the British film world was making slow progress. The Viennese novel, about a little girl whose parents were getting a divorce, created different problems in England than it would have in America. Also the phlegmatic tempo of the studio, with the long decision-delaying weekends and tea breaks, got on his nerves. But he was very fond of his co-workers, especially the young writer Christopher Isherwood.

Many refugees began to settle in Los Angeles. Arnold Schoenberg, who had returned to Judaism because of Hitler, arrived with his wife Gertrud and their adorable four-year-old daughter Nuria, to try to build a new existence. University professors and doctors were doing odd jobs while studying English, to pass the required examinations. One of Vienna's great orthopedic surgeons established himself as a masseur.

The French playwright Marcel Achard arrived to work on Maurice Chevalier films. Francesco and Eleonora Mendelssohn had told him to look me up. Dark, short, the near-sighted eyes hidden by enormous black-rimmed glasses—the biggest I have ever seen—Marcel conquered us all in the first second. My sons, Gottfried, my friends, the whole household surrendered to his warmth, his inexhaustible vitality and gaiety. Our affection included his wife Juliette. The Sundays in Mabery Road became a sacred rite for Marcel and no invitation from glamorous stars would tempt him away from the Ping-Pong matches and our various friends. They ranged from Johnny Weissmuller, then at the peak of his Tarzan fame—always involved in long conversations with the entranced Tommy—the "enfant terrible," Oscar Levant, Clemence Dane, Miriam Hopkins the actress, the MGM musicians Dimitri Tiomkin and Bronislaw Kaper from Warsaw and Lola his wife, both very Polish and nostalgic. Schoenberg and his wife would come, and Otto Klemperer, the conductor of the Los Angeles Philharmonic Orchestra, and Oliver would bring his new Hungarian wife, Ilonka. Gallantly forgiving my desertion, he had traveled in Europe for several months, met Ilonka in Budapest and married her. Though she was hard to beat in a Ping-Pong match, the marriage was a mistake and did not last.

Political discussions, verging on personal bitterness, were unavoidable among the Europeans and amazed the Americans. Gottfried participated in them as passionately and prominently as in Ping-Pong. Then, silver-haired and charming, Max Reinhardt arrived to stage A *Midsummer Night's Dream* in the Hollywood Bowl, and as a film for Warner Brothers. First, however, he went to Reno to get a divorce from Else Heims, the mother of his two sons, Gottfried and Wolfgang. Unfortunately the newspaper announced that he was establishing residence in Nevada, and this brought, with amazing speed, his wife Else to Los Angeles. Her unparalleled energy had succeeded for eighteen years in thwarting Reinhardt's attempts to divorce her and to marry Helene Thimig. Again Else was determined to win her fight. She was a strong and handsome woman, although the years of impassioned lawsuits had marred her beauty and embittered her life, while Reinhardt's success and world fame were hardly touched by them. The sons were devoted to both parents and wished their mother would face the inevitable. Gottfried implored her to agree to the divorce. Finally Else gave in, but he had to spend weeks haggling with lawyers and pleading with both sides.

Queen Christina was one of the last American films shown in the Third Reich. Friends and strangers wrote to me praising it for its pacifist tendency and "abdication of power."

I have repressed the memories of *The Painted Veil*; I only recall that the producer, wanting to stress the Chinese background, insisted on scenes with a statue of Confucius under a tree. For some strange reason he always called him "Vesuvius."

After *The Painted Veil* I had the good luck to be assigned to David Selznick, who was now at Metro and was to produce the next Garbo film. It did not take us long to hit upon the obvious: Tolstoy's *Anna Karenina*. David wanted me to collaborate with the English authoress Clemence Dane, a tall, heavy woman with classic features and dark hair tied in a Grecian knot. Her real name was Winifred Ashton. She wore long, trailing, chiffon dresses, had never been married and told me that she had never had a love affair. "So we shall rely on *your* experience, my dear Salka," she announced when we began to work on the script. "I have very little understanding for Anna Karenina. What *does* she want? Her husband is a perfect gentleman; she has a social position, an adorable child—but, of course, the poor thing is Russian!"

Dear Winifred, how "Russian" must I have seemed to her. But she was fond of me. I made her laugh and she listened to me, though she had the exasperating habit of stopping me in my tracks by correcting my syntax or insisting that I say "I shall" when I was convinced it should be "I will."

Hans and Peter thought that Winifred was "great" and Tommy adored her. They had long conversations because "he had the soul of a poet," and she gave him a marionette theater as a Christmas present. He immediately informed his father that he was writing a play about Adam and Eve and that the costumes would come from our fig tree.

Selznick found the screenplay we delivered much too long, the scenes Victorian, the dialogue too stilted, and he wanted changes. But Winifred in her impatience to leave thought it was perfect. She had a play in rehearsal in London and as Sam Behrman was between plays, David asked him to write the final script. It was wonderful to have Sam back, intense, moody and chain-smoking.

The filming started while we were still rewriting, but as we were always a few days ahead of the production everything moved smoothly. The director, Clarence Brown, was pleased, Garbo gave a wonderful performance, the atmosphere in the Selznick unit was harmonious and the rushes excellent.

When Sam asked me to dictate to the secretary the shots of Anna's suicide, I truly regretted that this was the last scene of the film. Walking up and down I described the night train approaching relentlessly—the lights from the carriage windows on Anna's face—her running down the embankment and throwing herself between the cars, then—a prostrated figure on the rails—the train disappearing in darkness—and last, a woman's handbag on the embankment.

"And that's what's left of a human being," I concluded, almost in tears, and turned to Sam who burst into roars of laughter. For years these words remained our special code. We signed telegrams and letters with: "What's left of a human being. . . ." They were our ultimate in *Galgenhumor*.

During all the editing of the film I stayed with Selznick. After

Anna Karenina he left Metro, and formed his own company. Thalberg had returned, not as head of the studio but with his own unit, and future Garbo films were on his program. As I was considered a Garbo specialist I moved to the newly built Thalberg bungalow.

Meanwhile more and more Europeans were drawn to California. One afternoon Gottfried brought for tea Friedrich Ledebur and Iris Tree, daughter of Herbert Beerbohm-Tree, a colorfully attired couple. Friedrich wore blue jeans, boots, red shirt, silver buttons on his Loden jacket: a happy mixture of a cowboy and an Austrian count. Iris was in a short red skirt and blouse, Indian beads around her neck and bracelets on her wrists, and a huge cowboy hat on the back of her head. Her very blonde hair was cut in a fringe over the eyebrows; with her blue eyes she was very lovely. Friedrich was the tallest man I have ever seen and the most handsome. Their six-year-old son Christian was in England in the care of his grandmother, Lady Beerbohm-Tree.

I immediately succumbed to Friedrich's unaffected old-world gallantry, his knight-errant charm, and Iris's impish sense of humor, her very special kind of poetic whimsy. The boys were enormously impressed that the Ledeburs traveled in a trailer, which looked like an Indian tent with rugs and skins and saddles and boots and God knows what. It was parked opposite the house and our new friends stayed with us two months and returned frequently ever after.

The atmosphere in the Thalberg bungalow was different from that in the rest of the MGM lot. Downstairs was his office and a reception hall, where the secretaries ruled. Upstairs were offices for the writers. On the third floor was a kitchen, a pantry and Thalberg's dining room. In the afternoon a Negro butler would knock at the doors to inquire who wanted tea or a highball. Thalberg's office was a long, wood-paneled room with a huge desk near the windows. Along the walls stood comfortable chairs and couches. One had to cross the full length of the room to reach the frail, small figure behind the desk, usually holding the telephone receiver in one hand while the other was jingling coins in his trouser pocket. After his long vacation and the trip to Europe, Thalberg had gained weight, looked healthier and was in a much better mood than I had ever seen him.

I had told him of an idea which I had for Garbo: Marie Walewska's love for Napoleon. He thought the political background too complicated for American audiences, but became interested after I had suggested Charles Boyer to play Napoleon.

Still, Marie Walewska had an illegitimate child by Napoleon, and before he decided to go on with the project, Thalberg wanted me to tell the story to the censors of the Breen Office. We met in the Thalberg bungalow, and when I was halfway through, the two gentlemen began shaking their heads. There was not only an illegitimate child but also double adultery.

Adultery was nothing new to the Breen Office. They had condoned it in other films. They also agreed that Thalberg had never offended "good taste"; however, this time they would not okay the story. "Then I'll go ahead without your okay," Thalberg said coldly. "This is a great love story and I am determined to produce it." It amused me to observe how the strong objections voiced by the censors had dispelled his doubts. The Breen Office retreated: "Only because it is you, Irving, we say go ahead with the script, but that does not mean that we will say 'yes' to the picture."

After they left Thalberg asked me: "How long will it take you to write the treatment?"

"I don't know. I have to read more. And then I have to ask you a great favor. I *must* have a leave of absence."

"Impossible. Why?"

"It's seven years since I have seen my mother, my family. Please let me write the treatment in Europe. I have to get out of Hollywood. . . ."

He looked at me curiously. I was sure that my personal life was not a secret in the studio. After a while he said: "I know. Sometimes you have to break away . . . Seven years, you said—it's seven years since you've seen your mother? I'll talk to Eddie Mannix."

Eddie Mannix was the Vice President of MGM, the second Almighty after L. B. Mayer. A former bouncer and boxer, he could be ruthless and violent, but he adored Garbo and also had a soft spot in his heart for me. After the first obligatory "no" he agreed to give me a two-month vacation and told me that I would remain on salary as I would continue to work for the studio.

And so at last I was on my way to Europe. But as things in life have an arbitrary timing, I was leaving with a divided heart, interrupting—perhaps breaking off—a relationship which had given me two years of great happiness: a happiness to which I could not hold on too firmly.

I arrived in New York on June 26, just in time to board the *Aquitania*, which was sailing at noon. As we were passing the Statue of Liberty a cable from Gottfried was handed to me. He had succeeded in driving his mother to Reno, and at last the divorce had taken place. As a reward for his travail he had invited Hans and Peter, with their French teacher, to meet him in Lake Tahoe and celebrate the event.

My excitement and impatience did not let me enjoy the calm and pleasant crossing. I was not going home. After my father's death Mama felt that the house was too big and lonely, too expensive to keep warm in winter, and had decided to transform it into smaller units, which she could lease. This made it impossible for Rose and Edward and their families to spend the summer at Wychylowka as in the good old days. Rose had written to me confidentially that the rent Mama received would never cover the cost of rebuilding. As the Gielens were anxious to escape the sight of swastikas and the strutting Saxonian Nazis for a while, they had chosen Porto Ronco in Switzerland for our family reunion. There, on the shore of Lago Maggiore, Mama, Edward and I would join them.

In Southampton, Berthold was waiting on the pier with Francesco von Mendelssohn. They had come from London in Francesco's bright red convertible. It was a warm, grayish afternoon, the sun breaking from time to time through the fine drizzle. The silvery haze, my emotional hypertension, Francesco's speeding, made everything unreal. Berthold seemed a stranger in this green and well-groomed landscape; the hedges, the parks and the meadows lovely but foreign, much more foreign than America had been years ago. This unexpected strangeness, after having touched the longed-for "holy ground" of Europe, flooded my eyes with tears: blinding and bitter they streamed down my face. Toward evening we arrived at the Dorchester, where Berthold had taken a room for me.

The air in London was suffocating. I took a shower and changed into my lightest summer dress; then joined Berthold and Francesco in the bar.

Although the Mendelssohns, Christians for six generations, were declared "Edel-Arier," Francesco and Eleonora had become voluntary exiles. Francesco maintained that the memory of the Jewish ancestor, the philosopher Moses Mendelssohn, obliged him and Eleonora to abandon the sumptuous Grunewald villa. Eleonora went to Kammer and made it a refuge for her Jewish and Leftist colleagues.

As always Francesco was happy and distressed, enthusiastic and restless. He planned to stage the *Three Penny Opera* in New York. I listened to him, not able to shake off my sadness, my "not belonging," although I was with Berthold. He was glad that at last I was in Europe. When Francesco left us we took a cab to a quiet Italian restaurant in Soho and talked.

He had finished *The Passing of the Third Floor Back*, his second film for British-Gaumont, and was preparing his third, *Cecil Rhodes*. He was much less nervous than a year ago, optimistic and in good spirits. I knew from his letters that he had met an English actress and they had become very close to each other. He described her as a rare person and a remarkable artist. In the years of Berthold's voluntary exile, I had been tortured by the thought of his loneliness. I was relieved that he had found understanding, companionship—love. His sister, the courageous Helen, had immigrated to England, and was working as a dressmaker to support her husband and young daughter.

London was filled with German refugees. Elisabeth Bergner had a sensational success in Margaret Kennedy's *Constant Nymph* and was acclaimed as the second Duse. Fritz Kortner and Johanna Hofer, Oscar Homolka and many others were furiously learning English. However the Allies had permitted the Germans to rebuild their fleet, Mosley and his followers paraded in the streets, and Berthold told me that watching such a demonstration Fritz Kortner had exclaimed: "My next screen test will be in Chinese!" Everyone hoped to go to Hollywood or New York, and was waiting for a visa to the U.S.A.

When Berthold left me, I was seized by an unbearable despair, a hopeless loneliness. I wished I had not come. Had I recklessly challenged fate? *Les absents ont toujours tord.*

Next day Berthold brought C. for lunch. She was distinguished-looking and exceptionally brilliant. She had problems in her work because theater and films in England were just as commercial as in America. I liked her immensely.

Later, in the lobby of the Dorchester, we ran into Max Reinhardt and Helene Thimig, married at last and happy. With them was Dr. Kommer, Reinhardt's pessimistic advisor. Kommer said: "You succeeded where I had failed for eighteen years," meaning that I had persuaded Else to divorce. But I protested. The credit was due to Gottfried and his impassioned pleas.

I also had to give a detailed report on Hollywood to Gottfried's older brother, Wolfgang, and his young wife, Lally. The brothers had a strong resemblance to each other, especially in their voices and the manner of speech. Both were conscious of their Reinhardt charm but Wolfgang used it more sparingly. Lally had left her "Aryan" family to follow him into exile.

It was no comfort to be told that there had never been such an oppressive summer in England. The grass in the parks was burnt and yellow. In her little automobile C. took me to see the historical places, but the sultry city depressed me; I could not breathe and was grateful when she invited me and Berthold to spend the weekend at her house on the Thames. It was a Victorian mansion with a large garden and old trees, going down to the river. Their refreshing coolness brought me back to life.

Berthold decided to show me Paris where I had never been. He wanted to visit all the shrines of the Revolution: from the storming of the Bastille to Napoleon. But Paris was as hot as London and having seen Notre Dame, the Tuilleries, the Cité, Versailles and the Trianon, we postponed our pilgrimage for a cooler season.

Our three days in Paris were friendly and nostalgic. We reminisced about Wychylowka and our trip to Venice; but our personal involvements were not mentioned, until I asked if he wanted a divorce. It would never change our relationship but make it easier for "the others." He objected angrily: "I believe in our marriage as I always have and we will find each other again. I know that we will grow old together."

I don't remember if it was at Brissago or Ascona that my sister was waiting for me. She seemed so unchanged that only after the first excitement had subsided did I notice the fine lines of worry on her dear, lovely face. They confirmed my fear of what life in Germany was like for her. In spite of Josef's deep concern and tenderness, the last two years must have been hell. The two children, Bibi and Michael, were beautiful and unconcerned.

The Gielens had rented a little villa in Porto Ronco and, in a neighboring one, rooms for Mama, Edward and me. Edward had a piano in his. He arrived with Mama the same evening, tired from an exhausting season but hardly changed in appearance. His little Margret was spending the summer with her mother. In the evening after the children had gone to bed, we sat on the veranda of the Gielens' house, as in the good old days, talking until late. Only the topics of our conversation had changed and were neither as abstract nor literary as years ago. Life had dealt us many blows and each of us had scars we tried not to show to the others.

Our youngest brother had stayed at home with Bella to make Mama's trip possible. Mama had aged a lot and did not hear well, but her charm and humor, her temperament and enthusiasm remained indestructible. She told us about her charities, how she went from house to house, shop to shop, begging for money, old clothes and food parcels for the poor. A Polish friend, a Christian, went with her; there was no anti-semitism yet among those in misery. "In a small town like ours, where people have known each other for generations, they don't change so rapidly," Mama told us. Still, the agonizing question: "What will the world do about the Jews . . . will it let Hitler destroy them?" came up again and again.

Mama and the Gielens supported me when I insisted that Edward should emigrate to the States. I was sure that he would have the same recognition there as in Europe, and I offered my help. But he was doubtful: "I am not the kind of virtuoso to have a sure-fire success in America. Of course I can play well," he added, understating as usual, "but I don't have that certain quality necessary for America. No—I am not being negative and it's not lack of courage, when I worry whether I will be able to adapt myself. You have to think soberly and be aware of the fact that my failure or my success will directly affect you. I suppose I would have possibilities as a teacher, though this too would be difficult at the beginning."

I had begged him to come first to Santa Monica with little Margret, live with me and see how his career developed. Of course, it was a crucial decision, to leave Europe and to start all over again. The Academy of Music in Florence had made him an honorary member; he had been offered a master class at the Academy of Vienna, he was giving concerts in London, Paris, Warsaw, Barcelona and Madrid. If it had not been for Hitler his recognition in Europe was assured and general. He told us that he had been invited to Russia for a very well-paid concert tour and to teach a master class in Kiev. Everyone who had been to the U.S.S.R. reported how well the artists were treated. "Alas," Edward sighed, "Russia and the U.S. have one thing in common—their passion for Tchaikowsky's piano concerto in B minor. . . ."

The days were passing much too fast. Sitting in the garden we would listen to Edward's playing, through the open window.

On one especially warm evening I said that it was tantalizing to be so near the glaciers and not to see them. All of us agreed that we were longing for cooler, more invigorating air and I easily persuaded them to make an excursion to the Engadine.

We left the children with Rose's devoted *Mädchen für Alles*, hired a car and drove over the San Bernardino Pass and Via Mala, to St. Moritz. We arrived in Sils Maria in the evening of August 1, the Swiss Day of Independence, and were greeted by bonfires, torchlight parades, singing and dancing in the streets. The full moon hung high over the snow-covered mountain peaks;

they were unbelievably beautiful. We were constantly on the move, picnicking in glades and on rocks, and Mama kept up with us, even on our longest excursions. I had urged Garbo to meet me in Switzerland but she did not dare to move from her hiding place in Sweden, because the reporters were as usual making her life miserable.

Finally I said good-bye to my dear family, promising myself that nothing would make me let seven years go by before we saw each other again. That neither time nor distance had estranged us was movingly confirmed by Edward:

> . . . Sometimes all kinds of reasons prevent us from finding the right words. More than ever we are apprehensive about our fate, and our helplessness to interfere with it. All my life this has distressed me in my relation to those close to me. How much more now after such a long time and under foreign skies. But what binds us, besides our inborn brother and sister love, is this deep "concern of the heart" we have for each other. I want you to know, before you return to America, that for all of us, as far as our emotions are concerned, the seven years of separation were as one day and that—even had it been much longer—we can continue an interrupted sentence without fearing that the other won't understand.
>
> Goodbye, now, my dear heart. I hope this letter will give you lighter and happier thoughts for the crossing. You are taking with you my love and the love of all of us.

Before returning to London I stopped in Paris to say good-bye to Marcel and Juliette Achard, the Feyders and Francesco Mendelssohn. On the Champs Elysées huge posters advertised Emil Jannings in an anti-British film. He was now a *Staatsrat* and most honored artist of the Third Reich. At a dinner party my neighbor exclaimed: "I don't see any reason why one should not work in Germany. The Jewish question concerns only the Jews." I got up and left. Marcel and Francesco followed me. Four years later, after the war broke out and the issue had become not merely a Jewish one, my hosts changed their attitude. During the occupation they went into exile.

The homecoming was glorious. I had been impatiently and lovingly expected and even the studio seemed pleased that I was back. Then the usual troubles began. I had to work with a writer who liked only Westerns and was utterly uninformed about anything that had ever happened in the world. It became obvious to Thalberg that our collaboration was a failure, and he chose his favorite writer and one of the most talented and expensive on the lot to work with me. Donald Ogden Stewart was brilliant and delightfully amusing; so amusing that it was hard to concentrate on work. With the exception of the story we were working on, we had many common interests and even some common idiosyncrasies. But he too had a deep dislike for Napoleon and soon wriggled out of the assignment. For a time I worked alone.

The 1936 presidential election was nearing; the Republicans hoped to overthrow FDR and the New Deal. A group of writers, among them Ernest Vajda, organized the Screen Playwrights to prevent recognition of the Screen Writers' Guild. Oliver became deeply involved in the ensuing fight, also Donald Ogden Stewart. A dedicated anti-Fascist, Don was now the chairman of the Hollywood Anti-Nazi League, which I also joined.

Thalberg did not like the Screen Writers' Guild; writers were not laborers and it was wrong for them to unionize. During our conferences, neglecting Napoleon and Walewska, we discussed politics and socialism which he considered evil. Once I could not resist saying: "What has a man of your talent and energy, Irving, to fear from socialism? With your organizatory ability, your obsession for work, you would always be the head of production and making better and more artistic films, and you wouldn't have to worry about financing."

He stared at me as if I were delirious. Then he began to relate his day from ten in the morning until eleven at night. The rushes —the story conferences—the consultations with the directors, the music department, the set builders and costumers—the telephone calls to China about the locust sequence in *Good Earth*, his talks with Paris to secure Charles Boyer. Then, having described his global activities he indignantly concluded: "All that I should do for five hundred dollars a week?" We burst out laughing.

Another interesting meeting occurred at that time. Having listened to the Sunday afternoon Philharmonic concert from New York, at which Schoenberg's *Transfigured Night* (*Verklärte Nacht*) was performed, Thalberg decided that Schoenberg was the man to write the score for *Good Earth*. Next day the producer Albert Lewin came to my office and asked if I could talk to Schoenberg. I explained that long ago Schoenberg had given up the style of *Transfigured Night* and had been composing twelve-tone music, which I doubted Irving would like. However, I promised to do my best to arrange a meeting. I knew that Schoenberg was having a hard time; he was giving lessons, which took many hours from his own work. I asked him if he would be interested in doing the scoring of *Good Earth*.

"How much would they pay?"

"Around twenty-five thousand dollars, I suppose."

I warned him that even if Thalberg wanted a composer of his stature there was no guarantee that he would not interfere. The offer was only worth considering if the twenty-five thousand would free them from financial worry.

A lot of protocol went on before the meeting was arranged and a studio car sent for the Schoenbergs. Thalberg promised me not to keep the great man waiting and he was in his office at 3 P.M. sharp. He wanted me to be present to translate in case there were any linguistic difficulties. At 3:30 there was still no sign of the Schoenbergs. Thalberg got impatient; the secretaries rang the house but were told that Mr. and Mrs. Schoenberg had left hours ago. Suddenly a man, who had been quietly waiting in the hall, approached the desk and said that he was Dr. So-and-So from Bad Nauheim, and that Mr. Thalberg had offered to show him the stages. He was waiting to be picked up by the studio car, but he suspected it was driving Mr. Schoenberg around the lot. Frantic telephoning stopped the tour and the Schoenbergs were brought to the office. Schoenberg had found it perfectly reasonable that he should be shown around the studio before deciding to work there.

We sat down in front of Thalberg's desk, Schoenberg refusing to part with his umbrella in case he forgot it on leaving.

I still see him before me, leaning forward in his chair, both hands clasped over the handle of the umbrella, his burning, genius's eyes on Thalberg, who, standing behind his desk, was explaining why he wanted a great composer for the scoring of the *Good Earth*. When he came to: "Last Sunday when I heard the lovely music you have written. . . ." Schoenberg interrupted sharply: "I don't write 'lovely' music."

Thalberg looked baffled, then smiled and explained what he meant by "lovely music." It had to have Chinese themes, and, as the people in the film were peasants, there was not much dialogue but a lot of action. For example, there were scenes like that where the locusts eat all the grain in the fields which needed special scoring, and so on. I translated what Thalberg said into German, but Schoenberg interrupted me. He understood everything, and in a surprisingly literary though faulty English, he conveyed what he thought in general of music in films: that it was simply terrible.

The whole handling of sound was incredibly bad, meaningless, numbing all expression; the leveling monotony of the dialogue was unbearable. He had read the *Good Earth* and he would not undertake the assignment unless he was given complete control over the sound, including the spoken words.

"What do you mean by complete control?" asked Thalberg, incredulously.

"I mean that I would have to work with the actors," answered Schoenberg. "They would have to speak in the same pitch and key as I compose it in. It would be similar to 'Pierrot Lunaire' but, of course, less difficult." He turned to me and asked if I remembered some verses of the Pierrot and would I speak them. I remembered very well: "*Der Mond, den man mit Augen trinkt. . . .*" ("*Augen*" high and long.) I reproduced it quite faithfully, watching Thalberg's face. He must have been visualizing Luise Rainer and Paul Muni singing their lines in a similar key. But he did not move a muscle of his face. "Well, Mr. Schoenberg," he said, "the director and I have different ideas and they may contradict yours. You see, the director wants to handle the actors himself."

"He could do that after they have studied their lines with me," offered Schoenberg magnanimously.

I thought that this would put an end to the conference, but Thalberg was fascinated by Schoenberg and asked him to read the screenplay of *Good Earth*. If he found some additional scenes, which he thought needed special music, he would like to hear his suggestions. Schoenberg took the script and he and his wife left.

After a pause Thalberg said: "This is a remarkable man. And once he learns about film scoring and starts working in the studio he'll realize that this is not like writing an opera."

"You are mistaken, Irving," I said. "He'll invent a revolutionary kind of scoring."

"He'll write the music on my terms, you'll see."

Next morning Trude Schoenberg telephoned me that the price of prostitution had doubled. For his complete control of the film, including the dialogue, Schoenberg was asking fifty thousand, otherwise it was not worth his time and effort. When I related this to Thalberg he shrugged and said that meanwhile the Chinese technical advisor had brought some folk songs which had inspired the head of the sound department to write some very lovely music.

Discussing the incident a few days later Schoenberg said to me: "*Komponiern heisst einen Blick in die Zukunft des Themas werfen.*" ("To compose means to look into the future of the theme.") I was very moved by these words.

The endless waiting for conferences, the lack of interest of my collaborators, who would not work as long as Irving was engrossed in something else, was undermining my morale. Wolfgang Reinhardt, sensitive and unassertive, had landed in Hollywood and got a job as Thalberg's assistant. He also was sitting around waiting. We spent many miserable hours talking about the hopelessness of the world and life in general.

"How could all this happen," I wrote to Berthold. "Why did we let it come to this senseless separation? Why can't we recapture our former life? I cannot bear any longer explaining to people why Napoleon did not marry Marie Walewska. Gottfried says that I am dramatizing myself. I know I have to pull myself together."

30

MY BROTHER-IN-LAW HAD a three year contract with the Berlin Opera House, but our meeting in Switzerland put an end to the forbearance of the Berlin authorities and he was peremptorily dismissed. Luckily he was immediately offered a contract with the Burgtheater in Vienna, which for the time being gave him and Rose a respite from Hitlerism. It was a great relief for me to know that they were out of hell and we could write to each other openly. Also to my great joy Edward gave in to my persuasions to emigrate with his daughter to the States.

They arrived in June 1936. Our neighbor across the street had a room with a piano, which I rented so that he could compose and practice undisturbed. I had rebuilt the garage, adding a room and bath for Peter, who longed to have separate quarters.

It was nice to have a girl in the family. Margret and Thomas were a few weeks apart in age and although he had forgotten his German and she had only a smattering of English, they established a friendly contact much more quickly than expected. She was a gifted child, quite extraordinary, musical and sensitive, but high-strung and used to being the center of attention. Edward adored her blindly. I was worried that it would be difficult for Margret to adjust to a predominately male family but she easily accepted with restrained graciousness the role of an only daughter. After a long, hard season, Edward was glad to rest for a few weeks. He had played two concerts in London and had seen Berthold, who was editing his film *Cecil Rhodes*. This and the perennial negotiations with Korda were delaying his homecoming.

Happy about Edward's arrival, Schoenberg was making plans for recitals, and Otto Klemperer invited him to play Beethoven's First Piano Concerto in the Hollywood Bowl. He introduced him to Mrs. Irish, chairman of the Los Angeles Philharmonic Society, and she asked Edward and me to lunch. I was surprised at how well Edward spoke English. The first thing Mrs. Irish said was that they needed publicity photographs and she suggested that he pose in a white apron and chef's cap, cooking spaghetti. "But I am not opening a restaurant," Edward defended himself.

"Musicians like to cook," declared Mrs. Irish. "The public identifies them. . . ."

". . . . with spaghetti!?" he interrupted, amazed.

But even without the spaghetti photo, his appearance in the Bowl was a success, and Klemperer engaged him to play another concert with the Philharmonic during the winter season. However, there were not many people interested in modern music in Los Angeles, nor advanced pupils to teach. His friends were in New York or still in Europe; there were not many people he liked to see, with the exception of the Polish musician Bronislaw Kaper, and Gottfried and Wolfgang Reinhardt. The latter were good chess players and so was Edward, who, as my mother used to say, had inherited this talent from our brilliant great-grandfather. Gradually Edward prepared to move to New York. Hollywood was a movie town and neither San Francisco nor Los Angeles showed any promise for him. For the children Santa Monica was Paradise. I knew this from my sons and now I saw it in Margret's ready acceptance of the great freedom and easy comradeship.

While I was explaining to "the best MGM minds" the partition of Poland and what Napoleon was doing in Warsaw in the year 1807, George Cukor was directing Garbo in *Camille*. Not often have I seen her as happy, glowing and inspired. I had told her what a profound impression Sarah Bernhardt had made upon me when I was a young girl and she could not hear enough about it.

Finally Thalberg, who still believed in *Marie Walewska*, called Sam Behrman to write the screenplay with me, and my hopes and spirits soared high, not only for the film but also for my own morale.

Sam arrived, as dear and whimsical as ever, and in spite of the Spanish Civil War, which broke out in July, Hitler's threats, and the appeasement policy of England and France, we finished in a reasonably short time a very good screenplay.

The Hollywood Anti-Nazi League had been founded by Prince Hubert von und zu Loewenstein, a progressive Catholic; a Mr. Breda who turned out to be no other than the Otto Katz whom we had known in Berlin as a communist; Rupert Hughes, a Republican; Eddie Cantor, one of the most popular stars; several studio executives, and, as I mentioned before, Donald Ogden Stewart, who was also the chairman. Breda traveled back and forth and appeared only sporadically. The members paid their dues and very little was going on, until one day Ernst Lubitsch told me that he was withdrawing from the Anti-Nazi League because it was dominated by communists. He advised me to do the same. I begged him to reconsider. After all, the Prince was certainly not a socialist, Breda was back in Germany risking his life and the Popular Front was the only way to fight Fascism.

"I know it from a reliable source that the Reds are controlling the Anti-Nazi League," insisted Lubitsch, and he mentioned a few names which made me laugh.

"But Ernst," I said, "what all these people do is sit around their swimming pools, drinking highballs and talking about movies, while the wives complain about their Filipino butlers."

"I am only warning you," he said. "I am getting out."

"And I am staying."

The difference in our beliefs never influenced our friendship.

The Popular Front extended into my family: Berthold had his own personal kind of socialism, Peter was a New Dealer, I was a "premature anti-Fascist," Thomas a Democrat and Hans a Trotskyite. The latter was in love with an attractive girl from a Mormon family, a few years older than he. She had embraced Trotskyism as her religion, clinging to it with the same fanaticism as her ancestors had clung to the Bible. Hans, who had been reading Lenin and Das Kapital instead of doing his homework, surprised me by graduating from high school and entered an extension course at the University of California in Berkeley. So far he seemed to be doing quite well, in spite of the news of the Moscow trials, with their inexplicable confessions and horrifying executions, and the growing Stalin terror. These were the days of meetings, and wherever one went one could be sure that a small group of girls and young men in blue jeans would be standing outside a hall or a theater, distributing leaflets which denounced Stalin and the tactics of the Communist Party. Often they were insulted and beaten up.

More than a year after my trip to Europe Berthold returned to Santa Monica. The boys were happy to have him back, especially Thomas. The big ones, though they loved him dearly, had their girls and their own problems and were not always available when, in the few short months of his stay, he wanted to transform them into Europeans. He was tense and unhappy because he missed C. and had not secured another film assignment, but he wrote wonderful poetry and, all in all, seemed in a much more conciliatory mood than on his previous visits. As always he enjoyed the beach, the conversations with Edward, visits with Bruno and Liesl Frank and Fred Zinnemann, who meanwhile had married a tall, blond and handsome English girl named Renée.

In September Hans went to study in Berkeley, and on the first free weekend, Peter and I decided to drive "up north" to find out how he was doing. I enormously enjoyed this excursion and the Sunday with my "big" sons. On the way home the car broke down and we had to stop overnight. Next morning as we were having coffee in a drugstore, we saw the newspaper with the headline: IRVING THALBERG DIES AT 37.

Only a few days before, Sam and I had finished our screenplay and we had talked to him. He was in a good mood, very pleased with the rushes of Camille. In the last months Greta and I had often mentioned how much happier he seemed. After my first clash with him about Queen Christina we had got along well and he had been always very cordial toward me. I felt terribly sad. His children were so small that they would not remember him.

It seemed likely that one of Thalberg's close associates would take over the production of Marie Walewska, and the heads of MGM wanted Garbo to express her preference. She did not know the new producers and left the decision to L. B. Mayer and Mannix, who in turn did not see eye to eye in the matter. Finally, as I remember, Mannix suggested Bernie Hyman.

Gottfried Reinhardt had been Hyman's assistant and had often told me that there was no nicer and more decent person on the MGM lot than Bernie, a close friend of Thalberg. Greta and I had lunch with him and she found him pleasant and sympathetic, but the question whether he was the right producer for our film remained unanswered. Again Clarence Brown, a veteran of Garbo films, had been assigned to direct her. Neither he nor Hyman had read the screenplay. Sam Behrman was on the verge of leaving, and told me, when I implored him to wait another week, that I had still not learned my Hollywood lesson—and if the studio wanted him they knew his New York telephone number. Still, he promised me to stay two more days. When I called him in the evening the hotel clerk said that Mr. Behrman had checked out.

Sam had been right: I had not learned my Hollywood lesson. Hyman was an important producer, who only approved screenplays he himself had supervised, and he disliked ours heartily. His great success had been *San Francisco*, in which the earthquake was a magnificent achievement of the "special effects" department. He was very sentimental, extremely kind and rather endearing; if it had not been for that, I could not have survived his indecision and endless procrastination. To some extent, because Hyman listened to him, Gottfried was helpful in preventing a disaster.

After several weeks of complete idleness, which could have been excused as mourning for Thalberg and reorganization in the studio but which were merely an inexcusable waste of time, Bernie told me that although he liked the story he did not like my and Behrman's script and wanted it completely rewritten. "Without me!" I exclaimed, but he did not want to hear of it. My resignation would be most disloyal to the film and to Garbo. After all, it had been my idea.

"What do you think of Sam Hoffenstein?" he asked.

"Very highly. I love his poetry."

"He is reading your and Behrman's script."

A few hours later Hoffenstein burst in to my office waving the blue-bound script and shouting: "This is the best screenplay I've ever read. It's brilliant—I could not put it down! Congratulations! Where is Behrman? I must send him a telegram."

Gottfried heard his shouting and came in. Hoffenstein repeated what he had said to me, adding more flattering adjectives and suggesting that we all go to Hyman. We had to tell him that not a word of the screenplay should be changed. I said that as I was involved it would be much better if he and Gottfried went alone. Ten minutes later Goldie, Hyman's blond secretary, called and said I should come to his office.

Bernie was sitting behind his desk, two girls in white uniforms attending to him, one to give him a manicure, the other a scalp treatment. He looked gloomy: "Sam says he likes the script as it is." Not reacting to Bernie's statement, I asked the girl who was rubbing his scalp if she could grow hair on bald spots. "Positively, yes," she said. Bernie, now more cheerful, launched into a long explanation. He had not said "Positively no." He admitted that there were some good scenes and lines in the script, but it had "no heart." It was sophisticated and cold. It did not make you cry. When "that man" was all alone on St. Helena—he meant Elba —waiting for "his Empress," and Marie arrived instead of her, "this should bring tears into everyone's eyes." I said that what we wanted to show was Napoleon's growing megalomania, his ruthless use of the Polish Legions without any intention of restituting their country, and Marie's disillusionment with the man she worshiped, her realization that he was an egotistical monster but whom she could not cease loving.

"If you want to feel sorry for Napoleon then let Garbo play him," suggested Hoffenstein. But Bernie said sternly: "I want this film to be the best Garbo ever made," and went off to lunch in the executive dining room.

Hoffenstein, Gottfried and I left the studio and drove to the "Little Gipsy," a Hungarian restaurant on Sunset Boulevard. After two martinis we felt much better and were more inclined to listen to Gottfried's analysis of Bernie's psyche. There was no. use resisting: the script would be rewritten even if William Shakespeare had been its author. It was imperative for Bernie's ego to start from scratch, because that way he could get used to the story and the characters, and this always took a great length of time. "For you Sam and Salka," he went on, "it will be leisurely work, pleasant, because you like each other and Bernie is a nice man. I am sure that you can save many scenes from the Behrman script, as in the course of time Bernie will become convinced that everything has been invented under his guidance. This may seem cynical to you and a waste of money, but that's not your responsibility. The more Bernie spends, the closer he is to becoming an executive. On the other hand, if you refuse the assignment, somebody else, much less scrupulous, will tear down Behrman's and Salka's script, and suggest another story, which Garbo will reject, and we'll have to start all over again!"

"Gottfried is right," said Hoffenstein and called for the wine list.

The Falange had split Spain in half. With the exception of a few calcified reactionaries, Hollywood was passionately on the side of the Loyalists and contributed thousands and thousands of dollars for ambulances, food, medicines and clothes. Ernest Hemingway, Vincent Sheehan, André Malraux and Ludwig Renn came to speak for Spain and crowds gathered in huge auditoriums to cheer them.

Before Malraux addressed a mass meeting in the Shrine Auditorium he was to speak at a few private gatherings. I gave a party for him, asking about fifty people, but twice as many came, anxious to meet him. He was tall, thin, his sensitive handsome face sometimes distorted by a nervous tic. He had as his interpreter Haakon Chevalier, a professor of Romance languages at the University of Stanford, who had translated Malraux's novels into English. (Several years later Chevalier had to pay dearly for his friendship with J. R. Oppenheimer of atom-bomb fame.) Berthold, home from his Gaumont-British work, introduced both men. Standing in front of the fireplace, Malraux urgently and passionately asked for help for the heroic struggle of the Loyalists and told about the great support Franco was getting from Hitler and Mussolini. His speech made such an impression that my guests contributed around five thousand dollars.

Next night, in the Shrine Auditorium which was packed to the last standing place, Malraux and Chevalier by their French-English duet carried away an audience of stars, producers, writers, doctors, lawyers, teachers, shop clerks, workers from the studios, the Douglas and Lockheed factories, and practically every German refugee in Los Angeles. Donald Ogden Stewart made a brilliant collection speech, which brought in a large amount of money. At the end Malraux thanked the cheering crowd, raising his fist in the communist salute. I turned around to see the effect and to my amazement saw ladies in mink rising and clenching their bejeweled hands.

Hemingway and Joris Ivens, producer and director of documentary films, were touring the States showing *The Spanish Earth* to compassionate, generous masses. Fifteen Hollywood stars gave a thousand dollars each for ambulances and medicine.

The rewriting of *Marie Walewska* became first a small, then a huge nightmare, but it cemented my friendship with Samuel Hoffenstein. Often I wondered how this Chassidic soul landed in Hollywood, but he made a lot of money. Hoffenstein's two volumes of verse, one called *In Praise of Practically Nothing*, had had great success and become very popular. Today, I am afraid, not many people remember them. Expressing himself in exquisite English, slightly tinged with an Irish brogue, he would surprise one by bursting into a Yiddish song or *Kol Nidre* and other Hebrew prayers. When intoxicated, he would improvise for hours in verse which, unfortunately, he forgot next day.

The filming of *Walewska* started before the script was finished, which gave our producer the chance to interfere and create dissent between the director and the writers. During the whole of *Anna*

Karenina Clarence Brown could not have been nicer to work with. Although not the most sensitive judge of a script, he was inventive on the stage, an excellent technician and competent in handling the actors. Napoleon and Marie went much against his grain, and we had to fight on two fronts. The one was Bernie's sentimentality and his addiction for ending each line of dialogue with a question: "You must be tired, aren't you?" "We love each other, don't we?" "It's a lovely day, isn't it?" (I am improvising the lines, as the script is MGM property.) The second was Brown's disgruntled obstructionism against the screenplay.

The film, released as *Conquest* in America, was more than three months behind schedule, cost several million dollars and was an exhausting experience for everyone, especially for Garbo and Boyer, who patiently suffered to the very end (although at doubled salaries). Thanks to Gottfried, Hoffenstein and I had a small victory; several scenes of the Behrman script were incorporated in the final version. But we also suffered a major defeat: Bernie found that the last farewell between Marie and Napoleon, before he boarded the *Bellerophon*, was not heartbreaking enough and as Hoffenstein and I were incapable of providing the right kind of "uplifting lines" he had asked Charles MacArthur to write another ending for the retakes. Of course we hated it.

In 1963 I saw *Marie Walewska* in London at a Garbo festival and I was surprised at how much better the film was than I remembered and how much the audience loved it.

Else Reinhardt, Gottfried's mother, was about to engage a German housekeeper and asked me to come and assist at the interview. I promised to stop by on my way to the studio. When I arrived she met me in the hall and informed me in a stage whisper: "*Nichts für mich!*" The woman was a refugee and educated; it would be embarrassing to have her eat in the kitchen. However, I should take a look at her. Frau Hardt was a pleasant-looking woman with a trim figure and very straight posture, her short hair prematurely white. I could see by the ironical expression of her blue eyes that she had heard every word Else had "whispered."

I knew that Garbo was looking for someone reliable to keep house for her and to ward off intruders and reporters. Having talked for a while to Frau Hardt it occurred to me that she would be right for the job. I asked her if she knew how to drive. "Of course. I drove from Berlin to Barcelona, beating the Nazis who chased me to the Dutch border." I invited her to come in the afternoon to my house and tell me more about herself.

She told me that she had been an executive-secretary in a publishing house in Berlin which her friend Annie von Bucovitch had inherited from her Jewish father. In 1933 the Nazis dispossessed her but offered Etta the management of the business, which she refused. Then, at great risk, she concealed a few thousand dollars, said farewell to her fatherland, and drove with Annie to Spain. They settled in Tossa near Barcelona, where they opened a boutique until the Civil War forced them to leave.

"We had," concluded Etta, "just enough money to take a very slow boat through the Panama Canal. As we were nearing Los Angeles I said to Annie: 'Let's not worry. I can always get a job as a maid for a movie star: Greta Garbo perhaps.'"

Just then Greta came in as if on cue and Etta stared at her as if she were an apparition. Later, having worked for Greta almost a year, Etta joined our household as my secretary, sharing the love of my Irish setters and untangling their silky coats, as well as my disturbing finances.

Annie von Bucovitch, Etta's friend and ex-employer, also faced the hardships of exile courageously. Raised in luxury and extravagance she worked, for very little money, in George Antheil's art gallery—a vain cultural effort for Los Angeles—in an antique store, and at the Warner Brothers' studio.

There were other refugees who arrived under more pleasant circumstances. Bruno Frank, the distinguished German novelist, had signed a contract with Metro. In 1933 he and his wife Liesl had moved to London, where they became great friends with Berthold. Liesl, young and pretty, with slant green eyes, was the only daughter of Fritzi Massary, the famous star of German musical comedy. They were well off, Bruno handsomely paid by MGM. Liesl, compassionate and warm-hearted, tried to help the refugees. With admirable energy and persistence she and Charlotte Dieterle founded the European Film Fund. All Europeans who had jobs in the studio gave one percent of their weekly salaries to the Fund. American writers, among them Dorothy Parker, Anita Loos, Alan Campbell, Samuel Hoffenstein, Sam N. Behrman, Donald Ogden Stewart, Herman and Joseph Mankiewicz, and others contributed. And after the war broke out they were also most generous in giving affidavits.

After *Conquest* was previewed Bernie told me to think about another story for Garbo.

"Only keep away from historical topics," warned Gottfried, "and convince Garbo to do a comedy for once." He was thinking of a story the Hungarian dramatist Melchior Lengyel had shown him. Lengyel was the author of *Czarina*, which for years had been played everywhere, and I cannot remember how many versions of it were sold to the movies. Always smiling, Lengyel would come to the studio with ideas and stories which he told very amusingly, in an absurdly concocted Hungarian English. The one Gottfried and Bernie Hyman liked best was *Ninotchka*, and the studio bought it.

Meanwhile I had read the biography of Marie Curie written by her daughter, Eve, and I thought that it would make a wonderful film for Garbo. When I told Bernie he looked aghast: "What makes you think Garbo will be interested in *that?*"

"I am certain she will." And as Greta was in Sweden I added: "Please let me send her a cable!"

He shrugged. "She's never heard of Marie Curie!"

Next morning came Garbo's answer: "Love to play Marie Curie. Could not think of anything better."

Since *Queen Christina* she had not expressed herself so positively and directly.

"You are incorrigible," sighed Gottfried, who was working on *Ninotchka*, and had persuaded Sam Behrman to write the screenplay.

"We will have two scripts ready when Garbo comes back," commented Bernie with reckless optimism.

Gottfried was now a full-fledged producer, though still under Bernie's executive thumb. Once more MGM had reorganized itself, nominating four Field Marshals, one of them Bernie, to command the lesser Generals of production. The only advantage of this reshuffle was that Bernie did not interfere during the writing of screenplays, only later after they were finished. The *Marie Curie* project had not been assigned to a producer. My suggestion of buying the book had upset the story department. Miss Corbeley, its head, had read the proofs and was convinced that none of the MGM stars would want to play a scientist. But Universal Studios bought it for Irene Dunne. As soon as Bernie heard of this, he moved heaven and earth to retrieve the rights from them. A deal was made: to get *Marie Curie* MGM had to buy some less desirable properties and paid two hundred and fifty thousand dollars—at that time an enormous sum—and Bernie decided I should write the treatment under his personal supervision. This meant endless waiting while he "familiarized" himself with the contents of the book, and constant interruptions by telephone calls. Luckily Mrs. Hyman had read *Marie Curie* and loved it.

I began to acquire a great deal of information about Polonium, Radium, radio-activity and the atom. Belatedly trying to correct my ignorance, I read scientific books, which fascinated me, especially Bertrand Russell's. "I have been an idiot," I would say. "Why did I not study physics instead of wasting my time in the German theater?" Berthold considered these remarks treason to our past. Now he was spending his summers in Santa Monica, always staying longer than he intended, annoyed that we were "never alone" and that it was "impossible to talk to each other."

31

I MET ALDOUS AND MARIA HUXLEY at the house of Anita Loos, the author of *Gentlemen Prefer Blondes*. Extremely tall and thin, his distinguished head with its soft brown hair bent forward, Huxley listened to people with an absent expression in his strange eyes. This expression remained also when he told amusing anecdotes (most of them very funny), and was probably caused by his eye trouble. His wife was slender and dark, not beautiful, with her sharp features, but interesting. She was a Belgian, and spoke with a strong French accent. They had a son, who was in school abroad. She told me that they both greatly admired Garbo.

A few days later Huxley and I were asked to lunch with George Cukor at Bernie Hyman's beach house. The table was set near the swimming pool and the absence of the hostess indicated that this was a business and not a social occasion. We sat down and Bernie asked Cukor to tell Mr. Huxley "how we see the Curie film." It was obvious that because of his success with *Camille*, Cukor was being chosen to direct *Marie Curie*. He had suggested that Huxley write the screenplay, but had no idea how Bernie saw the film. After a few rather vague sentences he interrupted himself: "It is much more important to hear what Mr. Huxley thinks about the idea."

Huxley said that he did not go much to the movies but that he was very much in favor of a film about the Curies. The discovery of radium was very photogenic and dramatic: the glowing glass tubes, the dark shack. . . "That's what Salka has been saying," said Bernie, disappointed. He wanted Huxley's "own approach to the material" and it did not have to be a scenario, just a narrative. He liked the love story but had found many of the incidents very dull and asked me to remind him which incidents these were; but when I started he was called to the telephone, and as Cukor also had to leave, Huxley and I decided to take a brief walk on the beach.

"You see," I shouted over the roar of the incoming tide, "the greatest problem is that Bernie does not understand the complete disinterest of the Curies in fame and personal profit. Poor as they were they refused one million dollars to patent their discovery. Now, how could they?" Huxley laughed: "Of course, this does not make sense!"

"My great hope is," I went on, "that you will compel Bernie to curb his imagination and stick to facts." Bernie returned and Huxley promised to write a treatment. Later Maria told me that the studio had paid him twenty-five thousand. . . . It was the same sum Thalberg offered Schoenberg for the scoring of *The Good Earth*.

I asked Bernie what I should do during the time Huxley was writing the treatment. I did not want to sit in my office twiddling my thumbs, and I felt that this was the right moment to ask for another assignment, which would relieve me for a while from the responsibilities of being a "Garbo specialist." I had read in a newspaper that a British destroyer had picked up, in stormy seas, thirty shipwrecked Spanish orphans, three nuns and two pregnant women. I had a very clear idea what kind of film this newspaper item, developed into a story, could make. William Dieterle was directing a Spanish Civil War film for Walter Wanger, so I did not feel too hopeless about my project.

When I told Bernie the story and said: "Orphans of the Spanish war," he sent me to a young producer, Frank Davis, the only one at Metro who would be interested. However, he warned me that as it had no big parts for stars the film would end up as a "B" picture. Nevertheless, Frank was all for it. Calm and practical, he was not swayed by optimism, but could be very persistent. The film had to show the suffering civil war inflicted.

For a while life and work went on quite happily, or at least, it seemed so.

A rich patron of music had invited Edward that summer to the Bohemian Grove in the Redwoods of northern California, a very exclusive Republican club whose members were all multimillionaires. He accepted only because his admirer assured him that such contacts were of utmost importance for his American career and one could not refuse. First he gave a concert in Carmel, then went to the Grove. From there he wrote me:

> . . . You've heard about Carmel. I read one notice (on the front page!) which seems almost *too* favorable. Still, everything went very well and they want me back for a recital of modern music. Now I am here in this "Grove" experiencing "*ein englisches Leben*" more in the sense of Great Britain than in *Des Knaben Wunderhorn* ("*englisch*" meaning also "angelic" in German). It is quite a shock to see these old men, the American variations on the theme of Dr. Mandl, wandering around and with a boyish predilection to piss on the thousand-year-old trees, saying "This truly is living in nature." Every second person explains to you at full length the profound "idea" of the Grove, which simply consists of the psychoanalytically complicated urge to escape from the spouse, drinking and a wild indulgence in dilettantism. I would have preferred to spend a week in a Trappist monastery, but I am afraid I have to stay here. The gentlemen were outraged when I said I would leave on the 27th. Once they capture an artist they hold on to him. They seemed deeply offended and my friend, Mr. L., explained in a long speech that "honoring" me to such an extent, the club expects me to participate in the great concert on Friday. The baritone Thomas from the Metropolitan Opera (an excellent singer) will also appear. And Saturday I *must* see "the Grove play," which is being intensively rehearsed and according to L., will be first: an unforgettable event; second: of greatest importance," because "all those who have power and money in the state will be present." It is true that from the ex-President, Herbert Hoover, the least person one encounters is a president of a railroad company. I don't know if such connections are really important, but as I am already here it is simply logical to stay. After all, Gulliver lived longer than three days with all kinds of peoples.

The week in the millionaires' Grove convinced Gulliver that social life and entertaining the rich was incompatible with his temperament and that he had to find a more dedicated musical following. He decided to go to New York or Chicago, preferably New York, where he would have contact with modern composers and where many of his former pupils and colleagues had settled. Sadly I realized that he was right. Margret stayed with us. Children adjust themselves quickly. Her friendship with Thomas and the certainty that her father would be back on holidays, reconciled her to the temporary separation.

Hans returned from Berkeley and enrolled at U.C.L.A., but I found out that he was not attending classes and spending most of his time in political discussions at the campus cafeteria. It also became increasingly noticeable that his hearing was impaired, which may have been one of his reasons for not following lectures. To me his affliction seemed an intolerable injustice. That this sensitive and brilliant boy should suddenly be isolated, deprived of normal contact with others, inhibited in the choice of his profession, was a blow which hit me harder than him. The doctors could only give it a name. They called it "otosclerosis," adding that it appeared during or after puberty and that twenty-five million people in the United States were hard of hearing. Statistics were no comfort. We were advised to consult a specialist in New York, and Edward suggested that Hans stay with him and continue his studies while he was undergoing treatments. I accepted gratefully, but cold, noisy and dirty New York was not a place to appeal to a young Californian. Hans came back home and we found a wonderful, dedicated man, Dr. Guggenheim, who took a great interest in his case and improved his hearing, although he was not able to restore it.

Peter was seventeen years old when he graduated from high school and insisted upon going to an eastern college. He was accepted at Dartmouth, but like Hans could not stand the East for longer than three months. He returned and enrolled at U.C.L.A., much more appreciative of old, lovely Santa Monica than he had been before. From time to time he threatened to give up his studies and get a job. I opposed it, convinced that my sons should get college educations as long as I could afford it. In his first attempt at financial independence, during the summer vacation, Peter became a filing clerk in the story department at David Selznick's studio. His boss, Val Lewton, told me later that it took him weeks to put the filing system back in order.

Before all these happenings, Aldous Huxley had finished the treatment of the Curie film and delivered it. It was instantly forgotten. *Ninotchka* had been pushed forward on the production schedule, but progressed at the usual leisurely pace caused by the chronic "recession." Bernie could not make up his mind who should direct it. Sam Behrman refused to stay in Hollywood and lucky Gottfried was sent to New York to work there with him.

Bruno Frank had been given my notes concerning the Curie film. He agreed with them but declined a collaboration because he preferred to write his treatment alone. I was surprised that no one mentioned the Huxley script, and on the next occasion, I asked Bernie what happened to it. Embarrassed, he admitted that he had had no time to read it but had given it to Goldie, his secretary, who told him "it stinks." As I did not share his faith in Goldie's judgment I asked him to show me the script, but days went by and I never received it.

Bruno Frank remained seven months on the assignment, then abruptly left MGM. Sidney Franklin took over the production and hired Scott Fitzgerald to write the screenplay. I hoped that at last somebody would be interested in what Huxley had done.

I had finished the outline of *The Cargo of Innocence* as my story was called, and was writing the screenplay with James Hilton. His literary standing and high salary guaranteed to some extent that the studio intended to produce the film. However by this time, the United States, England and France had abandoned Spain to her tragic fate, and our script was "temporarily" shelved. The activities for the Loyalist cause went on and I gave another party, this time for Ludwig Renn who movingly appealed to the conscience of the liberals. Again we collected some money, but much less than before. Hans's Trotskyite friends, forgetting their own disruptive activities in Spain, heckled Renn and accused the communists of breaking the socialist solidarity. And so the disintegration of the Popular Front continued, even on Mabery Road.

Like Ariadne's thread, the work on *Marie Curie* was running through the labyrinth of my life, dangling before me, incessantly interrupted, exasperatingly close to my grasp, then suddenly disappearing. Months went by . . . the Hitler menace grew.

I had breathed more freely after the Gielens had moved to Vienna; then the annexation of Austria endangered them again. All direct contact between us ceased.

I had applied for a Quota for my mother, besides collecting affidavits for others who were trying to escape from Vienna and Prague. Ludwig went to London. Karl Kraus had died before the holocaust he had predicted came true. Dorothy Parker, Herman Mankiewicz, Don Stewart, Miriam Hopkins, Sam Hoffenstein generously guaranteed with their bank accounts that none of my protégés would become a financial burden to the United States and I am happy to say that none ever did. It was impressive to see how rapidly men and women, who never before had worked with their hands, became "proletarians." That dramatists and journalists were drawn to Hollywood was obvious; American universities and colleges invited scientists, musicians and artists; doctors established themselves after miraculously passing exams in English; new Viennese restaurants and delicatessens flourished.

The occupation of Austria ended Max Reinhardt's European enterprises. Goering moved into Schloss Leopoldskron in Salzburg and the expropriated Reinhardt took a house on Pacific Palisades. He bore the loss of his theatrical empire with great dignity and opened a dramatic school on Sunset Boulevard. There he and Helene Thimig staged plays with inexperienced beginners unaware of the artistic importance of their master.

Max Reinhardt had a great liking for Hans and asked him to be his assistant and *dramaturg*. As Hans did not show any intention of continuing his studies, I was delighted that the Reinhardt school would give him the chance to prove himself, and that the theater was a stronger attraction than politics. The school slowly transformed itself into a theater, but its most talented pupils were immediately absorbed by the film industry. From London, Berthold wrote:

> As always, I forgot your birthday; not even these times make me conscious of time. Of course, your and the boys' letters arrived punctually on the *28th*, also the money. It was a beautiful birthday for me. I would have loved to have your photo. I don't have a good one and also the boys have changed. In the photos I have, they are so much younger.
>
> Now bulletins from the battlefield: my sister Paula is in a panic, she has to get out of Vienna. They dragged her to the barracks and made her scrub floors, wash dishes, make beds for the S.S., etc., etc. They jeered at her and she had to look on while they were beating an old Jew. She has written to you asking for an affidavit. Can you do it? Rose cannot write to you. Josef is constantly watched because of us, although he himself has been quite unpolitical. Kleiber engaged him to stage operas for a South American tournée. If only they could get out! Jacob Hegener * arrived emaciated after

* Berthold's publisher.

eight weeks in a Gestapo prison, also his seventeen-year-old daughter. Camil Hoffmann helped to free them through some foreign Embassy. The Jews don't arouse compassion in the world. Here in England an incredible indifference. Some papers are openly anti-semitic. Only the Quakers perform miracles of helpfulness.

Have my friends Christopher Isherwood and Wynstan Auden arrived in Santa Monica? As you remember, Christopher wrote the screen-play for Little Friend. Auden is a poet of great power; Isherwood one of the finest and most original writers. He observes very sharply, behind his mask of boyish charm. He lived in Berlin and speaks German. I find his Berlin Diary a stylistic masterpiece, the humor is quite devilish. You will like him. . . .

Do you remember how Edward had only one pupil in Hollywood? The same is with me—I am directing a one-act play with one actress, which will play only one night.

After Munich:

. . . It's just as well. My own feeling is that we are in a trap. . . . The war preparations here were pitiful. Everybody got a gas mask, they evacuated the children, and the rich people moved to the country. Had England fought I would have offered her my cadaver plus brain. Willi also volunteered his services. But when Chamberlain returned, Armistice Day scenes took place in the streets. Although the danger of war has passed a great depression remains. I got my extension for the American re-entry, and permission to work in England—all I need now is work. At the moment I am rehearsing a new play with Beatrix Lehmann: They Walk Alone. If it is a success and comes to the West End, it will bring me some money. Not enough though, as I have Income Tax debts. . . .

. . . That you are forced to live and work in Hollywood, whether you want it or not and whether you can stand it, because you are supporting all of us, Mama and others, is hard to bear, first for you, but even more for me.

32

Sam Hoffenstein used to say: "Wherever I go, I go too, and spoil everything." This was exactly how I felt. I had nothing but harassments and personal conflicts, in addition to bad news daily. In Porto Ronco, Rose had said to me: "With all your problems and responsibilities that you still have the courage to be in love impresses me as something truly admirable."

But my courage was deserting me. The years were piling up on me, but I loved to celebrate birthdays, even my own. As little as I worried about my finances and my health, so little was I conscious of my age. It was dissatisfaction with my work which made me despair. I could not bear the studio any longer; I longed for a respite from people who considered themselves superior only because they were overpaid.

In February, 1939, I became a citizen of the United States. Even I, who hate flag-waving and patriotic demonstrations, found it very moving, and repeated the oath of allegiance along with three hundred other people. I was hopeful that now I would get my mother and Dusko out of Poland. A few days later I was assigned to the producer Sidney Franklin, to collaborate on the screenplay of *Marie Curie*.

Mr. Franklin was a slight, inconspicuous man, nearing fifty and a dedicated Anglophile. His office looked like the drawingroom of an English country house. He constantly talked of the film he had made based on James Hilton's *Goodbye Mr. Chips*, which had had a British background, and was a great success.

There were four, sometimes five of us discussing the story, an international set up: Jacques Théry, a Frenchman, who did not give a damn; Mr. Harris, an American on loan from Fox, author of the Alexander Graham Bell film; the Austrian novelist George Froeschel, who alternated with another German refugee, Hans

Rameau; Claudine West, British, and with bad memories of me from the time of *Queen Christina*; and myself. No one was writing yet because we had not agreed on the "story line." Franklin's secretary was supposed to record all suggestions but only took down what Franklin dictated.

The conferences began at ten in the morning with the producer appearing last, changing into a jacket and stretching out on the couch, while we grouped ourselves around him. Invariably he would begin with: "Well, guys, last night, after dinner, I talked to Mrs. Franklin about the story and she agreed with me: no pretty girl would ever study chemistry or physics."

My colleagues waited until I automatically protested: photographs showed that Marie Curie was lovely in her youth. I argued, Miss West smiled enigmatically, Théry gossiped about Madame Curie's love life, Froeschel and Rameau made abstract and noncommittal suggestions. After two hours Franklin would admit that some pretty girls might study chemistry but not many.

Having settled that, we began the search for "motivation." At six P.M. we left the studio, certain that tomorrow's conference would again begin with "Last night after dinner. . . ." I informed Franklin about the Huxley script, and after he had read it he admitted that there were some good scenes in it. Also there was "one good speech" in the Scott Fitzgerald screenplay.

Gradually our conclave was reduced to three participants: Franklin, Walter Reisch and myself. Walter Reisch had written and directed successful pictures in Europe: *Escapade* with Paula Wessely had been bought by Metro and remade with Luise Rainer. I don't think Walter has ever forgiven me for suggesting *Marie Curie*. He constantly repeated that he hated bluestockings and intellectual women, while Franklin was gradually transforming Pierre Curie into a French Mr. Chips. At last we agreed that young Marie's weird interest in science could be "motivated" by her being a foreigner.

In summer Berthold returned from England, in good health but tense and nervous. He found the house too lively and moved to the room over the garage. As he had been away so long he had to get used to us. Luckily Edward was spending the summer at Mabery Road and his presence had, as always, a calming influence. In the evenings, as in the old times, we gathered to listen to his playing.

This was also the summer when Congressman Martin Dies and his committee announced that Walter Wanger's *Blockade*, Warner Brothers' *Juarez* and Metro's *Fury* were inspired by communists. Unperturbed by politics, we finally let Marie Curie, née

Sklodowska, "the girl with an impossible name," explain her devotion to science with: "I always wanted to know why the grass is green and the water wet." But we were deadlocked on another issue: the discovery of radium was not "spectacular enough for film audiences." It was not enough to show how in a miserable, badly equipped shack, two people stubbornly persisted in their search for four years. We had to find an answer to "did radium mean anything for the whole world?" "What was it good for?" It was not like Salvarsan, nor was it like Pasteur's vaccine for smallpox, nor did it cure diabetes. It was in an experimental stage; the treatment of cancer and radio-activity merely complicated the story line. Apart from all that, Sidney Franklin was doubtful about the correctness of Eve Curie's presentation. "She is not a scientist. It couldn't have been as simple as she writes. There must have been some kind of a gimmick." And Walter Reisch would say: "After all, they got the Nobel Prize." The comparatively primitive process by which the Curies isolated the new element was nothing sensational. There was no suspense, no competition, no false lead, no sabotage, as in a detective story. Poverty was the only obstacle and poverty was "dreary." I argued that the obsession of the Curies was a dramatic element . . . The moment when Pierre and Marie Curie entered their shack at night and saw a glowing substance in the glass tubes was a triumph of the human spirit.

Tired of arguments, Walter Reisch suggested that we ask a physicist at Caltech, and five minutes later a studio Cadillac took us to Pasadena.

Dr. Johst waited in his laboratory, at his side an atomsmasher. The small room had unpainted brick walls, a desk and two chairs; the cyclotron took up most of the space. Dr. Johst was middle-aged and tired; he stood behind the desk, while Reisch asked his questions. As I remember it, he started with the isolation of radium. Word for word, Dr. Johst gave the same information as Eve Curie's book and the encyclopedia. Franklin asked if there were no incidents of failure, false symptoms and wrong results. "The main problem was to get the pitchblende," answered Dr. Johst. Disappointed, Franklin asked the crucial question: "Has the discovery of radium completely changed the basis of science and has everything to start on another basis?" Dr. Johst was baffled. He murmured that every discovery leads to something new but he did not understand what we were after.

"We are after a gimmick!" I thought but refrained from saying it. Again Dr. Johst reiterated how the Curies had isolated radium, first as uranium then as a more radioactive substance, which Marie had called polonium in honor of her native country; then by special methods, she and her husband had found another radioactive substance, to which they gave the name of radium. The *Encyclopedia Britannica* mentions that the name was "happily chosen, for in its pure state radium bromide has a far greater activity—about two million times as great as an equal weight of uranium." This gave us some comfort and we left Dr. Johst.

In the car, after a gloomy silence, Sidney Franklin said: "This guy is a very small fish, otherwise he would not be in such a dirty, small office. He didn't say anything we don't know. We'd better look for somebody else."

At that, obviously out of despair, Walter Reisch exclaimed: "Why don't we send Salka to Paris to ask Irene Joliot-Curie, who is a physicist like her mother? Salka knows what we are after and she is the right person to interview Irene."

Franklin perked up. My heart was pounding. This was one of the things the studio adored: sending someone to the Antipodes, to the South Seas, to the Congo, or at least across the Atlantic. My eyes on Franklin, I held my breath. He nodded. Yes, that was a very good suggestion. My conscience made me remind them that it was summer, the Sorbonne and the Institute of Radium would be closed. "Then you must find out where Irene Joliot is and go there. Let me talk to Bernie. See you after lunch."

Reisch and I went to the Commissary and Gottfried and Bronek Kaper joined us for lunch. I told them that I was keeping my fingers crossed as I might be sent to Paris, and they turned green with envy. But I did not believe in such luck. The thought that having accomplished my mission, I might be allowed to go to Poland and see my mother and Dusko made me dizzy. I dismissed it.

"You will see," I said, "the studio will say 'no.' "

But the studio said "yes" and two secretaries typed pages of instructions for me, cables were sent to the Paris office and everyone was excited and kind and full of advice.

In two days I had my new American passport and a reservation on the *Normandie*, sailing on the last of July. Liesl Frank wanted me to look up and comfort those who were waiting for American visas. Berthold had a long list of messages for people I had to call in Paris and London. Hans and Peter envied me (Tommy was going to a camp and was completely preoccupied with his equipment). Expecting war to break out, Edward was worried.

On the Super Chief I read Mr. Franklin's instructions. They began with:

. . . The more we talk about it, Walter and I, the more we realize that we must consider our audience of primary school intelligence so far as this discovery of radium is concerned. I instantly considered myself in this same class.

FOR THIS REASON WE HAVE GOT TO REDUCE IT TO THE MOST SIMPLE TERMS, SO THAT WHEN YOU MAKE YOUR NOTES IT WILL NOT ONLY BE UNDERSTOOD BY THE AUDIENCE, BUT THEY WILL GET A *Thrill* OUT OF IT, AND WHEN LEAVING THE THEATER WILL SAY: "I KNOW HOW SHE DISCOVERED RADIUM, AND I WOULD HAVE DONE EX-ACTLY THE SAME IF I HAD BEEN MADAME CURIE."

Of great importance are the instruments that Madame Curie used in the discovery of radium. This, of course, as you know, is most vital.

. . . Ask whether we can say, in so many words, the following:

That if her discovery of radioactive minerals is a fact (that it still appeared doubtful staggered me) could they say that the basis of science will be completely changed and all experiments and everything that is done will start from another basis—that the very thought of *matter,* as scientists know it, will be changed?

Could she come to the conclusion, and voice it, that if they do not accept her theory, they are *a stumbling block* to the advancement of science?

Aware of how embarrassed "they" would be by such a threat I was determined to skip this question.

The next day I boarded the *Normandie,* the most beautiful ship in the world. After I had unpacked in my lovely cabin, I went on deck and suddenly was back in Hollywood: Norma Shearer; Frederick Lonsdale; Edward G. Robinson with wife, child, child's nurse; Pat and Charles Boyer; Bob Hope and his wife; Madeleine Carroll; Joe Cohn, boss of Columbia Pictures; buyers from Magnin and Bullocks, the great department stores in Los Angeles; Mr. and Mrs. Gilbert Miller—they were all going to Paris.

The weather was wonderful, everyone in elated spirits. I don't remember anyone ever reading the ship's bulletin or talking about Hitler. Happy to be going to Europe, I laughed with the others. The beautiful ship carried us rapidly eastward.

33

PARIS WAS DESERTED but lovelier than ever. The concièrges sunned themselves in front of their apartment houses, in large upholstered *fauteuils*, children skipped rope on the sidewalks, people promenaded with their dogs and cats and one woman took the air with a parrot perched on her shoulder. At the reception desk of the Plaza Athénée I caught a glimpse of my traveling companions, but was not to see them again for a long time.

I unpacked and called the Metro office. A woman's voice acknowledged my arrival, then advised me to "take it easy." The head of the office, Mr. Lawrence, was in the country, Mr. Monta, the lawyer, was taking a cure in Vittell. "But Monsieur Lapinère will see you tomorrow at your hotel."

I had just put down the receiver when Marcel Achard burst into my room, genial, beaming, with huge spectacles and with coat flying. We fell into each other's arms. It was wonderful to succumb to his infectious addiction to life. I had to report minutely about my "sons and lovers," then tell him what had brought me to Paris. Marcel said that he could help me. He and Juliette were good friends of Eve Curie. She was spending the summer in Dinard and nothing was easier than to arrange a meeting between us either there or in Paris. It would be more difficult to get hold of her sister. The mondaine Eve liked society, was young and gay, while Madame Joliot, a great scientist and admirable woman, was withdrawn and moody. Marcel thought that the best way to approach her was through Professor Jean Perrin, an old friend of the Curies.

I spent the next morning on the telephone trying to locate people who knew Marie Curie in her student days, but all in vain.

Metro provided me with a photographer and I began to look up the places where she had lived, studied, taught and experimented. We went through the empty lecture halls, laboratories and corridors of the deserted Sorbonne, and inspected from the outside the Institute of Radium, a modest building which I knew would never satisfy Franklin. The evenings I usually spent with Alfred and Lisl Polgar at the Deux Magots, or another café. Sitting around the tables were other refugees, immediately recognizable by their strained expressions. I remembered many from Berlin, from the Romanisches Café—all in a panic because of Hitler's threats against Poland.

The Metro office notified me that Professor Jean Perrin (Nobel Prize winner for his work on the atom) and Madame Irène Joliot were at L'Arcouëst in Brittany. A chauffeur-driven Renault was to take me there, then to Eve Curie in Dinard.

It was August 15, and all the French seemed to be on wheels. My elegant chauffeur was constantly exchanging: *"merde," "imbécile," "patate," "voyou,"* etc. with the other motorists crowding the roads. When we arrived at L'Arcouëst it was dark and late. There was no place to spend the night and after long, slow inquiries with monosyllabic innkeepers, my driver told me that we would have to take the ferry and sleep on the island of Brèhat. The prospect of an island and the ferry appealed to me. Next day a pale, misty sunshine revealed L'Arcouëst, an enchanting fishing village with dunes, firs and sandy beaches stretching far out after the retreating tide. We passed small, well-tended plots and old, gray farmhouses surrounded by low stone walls. Then among a few scattered villas, with large glassed-in verandas, was a modern new house which belonged to Professor Perrin.

A boy in bathing trunks admitted me to the hall. There was a lot of running and whispering behind closed doors, then a woman's voice calling: *"La dame de Hollywood, Papa!"* One of the doors opened and Professor Perrin, a friendly old man with a snow-white beard, invited me into a room with an enormous window through which one could see the dunes, the firs and a blue-gray strip of the sea. He was already informed about the reason of my intrusion, which made it easier for me to attack the most important issue and to ask if he could help me to meet Madame Joliot. I knew how reluctant she was to talk to strangers and said that I regretted to disturb her holiday, but the discovery of radium as presented in Eve Curie's book did not satisfy my producer. Obviously amused, Professor Perrin said that Eve's description was very accurate but, of course, she was not a scientist. He reiterated the details of the experiments Pierre and Marie had made, spoke of radioactivity, mentioned his own work on the atom, went to his desk and looked through mountains of papers, while I felt like an impostor. He was overestimating my understanding of science. He found what he was looking for; it was his own book with the title *L'Atome*, for which he got the Nobel Prize. He wrote a dedication on the flyleaf and gave it to me. The dedication was much too flattering. I thought at once of the cracks Walter Reisch, Franklin and Bernie would make when I showed it to them. My sons also would find it highly amusing. We were interrupted by a knock on the door and he went to open it. I realized that it was lunch time, and although my main errand had not been accomplished, I got up. Professor Perrin would not hear of my leaving and insisted that I stay. He led me to the dining room, where his daughter and son-in-law were already waiting at the table. As I remember there were also several grandchildren. I was introduced; then we sat down in deep silence. I felt I was not a welcome guest. After a while my hostess addressed me rather sharply: how was it conceivable that Hollywood dared to make a film about Marie Curie? Surprised, I answered that Eve Curie's book had been bought first by Universal then, upon my suggestion, Metro Goldwyn Mayer had acquired the rights to make a film for Greta Garbo. Unbelieving, she stared at me: "Impossible! Eve could not have sold her book to the films!" and she turned to her father. But he expressed pleasure that Garbo was to play Marie.

Madame Joliot was due in L'Arcouëst the next day and Professor Perrin promised to talk to her. Then he suggested that I should get in touch with Dr. Plotz, who was teaching at the Massachusetts Institute of Technology, or Princeton (I don't remember which). Dr. Plotz had been very close to Marie Curie in her last years. Professor Perrin asked me to come back on the following afternoon; by then he would have spoken to Irène Joliot.

The next day I went back to the Perrin villa, and the boy in swimming trunks ushered me into the room with the wide, open window. After a while I saw Professor Perrin among the firs, coming toward the house with a slender woman with short, gray hair. She wore a light cotton frock; her long, slim legs were bare and brown from the sun. Professor Perrin turned toward the dunes, but she walked straight to the open window and like a youngster, nimbly jumped into the room. She resembled her mother.

I rose to greet her. She said that she had received a letter from Professor Albert Einstein announcing my visit and I recognized Berthold's thoughtful concern. However, I felt greatly embarrassed by the convocation of world-famous scientists to assist Metro

Goldwyn Mayer in "reducing to most simple terms something which could be understood by an audience of primary school intelligence," especially when Madame Joliot stated that the mere idea of a film about her parents was repulsive to her. I answered that I respected her feelings, but that films about great discoverers, scientists and artists could contribute a great deal to an interest in enlightenment and education. Madame Joliot did not relent; she had seen the Dr. Ehrlich film and found it awful. She did not protest, however, when I said that although Dr. Ehrlich's "magic bullet" may have been oversimplified and in many things incorrect, it still had some merit, as it dealt with a taboo subject and showed dedication to the alleviation of suffering. The people who were producing the film about Marie Curie wished it to be dignified and truthful. She excitedly replied that her father, Pierre Curie, had an equal share in the discovery of radium and that her mother had always emphasized their unity. I assured her that the film would fully express this.

"Nevertheless, I cannot advise nor help you," Irène Joliot went on. "If I cooperate I forfeit the right to protest." Not in a position to take full responsibility, I remained silent. I was not even sure whether my own contribution to the screenplay would remain unchanged. Still following my instructions, I asked permission to photograph the Institute of Radium and the instruments Pierre and Marie Curie had used in their shack. She refused. The Institute of Radium was closed for the summer, besides it would again mean her tacit acquiescence. "The instruments are in the French Pavilion at the World Fair in New York. You can see them there."

Discouraged I left Madame Joliot. I did not agree with her, but I was on her side and lacked arguments to prove where she was wrong. She also recommended Dr. Plotz, adding that he was a kind, charming man, who liked to help. Smiling, she added: "He is an American, and fond of motion pictures." I resisted the temptation to mention that millions of Europeans and Asians went to see Garbo films.

The sun was gone when I arrived in Dinard at an old-fashioned but comfortable hotel, where I met Eve Curie for lunch. She was young, beautiful and very chic. The only resemblance to her sister was the high forehead and slim figure. She greeted me with warm friendliness, astonished when I told her that I had just come from L'Arcouëst, had seen Madame Joliot and that two Nobel Prize winners had pleaded that she receive me. Eve laughed. She was glad that I had talked to her sister before I met her. She knew the theater and film world and admired Garbo. She asked me about the screenplay. I answered that when I left America we were still "constructing the story line." In Bernie's name I invited her to come to Hollywood and work with us, but she refused for the same reason as Madame Joliot: she did not want to impair her right to protest. But she offered me an introduction to a Polish friend of her mother and with great warmth referred me to Dr. Plotz. Everyone seemed to love Dr. Plotz. We talked about Poland, where she had been while doing research for the biography. She regretted that I was not working with Sam Behrman for whom she had a high regard, and praised the Garbo films we had done together. On the hotel terrace we ran into Henri Bernstein, the popular French dramatist—tall, quite old, interestingly ugly and childishly conceited. He told me that he had doubts whether Garbo should play Madame Curie. In his opinion she was too glamorous and would be better suited for the heroine of his own last play, which he wanted me to read and recommend to MGM. So much for business, which he conducted almost automatically but with charm; after that he talked compulsively, gloomily and masochistically about Hitler's horrifying power and the huge success of Nazism and fascism.

I had asked Eve Curie about her childhood memories, but she said nothing I did not know. I gained great prestige with my driver when he saw me in the company of Henri Bernstein. "Un millionaire!" he respectfully informed me. In spite of his communist leanings he had a weakness for rich, self-made men, as long as they were not Americans.

We drove back to Paris via St. Malo, Mont-Saint-Michel and Caën, where he showed me medieval streets in which poor people still lived. They were so narrow that we had to leave the car and walk. The centuries-old, dilapidated, rotting houses exuded a hideous smell of excrement, poverty and dirt. Gray-faced women and ragged, emaciated children sat on their doorsteps like figures in Käthe Kollwitz drawings. Later, when I read about the bombings of Caën I had horrible visions of these houses and those people.

The difficulties of getting a French visa for my mother and Dusko were insurmountable. For hours I waited in line at the Mairie but could not overcome the red tape and, as Dusko insisted that I come to Poland and I had not seen him since the summer of 1927, we agreed that it would be easier if the three of us met in Warsaw. Before going to L'Arcouëst I had instructed the concièrge of the Plaza Athénée to reserve a seat for me on the plane to Warsaw via Copenhagen, intending to leave on August 23.

When I returned on the afternoon of the 21st the newspapers were announcing the Soviet German Non-Aggression Pact. I was told at the desk that I could fly only to Copenhagen and then see how to proceed to Warsaw by other means. And there was hardly a chance of getting a return booking before November. While we were talking, a telegram from Gottfried Reinhardt was handed to me. He implored me not to go to Poland; everyone was convinced that war was inevitable.

I phoned the MGM office and the chief, Mr. Lawrence, told me that Bernie Hyman also had cabled, worried about my trip to Poland, but that he had assured him that there was no chance of my getting there. I sent a long telegram to my mother. She answered that she and Dusko were dismayed, but she believed the political tension would subside. She would visit me in the States when her visa arrived. (I had applied for it as soon as I became an American citizen.) She added that so far Dusko, who was in the Reserves, had not been called.

My telephone kept ringing; people had heard that I was in Paris and desperate voices besieged me for help. I had heartbreaking visits from total strangers and I promised everyone to do whatever I could to get them affidavits.

At the MGM office the Hitler-Stalin Pact had changed everything. No one was interested in the film any longer; no one cared which scientists I should contact. Cables from Berthold and telephone calls from Bernie urged me to return at once. That was easier said than done, as all ships to the States were packed with Americans cutting short their European vacations.

The blackouts made Paris fantastically beautiful. With Alfred and Lisl Polgar I walked through the Palais Royal flooded with moonlight. We were overcome by a great nostalgia for the "good old days" when Paris was a *cité lumière* and when no Messerschmidts could drop bombs on her. Alfred and Lisl were certain that Hitler would attack Poland. I refused to believe it.

My American passport made me feel guilty, because my heartless adopted country refused entrance to the "oppressed, persecuted and poor." It was difficult to part with Europe at that moment but MGM had great influence and got me a cabin on the *Ile De France*, sailing from Le Havre on September 1.

I went to say good-bye to the Achards at their country place. The news on the radio was getting worse. Marcel drove me back to Blois, where I had to take the train to Paris. We arrived too early and had a drink in a little sidewalk café. On the other side of the street was a bakery. A lorry had driven up and soldiers were loading it with loaves of freshly baked bread. They were young recruits, morose, silent and subdued. Marcel and I looked at their boyish faces and had the same horrible thoughts.

The Plaza Athénée was deserted. The maids gathered in my room to discuss the worsening situation. They knew that I had intended to go to Poland to see my mother, and now, leaning on brooms or vacuum cleaners or sitting on the floor, they showed their sympathy. Our talks ended in tears and embraces.

On my last evening I had dinner with the Polgars; then we went to the Deux Magots. There were the usual intertwined couples on the boulevard, and the refugees, who now spoke in whispers. Those I knew approached our table and again I wrote down addresses and promised help.

The train to Le Havre left early. I was so exhausted that I slept until we arrived. Crowds were pressing toward the towering *Ile De France*. With the help of a kindly old porter I fought my way through to my cabin, which was a far cry from the one I had had on the *Normandie*. I wanted to send a telegram to my mother and went to the Radio Room on the upper deck. The operator stood outside and said that as long as we were in port he could not send any messages, but I had plenty of time to do it from the pier. I ran down the gangplank, found the telegraph office, but as I was writing the address the clerk stopped me: "*Pologne? Les Allemands sont en Pologne, Madame. C'est la guerre.*"

It took me quite a while to pull myself together; then I went back to my cabin. It was a blessing that we had not gone to Warsaw. I reread Mama's last letter: "Even if the war breaks out it will by-pass Sambor. It's too unimportant." The steward came and found me in tears. It was better to go on deck.

Hours went by; we were still moored at the pier. The air was hot and oppressive. I caught sight of Gina Kaus, the novelist, whom I had known in Berlin and seen recently in Paris. She, her two sons and her husband, Dr. Frischauer, were emigrating to America. "What are we waiting for?" her boys kept asking anxiously. Rumors were spreading that if France declared war the ship would not sail. Night came, tiny blue lamps, indicating stairs and companionways, were the only lights on. Two American ladies were loudly discussing the Salzburg festival. I went back to my cabin and waited in vain for the sound of the anchor being weighed.

Early in the morning we were called for life-boat drill. I put on my life jacket and went to my assigned place, where a large group had gathered. I was welcomed by Gregor Piatigorsky, the cello virtuoso, who with his wife and small child was returning to California. In the same lifeboat would be Nathan Milstein, the famous violinist, and his American wife. The conversation around us varied on the theme: would France and England go to war? or would the appeasers prevail?

The drill was over but the *Ile De France* remained motionless, her decks crowded with restless human beings, tortured by fear and uncertainty.

At last, at ten at night, the siren was blown hoarsely, the anchor weighed and the ship began to pull out. A bulletin was issued saying only that Poland was defending herself heroically; nothing about her allies. Everyone remained on deck to wait for the English newspapers, which would be brought aboard in Southampton. The crew began converting the library and the main drawing room into sleeping quarters for the additional passengers we were to pick up. Four hundred were expected; American students leaving Europe in a hurry.

At three in the morning the *Ile De France* anchored offshore and we could see faint lights. Wasn't Southampton blacked out? We waited another hour until we heard the motors of approaching tenders. The first to come aboard were Western Union messengers with telegram blanks and the English newspapers. The passengers pounced on them. I succeeded in getting hold of *The Times* and overwhelmed with emotion, I read the headline: ENGLAND AND FRANCE DECLARE WAR ON GERMANY. "At last!" exclaimed an American near me.

I cabled to my family in Santa Monica that I was sailing. I was not permitted to name the ship. Meanwhile the other tender unloaded a horde of Americans, young men and girls. They climbed aboard with rucksacks and suitcases, laughing and pushing, rough, handsome and healthy, joking about the U-boats. Had the *Ile De France* enough lifeboats? Where would they sleep? How about the bar? The whole thing was tremendous fun.

Next morning we were sailing full blast. My steward told me in great secrecy that the British ship *Athenia* had been sunk, close to the English coast. Later, back home, I heard how terribly worried they all had been, because they thought I was on her. (Ernst Lubitsch's ten-month-old daughter Nicola was aboard but was saved by her nurse.) At night on the dark ship people remained in their deck chairs, afraid to sleep in their cabins. The crew was grim and unfriendly: why should France fight because of Poland? We zigzagged for eight days on the north Atlantic, until one evening the lights on the *Ile De France* lit up brightly—we were in American waters.

As soon as I entered my hotel room in New York, Bernie's voice from the West Coast welcomed me back to America. He was overjoyed that I had returned safely, that I had not gone to Poland, and was most sympathetic about my mother and brother. Then he announced that the studio had decided to shelve *Marie Curie*; I should be thinking about a comedy for Garbo. He agreed that I stay a few days in the East to take action on behalf of my mother's visa. I called a friend in Washington who was close to the White House, and implored him to help cut the red tape. He said that in face of the rapid advance of the Germans, there was nothing to do but wait. I went home. Three weeks after she had been invaded, Poland surrendered. The State Department notified me that my mother's visa had been forwarded to the American Consulate in Bucharest. Then the Germans retreated behind the so-called Curzon Line, the Russians occupied the West Ukraine, and Wychylowka came under Soviet rule.

34

THE UNCONCERNED SUNBATHERS on the beach, their hairless bodies glistening and brown, the gigantic trucks rumbling on the highway, the supermarkets with their mountains of food, the studio with the oh-so-relaxed employees, the chatting extras pouring out from the stages at lunch time, the pompous executives marching to their "exclusive dining room" or to the barbershop, stopping to flirt with the endearing "young talent"—all these familiar scenes were a nerve-racking contrast to the war horror I constantly imagined. It did not help to tell myself that at least the bombings had ceased; what was life under Soviet rule like? The silence exasperated me. I also heard nothing from Vienna. All I knew was that my brother-in-law was staging operas in Buenos Aires; but had it been possible for Rose and the children to join him? I did not dare to cable her. Berthold had had reports that the German pogroms were nothing compared to the barbarism of the Austrian Nazis.

"Years of the Devil," my secretary Etta had written on the

folder which contained the tragic letters from Austria, Prague and France. How well I remember the evening after the Molotov report came out, when Bertolt Brecht and a friend, Ruth Berlau, were sitting by the fireplace in my home and I said how guilty I felt because I had been spared. Next morning I found under my door a poem Brecht had written:

Ich weiss natürlich: einzig durch Glück
Habe ich so viele Freunde überlebt. Aber heute Nacht im Traum
Hörte ich diese Freunde von mir sagen: "Die Stärkeren überleben"
Und ich hasste mich.

It seemed inconceivable that with their many connections, with British and American friends (influential politicians and foreign correspondents), Camil and Irma Hoffmann, these two kindest and gentlest people, had to die in Auschwitz. Camil's last letter, in his precise, neat handwriting, thanked me for an affidavit I had got for his son Jan, and concluded: "We are staying here in Prague in an old house, having renounced a vacation trip because of the rainy summer. We cannot complain of boredom: thanks to the 'world theater' there is no lack of distraction."

Later I was told that while they were interned in Theresienstadt the Nazis, giving in to international pressure, offered to release Camil but not Irma. He rejected the perfidious offer and they were both shipped to Auschwitz.

Walter Hasenclever committed suicide in France, Ernst Toller in New York. Berthold had seen him three days before he killed himself:

We had lunch together and he seemed so depressed that I hesitated to leave him. He told me about his insomnia and his utter hopelessness. I also had the impression that he needed money, but he denied it and now I read in the papers that he has left a substantial bank account. He was uncertain if he should go to England or stay in New York, and it was obvious that it was impossible for him to make any decision whatsoever. Nevertheless, I thought that he would conquer this depression. He showed such warmth towards me that I felt he had become more concerned for others and that in many ways he was beginning to find his true self. However, he no longer had the strength. In spite of his numerous contacts he was utterly alone and in spite of all his desperate activity people had lost confidence in him. One cannot stop thinking: if only he had not done it! But who can judge. . . .

This autumn of tears and anxiety brought also an unexpected joy. I had been reproaching Peter for spending more time on the tennis court than at his studies and one day he retorted. "How long can you support me?" I said: "Until you have a profession." "All right, let's make a deal," he said. "If I get a job I won't have to study! if I don't, I'll go back to school." "It's a deal."

Weeks went by and there was no indication whatever that Peter was looking for a job or playing less tennis, and I was confident that he would be enrolling at U.C.L.A. the next summer. Then, one evening, he appeared in tennis shorts, a racquet in his hand, and nonchalantly dropped a letter into my lap. It was from Harcourt and Brace, and said: "Dear Mr. Viertel: We are happy to inform you that your novel *The Canyon* has been accepted by us for publication." What's more, they offered him an advance. I was defeated.

The Canyon appeared in 1940, and critics unanimously expressed great hopes for the nineteen-year-old author. The book described a group of adventurous youngsters and adults, inhabitants of the Santa Monica Canyon, as it was when we first moved there. It was dedicated to "the foreign family up the street and to Anne." I never asked who Anne was.

After the war broke out, more Europeans moved into the Canyon. One of them was Christopher Isherwood, boyishly handsome, blue-eyed and, as Berthold had described him, with a great sense of humor. We saw a lot of each other as we also had friends in common: the Huxleys, Iris Tree, John Houseman, Klaus and Erika Mann. MGM signed him up to write screenplays, which he seemed to enjoy for a while. As the war went on he left to work with the Quakers. I felt that, at that time, he was going through great emotional strain.

Andrew, a thirteen-year-old refugee, son of Leonhard Frank (author of *Karl und Anna* and *Die Räuberbande*), joined our household. His parents were divorced. The mother, Lena, was in the East, struggling for a new existence, and until she could achieve it I offered to take care of Andrew. He was Tommy's age and extremely intelligent and lovable. Then Berthold's niece Susan, his sister Helene's daughter, arrived with an eight-month-old son. Her husband, St. John Mann, was an officer in the British Navy. As his duties took him far away from England, she and the baby came to stay with me. Of course Etta worried about the permanent overdrawing of my bank account, but admitted that there was nothing else we could do.

Ninotchka was in full production. Lubitsch came to my office every day, telling me what scenes they had shot and how wonderful Garbo was. And he maintained that considering his bitterness about the Stalin-Hitler pact, the film was not anti-Soviet. Piled up on my desk were novels and plays which the story department thought "excellent Garbo material."

I don't remember what provoked Gottfried and Sam Hoffenstein to urge me to take an agent, but they were convinced that Paul Kohner would represent my interests better than myself. I had known Paul since our early days in Hollywood when he was a producer at Universal, and as our large household urgently demanded a greater income I said that I would be glad to have him as my agent. Paul agreed that I was underpaid: six hundred and fifty dollars a week was peanuts and I deserved twice as much. I was sending hundreds of dollars to Europe as well as large sums which, from time to time, unknown people with Jewish names, in Sweden or Switzerland, requested for my mother. It was impossible to investigate these demands; I refused to risk my mother's safety because someone might be taking advantage of me. (Later I found out that Mama and Dusko had received only a fraction of what I had sent.) Also Christmas was approaching and there was a long list of people I had to remember.

On the day Kohner was supposed to discuss my contract with Eddie Mannix I came home just as the telephone rang, and picked up the receiver. Steeling himself to firmness, the story editor informed me that he was taking me off the payroll. I remember that I said "thank you," although I still don't know why. Then he hung up.

As soon as I recovered from the shock, I phoned Kohner. He was flabbergasted. He said that Mannix had angrily refused to raise my salary, but that he should also fire me was quite unexpected. Gottfried came and reported that Mannix was furious that I had let an agent "barge in between us." After all, for seven years MGM had voluntarily increased my weekly check.

"She should see if Kohner can get her a better job," he shouted.

Bernie phoned and advised me to apologize to Mannix, but I refused. It was my right to be represented by an agent. Paul Kohner took up the challenge and said he would get me a job in another studio. It would take some time, as Christmas was so near. I had to be brave and optimistic. Roosevelt's reelection to a third term, with Henry Wallace as Vice President, was a comforting victory. For the first time in my life I voted and took an "active part in democratic procedure." My now twenty-one-year-old Hans, although pleased that Roosevelt had won, had voted for the Socialist Norman Thomas.

The work at the Reinhardt studio had taken Hans away from politics, but the murder of Trotsky in Mexico brought him, and me also subsequently, in contact with the young Trotskyites again. At first it appeared that Trotsky was only dangerously wounded and his adherents tried sending a famous Los Angeles brain surgeon to Mexico. They needed money and asked me if I could help. As I was already unable to pay my own expenses I thought of Ernst Lubitsch and Edward G. Robinson. Lubitsch had never said "no" when I asked him for money, and Robinson, who knew Trotsky personally from a visit to Mexico, had told me repeatedly how impressed he had been with the old man. Ernst gave me a hundred dollars in cash, Robinson a check for a hundred and fifty, made out in my name, and I added a hundred myself. But Trotsky died that same day and the distressed young people begged me to send the money to his widow. I am mentioning all this not because I want to give the impression of having been close to a historical event, but because my natural and human action was to have unforeseen consequences later, in the McCarthy era.

Worries and anxieties multiplied. In spite of the repeal of the embargo, Peter was sure that America would remain neutral and that he would never have a chance to fight the Nazis. "Your boys are not going to be sent into any foreign wars," Roosevelt promised American mothers. So Peter secretly tried to enlist in the Canadian RAF. He was rejected twice because his eyesight did not meet the requirements of the recruiting board. The third time he told me frankly that he was going to Vancouver and invited me to accompany him part of the way. It was June and we drove through the Yosemite Valley, along the Merced river swollen by hundreds of cascading waterfalls, its banks a jungle of fragrant wild lilac. This exuberant bloom could not dispel the visions of destruction and death into which my son was so eager to rush, just as life was offering him so much. I understood his decision but I did not want him to enlist in a "foreign" army; as a matter of fact, unheroic mother that I was, I did not want him to enlist in any army. I dreaded the thought of his being a pilot and my only hope was that my former housekeeper, Jessie's husband, was on the recruiting board. War or peace, the world is rather small when you think of it. Peter came home, as the only job offered him was in the coast defense artillery for which he had no taste; and for the time being I could breathe again.

To better my financial situation I was contemplating all kinds of moves. My favorite plan was to forget about the movies or stage and to open a restaurant either in Santa Monica or in Beverly Hills, but preferably in the Canyon. My friends praised the food in my house extravagantly and I had great success as a cook, but even the generous Ernst Lubitsch refused to finance me, saying: "You'll be feeding the whole town for nothing."

I thought of a hotdog stand which according to my sons, would be a "gold mine," or a goulash wagon on the beach; but all these plans provided only amusement at the dinner table and a lot of teasing from Gottfried, who prophesied that after a few weeks of punitive exile I would return, a prodigal daughter, to Eddie Mannix's open arms. Looking back I don't know whether it was lucky that Paul Kohner sold "my services" to Warner Brothers. For the moment it was a triumph and an enormous financial relief. Nevertheless in the long run the hotdog stand might have given us more permanent security. Anyway, I got an assignment which paid a thousand dollars a week. The mortgage on the house was taken care of, at least temporarily; and I could afford to raise the wages of the young refugee couple, Walter and Hedy Herlitschek, who kept house for us. (They changed their name to Herley as soon as they touched ground in the U.S.). Walter had been a salesman in a chic haberdashery shop in Vienna, Hedy a dressmaker; now she was a cook, Walter a "butler-chauffeur." Without bewailing their prosperous past, the majority of refugees grabbed any kind of work to provide for their families and the old and sick they had to leave behind and for whom the gates of the promised land would never open. It was easier for the women to get jobs, and many supported their men and children by catering at parties, and introducing the *Sachertorte* and *Apfelstrudel* to American palates. They washed, cleaned and sewed. As the defense industries were absorbing more and more workers and giving greater opportunities to Negroes, the demand for "domestics" benefited the refugees.

In May, 1940, Berthold wrote from New York:

Dearest Salka: I am not reproaching you for not writing long letters, as I know how busy you are, but in times of great and small failures the ear becomes sensitive to voices which do not penetrate the distance. By "small failure" I mean our production of *The Gray Farm*. The great failure is the world tragedy which destroys so many and so much. It's true that the ultimate decision has not fallen. Don't be upset when I confess, only to *you* and to no one else, that the imminent conquest of Paris does not aggravate my diabetes so much as the bombings of London and Berlin. It is impossible for me to mourn empires and cathedrals. I mourn only the people, confused, misled and apostatical as the human race might be. If the entire so-called culture would become one huge heap of rubble and a new world, cleansed of the Nazi pest, would emerge, my days would end in complete happiness.

I have not heard from C. From Helene only one letter. Have you any news from Mama? For the moment she seems safe. However, the final reckoning between Nazi Germany and Soviet Russia will inexorably come. Perhaps some people, the poor like my old aunt Nelli, can be saved by their kindness, harmlessness and proletarian sanctity. Those are their three guardian angels. Also Helene belongs to those dear venerated souls, which nothing can defeat since they are poor, so poor that they have given up the last shred of Jewish bourgeois pretentiousness.

As for me: *The Gray Farm* will close in a week. Until now the audiences like it and are not influenced by the bad reviews. I see Edward often; it always purifies my soul. I miss Tommy.

And often I think of what Gottfried is going through in these tragic days of Hitler's victories. Please give him my sympathy. It's noon, and again the horrible Job's messages: "The Germans are attacking in torrents of manpower." "General Gamelin has issued an order to his soldiers that they must let themselves be killed on the spot."

Can this onslaught be stopped or is all resistance, as far as the old world is concerned, ten years too late? Perhaps Europe must be given up, although the confrontation with Russia and the Slavic world is unavoidable. Will this happen in our lifetime? Everything will be decided with terrific speed in the next few years. Last news: the British are bombing Germany.

I embrace you and the sons.

Your,
Berthold.

In the late summer of 1940 a letter from my mother arrived, written on March 12th. She wrote in French and complained about lack of news from me, having only received my cables. She was well and had moved into a "petite maisonette" not too far from Wychylowka which had been "nationalized." All five of them: Hania, little Adam, Viktoria, Dusko and Mama, shared one room and kitchen.

> However, everything has a good side: Dusko has a job. The Soviets made him chief of the physical culture section and he has an office and a secretary. He works from eight in the morning until three in the afternoon, and for an extra salary he also coaches the soccer team "Spartacus." His Russian superiors appreciate him and in spite of all the horrors we went through, I am thankful that he has become a responsible human being. I have no words to describe Hania's selflessness and sacrifice; she has been wonderful. She and Viktoria are employed in a cooperative. Adam goes to school. He is a dear boy and a very good pupil. Alas, I am over the age limit to apply for work, but am keeping busy in our little household. There is no anti-semitism and no discrimination, but there are many things about which I'd rather talk to you and Edward personally. The worst were the bombings. No one can imagine the horror of that. Write soon, my dearest children. How are the boys, Margret, Berthold? I have no radio, no newspapers—we are cut off completely . . . Perhaps one day I will see you, but when? Which ocean could I cross? . . . [And then a sentence which made me laugh and cry:] Is the film about Marie Curie Sklodowska finished?

At last, the State Department notified me that Mama's visa had been forwarded from Bucharest to the American Embassy in Moscow. I cabled her to apply for permission to leave Sambor. Letters always took two or three months. To my indescribable joy, Rose and her children, who had been in great danger in Vienna, were on a Greek steamer on their way to Buenos Aires, where Josef was waiting for them.

It was toward the end of my Warner Brothers assignment that my secretary excitedly announced a call from Mr. Mannix and his rasping voice shouted: "When are you coming back? Don't you miss me? Have you finished your script?"

"I am finishing this week."

"Well, come and see me. Don't sign with anybody before we have a talk, but don't send me Kohner!"

Paul Kohner was generous. He said he would not represent me if I returned to MGM, but that I should insist on the same salary I had at Warner Brothers. Determined to stand my ground I went to Mannix. He embraced me, said he loved me and that MGM was one big family to which we both belonged, and I needed no agent as long as he, Mannix, was taking care of me! I said that Mr. Kohner got me a very good job at a much higher salary. But Mannix explained that for the thousand dollars I had been earning at Warners, I would pay higher taxes, plus 10 percent to my agent, and would keep much less than the seven hundred and fifty he offered me. His mathematics were compelling. As I could neither add nor subtract as rapidly as he, I gave in. We embraced and kissed. Outside his office I realized that the seven fifty were by no means tax free. . . .

And so, much to Greta's pleasure, I returned to the "MGM fold" and to the perennial search for a Garbo story. There was one subject which we both liked very much and thought would make an interesting film. It was a novel by the Los Angeles writer, Scott O'Dell. The locale was northern California, in the wonderful country around San Jose. When I suggested the book, Bernie seemed interested, mainly because he immediately conceived the slogan: "Garbo plays a Western." But as he preferred to make films in the studio, his addiction to farce and operetta won out. I had no help from Gottfried, always capable of swaying Bernie, because this time he shared his views. What they all would have liked best was a sequel to *Ninotchka*.

Resigned, I gave up arguing and half-heartedly suggested a comedy by Ludwig Fulda, *The Twin Sister*, an old standby of the Vienna Burgtheater. Sidney Franklin was the producer. Years ago he had made a silent film based on the same play. As George Cukor was to direct it, Garbo agreed. The setting of the original play was Italy during the Renaissance, and I shared the task of making it contemporary with the well-known German actor and dramatist, Curt Goetz, who, preferring a substantial weekly check in Hollywood to a success in the Third Reich, had come to America. As he barely spoke English he was hopelessly handicapped in adapting his witty lines to American humor, and was replaced by Walter Reisch who, though not exactly a humorist, had a feather in his cap as one of the five authors of *Ninotchka*. To give everyone his due, these authors were: Reisch, Billy Wilder and Charles Bracket, then Melchior Lengyel as the inventor of the original story and S. N. Behrman for the "additional dialogue." The "Lubitsch touch" was acknowledged by all concerned.

At the time when each day brought news more horrible than one could bear, it was not easy to manufacture a silly comedy. I wrote to Berthold,

> These last days were so awful, that I could not write nor work nor think coherently. In growing despair we remained glued to the radio. Gottfried is quite close to a breakdown. I don't have the heart to remind him of what I said before the outbreak of this war, for which he and Bruno Frank had so ardently prayed. It appeared quite possible to me that the Germans could be victorious, at least, as long as America was not involved. Now everything is more gruesome than we can imagine. Somebody in the studio was saying yesterday that when the 75 mm's started to shoot into the German tanks, the screaming of those burning inside drowned the roar of the guns. What an inferno the world has become! And London! One can only pray for those dear to us and for all the unknown who have become so dear through their suffering.
>
> Meanwhile, the conferences with Franklin have become so dreary that Walter Reisch blew his top. The result is that Franklin does not want to produce the film. Mannix called me to report to him and I supported Walter's outburst. Now we are waiting for another producer to take over.

After the fall of Paris, the League of American Writers and the Emergency Rescue Committee took steps to save, at the last minute, the German intellectuals who had fled to the south of France. With the help of Dorothy Thompson and Mrs. Roosevelt, Herman Budzislawski of the *Weltbuehne*, Schwarzschild, publisher of the *Tagebuch*, and the composer Hanns Eisler, received their visas; and the major studios hired, at a minimum salary of one hundred dollars a week, such renowned novelists as Heinrich Mann, Alfred Doeblin, Leonhardt Frank, Wilhelm Speyer, Alfred Neumann, and the journalists and critics Alfred Polgar, Walter Mehring, Jan Lustig and George Froeschel. Emil Ludwig, Franz Werfel and Lion Feuchtwanger rejected the offer, as their books were selling well in America. Hollywood could now boast of being the Parnassus of German literature, inasmuch as Thomas Mann had also become a resident of the Pacific Palisades. Alfred and Lisl Polgar had come from Lisbon and had been spared the ordeal which Heinrich Mann, his wife Nelly, the Werfels and Thomas Mann's son Golo went through crossing the Pyrenees on foot, the Gestapo close behind them.

It is unpardonable of me not to remember on what occasion I was introduced to Thomas Mann. It must have been at a meeting or banquet for some cause, most likely the Emergency Rescue Committee of which he and Dr. Kingdon, President of Newark University, were the chairmen. A slight man of medium height, he wore his hair parted on the side and a neat graying moustache under the jutting nose. He had the reserved politeness of a diplomat on official duty. His speeches, delivered in a careful, literary English, impressed the Americans, especially the younger generation, with their elevated intellectual content; and they were the pride of the refugee intelligentsia, anxious to preserve their cultural heritage. Frau Katja, his wife and the mother of his six children, accompanied him everywhere. Erika's beautifully-shaped head with the boyish haircut and dark eyes could sometimes be seen in the photos taken at banquets, meetings and lectures, but as a war correspondent she was rarely in the United States.

It was through Karl Kraus that Berthold met Heinrich Mann, one of the few contemporary writers whom Kraus appreciated. Mann's satirical masterpiece *Der Untertan*, portrayed especially well the German subservience to militarism and nationalism. Later Heinrich Mann's pacifist-socialist convictions and his early awareness of Teutonic racism made him a great influence in the Popular Front movement. In America, he was overshadowed by the fame of his brother. He was nearing seventy when, thanks to the Emergency Committee, he became a screenwriter at Warner Brothers. With his distinguished looks and the manners of a nineteenth-century *grand seigneur*, he appeared an odd figure in the Burbank studio. The German game: "Who is the greater writer, Heinrich or Thomas Mann?" continued to be played by the emigrants. Those inclined toward the left were for Heinrich, the more conservative for Thomas Mann.

At least thirty years younger than her husband, Nelly Mann was a voluptuous, blond, blue-eyed Teutonic beauty with red lips and sparkling teeth. Her sometimes ribald manner confirmed the rumor that she had been a barmaid in Hamburg. But even those she shocked had no doubts about her devotion to her husband. She drank secretly, slipping out to the bathroom or kitchen, coyly refusing the drinks offered at parties; then insisted on driving Heinrich home, to which he heroically consented.

Heinrich Mann's seventieth birthday was approaching and the "German writers in exile" felt that some notice should be taken of this event. Unfortunately, on the same day in March, 1941, Thomas Mann was to receive an Honorary Doctor's degree from the University of California in Berkeley. Immediately afterward he had a commitment for lectures, and would not return to Los Angeles until the end of April. After long diplomatic negotiations, the dinner had to be postponed until May. A major disagreement ensued as to whether it should take place in a restaurant or a private home. I called Berthold in New York and asked him whether I should not offer our house for the celebration. He was all for it. Lion Feuchtwanger and Liesl Frank were both delighted and promised to give me a list of guests, which had to be accepted by Nelly. She and Alma Mahler-Werfel were feuding and Nelly disapproved of everyone who was friendly with the Werfels. Finally the Feuchtwangers succeeded in arranging a truce and forty-five persons were invited. I set a long table in the living room; it could be removed quickly after the dinner was over. Decorated with flowers and candles it looked very festive.

Heinrich sat on my right and Thomas Mann on my left, Nelly was opposite us, towering over the very small Feuchtwanger on her right; on her left was Werfel. Everyone else was seated strictly according to age and prominence. I had begged Berthold to send me a telegram which would welcome Heinrich Mann, and I hoped to get it before dinner. Good, faithful Toni Spuhler took over the kitchen and managed very well, in spite of the many refugees who, awed by the importance of the evening, had insisted on giving her a hand, and also helping Walter and Hedy to serve. For them Heinrich and Thomas Mann, Alfred Neumann, Franz Werfel, Alfred Polgar, Lion Feuchtwanger, Alfred Doeblin, Walter Mehring, Ludwig Marcuse, Bruno Frank represented the true Fatherland to which in spite of Hitler they adhered, as they adhered to the German language.

We finished the soup and as the telegram had not arrived I made a speech, which had the virtue of being very brief. Bruno Frank and Feuchtwanger were to speak after the main course and I motioned to Walter to go on serving but he discreetly pointed to Thomas Mann, who had risen and was putting on his spectacles. Then, taking a sizeable manuscript out of the inner pocket of his tuxedo, he began to read. I assumed it was at least fifteen pages long and I was right, because many years later Thomas Mann mentioned this speech in a letter to his son Klaus, offering it as an essay for the periodical *Decision*. It was a magnificent tribute to the older brother, an acknowledgement of Heinrich's prophetic political wisdom, his far-sighted warnings to their unhappy country, and a superb evaluation of his literary stature.

We hardly had time to drink Heinrich Mann's health before he rose, also put on his glasses and also brought forth a thick manuscript. First he thanked me for the evening then, turning to his brother, paid him high praise for his continuous fight against fascism. To that he added a meticulous literary analysis of Thomas Mann's *oeuvre* in its relevance to the Third Reich. I no longer remember all the moving and profound thoughts expressed in both speeches. It gave one some hope and comfort at a time when the lights of freedom seemed extinguished in Europe, and everything we had loved and valued buried in ruins. At the open door to the pantry the "back entrance" guests were listening, crowding each other and wiping their tears.

The roast beef was overdone and Toni was upset, but the guests were elated and hungry and did not mind. Bruno Frank's and Lion Feuchtwanger's speeches were brief and in a lighter vein. The dessert, my chocolate cake, a "speciality of the house," was served and disappeared rapidly. Toward the end of the dinner Martha Feuchtwanger spontaneously offered a toast, "To Nelly, who saved Heinrich Mann's life, practically carrying him in her arms on their rough trek through the Pyrenees. She supported him with her loving strength and gave courage to us all."

Nelly hid her face in her hands when we surrounded her to clink glasses and then, screaming with laughter, pointed to her red dress, which had burst open revealing her bosom in a lace bra.

Berthold's telegram was handed to me after we had left the table. I read it aloud and Heinrich Mann suggested that all the guests send a greeting to the absent host. While everyone gathered to sign his name, I said to Bruno Frank how touched I was by the wonderful homage the brothers had paid each other.

"Yes," said Bruno. "They write and read such ceremonial evaluations of each other, every ten years."

35

THE DEFUNCT HAPSBURG MONARCHY must have been much more broadminded than the Legion of Decency and "The Catholic Interest Committee of the Knights of Columbus of Manhattan and the Bronx," who both maintained that our comedy was glorifying adultery.

The Two-Faced Woman had this plot in common with the original *Twin Sister*: to test her husband's fidelity and refresh his subsiding ardors, a young woman impersonates a non-existing twin sister, whose mondaine, flighty, capricious personality contrasts with her demure and less superficial self. The experiment succeeds and dismayed she sees him fall head over heels in love with the invented twin.

Gottfried Reinhardt was the producer, under Bernie Hyman's executive control. George Cukor directed, Sam N. Behrman and I wrote the screenplay with Mr. George Oppenheimer, who having participated in the creation of Marx Brothers comedies was an expert in the farcical situations to which Bernie was so devotedly attached. As nothing divides people more than difference in their sense of humor, it was a miracle that my friendship with Gottfried survived the severe test. Sam Behrman's authority and intervention prevented many bitter feuds. But the attacks upon the film were unjustified; it was also not true that it had "degraded" a great actress. I saw it in London, twenty-five years after it was made, when age and events had made me objective and even indifferent. I found the audience amused and appreciative; I thought that it had very funny scenes and, thanks to Sam, excellent and witty dialogue. But I thought that Garbo was miscast. Unlike *Ninotchka*, in which Lubitsch had humorously exploited her unique personality, *The Two-Faced Woman* demanded a flippant comedienne. Nevertheless Garbo's beauty and charm were prodigiously rewarding even in this unimportant film.

The assertion that *The Two-Faced Woman* "glorified incest and adultery" appeared preposterous even to Louis B. Mayer, and he invited Archbishop Spellman, who was visiting Los Angeles, to see and judge the film. After a lunch with the executive his Eminence had a wonderful time in the projection room. He gave the film his blessing but suggested that we add a scene, showing that the husband knew all along that the twin sister was his one and only wife. This change did not improve the film.

My next job was *The Paradine Case*, a classic murder novel, which was not for Garbo; but Victor Saville, the producer, would have been delighted had she shown any interest, and the star role would have been rewritten for her.

A "junior writer," Miss Polly James, was to help me with linguistic problems. We liked each other and the work went pleasantly and smoothly ahead.

One day I read that Lawrence Steinhardt had been appointed as U.S. ambassador to Moscow. Garbo had met him when he was assigned to Stockholm and she thought that perhaps he could precipitate the visa for my mother. He answered her cable immediately: ". . . I shall do everything possible to facilitate the departure of Mrs. Steuermann as soon as her immigration case has been established in the Consular Section of the Embassy . . ."

In February, 1941 I had received a telegram signed by Viktoria, which asked me to cable fifteen hundred dollars to a Mr. Konrad Styckgold in New York, and immediately notify her that the required sum had been sent. The cable ended with the mysterious words: "The eternal road. See you soon. Viktoria Holowka." I cabled the fifteen hundred dollars and on May 30 another cable from Dusko notified me that Mama had left for Moscow to get a Japanese visa, and that she would embark in Kobe on the S.S. *Cleveland*, sailing on July 20. Immediately I mailed a check to the American Embassy for her passage and held my breath. However new rules and regulations relating to visas became effective on July 3, and my friend in Washington informed me that "from now on all decisions were made by the Department of State and not by the consuls abroad." He promised that he would do everything to get the authorities to reapprove the visa quickly and notify Mr. Steinhardt. Meanwhile, it was impossible for Mama to sail on the S.S. *Cleveland* as the Soviet government withheld her permission to leave. She was seventy-three, did not know a soul in Moscow, and the thought of her anguish and loneliness haunted me. I kept sending money and telegrams to the U.S. Embassy.

I'll never forget one night when Hans and Thomas had induced me to go to the movies in Hollywood. As we left the theater we heard the newspaper boys shout: "German armies invade Russia." First I did not believe the headline; then my next thought was of Dusko in Sambor and my mother in Moscow!

The next morning, it was a Sunday, I got a cable from Dusko, asking me to send "the same sum as for Augusta," but the banks were closed and the telegraph office refused to forward money to the war zone. I tried all day Monday, but all connections with West Ukraine were cut. My only hope was that Dusko had fled with the retreating Soviets.

Soon after these events Lawrence Steinhardt arrived in Los Angeles and visited MGM. Greta brought him to my office. He was very sympathetic and said he knew my mother, as she often came to the Embassy. "We are all greatly impressed by the charming old lady. The Russians occasionally ask favors of us and on the next occasion I will insist that they let your mother leave the country." He kept his word.

The following letter arrived late in July. It was dated June 16, 1941.

Moscow, Hotel National. June 16, 1941

Dearest, dearest Edek and Salka: This is now the third week that I am besieging the Police Department to give me permission to leave Russia. They say I will have to wait until I get an answer to my application and then it is not at all certain that it will be positive. At the American Embassy they are very attentive to me. Mr. Steinhardt received me with utmost friendliness and told me that he had seen you, darling Salka, and promised you to do everything in his power to get me to America. So there is nothing else to do but to wait patiently, which is not easy.

In the first few days alone in this huge, beautiful city, I thought I would go insane and did not dare to leave the hotel. But my love for music saved me. There are concerts every day at the music schools, where one does not have to pay and I can listen to remarkable pianists. Yesterday, a certain Bublikow, a pupil of Igunow, made a great impression upon me. He played Schumann's *Waldszenen* and Rachmaninoff's third concerto and was really marvelous. I am also going to hear Portnoj play a concerto by an Armenian composer.

Portnoj does not cease to regret that you, Edward, are not here, as it is an Eldorado for artists. Your pupils Muenzer and Koffler have great success; they play in Leningrad, in Kiev, in the Crimea. Their concerts are well organized; they are paid a lot of money and don't have to worry about anything. Yesterday I went to hear the Bach-Schoenberg Cantata performed by a new young conductor. I did not think he was an interesting personality.

There are many theaters and you can see *Othello* in Armenian, *King Lear* in Yiddish, *Maria Stuart* in Russian. What the Russians have achieved is very impressive, but one has to be young here and able to work hard. For old people like me, life is very bitter because we are useless. I hope this exit permit will come soon! Salka is spending large sums to get me out and I am stuck in this hotel room for which I have to pay twenty-four rubles. However, the hotel has one advantage: it is close to the American Embassy, even on the same side of the street. The streets are so wide and there is such traffic that I have to gather all my courage to cross. Luckily the music school is not too far away and on a narrower street. I also have my meals there in the students' canteen, which is clean, simple and cheap.

My only hope is that Dusko will now work more intensely and not rely upon Salka's checks. This was the main reason for my leaving. I would gladly travel third-class on the Trans-Siberian but they say at the Embassy that I would not be able to stand eleven days and eleven nights on a hard wooden bench. However, my trip from Lwow to Moscow (two days and two nights third-class) was not bad at all.

The young lady at the Embassy, a Russian Jewess from Odessa, saw from my passport that I was born in Mogilev and the name Rafalovicz impressed her. Now she comes every day to take me to lunch. I am really very grateful, because it is sad to be so alone. I am counting the days till our reunion, my dear children.

The letter arrived while the Nazis were rapidly advancing toward Moscow. I sustained my faith in Russia by reading *War and Peace*.

In August a telegram from Washington confirmed that the

"visa case Augusta Steuermann had been approved by the Inter-departmental Committee," and Moscow notified. In the bombed city my mother still waited for permission to leave the country. Finally, in early September, Steinhardt cabled me that she would leave on the Trans-Siberian to Vladivostok, and from there on a steamer to the United States. I assumed that she had a cabin on one of the new Lend-Lease ships.

It took two months of anguished waiting before a telephone call from the Immigration Office in Seattle reached me at the studio, and a friendly voice requested me to stay on the line because "a very dear person" wanted to talk to me. As it was unusual for the Immigration officers to call a passenger "a very dear person," I knew that it could only be my mother. It was her seventy-fourth birthday; she had just disembarked after a six weeks' sea voyage and ten days on the Trans-Siberian train. Her voice sounded gay and fresh, as if it had been the shortest trip she had ever made.

As Soviet ships crossing the Pacific could not send radio messages, my mother had not been able to let me know when and where she would arrive, and I could not meet her. But the new Soviet-American friendship had prompted the Immigration authorities to welcome her, a Soviet citizen, with warm-hearted, American hospitality and to give a birthday party for her. The Polish interpreter, Madame Jasny, put her on the train to Los Angeles, and two days later with my sons and Etta, I was waiting for her at the station.

I cannot describe what I felt when I saw an emaciated, old woman emerge from the Pullman and recognized that it was my mother. She had been strong and vigorous when I had seen her in Switzerland, now I was holding a trembling, worn-out creature in old tattered clothes. The most pitiful sight were the "new" shoes she had bought in Moscow. They alone told the heartbreaking story of the suffering of the Soviet people.

After we had calmed down, Mama explained her trembling: "The bombings—" she said, apologetically. "First at home and then in Moscow. It is the most horrible experience, believe me. Imagine what the people go through in London!"

I couldn't wait to feed and dress and pamper her. When she began to gain weight and to recover her strength, her trembling subsided, although it never completely left her. California enchanted her. She admired the flowers, the ocean, the abundance of fruit, "and what a blessing that you never have snow." But Dusko, Hania, Viktoria, Adam, and her old friends were constantly on her mind. During her stay in Moscow, until the German invasion, she had been in steady contact with them. "They wanted me to leave," she told me, "because if anything happened it would be easier for them to move. After all, I was a burden, and then I wanted to see you, Rose and Edward before I died."

She assumed that once the German advance was achieved, a local Ukrainian administration would take over Sambor. An independent pro-Nazi Ukraine was one of Hitler's aims. My mother hoped that Viktoria, who had married a young Ukrainian, would be able to protect Hania and the boy. But the Jews were doomed and Dusko could do nothing but flee with the retreating Russians.

She liked to talk about her two years under Soviet rule. She had attended courses teaching the Soviet constitution, which she found idealistic and which promised people a better future. "However," she sighed, "as in all religions, on paper everything looks different than in practice." The population was told to choose whether they wanted to be Polish or Russian, and luckily she, Dusko and her household opted for the Soviets. Those who opted for Poland were immediately deported to unknown places. The Russians had "nationalized" Wychylowka, depriving her of the house and all her possessions, but such was "the system." Otherwise, she found them friendly, good-hearted and severely punishing anti-semitism.

When the news spread that I had got my mother out of Russia, friends and acquaintances wanted to hear about her experiences and I had to give a big tea party. Everyone brought friends. The ladies crowded around Mama, expressing admiration for her English, which she was just learning to speak; but after a while I noticed that only Bertolt Brecht and his wife Helli were paying attention to her. Some others even neglected to say good-bye to her. Old age even gallantly borne frightened them.

Brecht and Helli (the actress Helene Weigel) with their children, Stefan and Barbara, had arrived in California in July, preceding Mama by three months. Their journey from Finland, Moscow and Vladivostok, then on a Swedish ship via the Panama Canal to San Pedro, was even longer than hers. This was the disastrous summer of Hitler's victories and we spent many evenings together trying not to abandon hope. Hanns Eisler, whom I had known in Vienna when he was studying with Schoenberg, was an old friend of Brecht and he and his dark-haired, petite wife Lou were often with us. They were already acclimatized to Hollywood, and popular in American literary circles: Eisler because of his brilliant mind and jolliness, Lou because of her humor and intelligence.

The high rank Brecht now occupies in world literature does not need any restating in these personal recollections. His work and its influence are discussed every day in newspapers, essays and critical works. Books about him are written in many languages and his plays are performed everywhere in the East and West. It was not so in Hollywood. Life was hard: "Every morning to earn my bread I go to the market where they buy lies. . . ." he wrote.

After the Reichstag fire Brecht and his family had fled first to Denmark, where they were guests of the venerable Karin Michaelis, whose novel *The Woman of Forty* had shocked my mother's generation. When Hitler invaded Denmark and Norway they went to Finland, where they got their U.S. visa and, as the Nazis were then marching into Russia, Brecht and Helli with their two children left for America. Brecht's friend and secretary Margarete Steffin, Karin Michaelis and Ruth Berlau, a Danish actress, went with them. The hopelessly ill Margarete Steffin died in Moscow.

The Brechts rented an old wooden bungalow on Twenty-sixth Street in Santa Monica. It was very simple but spacious. Of the two large rooms on the first floor, one became Brecht's frugally furnished workroom, the other the living room. At the back of the house was a lovely garden with flowers and fruit trees.

Neither Brecht nor Helli had changed much since our Berlin days. His black hair, combed down and cut straight above the forehead, made his thin face resemble a Chinese sage, although the aquiline, fine nose remained irrefutably Caucasian. The mouth, with its thin, tight upper lip over rather bad teeth, had a deceptively mild expression; behind glasses, the dark deep-set eyes looked sceptically humorous. The leather jacket he used to wear in Berlin was replaced in California by a gray flannel shirt with a straight collar and was tailored by Helli. She had acquired many skills and had become the all-around working woman and mother: sewing, cooking, gardening and washing. After a long day's chores she would stay up half of the night, serving tea and homemade cakes to visitors who came to discuss the war and to quote Brecht later. Hollywood actresses who met Helli at the Chaplins' or in my house were amazed when I told them that she was their distinguished colleague. "She certainly doesn't look it," concluded the flighty ones, after they had scrutinized her face and straight hair pulled back in a tight knot. Exile, hard work and the difficult, although unswerving, relationship with Brecht had left their mark on the bony, strong features which never wore make-up.

To the "film colony" the Brechts were strangers, an odd European couple who did not speak English (although Brecht understood everything and could follow discussions). But he refused to express himself stumblingly in an alien tongue, unlike Hanns

Eisler who, unconcerned about grammar and his atrocious accent, enlivened the dullest parties.

Brecht's contribution to the Hollywood output was very small indeed. *The Hangmen Also Die*, a Fritz Lang film for which Eisler wrote the music, went through the usual grind, and Brecht withdrew his name from the screenplay. *The Visions of Simone Marchand*, on which he collaborated with Feuchtwanger, was sold to MGM but never made into a film. However he worked on his poems and the plays, *Mother Courage, Arturo Ui, The Caucasian Chalk Circle, Schweik* and *The Good Woman of Tse-Tsuan*.

The German colony was divided into several groups, but Thomas Mann remained the representative, towering literary figure, his influence reaching as far as Washington D.C. Bruno and Liesl Frank had been close to the Mann family for many years and the friendship continued in Hollywood. The Feuchtwangers, Franz and Alma Werfel, the Bruno Walters and Liesl Frank's famous mother, the musical comedy star Fritzi Massary, belonged to this circle, also the Dieterles. Then there was a devoted admiring group around Fritz Kortner.

The Polgars who did not belong to any group, spent their Sundays on Mabery Road. Max Reinhardt and Helene Thimig were preoccupied with the Workshop and the planning and preparing of its productions. They entertained rarely but these occasions were usually exceptionally pleasant. One evening I was invited with Sam Behrman, Franz Werfel and Alma, Mr. and Mrs. Erich Korngold and Gottfried. The Stravinskys came later, missing a marvelous dinner. They had never met Alma before. Remembering her position in the musical world, and forgetting Werfel, she rushed toward Stravinsky, announcing: "I am Alma Mahler." She was an imposing woman, still blond with large blue eyes and the old-fashioned charm of a Viennese beauty. The two great composers, Stravinsky and Schoenberg, avoided each other ostentatiously, and in fact only shortly before Schoenberg's death did they mutually acknowledge their importance. Later Stravinsky paid great homage to Schoenberg and to his music.

During his first years in Los Angeles, Schoenberg was teaching counterpoint at the University of California. His classes were crowded not only by students but also by jazz musicians of whom many also took private lessons from him. Edward used his summer vacations in Santa Monica to rehearse and prepare performances of Schoenberg's compositions, one of which, the "Pierrot Lunaire," took place in our living room, with Schoenberg conducting and the lovely Erika Wagner (Mrs. Fritz Stiedry in private life) speaking the text. All the literary and musical elite was present, among others three famous conductors: Bruno Walter, Otto Klemperer and Fritz Stiedry. The applause was not unanimous, but it was led by Thomas Mann, clapping his hands heartily while Bruno Walter whispered into his ear, obviously disapproving. That same winter Leopold Stokowski conducted Schoenberg's piano concerto in New York, with Edward as soloist. It was an almost unopposed success for everyone concerned.

The German invasion of Russia and the help America was sending to the Soviets had changed the attitude of the American Left, split during the Stalin-Hitler pact. In November, when the Germans had reached Sevastopol and Rostow, gloom settled on everyone. But in December the Soviets reconquered Rostow, relieving Moscow, and their offensive gave hope that the tide was turning. To this hope my mother and I clung persistently and desperately, praying for Dusko, Hania and Viktoria, and the millions of Slavic and Jewish people.

On one of the gray December afternoons I left the studio quite early and trying to fight my dismal dejection, I drove to the Santa Monica pier.

The clouds above the horizon had broken up and become purple, mauve, pink and silver-gray; the sun in their midst was like an enormous orange. I walked down the deserted pier, watching the orange ball disappear in the clouds, then suddenly come out blood-red and sink into the dark water. At the very end of the pier a young girl was sitting on the wooden planks, her legs in torn, faded jeans dangling through the railing. She wore a man's shirt, wide open, showing firm, round breasts. In one arm she held a fat baby which was sucking avidly; in her other hand a fishing rod, its line stretched far out in the water. She was watching the float with great concentration. I could not tear myself away from this sight of complete calm and satisfaction.

Next morning I took my mother for a drive in the open car along the Pacific and we listened to the Sunday concert from New York, which came over the radio. It was a combination of two of Mama's great pleasures. Arthur Rubinstein was just finishing the first movement of the Tchaikowsky Piano Concerto no. 1, when the broadcast was interrupted and the announcer said that early in the morning Japanese airplanes and submarines had attacked and sunk the American fleet in Pearl Harbor.

36

ALL THE JAPANESE LIVING IN CALIFORNIA were sent to concentration camps or, as they were politely called, "internment centers." Then Hitler declared war on the United States, and German refugees had to register as enemy aliens and to observe an 8 P.M. curfew. Thomas Mann and Albert Einstein appealed to the President: "The earliest and most far-sighted adversaries of the totalitarian governments, who have risked their lives by fighting and warning against forces of evil are now subjected to a humiliating treatment."

Strangely enough, there was no curfew in the East, where the "Bund" and the "Silver Shirts" had an impressively large membership of racists and pro-Nazis of German origin. In Hollywood most refugees goodnaturedly accepted the restriction of their liberty. They observed the blackouts and spent their evenings at home, convinced that a "fifth column" existed and caution was necessary. My former colleague from the Reinhardt theaters, Alexander Granch, used the time to write his moving memoirs. The younger men rushed to enlist in the army, which automatically made them American citizens.

Many of my friends, among them Annie von Bucovich, left Los Angeles to work at the Office of War Information. The Coordinator was our friend John Houseman, a producer at MGM.

I was visited several times by the FBI—strong, handsome young men, who would have served their country better in the Marines rather than in harassing the refugees. I specifically remember their inquiry about Annie:

"Is the lady a communist?"

"No, she is not."

"She is a Russian . . . ?"

"She is neither a Russian nor a communist."

"She is anti-fascist?"

"Yes, she is."

The FBI man shook his head disapprovingly. "Oh, you people," he said with a deep sigh. "You are anti-fascist but I have never heard one of you say: I am anti-communist."

"Whom do you mean by 'you people'?" I asked belligerently. "The refugees? They were the first victims of the Nazi horror, the first enemies of the regime with which the U.S. is at war. And aren't the Russians our allies?" But I realized that my outburst was a waste of time and energy, so I assured him once more that Annie was not and had never been a communist and had never read a word of *Das Kapital*.

Gottfried was in uniform almost immediately. The Army could not be persuaded of his usefulness in "intelligence" or "psychological warfare" and after basic training, he was assigned to the Signal Corps to write scenarios for films glorifying the building of latrines, rifle cleaning, prevention of V.D., and all things vital to warfare. The only redeeming feature of this uninspiring but necessary work, was that his outfit was stationed at the Astoria Film Studios in Long Island, and he could live in Manhattan.

When the United States entered the war Peter was under contract to David Selznick, but loaned out to write a film for Warner Brothers. He did not wait to be drafted but enlisted in the Marines. I was greatly distressed that he had chosen the toughest branch of the U.S. forces and blamed Oliver for influencing him. Oliver denied it but said that he approved of Peter's decision. "The Marines are our elite corps," he told me. "Their training is rough, long and severe, but it provides greater safety and more opportunity for individual initiative." I was skeptical about the "safety" and the words "individual initiative" made my blood freeze.

Oliver had married again, but this time he had made a more congenial choice. Charlcie was an attractive Southerner from Alabama, generous, warm-hearted and not as competitive as her predecessor, except when they played Bridge. They had moved into a house on Mabery Road and we saw each other often. I could not share Oliver's enthusiasm about the Marines, not even after I had received an impressive gilded certificate that my son had passed successfully the "mental, moral and physical examination required for a Marine . . . On behalf of our President, Secretary of the Navy, Commandant of the Marine Corps and Officer in Charge of Western Recruiting Division." I was heartily congratulated "for being able to furnish a son who measures up to the high standard required for enlistment in the United States Marine Corps."

The words "son" and the "two" of the date 1942 had been typed in.

Berthold, in New York, reacted better to Peter's enlistment than I expected: "Peter wrote me a very moving letter, which depicts clearly the fixation under which he labors, as, more or less, we all do. He cannot divert his eyes from Hitler's gorgonian features, he is compelled to face the monster, man to man, as in a duel, otherwise his own existence will become worthless to him."

All this was true and irrefutable and, as always, we both felt alike; still it was hard for me to control my growing depression and anxiety and continue writing scenarios. It tortured me to think that Peter had become a tiny, passive particle in an immense, grinding mechanism, never knowing where and how it might evolve and—I pushed away the thought that he could be killed— how it might change him. I loathed people who said: "The Marines will make a man of him." The training alone: this teaching of killing, of brutality, the drill sergeants demanding that it be done enthusiastically, was amply gruesome. I had seen war and fervently hoped never to see it again. Now a demented maniac, and the endemic German nationalism forced me to admit that this one had to be fought and suffered to the bitter end. And I had "furnished" a son to participate in it.

Because of his impaired hearing Hans was not called. He was still with the Reinhardt Workshop and getting more and more involved with the theater. He played a comedy part in *Jederman*, which the Workshop produced.

He wrote to Berthold,

> My best (?) lines, usually brought on in the audience a silence that you could cut with a knife. But on the second night, somehow my timing and everything else clicked perfectly and I got laughs just about every time I opened my mouth. Reinhardt was very pleased and said that I should remember that night, for it was my birthday as an actor . . . I do not know whether it is good or bad that the theater fills me as completely as it does. But I definitely feel: "Here I belong, this is my place in life." I have tried to get away from it, but have always been driven back . . . I think I should make my work such as to bridge that old contradiction * which we have talked about so much, and to build my place in life so that I do not have to reproach myself.

* He obviously meant the contradiction of being a socialist but removed from the realities of the life of the working class.

> . . . I am thinking of going away from the theater for
> a short while, into a more "primary" occupation, in
> order to live as most people do. . . . Concretely, this
> means some kind of industrial work. I know you will
> say (and rightly) "What, again!" But this time the
> perspective is different. What do you think?

And without waiting to know what his father thought he went
to work in the shipyards. He would come home unshaven and
grimy, a helmet on his head, every inch "the worker." One day he
phoned that he would bring a friend for dinner. I was expecting
the Huxleys and had promised Maria that we would be alone.
Hans pleaded with me; Norman was an admirer of Huxley and it
would be "a great thing" if he could meet him. I softened and
gave in, admonishing Hans that they should not be late.

As usual the Huxleys arrived on the dot and we were drinking our
sherry when Hans and Norman, a frail, short, ungainly young Jew
from Brooklyn, made their entrance, looking as if they had
emerged from the bottom of a coal freighter. Only good manners
prevented Maria from wincing, when Norman, with a "toity toit"
accent thanked me for the invitation.

At dinner the young people kept silent, while Aldous talked
about cheese. He not only knew every kind of cheese, but also the
history of its origin. His knowledge and memory were awe-
inspiring. After dinner the conversation switched to films and
Maria wanted to know if I had an interesting assignment. I said
that I had an idea for a Cagliostro film. Aldous was very much in
favor of it; he himself thought that Mesmer and his experiments
with animal magnetism and hypnosis were "extraordinary." He
told us about some phenomena which sounded quite uncanny,
and named several books I should read, when unexpectedly Norman corrected him about the author of one of them. I forget the
name and the issue; all I remember is Aldous's exquisite Oxford
English cutting sharply through Norman's nasal Brooklynese and
with a few withering words putting him in his place. But, un-
withered, Norman stood up to his idol. A conspicuous tremolo in
his voice betrayed his nervousness as he said bravely: "It's easy for
you, Mr. Huxley, to ridicule me, who never went to college; nevertheless, I've read a great deal about occultism, Mesmer and others,
because it fascinates me." Suddenly Huxley's face lost its haughty
expression and became soft and embarrassed. It seemed to me that
he blushed. Leaning forward, he put his hand on Norman's arm
and warmly apologized: "I really am sorry. Of course you are right,

please excuse my remark. I should have mentioned. . . ." and on went the discussion, now on quite equal terms.

After the Huxleys left the transfigured Norman exclaimed: "I felt like throwing myself on the floor and letting him walk on me to the door." Soon afterward, Norman died very young and several years later I came upon one of Huxley's short stories written in his youth, which shocked me by the rather crude anti-semitism one of the characters expressed.

Before he left for his training, Peter invited me to have dinner with him at a restaurant on Sunset Boulevard, as he sometimes did when he wanted a quiet tête-à-tête with me. When I arrived I found Harold Clurman waiting for me at the reserved table, and was pleased that he was dining with us. We ordered our drinks; then Peter appeared with a young woman, Virginia Schulberg. I had met her before; she was the wife of Budd Schulberg, son of the Paramount executive. Budd's first novel, *What Makes Sammy Run*, was much talked about. Virginia was strikingly lovely, her figure neat and slim. She walked and moved with an exceptional grace. The shoulder-length dark hair was held back by a black velvet ribbon; she wore no make-up, and with her shining eyes and rosy complexion she had an aura of wholesomeness and outdoor living, although at the moment, probably because of me, she was so tense and nervous that it made everyone uncomfortable. I knew immediately that she and Peter were in love. In spite of Harold's efforts, the dinner lacked gaiety. With Peter leaving in the next days this was quite understandable. "Jigee," as Peter and Harold called her, did not talk much and left soon. Peter was to meet her later, after he had driven me home. As soon as we were alone I asked if his infatuation with Virginia was as serious as it appeared. He said yes, and that she intended to ask Budd for a divorce. "She is a wonderful girl, Mother."

Peter was twenty-one and although his book had been a literary success and he had had film jobs, his ability to support a family, especially now as a Marine private, was, to put it euphemistically, dubious. Virginia was twenty-six, she and Budd had a two-year-old girl, and since her marriage she had lived the luxurious, carefree life of the Hollywood rich. But I have never considered economic security more important than love.

In the following days most of my time was spent with Jigee in the parking lots of office buildings, waiting for Peter who had endless last-minute errands. We used these hours to get acquainted with each other. She had heard all sorts of opinions and judgments of me, some harsh, many exaggeratedly admiring. I knew less about her, but I foresaw that she would need a lot of courage to face the future. How would Budd take it? And Peter somewhere on the other side of the globe . . . it might be months, perhaps years, before they could live together. While we were thus sharing sadness and anxieties she became very close to me. We both knew that once Peter was gone we would need each other. At the moment things were not too bad: Peter's camp was near San Diego and we could visit him on Sundays.

Jigee went to Mexico and returned shaken and unhappy but determined to leave Budd. She told me she could not feel guilty for loving Peter and that the failure of her marriage was not her fault alone. This was probably true, but the Schulberg family disagreed with her on that issue.

The boot camp was a rough experience for Peter and the more I heard of the "Marine spirit" the more I loathed it. No, I was not made to be the mother of a Marine. He shared his tent with four other boys, all from an orphanage in Texas and none older than seventeen. Until they were recruited they had known nothing but life in the orphanage. They made ugly, anti-semitic remarks and Peter told them to cut it out, and that he was a Jew. They were deeply shaken and confessed that they had never seen a Jew before. For days they went out of their way to show him their repentance, cleaning his boots and rifle and doing all the disagreeable chores for him.

Jigee's parents were working-class Americans, ruined by the Depression. The father, Robert Ray, a handsome man but twenty years older than his wife Henny, was always talking about the happy days when he traveled with his parents in a covered wagon. These memories must have left in him an unceasing restlessness and when I knew him in his old age, and divorced by Henny after twenty-five years of marriage, he was moving back and forth in his trailer, from Santa Monica to the Mojave desert, looking up old pals from his prospecting days. The trailer had become a substitute for the covered wagon. He was a distrustful, lonely man, full of prejudice against Jews, Negroes, Hollywood, his sons-in-law, and the whole "damned, new-fangled" twentieth century. But he adored his daughters. Henny was a hardworking housewife if ever there was one, and a romantic. Having divorced Robert she married her "high school sweetheart," a night clerk in a modest beach hotel, who played the violin and wore his hair long. It was snow-white.

The Rays' two daughters, Jigee and Anne, were helping their parents financially. Anne, the elder, was handsome, vivacious, very witty, but not as lovely as Jigee. She had a good job as an execu-

tive secretary, was efficient, independent and very much in love
with a young, successful screenwriter, Melvin Frank, whom she
soon married. Before she met Budd Schulberg Jigee had been a
dancer in the Paramount chorus. Budd's mother, Ad, had had
strong reservations about the marriage and after it broke up,
warned me of Jigee's "destructive character." But the broadminded young generation, Budd's sister Sonja, and Stewart his
younger brother, remained her friends. Later I understood that
what Ad called "destructive" was Jigee's negativism, her quick
"giving up," an admitted distrust of herself and a frequent mis-
conception about the motives of others.

As long as Peter was in training Jigee used to meet him in La
Jolla or Coronado beach, close to his camp, and spend Sundays
with him. On other days she would come to see me with her little,
curly-haired Vicky. We spent Sundays on the beach. When I was
taking a walk Vicky would usually appear at my side and silently
slip her hand into mine, trying to keep step with me; with this
handclasp she also took hold of my heart.

But even the training of a Marine comes to an end, and Peter
was shipped to the Pacific. My dreary, unsatisfactory work was no
distraction nor remedy for the persistent worry about his where-
abouts and assignment, the longing and uncertainty. We guessed
that he was in New Caledonia, undergoing further training. Jigee
and I shared his news and forwarded it to Berthold, who, between
outbursts of energy and frustration, was trying to find a foothold
on rocky, slippery Broadway. After he had staged *They Walk
Alone*, in which Elsa Lancaster appeared in the part created by
Beatrix Lehman, he was preparing a play with Oscar Homolka.

His book of poems, *Fürchte Dich Nicht*, came out and received
great praise. Heinrich and Thomas Mann, Alfred Polgar and
Herman Broch wrote enthusiastically about it in refugee newspapers and weeklies, which were the intellectual sustenance of the
emigrants. He had found a happy relationship with a Viennese
actress, Elisabeth Neumann, also a refugee, a courageous, loving,
cheerful human being. I had met her when I was in New York for
a few weeks vacation. Berthold was much more at peace with
himself, and also with me and Gottfried. We saw each other
often, and also Edward when he could tear himself away from his
lessons and rehearsals.

Max Reinhardt was in New York, staging *Rosalinda*, which was
nothing else than good old *Fledermaus* rewritten and revamped by
Gottfried and another G.I. It turned out to be Max Reinhardt's
last success. As I remember, it ran for more than a year. Gottfried
and I went to Toscanini's NBC broadcasts, to which Eleonora

provided the tickets. We were happy; the Russians were winning the battle of Stalingrad.

There was no visible effort at MGM to find a new story for Garbo, until one day Bernie Hyman asked me excitedly to come to the projection room and see a Russian film, which a European producer, Mr. Rabinowich, had imported and intended to show in the States. The title of the film was *The Girl from Leningrad*. It was a moving, simple story about a wounded soldier and a nurse, made during the Russian-Finnish war, but changed into the Soviet-German conflict. The menacing presence of the Nazis was not so much seen as constantly felt, in the black winter forests which could just as well have been somewhere near Leningrad. I asked Greta to see the film, and she was very impressed. However, MGM decided against it. Perhaps Garbo's enthusiasm was not emphatic enough, or they did not want to make a film sympathetic to the Soviets, or L. B. Mayer felt compelled to glorify the deeds of the Red armies in his own way. *The Song of Russia* was chosen instead of *The Girl from Leningrad*. This story had been concocted by director Gregory Ratoff, a gregarious White Russian with a hilarious accent, and two leftish screenwriters. Anna Louise Strong, for many years a Moscow correspondent to American papers, was called in as "technical advisor." I saw her often in the corridors of the Thalberg building: a large, white-haired woman leaning heavily on a cane, flanked by her collaborators (one of them later recanted his "sins" before the Committee on Un-American Activities). The story was not merely a tribute to the sacrifice of the Russian people; it was also intended to exploit the then much publicized Garbo/Stokowski romance. Ratoff told it in a nutshell: "Russian girl falls in love with famous American conductor, who arrives in Russia to give concerts but gets involved in the scorched earth policy." Mr. Ratoff wanted me to convince Garbo to play the girl, "a magnificent role and written especially for her." He described the scenes in which she sets the torch to the harvest, while her lover conducts Tchaikowsky's 1812 Overture. "Garrrbo is making scorrrched earrrth," cried Gregory, carried away and rolling his rrr's. "All alone she scorrrches the Rrrussian earrrth, while Stokowski—I mean, Rrrobert Taylor—conducts."

Ultimately *The Song of Russia* was played by Susan Peters and Robert Taylor. I did not see it, but even the most fanatical pro-Russians assured me that it was perfectly dreadful. Nevertheless, it became one of the many unjustified accusations of communist infiltration of Hollywood, which L. B. Mayer had to explain before the Committee on Un-American Activities.

And so the search for a Garbo story continued with the usual frustration, until Bernie Hyman, who had Garbo's interest sincerely at heart, suddenly died at the age of forty-two. Despite his procrastinations and sentimentality, he was kind and a real friend.

37

STALINGRAD, THE DEFENSE OF LENINGRAD, the landings in Africa and Italy, the relentless bombardments of German cities, all led us to believe that the end of Hitler was nearing. But any hope of a national uprising, an anti-Nazi underground movement—based on Breda's predictions—proved to be in vain. The Gestapo was monstrously efficient and the working class accepted with inexhaustible docility the demolition of their homes, terror, misery and death.

In 1942 the Molotov Report revealed for the first time the atrocities in Poland and Russia, but most Americans refused to believe it, saying: "Soviet propaganda." I was hiding the gruesome reports from my mother. As long as Sambor was occupied by the Germans I tried to convince her and myself that Dusko had escaped with the Soviet garrison.

The Japanese were in the Philippines, spreading so far out over the islands of the Pacific that they threatened Australia. We did not know where Peter was. The mail was slow and irregular.

Then ultimately the unavoidable but predictable occurred: Gottfried's falling in love with a young woman he was soon to marry brought an end to our relationship. It is senseless to compare one's own grief with the enduring horror suffered by millions, but the consciousness of unspeakable tragedy makes sudden loneliness even more desperate and hopeless. It was difficult to extricate myself from an involvement which, for ten years, had been a vital part of my life. I was very fond of Wolfgang and Lally and, in the years they had lived in California, Max Reinhardt and his wife Helene had shown me affection, friendship and sympathy, which I fully returned. Else, his former wife, was a friend in spite of our

long established disagreements about love and divorce. She had
been a daily visitor in our house, and Mama, who had admired her
on the stage, was always glad to see her, amused by her eccentric-
ities.

The constant changes of residence had delayed Berthold's
American citizenship, and to achieve it at last he decided to return
to Santa Monica for six months, and just as he had resented my
past happiness he now resented my sadness. "Whoever touches
your heart does not foresee that he is unleashing an avalanche!" he
told me bitterly.

Max Reinhardt's seventieth birthday was in September, 1943.
He celebrated it in New York in excellent health and hardly looking his age. A few months before he had staged Irwin Shaw's *Sons
and Soldiers* which, alas, had not been a success, and he was planning with mellow resignation a production of Offenbach's *La Belle
Helene*. The last time we saw each other he wryly admitted that
he would prefer not to be regarded in America as "a specialist in
musicals."

A few weeks later Wolfgang told me that his father, who had
never been ill in his life, had lost his speech. After a few weeks he
was better and it seemed that he would recover. But another
stroke paralyzed his right side and when his wife arrived from
California, he was dying. Both sons were with him, while we in
Mabery Road—Berthold, Else, forgiving at last, Lally, Hans and
Mama—were waiting in the living room, hoping against hope.

For Else, Max Reinhardt remained the only man in her life; for
Lally, a myth, whose indestructible charm she constantly discovered in Wolfgang; for Hans, a master, the first one to give him
sympathetic encouragement. To Berthold and me he had always
been, in one way or another, an enormous influence in our artistic
life, even when we opposed him. To be "discovered" by Reinhardt
had meant more to me than the best contracts at royal theaters.
However, in Hollywood the glory was gone and it always gave me a
jolt when I heard a nasal voice call him "Max." The Workshop
with its young, raw and inexperienced students, made it impossible
to stage unforgettable performances, but on that long October
night, while we waited for the call from New York, I remembered
an incident I had witnessed one evening when Reinhardt was
rehearsing a Maugham play. The unassuming Workshop auditorium was almost empty, only a few students were lolling about in
the chairs, backstage someone was banging the piano. Reinhardt
was showing a young man how to play the scene preceding the

last-act curtain. The action was silent; everyone has left, only the butler tidies the living room, empties the ashtrays into the fire-place, drinks the liquor left in the glasses, puffs up the pillows on the couch and blows out the candles. All this is done with musical accompaniment. With inimitable grace and precision, Max Rein-hardt was acting this pantomime in perfect timing to the slowly descending curtain. I was watching in breathless enchantment and was loath to have the curtain come down. . . .

We jumped when the telephone rang. It was Gottfried to tell us that his father was dead.

In the summer of that year I left MGM. The producers offered Greta screenplays which she did not find suitable and everything I suggested, with or without her consent, was persistently rejected. There was no Thalberg, no Selznick, no Bernie Hyman to talk to. One day Louis B. Mayer asked me to come to his office. In a very melodramatic tone he accused me of being a heartless highbrow. "If I would ask you to write a scene for Greta" he pronounced it Greter "in which a poor mother prays for her dying child, you would smile contemptuously and say it's corny, wouldn't you? Such a scene would never bring tears to your eyes!"

Amazed at this assault I said: "What makes you think it would not, Mr. Mayer? It depends on the scene and the story!" I broke off, embarrassed. Nothing in the world would have made me say that a Metro film *could* "bring tears" to my eyes.

He went on telling me that Joan Crawford blindly followed his advice and had fared very well by it, and "that poor little girl, Judy Garland, she always does what I tell her; even Norma listens to me—only Garbo is difficult. I am her best friend. I want her to be happy—she should come and tell me what she wants—I'd talk her out of it!"

I told Greta about my interview with L. B. Mayer; however, she thought it pointless to see him unless the studio had a story for her.

A few days later Mannix explained to me in a friendly talk that, much as he was trying to please Garbo, she and he did not see "eye to eye in the choice of film material." Then I mentioned that it seemed the story department had very little use for me. He denied this vehemently: as soon as I had a "good story" and Garbo really wanted to do it, he would consider it with the greatest attention, provided he could find the right producer for it.

I returned home discouraged and depressed, obsessed by the thought of getting out of Hollywood. Berthold casually remarked

that it would do me good to see Edward, Eleonora von Mendelssohn, Sam Behrman and my other friends. I asked for two weeks
leave of absence. I was told to wait, but as no one seemed to care if
and where I worked, I decided to go to New York anyway. Before
leaving I gave the necessary instructions at home; alas, without
taking into consideration Berthold's absentmindedness. I had been
gone a week when the story department called and Berthold answered the phone and said: "Mrs. Viertel is in New York." I
returned jobless. Mannix assured me that he understood my desire
to escape for a few days, that I had always been conscientious and
that any time I needed a friend or wanted to come back to the
studio, he would receive me with open arms. I am convinced he
meant it.

There were great changes in our household. Etta had gone to
New York, Susan Mann and little Andrew were in England to be
near husband and father, Margret had brilliantly passed her high
school exams and Edward wanted her to continue her studies in
the East. Walter and Hedy had left and I was keeping house,
cooking, cleaning, gardening, and writing a story with Polly James.

A few jobs were offered me, but they were always connected
with speculations on getting Garbo. An agent told me that it was
difficult to secure an assignment for me because I had been "identified" with films like *Queen Christina* and *Conquest*, which had
only made money in Europe. *Conquest* especially had been very
costly.

Shortly before Christmas Peter came home unexpectedly. He
had been assigned to Officers' School in Quantico, the Marine
base on the East coast. But first, he and Jigee would get married.
He was thin, brown, but unchanged and "he had been lucky": he
had participated in the landing at Bougainville. After he left, his
outfit had suffered great losses at Tarawa. When he was sailing
home aboard a destroyer, it was hit by a Japanese bomb but only
slightly damaged. He was convinced that the Marines "were great"
and he was glad that he had joined them. I, too, was glad: first because he was alive, second because he was going to stay in the
States for a while. As long as he was not on a destroyer or landing
on a Japanese-occupied island—I had every reason to be glad.

The marriage took place in our living room. A Santa Monica
judge performed the ceremony. There were only a few guests besides our two families: Melvin Frank, who, in a week, was to marry
Jigee's sister Anne, Oliver and Charlcie Garrett and several friends
of Jigee. Berthold, extremely fond of his daughter-in-law, was
happy and so was I, although early next morning Thomas had to

present himself at the induction center in Fort MacArthur. It was his last evening at home. He was eighteen and had been drafted.

The solemn vows did not fail to bring tears to my eyes and Jigee laughed: "What an old-fashioned mother you are!"

"Probably I am," I admitted.

Mockingly she warned me: "You must not be sentimental, dear . . . I know it won't last." I was shocked; it was only a minute since she had said "Yes." "How can you talk like that?" I exclaimed.

"I am five years older than Peter."

"Don't be silly. Now *you* are being old-fashioned! You can't believe it matters!"

She shrugged, then kissed me and we both cried. Then we looked at each other and burst into laughter.

It was dawn when I drove Thomas to the bus which was to take him to the induction center. Several shivering young men with small suitcases were already waiting. Later he phoned that if we wanted to say good-bye to him, we could see him off at the downtown railroad station, because he was leaving for a training camp somewhere in Alabama. I drove with Berthold to Los Angeles and we lined up on the platform with a large crowd of parents and sweethearts. We waited patiently for half an hour then we heard marching and commands and a long column of youngsters in ill-fitting uniforms passed by. They halted for a moment, and the women surged forward, calling the names of their men. I could not see Tommy and I was desperate. I was sure we would miss each other.

"There he is," cried Berthold suddenly and there was Thomas looking so bewildered, so boyish, so lost and so darling next to a huge beefy sergeant or corporal or whatever he was. The man was making himself important, shouting and commanding. I broke out of the line, ran up to Tommy and threw my arms around him, kissing his hot sweaty cheek. The sergeant yelled. Then again someone in front shouted and the column moved on. Marching out of step, Thomas waved to me and to his father; then we lost him among the uniforms.

I was shedding torrents of tears as we drove home, which made it difficult to watch the road. Berthold smoked nervously and tried to comfort me. He reminded me how Tommy always adjusted himself to a situation, even when he was small and heartbroken, as for example about Nena's leaving—poor Nena, her son in the Wehrmacht was now the enemy. I cried that Thomas was too trusting, too kind and unaggressive. I had not brought my sons up for the cursing and the cruelty and the killing. Berthold kept saying that Tommy would be all right. Then he tried to remember a poem Tommy had written when he was nine years old:

> "The hills are robed in forests.
> At the top of the mightiest hill of all
> A tower stands
> From which man can see
> Pastures of green,
> Of which horses and cows dream
> And where plenty is raised.
> At the south is an inland sea
> Bubbling, cool and refreshing
> Like Coca Cola."

Coca-Cola was Tommy's favorite beverage. We laughed and Berthold said again: "He'll get along."

I had some success with my freelance writing and sold a story to Paramount; it helped to pay the taxes and gave us a short respite from mortgage worry. Hans was in San Francisco, where he was finishing a course for machinists. He wrote me:

> I had a talk with the instructor and he began by saying that he considered it impossible to turn out machinists in three months, that I was not ready to go out, and that he felt he could not recommend me. Then he went on, he did not think I was cut out for this sort of work and perhaps I should try something else. I told him that I was determined to make a go of it and that he should give me three more weeks of trial. He agreed to this . . . His attitude has become much friendlier; he has helped me and right now I run the best lathe in the shop and I feel a great pride and happiness in the beauty of its power and accuracy. I know it sounds silly and literary, but that's what often happens when you try to put feeling into words. But there is a sense of achievement when you start with a rough and dirty bar of steel and after several hours make it into a smooth, clean piece of useful machinery. . . .

He got a job in the aircraft industry.

Virginia (Jigee) and little Vicky had gone East, to be near Peter while he was in Officers' School.

Suddenly the house was empty without the young. Mama, Berthold and I had our meals in the small breakfast room; and like in a Strindberg drama, Berthold's frustrations and my unhappiness created tensions. At night he wrote until very late, and he would come to my room as soon as he saw the light of my lamp and, smoking incessantly, walking back and forth, he would talk, prophesying conflicts between the Soviets and America.

He had finished a play, and had read it to Thomas Mann and Hoffenstein; their warm appreciation gave him the impetus to return to New York and show it to producers. Suddenly he was in a great hurry, did not have time to put his papers, letters, manuscripts in order, and in a room where everything was upside down and in utmost chaos I packed his suitcases. Finally we left for the station. The train was called *The Challenger*; it was slower but cheaper than the *Super Chief*. We walked up and down the platform, then embraced each other for the last time. Again he spent the long trip writing letters, intensifying our contact as the distance between us grew.

March 15, 1944. Dearest Salka: This night I was able to sleep, but not the first one. It was so terribly difficult to leave you with all your uncertainties. Lately one blow had followed the other, bad luck upon bad luck. Perhaps I have so blindly grabbed at this chance to go to New York because it was completely *against* my feelings. One becomes discouraged (not you!).

The trip to the station and the few quiet minutes with you helped me as nothing has in a long time. Arm in arm with you one can "challenge the whole world . . ." I will not be away for long, unless the play is produced, which would be a stroke of luck. I *can't*, after all the long, harrowing work, neglect this chance. For many years you have given me the possibility to do my literary work: in the drawers of the bureau in my room, on tables, chairs and in cupboards, among newspapers and books, are manuscripts and loose papers containing the lyrical output of my whole life, which one day will justify me before my children. In various folders, notebooks, copybooks are fragments of novels, speeches, essays, outlines, aphorisms, some even sorted out. I hope Mrs. Scott (the cleaning woman) has not swept a great part of it away. It would be best if you left the room as it is, until I come back, which will probably be in four weeks. I shall be longing for Mama.

Don't you think that our talks did her a lot of good?
Write soon.

I love you since ever and for ever—Your Berthold.

38

A RUSSIAN SHIP COMMANDED BY a woman captain and "manned"
only by women, arrived in Los Angeles harbor, and everyone went
wild. There was a great meeting at the Shrine Auditorium, proc-
lamations of enduring Soviet-American friendship; Charlie Chaplin made a speech and kissed the handsome, bosomy captain, and a
few days later Mr. Lester Cowan, the producer of the successful
film *G.I. Joe*, invited me to lunch at the Beverly-Wiltshire Hotel
to tell me about an idea he had for Miss Garbo.

I met an energetic, dark-haired young man, and the project he
eloquently described sounded very appealing. He wanted to produce a film about a woman skipper of a Norwegian boat played by
Greta Garbo, and I should provide the story. He had a sizeable
ship at his disposal and also the warm support of the Norwegian
Ambassador in Washington. All this sounded very exciting and
Greta agreed to meet Mr. Cowan. We had lunch with him, during
which he presented his project in greater detail. Garbo was very
interested but repeated that she would not sign a contract until
she had read the finished shooting script. Cowan said that he
would take the gamble as he firmly believed in his project. Next
day he asked me to write the story. We signed a week to week
contract at a thousand dollars a week, and I became immersed in
newspaper clippings and all the reports Cowan had received from
the Norwegian Embassy. It did not take me long to come upon a
fascinating incident: the escape of the coastal steamer *The Galte-
sund*. Ten years later it was wonderfully reported by A. J. Liebling
in the *New Yorker*.

I had to invent the reason why our ship was commanded by a

woman, also invent a love story, but as everything had a real purpose—the Resistance—it became true and exciting. Cowan had engaged the renowned maker of documentary films, Joris Ivens, as technical advisor. Joris was a stimulating collaborator and after a long, long time I was certain that I was doing something worthwhile.

The story outline was approved by Garbo, with the usual reservation that her consent to play the leading role depended on the screenplay. Encouraged and hopeful, Lester Cowan decided to hire Vladimir Pozner, a French writer of Russian descent, whose contract with Warner Brothers had just expired. He thought that the three of us would make a very happy "collective." He was right. Our work progressed so harmoniously that I felt a superstitious fear that the "collective" would not last. Pozner, his attractive wife Ida, and their two children were daily guests on Mabery Road. We worked at home and Garbo often came to "inspire" us. After two-thirds of the script was finished Cowan decided that this and a synopsis of the rest should be sufficient for Garbo to make up her mind. He himself was very pleased, especially after he had shown it to people and the "reaction" had been "favorable." But, to his and our dismay, Garbo refused to play in the film. She gave no reason. Cowan offered to have the screenplay rewritten by other writers, but she remained adamant.

I had been concentrating so completely on my work and my personal conflicts that I was only superficially aware of the red-baiting which began to occur in Hollywood. To my utter amazement, I learned that Greta had been warned that it was only a matter of weeks before Norway became a communist country, and also that I was "under the influence of the Reds." Her agent, Leland Hayward, first enthusiastic about the story, declared that war films were "outdated and nobody cared to see them." The "Reds" could only be Pozner and Ivens and they had been signed by Lester Cowan. Neither of them ever waved the "Marxist finger" at me with such humorless, school-masterly severity as some of my American colleagues. It was no news to anyone that I abhorred nationalism, militarism, fascism, torture, concentration camps, genocide, starvation and the unspeakable sufferings of mankind, inflicted to create a superior race or a classless society. But I never equated Stalin with Hitler, nor communism with Naziism, and I optimistically believed in the victory of reason, which would ultimately defeat white, red or black global bestiality.

This confession of my political creed seems necessary for the understanding of my future troubles.

Garbo's refusal was a severe blow to Lester Cowan's project, but he kept us on the payroll until we had finished the screenplay. There was a chance that MGM would buy it. Mannix had read it and called me to say that he thought it was an excellent piece of work but MGM was "afraid" that, as we were winning the war, the public did not care about the resistance to the Nazis any longer.

And so another hope for a Garbo film was gone. I returned to my domestic preoccupations, to "writing on spec," and trying to solve the eternal dilemma of my economics. Elisabeth Neumann, Liesel, had arrived to make a film test and we spent several days discussing our common cause: Berthold. Then I wrote him:

> My dearest Berthold: I have come to the conclusion that it would be best for you if we got a divorce. You know very well that this would never change our relationship. Liesel is such a brave, dear person and has no other wish than to live for you and with you. We must only agree about the reason for our "parting." Mental cruelty or incompatibility, awful as it sounds, would be the simplest. Please, Berthold, don't be sentimental and superstitious! I am sure that life in this puritanical country will be much easier when you and Liesel are married. And as far as both of us are concerned, we will remain the same to each other as long as we live.

In his delayed answer Berthold told me he had no desire to discuss a divorce as other, more important things had come up: Thomas had finally confessed that in his determination to be a good soldier he was going through hell. I had sensed this, although his letters to me always sounded cheerful, but with his father he was more candid. He admitted that in spite of the utmost effort it was impossible for him to keep pace with his comrades in running, shooting, digging, taking cover. Just before being shipped overseas, his platoon commander went to the major in charge and advised that the army should not send Thomas into combat as it would mean sheer suicide for him. The major called Thomas and the first question he asked was: "Are you a Jew? Are you trying to get out?" The interview was conducted in such a tone that Thomas insisted on remaining with his company, and repeated the three months of basic training under the most grueling conditions. Finally, upon the insistence of his CO he got a thorough medical examination, which established that because of a slowed down coordination he was unfit for combat. A few weeks in New York with his father seemed a due compensation for ten months of soldiering in Alabama. Meanwhile the war was coming to an end. In autumn our warrior received an honorable discharge, returned home and enrolled at the Junior College of Santa Monica.

Shortly before Christmas I ran into Nelly Mann. She was laughing and joking and we made a date for lunch, but next morning she cancelled it. A few days later Katja Mann telephoned to say that Nelly had died. She had broken a probation for drunken driving and in her panic about appearing in court, she put an end to her constant tussle with the police, her struggle with a language she could never learn, her fear of aging, and her losing battle with liquor.

She was to be buried at the peaceful Woodland Cemetery, which we so often passed driving on Pico Boulevard.

The December sun was warm and pleasant. Nobody was there when I arrived; the earth mound at the freshly-dug grave was covered with an artificial lawn, such as they use on movie sets. On one side were six chairs and I sat down and waited. After a while a limousine-like hearse swung noiselessly and swiftly toward the grave. Two men took down the coffin, put it on a wheeled contraption, scattered a few gladioli on the top and placed it over the width of the grave. Then they stepped back and I could hear them quietly talking about baseball. Nelly in her coffin and I, sitting opposite her, waited patiently. Slowly the funeral guests began to gather. Thomas and Katja Mann, the Feuchtwangers, Helli Brecht, Ludwig Marcuse, Liesl Frank and I; also Toni Spuhler, who had befriended and helped Nelly in her personal and domestic troubles. The last to arrive was Heinrich Mann, large, heavy, stooped by grief. After a long pause the undertaker, a solemn young man, looked at his watch. There was still another ten minutes until the appointed hour and if anyone wanted to say a few words . . . Vehemently Heinrich Mann shook his head and the young man stepped back. After another moment of indecision he cleared his throat, took out a prayer book and with a reproachful look at us all began to read "The Lord is my shepherd." He read fast and without punctuation. When he had finished, we got up and waited for the coffin to be lowered into the grave. But such realistic and distressing things do not take place at a Hollywood funeral: to become dust to dust, ashes to ashes, the dead wait until the mourners have discreetly withdrawn.

The solemn young man shook the widower's hand and left. With a tearing, muffled sob, Heinrich Mann turned, and covering his ravaged face with his handkerchief, stumbled away. It was gruesome. Katja ran after him, took his arm and led him to her car.

"They should have had a priest," said my mother when I told her about the funeral. "That's what religion is for. It gives funerals more dignity."

"Dearest, dearest Berthold," I wrote. "Nelly's death was the last, sad event of this depressing year. The new one must be better. I wish you, Liesel, Edward, Margaret and Hans, my big Hans who is now with you, a very happy Christmas. I embrace you all in endless love. The cigarettes, which I bought on the black market, are a reluctantly-given present and against my conviction, but if they make you happy. . . ."

39

THE WAR YEARS WERE TELLING on my mother. After the liberation of Sambor there was no response to our attempts of communication. We both had bad premonitions, but to each other we pretended that common sense had persuaded Dusko to flee with the retreating Russians. The other, humble working people like Hania, her son Adam, and Viktoria, were not Jews, and to some extent protected by their Ukrainian nationality. It was impossible to conceal from Mama the pictures of the concentration camps, which appeared in newspapers and *Life* magazine. On such days she stayed in her room and I would find her in her chair by the window, her elbow on the armrest, and her eyes covered with her hand. An open book was always in her lap. When I approached she would look up and say: "I am only resting my eyes." She was reading *Albertine Disparue*, and she insisted that it fascinated her. Having taken it at random from the bookshelf she refused to start with *Swann's Way*. "It is too late for me to go through the whole of Proust."

She liked to keep me company when I was cooking and she chopped and peeled whatever was necessary. This always brought back memories of Polish and Russian recipes, Papa's likes and dislikes and Niania's wise old sayings—Niania had been dead for many years—but Mama remembered them well and they were as apropos in California as they had been at Wychylowka. After a while we would cease talking and plunge into our separate gloom. The evening broadcasts of the Southern California Gas Company were a blessing. We listened devotedly to music. She was touchingly grateful for the least bit of attention, especially if shown by her grandsons. It was difficult for her to follow a general conversation and she refused to wear a hearing aid, but when Edward arrived to spend his summer vacation with us she immediately was rejuvenated and even her hearing improved. Edward was now recognized in America as a master performer of contemporary music, his reputation as an outstanding teacher was established, and in summer pupils followed him even to California. Mama was proud but not completely satisfied. Her musicality, this first, great source of artistic experience in our youth, did not readily appreciate the twelve-tone system. She understood Mahler and Debussy. Schoenberg, Alban Berg and Webern depressed her. She liked the *Gurre Lieder, The Transfigured Night,* some pieces of *Pierrot Lunaire;* for the rest, she confessed: "It's hard to understand." She considered it a handicap to his career that Edward had chosen to be the prophet of this Messiah.

That summer Clara Silvers, a very lovely girl with black hair and dark eyes, was a frequent guest in our house. She was Edward's pupil and one did not have to be a keen observer to notice that she and Edward were in love. But as he was thirty years older, Edward fought hard against his feelings. Clara's devotion, her love and understanding for his artistic struggle were victorious. All of us, Mama, Berthold, Rose in far away Argentina, and I, received her lovingly into the circle which had always bound us so intensely together. Edward's second marriage brightened Mama's last years.

When Berthold and I said farewell at the Los Angeles station, when arm in arm with me he wanted to challenge the world, we did not know that it was to be the last time we would be together. Letters, telegrams, telephone calls continued, but trips across the continent were too costly. All Berthold and Liesel could afford in summer were a few weeks in the country, somewhere in the East, while I was tied to the house by lack of money and taking care of Mama. And so another year went by, a year in which I found that detours, although leading to a desired goal, can become too long and too arduous. I had been scrubbing, washing, ironing, cooking, digging and weeding, while a book was emerging slowly but clearly from dreams and memories. It was like brushing away cobwebs in an unused cupboard. But when, exhausted from physical work, I sat down at my desk, I felt as if thick gray ashes were choking a smoldering log. Why didn't I let the house go dirty, neglect the garden, the dogs? I could not. It was Niania's heritage, her tidy peasant mind that had a firm grip on me and made me loathe disintegration. I wrote to Berthold:

> I woke up this morning and looked at the ocean. It was leaden gray, the whole canyon shrouded in fog. I went downstairs to make breakfast; then the telephone rang and Else Reinhardt said in a choked voice: "Have you heard? Roosevelt is dead." My knees gave way, just like when we had the earthquake.
>
> I am sure you also are terribly sad. I know we are winning the war and I know Roosevelt's death will not affect its outcome, but it is as if one had suffered a great personal loss.
>
> Dear Berthold, you must not reproach me when I do not write often. Fatigue—I could call it "combat fatigue"—prevents me. My letters would be depressing, but I know Mama writes for me. She is well and my "paying guest," Ruth Berlau, who moved into the room next to the garage, amuses her.

Ruth Berlau was Brecht's friend and secretary. She was young and attractive and her faulty German, with a Danish accent, made everything she said original and funny. Brecht was working with Charles Laughton on his *Galileo*; Laughton translating it into English and completely hypnotized by the author. He carried the manuscript under his arm to read aloud at the slightest provocation. Only, when Brecht was around he confined himself to Shakespeare or the Bible.

Helli Brecht and I went on shopping expeditions. My brave little convertible did not use much gasoline and we would drive downtown to the Grand Central Market. There, for ten or twelve dollars, we could buy food for a whole week. The Grand Central Market was, and I assume still is, enormous, interracial, multilingual, unbearably crowded, cheap and fascinating. At the stalls previously owned by Japanese, Mexicans and Filipinos now stood behind mounds of fruit and vegetables. If only one could send some of it to Europe.

Peter was now a lieutenant in the O.S.S. (Office of Strategic Service) in Germany. He described in his letters the misery and the terrible destruction: and of course, no one had ever been a Nazi. The fierceness of the hopeless "last stand" contradicted this. The Russians were in Berlin. The well-known streets were now a bloody, senseless battlefield. But to prevent one from having pity for the German people, new concentration camps and Gestapo murders with their infernal gruesomeness were discovered. When finally Hitler and Goebbels killed themselves in the bunker, a British newspaper quoted Shakespeare: "The day is ours, the bloody dog is dead." Still, the day was not ours and bloody dogs were still on the loose.

The war in the Pacific went on and the U.S. Draft Boards were recruiting and reclassifying. When the 4F's appeared for new physical examinations Hans came home and announced: "Mother, they've taken me!" He said that he had presented himself without his hearing aid and had been declared fit. I had never seen him so happy. However, at the induction center he could not manage without his helpful device. For a while no one paid attention to it; some of the soldiers thought that it was a new kind of walkie-talkie, until one day his lieutenant stopped him, exclaiming: "Man, what are you doing in the army?" and sent him to the commander. Later Hans, in his reserved manner, repeated to me the dialogue he had with the benevolent superior, in which he punctiliously tried not to appear "a flag-waving idiot." He insisted that he wanted to serve, mentioned his good knowledge of German and his fair one of French and was immediately assigned to the Counter Intelligence Corps (C.I.C.), which urgently needed bilingual men. He was sent East for his training and a few weeks later shipped to Germany. Needless to say, he was excited. As correspondence with German citizens was still forbidden, I had asked him to take a letter to our dear old Louise Wenzel and mail it abroad. I knew she had been bombed out and I had been thinking of her with great concern.

Shortly after Hans left, Brecht drove up one morning in his battered Ford and said that it was utterly ridiculous to have financial worries, when he and I could put our brains together and invent a saleable film story. I was very flattered that he considered my brain good enough to be "put together" with his, but he was not joking; he suggested that we work two hours a day and write a strictly commercial story. We were to commit ourselves to abide by the rules and respect Hollywood taboos which, after my years at MGM, I thoroughly knew. "Why shouldn't we be able to do as well as any Hollywood hack?" he asked.

"Because what the producers want is an original but familiar, unusual but popular, moralistic but sexy, true but improbable, tender but violent, slick but highbrow masterpiece. When they have that, then they can 'work on it' and make it 'commercial,' to justify their high salaries."

Brecht bit into his cigar and assured me that we could write our story in such a way that they would not notice what a highbrow masterpiece it was. But we had to proceed scientifically, soberly and objectively. I felt that his suggestion was prompted by his desire to help me and to cheer me up, and I was very moved.

The first thing we promised each other was never to consider anything from an ideological or "artistic" viewpoint. We had to be shrewd and invent situations and characters for the Hollywood market. We must begin with a survey of stars who needed "vehicles." Everyone was writing war stories and there was not much material for women stars, so it had to be "a woman's story." Garbo was out of the question; she was too special. We had to think of a simple, humorous, warm, ordinary personality (he thought Gene Kelly had these qualities, but he was not a woman star)—Barbara Stanwyck? Myrna Loy? Well, we had to have the story first, then worry about casting. Whatever ideas we tried, whatever subject we broached, we always came back to the war, and finally our main character emerged as a heroine of the French Resistance. All I remember now is that her husband was a prisoner of war in Germany and returned after France was liberated. But before leaving Paris a vengeful SS officer had shaved the young woman's head to make her appear as a "collaboratrice." This was the premise and the main conflict of the story. Brecht insisted that for the larger part of the film the actress playing the role remain hairless. I pleaded that at least she wear a scarf and reminded him of our pact, but his only concession was that at the beginning we see her brushing her long hair. The more we discussed it the more stubborn Brecht became about the clean-shaven scalp of the leading lady, and soon I also got used to it, comforted by the thought that as the film went on the hair would grow at least half an inch.

In due course we discarded our basic agreement. We found that we needed the advice of someone who knew France and the French better than we, and I suggested Vladimir Pozner. Brecht was pleased to enlarge our "unit" and we both agreed to share our future riches with Volodja, evenly dividing by three the impressive sum we expected to get. He liked our story and every morning at ten we met in my house, working until one p.m. We nominated Frieda, the dachshund Jigee had left with me, as our producer.

Frieda was fourteen years old, very fat and moody. She hated and tyrannized over my two big dogs, Sherry and Prinz, who, awed by her authoritarian manner and sharp bark, withdrew at the mere sight of her. She barely tolerated the members of my family, but adored Brecht. In the morning she waited for him and when she heard his car, she quickly took her place on the living room couch.

Approximately every half hour she would jump down, waddle over to Brecht, sit up on her hind legs and look at him expressively. Obligingly, he would rise from his chair, escort her to the glass door leading to the garden and open it for her with a deep bow. Then, after a pee on my poor lawn, she returned, scratched at the door and Brecht would get up, cross the room with his light, swift steps and again with exquisite politeness hold the door for her to come in. Neither I nor Volodja were permitted to interfere with this ritual. In her wicked flirtatiousness Frieda interminably prolonged her entrance, exploiting to the hilt Brecht's attention. I even noticed that she often went out for no other reason than to observe him through the glass door. He was indignant when in protest against her constant exits and entrances I locked her in my room.

We finished the outline and dictated the story to Tamara Comstock, a young friend of mine, an American, who was also the umpire and peace-maker when the three of us showed conflicting preferences in our English vocabulary. But it turned out a good story and we believed in it. Alas, no studio wanted to buy it and no star could be induced to shave her head.

I have often been asked: "What kind of person was Brecht?" and I can only say: "He was a slight man, polite and considerate, who never uttered a banality. When he expressed an opinion, it was always as extraordinary and original as his poems, his prose, his plays." His complete lack of pose was his most striking attribute, also his shrewd humor and, if there is such a thing, his elusive simplicity. In heated discussions he remained deceptively calm and polite, although he could be very sharp, sarcastic and impatient. Often he would smile his Chinese smile, but not laugh, I mean *really* laugh loud and heartily like, for example, his wife, whom he always spoke of as *die Weigel*.

It is not easy to be a domestic slavey, but Helli never complained. Fifteen years later, in Paris, I saw her play *Mother Courage* with the Berliner Ensemble. The Sarah Bernhardt Theater was packed and after the last curtain the audience stood and cheered. When I went backstage Helli, in the dressing room of the great Sarah, was sitting in front of a huge gilded mirror, press photographers crowding around her clicking their cameras. The room was filled with French, German and English-speaking admirers and many who were curious to meet an actress "from behind the Iron Curtain." She saw me, extricated herself from the crowd and embracing me, exclaimed: "I am glad you could see that I can do something else besides bake a *Gugelhupf*. . . ."

Shortly before National Socialism collapsed, Brecht, Heinrich

Mann, Feuchtwanger, Alfred Döblin and Berthold founded the
Aurora Verlag in New York, which was to publish books for the
hoped for "new Germany."

That year, 1945, was Berthold's sixtieth birthday. Two actresses,
Eleonora von Mendelssohn and Mady Christians, headed a committee, and for some technical reason decided to celebrate it two
months before its actual date which was in June. Berthold's report
to me showed how pleased he was with the evening.

> Dearest Salka: You cannot imagine how happy you
> made me, with your letter, and Tommy with his poem.
> I wrote to Mama and have sent her the *Austro-
> American Tribune* with the review of the evening.
> Edward played beautifully, Eleonora read my poems,
> Polgar made a charming speech and did not forget to
> mention you, which moved me especially. Bassermann
> was simply marvelous, and a great event. Homolka read
> a scene from my play. Mady Christians as the "chair-
> man" was so excited, as if this would be her most
> decisive première. Piscator painstakingly enumerated
> every play I have ever done on the stage. The list
> seemed endless and boring, but the audience was
> interested. At the end I had to speak and said that I
> consider this celebration a symbolic homage to all who
> are in exile and that today one should be twenty years
> old, not sixty. It's a shame you were not there. I wish
> you could see all the letters and poems. Garbo came
> and was much noticed but not bothered. She called me
> afterwards and the next day we lunched together. Now
> she is on her way to California. You must have received
> the telegram Karin Michaelis, Ruth Berlau and I have
> sent you . . . The most heart-warming letters came
> from Thomas Mann, Dieterle, Einstein, Vicki Baum,
> Hanns Eisler, Feuchtwanger, Karin Michaelis, Renoir,
> Stiedry, Alfred Döblin, Ludwig Roth, Otto Zoff, Zuck-
> mayer, Upton Sinclair and, of course, Heinrich Mann
> and Brecht; also from Kortner, although stressing the
> "differences." Perhaps the dearest of all was Bruno
> Frank's letter. His beautiful poem came too late to be
> included in the program. Next morning at breakfast
> Liesel and I wondered where to get the housekeeping
> money for the coming week. Please don't be alarmed,
> there are all kinds of prospects. Also, don't worry about
> the summer—we have taken a house in Vermont. I am

too superstitious to speak about the things I am planning. Is it true that you may go to London to do Shaw's *St. Joan* for Greta? Have you and Virginia any news from Peter? This letter goes on without paragraphs because of the joyous feeling you gave me with yours.

I had not written to Berthold about the *St. Joan* project because it was still at a preliminary stage. Gabriel Pascal and Wolfgang Reinhardt had approached Garbo about it. This was the same Gabriel Pascal who had bought my first film story, when our *Truppe* collapsed, and to whom G. B. Shaw gave the rights to film his plays. He came to Hollywood and we had several amusing and almost promising meetings. The only memento left of our negotiations is the following cable:

SALKA VIERTEL 165 MABERY ROAD SANTA MONICA CALIFORNIA WILL YOU GIVE GRETA FOLLOWING MESSAGE QUOTE HAVE ARRANGED ON GRANITELIKE BASIS MAKE BEST PICTURE EVER MADE WITH YOU FROM JOAN STOP ALL INTRIGUES OF OTHER PRODUCERS MAJOR COMPANIES ETC MAKE ME SMILE BECAUSE I KNOW YOU FEEL THE SAME AND ARE CLEVER ENOUGH NOT LET YOURSELF DOWN IN THIS DECISIVE TURNING POINT OF YOUR CAREER STOP I AM WITH YOU FAITHFULLY AS YOUR PRODUCER AND THERE IS NO OBSTACLE WHATSOEVER THAT I CANNOT LAUGHINGLY OVERCOME UNQUOTE DEAR SALKA CABLE ME YOURSELF HOW MANY WEEKS YOU NEED FOR DEFINITE SHOOTING SCRIPT I FEEL IT WOULD BE MORE LOGICAL IF YOU COME ALONG WITH WOLFGANG AS SOON POSSIBLE AND WORK WITH ME HERE ON SHOOTING SCRIPT BECAUSE I MUST HAVE EVERYTHING PREPARED ON BASIS OF SHOOTING SCRIPT BEFORE I LEAVE TO FETCH GRETA AFFECTIONATELY

GABRIEL PASCAL

I kept the cable because I have been always sentimental about Pascal since he had told me that he was a Gypsy.

My dearest Salka [wrote Berthold]:   June 1945
    It was quite insane to take over the play (Brecht's *The Private Life of the Master Race*) and to work incessantly for eight days and nights under most absurd circumstances, knowing that it was *impossible* to achieve a good performance. Nevertheless, those incredibly tense eight days made me feel young again and, at least, I have introduced a few new American actors. Two of them even had success. It impressed Brecht that I immediately lost the check I received as the reward for my sin, and essential for paying the rent. (I got it back.)

I liked working with Brecht. In the most desperate emergency he remains a man—utterly unhysterical. Edward was most critical but, as always, objective and swayed neither by love nor hatred—the Incorruptible, God bless him.

Today I shall see Polgar for the first time since Bruno's death. It affected him deeply. It has also shaken me to the roots of my being. How is Liesl bearing up?

Your Berthold

Sad and unexpected as Bruno Frank's death was, I was comforted by the thought that he had lived long enough to see the crumbling of the Nazi power. Thomas Mann said: "He was a 'Sunday's child' even in his death." Resting after lunch, he died in his sleep. I went to Liesl and found her sitting at his bedside, staring at him uncomprehendingly. The peaceful expression, the smile on his face, showed how, painlessly and without struggle, his life had ebbed away.

Soon after Bruno, Franz Werfel, ill for some time, died of a heart attack. It seemed as if he also had kept his strength up to see the day of the German surrender.

Six weeks later Peter got leave of absence. In the last months of the European war Jigee and little Vicky had been staying with me and now, with Peter home, the house became much livelier and everyone was much happier. Mama read fairy tales to Vicky, who, with great seriousness, corrected her English pronunciation. In his free time Thomas, Vicky's favorite vehicle, carried her piggyback around the block.

Also back from the wars were Irwin Shaw and Robert Capa. Irwin was already much admired and praised for his short stories in the *New Yorker* and had begun to work on his novel, *The Young Lions*. He and his lovely Marian were addicted New Yorkers, but used to spend part of the year in California, where Marian had her family, and Irwin was wooed by the studios. Broad-shouldered, athletic, full of exuberant vitality and always ready to laugh, he and the graceful, poised Marian were an engaging couple, most welcome on Mabery Road. Robert Capa made meteoric appearances at which first we clashed but afterwards became great friends. Oliver Garrett, who had been in Africa for the Office of War Information, told us about his experiences with the Vichy Generals. One of the more pleasant things which had happened to him in North Africa was his running into Françoise Feyder doing propaganda for the Free French. "How is Salka?" was the first thing she wanted to know.

Then just as everything appeared a little more hopeful, the Atom bomb was dropped on Hiroshima—loathsome, horrifying as all the atrocities of the Second World War. Some people, among them my own friends, whose humanity and compassion I had never doubted, thought that the thousands of burned bodies in Hiroshima and Nagasaki were less terrible than a prolonged war, and the sacrifice of thousands of American lives. Some saw the great promise that the channeling of atomic energy held: warmth to the Arctic, cooling of the African desert, abundance for barren countries. Mercifully the future, although menacing, is unknown to us. Fumbling, we try to cope with the sins of the past and their reverberations upon the present.

Christopher Isherwood's *Prater Violet* was published and had a great success. Its hero, Dr. Bergmann, modeled on Berthold, received extremely flattering tributes. One critic wrote: "Dr. Bergmann is a lion molested by flies." Berthold commented:

> These are the outbursts I had in London, which Christopher remembered, and which now tell a belated truth. I am concluding my career as a tragic Punch. But I am happy for Christopher that the tortures we endured together during the filming of *Little Friend* have not been in vain. As Wedekind says: "*Frau Poesie schafft ohne Graus, beneidenswertes Glück daraus.*"

40

IT HAS BEEN SAID OF HOLLYWOOD that once you are "down and out" your friends abandon you and, lonely and poor, you spend your evenings grieving for those glorious days, when you were invited to Pickfair. This was not true in my case. The loyalty of my friends remained unwavering. Actually, it was during the lean years that

290 · SALKA VIERTEL

165 Mabery Road established the reputation of a "literary salon," and I myself—to borrow Sam Behrman's expression—of a "salonière." This was mainly due to the informality and the haphazard intermingling of the famous with the "not famous" and the "not yet famous."

I had met Charles Chaplin in the Thirties; we had been seated next to each other at a dinner party once or twice, the first time after he had finished filming *The Great Dictator*. He was possessed by his work, and it was captivating to watch his never-ceasing absorption, his constant improvising of situations.

When Chaplin became the victim of a witch hunt, we saw each other quite often. A desperate girl, urged by a Hollywood gossip columnist, had filed a paternity suit against him with all the sensational trimmings which made it a criminal case. For the patriots of the Right it was the occasion to punish Chaplin for having remained a British subject, and for his flirtations with the Left.

It was also the year of Churchill's "Iron Curtain" speech and Senator McCarthy's investigations of communism in the U.S. Invisible and powerful, the FBI was practically in control of the studios. However, those worried about fascist trends in the country were relieved when the jury at the Chaplin trial—they looked rather grim in the newspaper photos—returned with the verdict "Not Guilty!" "It's still a free country, Charlie," said a woman juror, warmly clasping Chaplin's hand.

He married Oona O'Neill soon after the trial. I met her at a small dinner party given by Tim Durant, an old friend of Charlie's. She was eighteen, beautiful, poised like a Goya princess, and expecting her first child. Charlie was reenacting the whole trial, playing the judge, each of the twelve jurors, the district attorney who fascinated him, and his own lawyer, whom he deeply disliked. For an encore he repeated his already famous speech for Russian War Relief, which had so greatly augmented his troubles.

My sons had left me. Hans was still in Germany and Thomas had gone to Vermont to study at the University in Burlington, "working his way through college" as a handyman in the hotel where he also roomed. It was difficult to imagine my impractical dreamer "handy" for any hotel, but he seemed to manage. I knew that the main reason for his studying in the East was to be near his father and to spend his holidays with him.

Many of my friends had settled in Mabery Road. Fred and Renée Zinnemann, with their little son, lived at the ocean end of the street; Oliver and Charlcie Garrett bought the house next to them; Christopher Isherwood moved into my garage apartment. He still looked like an adolescent; one could detect the fine lines around his blue, wide-open eyes, only because they were lighter than his sunburnt face.

In the morning, on his way for a swim, he would stop by for a cup of coffee and a chat, thus reviving for me the old Wychylowka breakfast tradition. The chat would transform itself into an absorbing discussion, which on my side tended to be rather emotional. At this time I was "unbalanced" to say the least, but Christopher had unlimited patience and understanding. Then one of us would say something atrocious and hilarious, and suddenly we laughed and the world became bearable again.

One evening I had guests for dinner, Donald Ogden Stewart, now married to Ella Winter, the widow of Lincoln Steffens. She asked: "Isn't there a house nearby we could move into and be your neighbors?"

"You can have the corner house," I said. "The one opposite the Zinnemanns. It's for sale."

The Stewarts only came to Hollywood when Don was writing a film. In spite of her anthropological curiosity about the "Hollywood people," Ella, a handsome brunette and passionately political—her book about Russia, "Red Virtue," was a best seller—was never at ease with them, but she acquired a kind of *Galgenhumor* about the movies as Don loved living in California. Also the four-figure weekly checks were not to be sneezed at, especially by a generous man who never failed to come to the aid of friends and causes.

The next morning, as I was preparing breakfast, the Stewarts stuck their heads through the kitchen door and announced that they wanted coffee and that we were neighbors. They had just bought the house on the corner. Amazed that the real estate office would open so early, I was very pleased.

Immediately after his demobilization Peter and Jigee decided to realize their long-cherished dream of having a ranch. Somehow Jigee liked to picture herself as a pioneer woman facing the rugged life; Peter loved the outdoors and physical work. There were still some unexploited places along the coast and he found fifteen acres of most beautiful land in Zuma Canyon, twenty miles north of Santa Monica, and only half a mile from the ocean.

It was taken for granted that the two pioneers would build their house themselves, but luckily they had good friends of whom one was a carpenter and the other a plumber. I remember that one day, when I drove out to see the progress they were making, I found Jigee sitting on the roof, nailing down shingles, and Peter, helped by his friend Robert Parrish, dragging and hewing the frames of doors and windows. Vicky, her hands full of nails, was helping too. I believe that this was the happiest time of Peter's marriage.

I had not met many women as intelligent and spontaneously warm-hearted as Jigee. I knew that she was fond of me, however, in Peter's presence she would often become tense and sharp. It took me a while to realize that she was jealous, even of me. Also she became restless and dissatisfied, and the pioneering in Zuma began to lose its charm. When Peter signed a contract to write a film in Switzerland—it later emerged as *The Search* with Montgomery Clift—she was glowing with excitement, as she had never been to Europe and was eager to see it with Peter. For a brief moment she had pangs of guilt toward Vicky, who would stay in Zuma with her grandmother Henny, and Arthur.

Only a few weeks after Jigee and Peter were gone, Melvin Frank, Henny's son-in-law, phoned me one night that Henny had had a stroke and was in the hospital. Anne was expecting the birth of her second child at any moment and they would be grateful if I drove out to Zuma, first thing in the morning, to look after Vicky. Grandpa Ray had stayed with her overnight.

When I arrived at the white ranch house under the sycamores, Vicky, unkempt and unwashed, was standing on tiptoe at the kitchen stove, stirring the porridge. She was a wisp of a child with dark eyes and a halo of short golden curls; on the floor were little mounds of shells, stones and gulls' feathers she had collected on the beach. Grandpa Ray was looking for something in the frigidaire. I convinced him that they should come with me to Mabery Road until we knew more about Henny's condition. We gathered the shells and feathers, left a note for Arthur, took Bo, the Alsatian, locked the doors and drove home.

All day we waited for news. Finally Grandpa, who could not bear "sittin' around and doin' nothin'," went to the hospital to find out for himself.

Vicky was already asleep when Anne arrived with Melvin. Henny had died without regaining consciousness. They had cabled Jigee, urging her to return immediately. I thought that even in her sorrow it was essential for Jigee to be with Peter, and anyway it would take her ten days to come back. I said that I would be happy if Vicky stayed with me. I wrote this to Jigee and she answered how grateful she was and how terrible it would have been for her to leave Peter.

After the first shock subsided, Grandpa left for the desert. Anne was sad and cried often, but soon her little Liz and the new baby boy absorbed her completely. Vicky became the center of Mama's and my preoccupation, which pleased her greatly. Christopher thought I spoiled her; he believed that children should be seen but not heard.

The pleasant domesticity was interrupted by a call from Henry Blanke, producer at Warner Brothers, who wanted me to adapt a novel, *Deep Valley*, and write the screenplay. It was a strong and simple story. The demands of my household were easily solved, as I was earning money again! Anna, a refugee from Vienna who had often helped out in an emergency, moved in to take care of my menage and menagerie—dogs, cats and Vicky's turtles—and I could also afford a gardener.

Work in the studio was pleasant; Blanke, intelligent and cultured, was easy to talk to and the atmosphere in the writers' building, due to the influence of John Collier, very cheerful. An Englishman, he had introduced the four o'clock break for tea, which turned out to be a great success. We gathered in his office, and his secretary brewed pot after pot for the ever increasing number of writers who discovered a taste for it.

One expected the author of the weird *Fancies and Goodnights* to be somewhat "odd and eccentric," but John was nothing of the kind. He had a round pink face, neatly parted dark hair and periwinkle eyes. Natural, simple, interested in people, he also was an inspired cook.

I had to give away my dog, Prinz, who had become unmanageable and attacked children, and it made me sad. My secretary at Warners drew my attention to an advertisement in the *Tailwaggers*, a magazine dedicated to the welfare of dogs. The owner of a four-months-old English sheepdog was looking for a good home for him. Of all breeds I loved the shaggy English sheepdog most, and unable to resist I called to ask when and where I could see the puppy. "Any time," answered a woman's polite voice.

Oliver, who had a meeting at Warners, offered to drive me. After some impatient searching in North Hollywood we found a deadend road and a bungalow with the obligatory hibiscus bushes on the front lawn. A young, very pregnant woman stood on the porch waiting for us. She showed us into the living room, where a disconsolate three-year-old girl was clinging with both arms to the most beautiful dog I had ever seen. He was so big that I could not believe it was the four-month-old puppy; the thick, shaggy coat made him look like a medium size haystack. His color was deep, charcoal-gray with a lighter underbrush and a white mop hid his eyes; one sensed their intelligence.

"I don't want Timmy to go!" sobbed the little girl.

The mother explained to me that with the new baby coming they had to move to another place, where it was impossible to keep a big dog. "Children forget so quickly . . . we'll get her a kitten."

I could see that she was most anxious to have the whole thing over with. Oliver's sports-roadster stood in the driveway. She whistled. "Timmy adores going for a ride." The dog came running and as soon as he saw the car went berserk with glee and jumped into the back seat. I could hear the little girl crying and I wanted to comfort her, but the mother stopped me, saying we should leave quickly. Timmy did not even look back as we drove away.

Standing on the back seat like a conqueror, he put his soft paw on my shoulder. His white mane was blowing in the wind, his tongue was out, and I adored him.

Timothy's reception at home was not enthusiastic. Anna's only comment was a sharp: "What, another dog!" Mama found him too hairy and too emotional. Frieda the dachshund fascinated him, but I was the center of his universe and he never left my side.

Peter and Jigee returned from Europe, reclaimed Vicky, and settled down in Zuma. Jigee seemed happy; Peter had finished his novel *The Line of Departure*, and took a job, as I remember, with Twentieth Century-Fox.

The Nuremberg Trials were coming to an end and the pitifully small groups of survivors of Dachau and Auschwitz began to arrive in the States. The tattooed numbers on their wrists, the eyes which still reflected the horror, haunted me in sleepless nights.

There was no news from Sambor. In New York Edward contacted Jewish organizations which were tracing concentration camp survivors. I telephoned the Soviet ambassador, Mr. Umanski, in Washington, to ask his help, as Sambor was once more under Soviet rule; but I could not get through to him. A woman from Sambor informed me that she had received an unverified report about her own brother, a friend of Dusko. Apparently both had tried to escape by jumping from a train taking them to a concentration camp and were killed by the S.S. I did not tell my mother. Each morning I exerted all my cunning to get to the mailbox before she came downstairs. In that way I succeeded in intercepting a letter addressed to her. It was from Viktoria.

Scribbled in pencil on a page torn from a notebook, she wrote that she was anxious to know how we all were, how we had survived the war and added that she was sorry to give us bad news about Dusko: "In 1943 he came to my house begging me to hide him, but as we are living in a rented place I could not do it, and since the last German *Aktion* I have not heard from him again."

She was not on speaking terms with Hania, who had left Sambor with Adam. She, Viktoria, and her husband, were well. They had four children and "would Salka, who had always been like a sister to me, send us a food parcel?"

A cold horror took hold of me. The German word "*Aktion*," the only one clearly written and correctly spelled, killed all my hope that Dusko was alive. I prayed that the story of his desperate escape were true, that he had been spared the gas chamber. All her life Viktoria had been a member of our family, and the callousness of her report was so shocking that it took me a long time to recover.

I wrote her that she had forfeited the right to appeal to my sisterly feelings. She had cruelly denied shelter to a hunted Jew, whose father and mother had given her love and devoted care since she was born, and that she had allied herself with murderers and torturers. My tears stained the paper and I had to stop. Could I reproach this cowardly woman for not risking her life? Hadn't others, more powerful than she, stood by indifferently when these unspeakable horrors took place? She was only one among millions. And to think that it was the same little Viktoria, who in her nightshirt had followed me to Papa's room and climbed on his bed and like a bird ate the corn kernels from his hand.

I tore up the letter, mailed a CARE package to Sambor, and never told Mama what Viktoria had written. But Mama must have sensed that I was keeping bad news from her. She stopped going to the mailbox, her trembling got worse and she could no longer write to Rose and Edward. Her attempts to type were touching but unsuccessful. While I was in the studio Else Reinhardt and Miss Wiesen (short for Wiesenthal from Augsburg), a new friend and courageous soul displaced into Hollywood households, used to come and keep her company.

In the evening she would talk to me about people who were dead long ago, like old Lamet, the tall, white-bearded Jew, who had owned the inn at Wychylowka.

"He died on a cold, sunny, winter day—a Saturday," Mama said. "They all had gone to the synagogue and left him with his great-grandchildren, two little girls of four and five. He was sitting on the bench by the stove, and the little girls were singing and dancing on the bright spot the sun made on the floor. Their mother came home and said something to old Lamet, but he did not answer. She saw that he was dead. He had a beautiful death . . . You remember how many children and grandchildren they had?" I remembered and I thought of "the last German *Aktion*" in 1943.

41

THE SCREENPLAY OF *Deep Valley* was almost finished when the studio workers went on strike. It started with the set dressers demanding higher wages and recognition as a separate union, then the carpenters, painters and readers (story analysts) joined. The latter and the cartoonists—young men and women in blue jeans, and pullovers, red scarves around their necks, cigarettes sticking in the corners of their mouths—were conspicuously the fermenting element of the "revolution." Sympathetic to their cause, I contributed to the strike fund.

Then pickets lined up in front of Warner Brothers and writers and secretaries had separate meetings in the cafeteria opposite the studio to decide whether they should cross the line. One of the writers suggested that we had better wait and see what the secretaries decided, because he "could not dream of working without his secretary." This sounded convincing and we stepped out onto the sidewalk to watch what the "girls" would do. About thirty of them came out and for a while they stood undecided, watching the slowly moving pickets and the studio police, who were protecting the entrance. Finally an energetic young woman threw back her head, said "What the hell!" and ran defiantly across the street and through the passive picket line. The others promptly followed; only two, one of them my secretary, hesitated. I went up to them and asked what had happened at the meeting. They told me that at first most of them sympathized with the strikers but one girl, who had worked for Ayn Rand, swayed them by insisting that the strikers were just a bunch of communists and that a decent person had to be against them. . . .

The writers decided to stay out until the mass picket lines were withdrawn, but the writer who had been collaborating with me on the final version of the screenplay, declared that he refused to be "intimidated" and would be on hand in his office. I said I would not, and Henry Blanke, our producer, suggested that we work at home and have our conferences at his house.

It was customary at Warner Brothers that when a film was to be previewed the producers, director, writers and technicians (but not the actors) who had worked on it dined with Mr. Warner. And so after *Deep Valley* was finished, I was invited to the executive dining room before we all took off to one of the Warner Brothers' theaters on the periphery of Los Angeles county. The atmosphere around the table had the same ostentatious "camaraderie" I had noticed at similar functions at MGM. I imagine such also must have been the *Gemütlichkeit* when Stalin's staff was dining with their boss.

Mr. Warner was telling us about the communist menace and that thousands of Jews had been killed in Russia. He asked me how my mother escaped. I said that my mother had lived two years under Soviet rule, and that in my hometown, Sambor, Jews had been treated decently during the Soviet occupation, and that official anti-semitism did not exist. My collaborator interrupted smilingly: "Salka is a communist, Mr. Warner." It was supposed to be a joke—but it prompted Blanke to jump to my defense: "She is not!" he said. "One need not be a communist to say that Soviet anti-semitism is not to be compared to the horrors the Nazis committed."

I said: "It is just as unconstitutional in Russia as it is here, but uncontrollable in individuals." As no one could deny that anti-semitism existed in America the discussion ended.

The preview was a success, and Mr. Warner especially expressed his great satisfaction with the screenplay. This was the last time I was to work at a major studio, but it took me several years to realize why.

I had paid off debts and a large part of the mortgage, my name was on the credit list of an interesting film, and my agent was optimistic about my future employment. For a while I could have managed with the money I had earned, if the U.S. Treasury had not suddenly dug up past taxes that Berthold still owed. Only a new mortgage—"refinancing" the bank called it—could save the house. "I have always depended on the kindness of strangers," says Blanche Dubois in *Streetcar Named Desire*—well, so have I: a New York dramatist, as I remember one of the first clients of the now legendary Mr. I. P. Lazar, had signed a fabulous contract with one of the studios, and wanted a house near the beach. The rent he offered me was enough to pay the monthly installments on the mortgage and also left a small sum for food, telephone and gasoline. Mama and I liked fruit, vegetables and cottage cheese, and we could also afford a pound of meat for Timmy, who was no longer a puppy.

My tenants had no need for the garage apartment and as Christopher had left on one of his long voyages, this time to South America, I decided to move to his room. Mama preferred the one downstairs, previously Peter's den, panelled with pine, with bookshelves and all the books she wanted to read. Each of us had a bathroom. The roof-deck provided a grand view of the sea and the Canyon. There I cooked our meals on the electric plate, a present from Greta. To ease the transition from bourgeois comfort to narrow bohemian quarters, Aldous and Maria offered me and Mama a house they had in Wrightwood, a mountain resort on the edge of the Mojave Desert. They insisted we take it for a few weeks as they themselves had moved to another one more suitable for them. Of course Timmy was also invited. That summer Edward could not come to Santa Monica. He and Clara had only a brief holiday and were spending it in Canada. Their absence, and a tragic event which no longer permitted me to see my niece Margret, increased the sad emptiness of this summer. Mama was very depressed and I thought a change of scene would be good for her.

In a remote way Wrightwood reminded me of the Carpathian Mountains. Its landscape was not yet spoiled by real-estate billboards, and bungalows and log cabins were haphazardly scattered in the woods. Instead of the smell of wild berries and mushrooms, one was rewarded with dry whiffs of sage, which the wind blew from the desert.

We had a lot of space in the house and I induced Greta to come to Wrightwood and stay with us. The Huxleys and Krishnamurti, the gentle philosopher from Ojai, Friedrich and Iris Ledebur, with their adolescent son Christian (still "Boon" to us), were also in Wrightwood. It was one of Friedrich's endearing qualities to attach himself to saints and philosophers, although he himself rarely showed mystic inclinations.

After our return, undaunted I settled down to work on an original screenplay. On Sundays Mama and I would drive out to Zuma where the younger generation gathered: Irwin and Marian Shaw, who spent their summers in a beach house not far from Peter and Jigee, and a charming young couple, Bob and Cathy Parrish. There were picnics and hotdogs and much reminiscing about the war. Very few of the young writers and directors were interested in Brecht's *Galileo* which was performed at the Coronet Theatre in Beverly Hills, directed by Joseph Losey. Charles Laughton, who

had translated it, was a superb Galileo; otherwise the performance was uneven. But many scenes were very impressive. The
Beverly Hills audience did not understand the play nor did it care
for it. The success of *Galileo*, just like Brecht's and Losey's, had to
bide its time.

Our modest quarters limited my hospitality; nevertheless friends
dropped in for tea and a chat on my "terrace." Restless and up-
rooted, Eleonora and Francesco Mendelssohn would appear during their brief visits to California; Eleonora persisting in her
heroic determination to gain a place in the American theater,
Francesco either terribly depressed or unduly elated, too eccentric
even for Hollywood. Both had nobly rejected the idea of returning
to Berlin: "The name Mendelssohn obliges." The Grünewald villa
was a heap of ashes but the Rembrandts, Titians, Corots, van
Goghs and Goyas had been saved, and restored to their Italian
mother.

It was around that time that George Schlee became an increasingly important influence in Garbo's life. A Russian lawyer, he had
emigrated to the United States and was managing the *maison de
couture* of his talented wife Valentina. Broadway actresses and the
most exclusive of "The four hundred" were dressed by her. Educated, intelligent and hospitable in the old Russian manner, Schlee
was well liked in society, and literary and artistic circles. He persuaded Garbo to spend part of the year in New York, trying to
alter her rejection of a more social life. The summers always
brought her back to California and she would rent a house in
Santa Monica or Beverly Hills. Perennially beautiful, she would
appear unexpectedly to fetch me for walks on the beach, and
wistfully we would discuss a vague idea for a film no one would
want to make. However, it appeared we were both wrong, because
one day George Cukor called and invited me to lunch. It was ages
since I had seen him. As always, he was bubbling with ideas and
good humor. He began telling me how disgraceful it was that in six
years MGM had not been able to find a story for Garbo, their
greatest and most international star. He had just read a biography
of George Sand and was certain that it contained all the romantic
elements for a Garbo film. I had never thought of Garbo as
George Sand but Cukor's enthusiasm was infectious. When I was
fourteen I had devoured her interminable novels *Indiana* and
Consuelo, and I remembered my grandmother's indignation about
her morals. Nevertheless, I thought that most of George Sand's
biographers were biased, condescending and ironical. Only a few
condoned her many lovers, her trousers and her socialism. Cukor
suggested we talk to Garbo. She was in favor of the project.

Luckily, a friend and neighbor in the Canyon had rescued from the Nazis some of his valuable French books, and lent me George Sand's letters to Alfred de Musset, Chopin, Liszt, to her lawyer, to the tutor of her children and to her despicable husband. More dramatic and interesting than the well-known relationship with Chopin was her passionate affair with the young, dissipated, alcoholic genius Alfred de Musset. George Sand's *Elle et Lui, Leone Leoni, Le Journal Intime*, Musset's poems, his *Confessions de l'Enfant du Siècle*, and all those grandiose outbursts in their letters had recorded, as on a fever chart, the ups and downs of a love they considered immortal. What an advantage it was for posterity that they had no telephone!

It took me more than six months of intense work to write a film treatment. As Cukor predicted, great interest was immediately shown by British Independents. In Hollywood Walter Wanger, in association with Eugene Frenke, took an option on my script. Afraid of the technical difficulties and the hardships in post-war Europe, Garbo chose them as producers. However, having seen *La Duchesse de Langeais*, a French film (with Edwige Feuillère) from a distinguished screenplay by Jean Giraudoux, Wanger, for the usual Hollywood reasons, found the Duchess more "worthy of Garbo" than the less blue-blooded and more Red-oriented George Sand. As my main objective was that Greta resume her artistic career, I did not try to argue. I told myself that it was much safer to remake a French film than plunge, under Wanger's guidance, into the vortex of George Sand's passion. George Cukor bowed out. Wanger engaged Sally Benson, the author of *Junior Miss*, to write a new screenplay of *La Duchesse de Langeais*. Garbo was unhappy with it and Wanger promised it would be rewritten, but the film proved difficult to finance and the project collapsed. The display of dilettantism, inflated egos, incompetence, and a hypocritical, indecent disregard for the sensibilities of a great actress had been unsurpassed, even in the history of films. It made Garbo once and for all renounce the screen.

The "Hearings of the U.S. Congressional Committee Regarding the Communists' Infiltration of the Motion Picture Industry" had started in Los Angeles. Only the satirical genius of Karl Kraus could have done justice to the personalities of Congressmen J. Parnell Thomas, Rankin and Stripling, and their utterances. The investigations were timed to influence the forthcoming Presidential elections. A third party emerged in American politics, supported by "Arts, Sciences and Professions" and called the Progressive Party, which nominated Henry Wallace.

As the film workers' strike went on, through many phases and jurisdictions, the Un-American Committee subpoenaed writers, actors, and union organizers suspected of Leftist activities. Jack Warner and L. B. Mayer had to explain why they had made such subversive films as *Mission to Moscow* and *Song of Russia*. William Wyler's *The Best Years of Our Lives* was attacked but spiritedly defended by its courageous director and producer. "Friendly witnesses"—self-appointed Redbaiters—eagerly denounced their colleagues. On television one could see chairman Thomas's bloated face and hear his voice, which he drowned by the incessant pounding of the gavel. Was it possible that there were people who had voted for this man?

The hearings in Los Angeles preceded the big show in Washington, where nineteen writers and directors had been subpoenaed. "Progressive" Hollywood protested and formed the Committee for the First Amendment. More than five hundred prominent Americans signed a protest against the hearings. Large sums were given for publicity and nationwide broadcasts. Thomas Mann was cheered when he addressed a meeting, saying: "I have the honor to expose myself as a hostile witness. I testify that I am very much interested in the moving-picture industry and that since my arrival in the United States nine years ago, I have seen a great many Hollywood films. If communist propaganda had been smuggled into them it must have been most thoroughly buried. I, for one, never noticed anything of the sort . . . As an American citizen of German birth I finally testify that I am painfully familiar with certain political trends. Spiritual intolerance, political inquisitions, and declining legal security, and all this in the name of an alleged 'state of emergency' . . . That is how it started in Germany. . . ."

Of the nineteen summoned to Washington, eight were quietly dropped from the list of the Un-American Committee, the others became the Hollywood Ten. The eleventh, Bertolt Brecht, was an alien and took a different stand. I listened to the radio. Extremely punctilious about the interpretations of his poems, which the Committee suspected were Marxist, he explained to Chairman Thomas: "Of course I studied Marx. I do not think intelligent plays can be written today without such a study."

The Committee was baffled, but did not permit him to read a statement. They asked if he knew Gerhard Eisler, a German Communist held on bail by the U.S. Immigration authorities, and a brother of Hanns. "Did Eisler visit you when he was in Los Angeles?"

"Yes," said Brecht, "he did."

"To what purpose?" asked Mr. Thomas suspiciously.

"We used to play chess," said Brecht.

"Did you discuss politics?"

In his calm, friendly voice Brecht answered: "Yes, we also discussed politics."

I could hear the audience laugh, the pounding of the gavel, and then the sixty-four-dollar question (I have never found out why it was worth sixty-four): "Mr. Brecht, have you ever been or are you now a member of the Communist Party?"

"No," said Brecht. The Committee was utterly unprepared for this, and even some of Brecht's friends were surprised. The Chairman could do nothing else but thank him for having been a cooperative witness. Immediately after the hearing Brecht boarded an airplane, which took him to Switzerland. Then he went to East Berlin. Several weeks later Helli sold the house in Santa Monica and followed with the children.

Hanns and Lou Eisler were threatened with deportation and detention in a "Lager" in Germany. Again a committee, to which I belonged, collected money to help them. Hanns's worst misfortune was to be the brother of Gerhard Eisler, and to have a monster as a sister. She denounced him and Gerhard to the FBI and wrote hate-filled and well-paid articles against them which made the front page in leading American newspapers.

Gerhard Eisler was arrested, but jumped bail, and under the very nose of the FBI, left the United States on the Polish ship *Batory*. Immediately, headlines accused him of being an atom spy, which did not improve his brother's situation. In an indignant article, "Cry Shame," published in the *Nation*, Martha Gellhorn described the treatment Hanns Eisler had received from the Un-American Committee. Finally, through the intervention of Professor Albert Einstein, Heinrich and Thomas Mann, William L. Shirer and President Benes, he and Lou were granted permission for a stay in Czechoslovakia. They were deported and had to sign a declaration promising never to return to the United States, nor to Cuba or Mexico; which was rather strange as neither of these countries are a part of the United States.

I no longer saw those who still represented glamorous Hollywood. Ernst Lubitsch and Sam Hoffenstein died that same year. Embittered, disgusted with Hollywood, post-war Germany, and the whole world, Sam rarely left his house. From time to time he would ask two or three intimate friends for dinner, usually a young screenwriter Elisabeth Reinhardt (no relation to Max) and me. The evening would start with martinis, of which Sam took too many; then he made us laugh with his outrageous blasphemies, uproarious improvisations and solemn Hebrew incantations.

Then, invariably, he would become "Swiftian," aggressive and bitter, and abused everyone and everything. One morning Elisabeth rang me, in tears. Sam had phoned her at four in the morning, asking her to come; he was alone and feeling ill. When she arrived he was slumped at the telephone, dead. It was a great loss for us all.

After two years in the service, my Hans was demobilized but decided to stay in Europe and spend a few months at the Sorbonne, which was offering foreign students a course in French culture. At this time the prospect of producing the Georges Sand film abroad was still acute, and we looked forward to a reunion. En route I would stop in New York to visit with Edward and Berthold. It depended on my contract whether I would leave my mother with Edward and Clara, or in good care in Santa Monica.

Hans wrote from Paris:

> After all these months in drab, poverty-stricken and destroyed Germany, it was like being back in the world again. I realize now that the peculiarity of Germany lies *not* in her present state of prostration. I have been living among people who for twelve years had been completely cut off from the flow of world thought, and those of my age had grown up behind a new kind of Chinese wall, which in its way was even more impenetrable.

As he could not get batteries for his hearing aid in Paris, he went to London and appeared, lugging his suitcase, at the flat of his aunt and uncle, Helene and Willi Bruckner. They had last seen him when he was seven years old, and received him with great joy. They insisted he stay with them although the procurement of food was a major problem—I tried to alleviate it by sending food parcels. In her eagerness to keep Hans in London, Helene at once began scheming to find him a job. She had established herself as a successful designer and dressmaker, although not as prosperous as to suit the wishes of her generous heart. Both she and Willi were very popular among the German emigrés, of whom many had achieved influential positions in the theater and the BBC. Quite a few, like Heinrich Fischer, our former *Dramaturg* of *Die Truppe*, knew and admired Berthold. Hans was introduced to the chiefs of the German section of the BBC, and invited to write and deliver ten-minute broadcasts to Germany.

The BBC also wanted Berthold to direct their German programs. The Schauspielhaus in Zurich, the Volksbühne in Berlin and the Staatstheater in Dresden all offered him contracts. A newspaper wanted him as editor. Many who hoped for a de-Nazified Germany urged him to return. Hans urged him to tear himself away and come to England. The BBC notified him that his contract and working permit had been mailed and that he would have to leave very soon. There was no time for good-byes. Would we meet in London or Paris, or—yes, where?

Berthold had told me that the letter from Dresden included an offer for me—a contract to act and direct at the Staatstheater. But I never considered going back. My mother was too old to be exposed to radical change, my sons were Americans, and the only place I had become attached to was that small promontory above the Pacific Ocean with winding Mabery Road. I did not believe that all Germans were Nazis; but that even those who had had Jewish friends had tacitly accepted their disappearance, the unspeakable horrors and the mass exterminations made it impossible for me to return. I was aware of the heroism of those who had never been swayed. Paul Wegener, Edward von Winterstein, Gerda Mueller, a few of my former colleagues, our dear Louise Wenzel, they had all remained uncorrupted. A long list of children's names, which I had received from Helli Brecht, was most persuasive. All these sick and undernourished Annemaries, Ingrids, Gerdas, Heidemaries, Gudruns and Kristas, interspersed with Karl-Heinzes, Bernds and Klauses, had next to their names: "Father beheaded—father died in concentration camp—father executed for high treason—father hanged for contributing to the demoralization of the army," and so on and on. There were also two beheaded mothers.

And just to show the insane repercussions of the Cold War, I must mention that when I asked people, who during the siege of Stalingrad had generously contributed to the Russian War Relief, to give me a check or old clothes they refused because "communists would get them."

It seemed sensible that Berthold should go alone to London and see how things turned out. Then if he decided to stay, Liesel would join him. As usual, in his letters he was pleased with the tempting offers and at the same time apprehensively cautioning himself as everything seemed a plunge into darkness. Finally he made a decision and suddenly mentioned a subject he had once declared taboo: our divorce. He reminded me that:

> In your kind concern you have several times suggested a divorce, but I was always against it. However,

should I really go to Europe, to London or Switzerland
—I am still not sure where—I am afraid that, as you
have rightly foreseen, such a formality could be necessary. As long as I am married to you, Liesel and I
cannot travel together. Surprisingly, she wants it,
although living with me is certainly more trying than
ever. I don't have to tell you how devotedly she has
taken care of me—always cheerful and good-natured.
This and her utter absence of pettiness makes our
existence happy and easy . . . I don't know where I'll
end up: Austria or Germany, or will I return to America? No one can foresee. All I hope for is a few creative
years; then whatever happens I'll be content. I am not
depressed, merely fatalistic. Tell me what you think of
all this. But more than anything I wish to see you.
Again it's the money. If only you could come to New
York.

Not only could I not afford the trip to New York, but I could
not leave Mama alone in her little room. She needed much more
care now. Also I had to apply for the divorce. I asked Larry Beilenson how we could get it over quickly and painlessly. Soothingly
phlegmatic, Larry said that he did not see any reason to hurry.
Speed was a matter of money and, as we were too poor for
Nevada, there was only the "normal" procedure in Los Angeles or
the disagreeable one in New York. I explained Larry's reason to
Berthold, who answered:

I understand that Nevada or Mexico are too costly,
and I firmly refuse to submit to the performance of an
"in flagranti" necessary in New York. Further, I do not
wish either of us to charge incompatibility or mental
cruelty. If the worst comes to the worst, let's have
desertion.

This was truly Berthold; no aspersions upon the insoluble bond
of our hearts and souls was permitted, no "incompatibility" or
"mental cruelty" should ever cast a shadow upon it—desertion was
more like an act of God.

I'd have preferred that all that was unnecessary.
However, once Liesel and I decide to keep house in
countries like England, Germany and Austria, everything becomes so difficult, so unhealthy and expensive,
that one has to comply with the rules.

And so Larry Beilenson filed my suit for divorce in Los Angeles.

Leaving America seemed to Berthold like a second emigration, or like a return to somebody once very dear but now disfigured and scarred by a horrible disease.

In late September Tommy came from Vermont to say good-bye to his father. I said farewell on the telephone. It was more than three years since Berthold had left, and as always, his voice seemed to bridge the distance and the years. This time it sounded blurred and so far away that I could hardly hear it . . . I was terribly upset and forgot what I wanted to say. . . .

I have a snapshot of Berthold and Thomas standing on the deck of the *Queen Mary*, the son towering over the father, who is smiling broadly into the camera, while Tommy looks down at him with great tenderness. . . .

The District Court of Los Angeles took its time about the divorce, but on December 27, 1947, I was able to dispatch the following news to London:

Dearest Berthold and dearest Hans: Forgive me for not writing for such a long time. I washed my car with a new kind of cleaner and it caused a terrible rash on my hands, which drove me insane. Finally the doctor gave me something which helped and now it is almost gone. This is an explanation and not a complaint.

The divorce was on the 20th. The judge was rather unpleasant because I refused to accuse you, Berthold, of "abuse and cruelties." It made him suspicious. I said that you didn't want me to go with you to England. You will read all this in the documents they are sending you. Renée Zinnemann was my witness. Everything was done in a most civilized way. As Renée had seen you in London, the judge wanted to know whether you had told her that you loved another woman, and she confirmed this. Of course, no names were mentioned. He was also suspicious because I did not ask for alimony. "Are you sure you have been a good and faithful wife?" he sternly inquired, and my lawyer, Larry's associate, said quickly: "She has, your Honour."

You know how little respect I have for the institution of marriage and for property. Thirty years ago, when I married you, I was convinced that our relationship would be exceptional in our absolute truthfulness toward each other. I loved you and I shall always do so. We have held together and belonged to each other through all the storms. Nothing will ever change that. Everything has been unerringly true and will remain true to the very end.

Leaving the court I suddenly thought of that afternoon in Pasadena at Mrs. Gartz's house—you remember? It was our first year in America and Upton Sinclair took us there for tea. A wizened old lady, a friend of Mrs. Sinclair, was telling fortunes and insisted that you let her read your palm. She was terribly impressed, said you were a genius, that you would leave California and that oceans and countries would separate you from me. Also that you would marry again. She refused to tell my fate. I told Renée of this prophecy.

[Then abruptly turning from clairvoyance to realities, my letter continued:]

Fritzi Massary wants to give you a Christmas present and I advised her to send you a food package; so don't be surprised when you get five dozen eggs from Canada. Write her your thanks to New York, care of Liesl Frank: they are spending the holidays together. On the first of the year I am sending you and Hans food parcels. I will notify Liesel, your Liesel, about the divorce. I embrace you and Hans lovingly. Salka.

Berthold replied:

Had the judge known my feelings towards you, he would *never* have granted the divorce, because in most marriages a relationship such as ours does not exist. You must know that I consider this formality an act of your kindness and utmost generosity and it makes you more lovable than ever. It moves me deeply as it only strengthens our bond. But I must admit that it made me very sad. It aroused a whole world of thoughts and emotions, *which belong only to you and are indisputably yours as long as I live* . . . I long for you and I worry about you terribly.

I love and respect you, and always more and more, but that does not help . . . Divorce or no divorce, what difference does it make? If only you were happier. . . .

The last sentence surprised me. I was not unhappy. I was exhausted, impatient, frustrated, often desperate, overworked; but my life still had moments of joy, of sensuous and intellectual pleasures. Even getting old was no threat. I never had the temperament nor the leisure to become aware of it.

42

LOOKING THROUGH NOTEBOOKS, letters and diaries, it occurs to me that as the years went by, my life ceased to be solely my own. It became like the estuary of a big river into which other streams flowed. I could not influence their course but I was affected by it. First there were my sons; the confiding, although not entirely candid Jigee; and Edward, who luckily had his young, strong and utterly devoted Clara. Then Berthold, whose bitter years of exile were rewarded by the heart-warming reception in London, soon to be followed by a series of great successes in the German theater. He had married Liesel and his letters sounded happy.

After my tenants left, my mother and I moved back into the house. Thomas, "our American Parsifal" as Berthold called him, returned, to continue his studies in Los Angeles. Then the fog and cold drove Hans out of London and he decided to use his "G.I. Bill" to enroll at the University of California. But when William Dieterle, who had always appreciated Hans's talents, asked him to prepare material for a planned production, Hans was immediately seduced, and divided his time between films and ancient history. The return of my sons drew, in succession, many young women to the house, some charming, some less so, one even with an adorable little daughter; but she stayed only a short while.

Then a friend told me that a young couple could not find a place to live, because the wife was white and the husband a Negro. She was sure that they would like to have my vacated garage apartment; and so Lynn and Carlton Moss, two very attractive and remarkable people, came into my life and into my crowded heart. In 1947 Civil Rights were still merely on paper and California not the most tolerant of the States. After his discharge from the army, Carlton was making educational films for Negro grammar schools. Lynn had been acting in radio plays and television, until she was blacklisted and forced to take all kinds of strenuous, badly paid jobs to make a living. For Thomas, who missed his father, Carlton was a godsend, a close friend and advisor. My mother also adored the Mosses.

In all the years I had lived on Mabery Road, I had exchanged merely friendly nods and brief greetings with my next-door neighbors, Mr. and Mrs. Ferris, an old retired couple. Aloof and gentle, they did not even reproach me when my dogs dug a hole under the fence and killed their pet duck, Matilda. Lynn and Carlton had lived for some time in the "Schloss," as Carlton called the house (pronouncing it "slush"), when early one morning, as I was watering my roses, I saw Mrs. Ferris cutting flowers in her garden. I wished her a pleasant day; she called back: "Oh, I am so glad to see you," and came to the fence with a huge bunch of sweetpeas. "I'd like you to give this to your mother." I thanked her and said that my mother would be enchanted with the lovely bouquet. Then Mrs. Ferris asked: "That nice couple over your garage, are they staying with you for any length of time?"

"As long as they wish it," I answered defensively.

But Mrs. Ferris had more on her mind and slowly and hesitantly it came out. "You know that Mrs. A., the lady who owns that large Spanish house down the road, has been canvassing for signatures to protest your renting to Negroes?"

"No one can tell me who should or should not live in my house . . ." I burst out angrily.

Mrs. Ferris reached over the fence and put her hand on my shoulder. "Don't get excited! I want you to know that no one signed. We, the property owners on this side of the Canyon, had a meeting"—apparently I was not considered a "property owner" as I had been excluded—"and my husband told them: 'These are friends of Mrs. Viertel. We are pleased she is our neighbor.'"

Moved by the unexpected support, I thanked Mrs. Ferris profusely. But she had not finished. Taking a deep breath, she shook her head and looking reproachfully at me, added: "Yes, that's what my husband told them, regardless of the fact that we've seen you driving around with that 'Roosevelt for President' sticker on your car."

Dear Mrs. Ferris! This was the only time in my life I regretted not being a Republican.

Berthold's impatient desire to go to Germany was unexpectedly fulfilled. The BBC sent him with a large staff to report about the Ruhr Valley and the cities on the Rhine. The first was Dusseldorf, with its memories of our life together:

There are no words to describe what this place looks like. No words, no photography can give you a glimpse of the total destruction. That's what totalitarian total war looks like, and that's how the whole world will look after the next one. The Schauspielhaus does not exist anymore. I cannot tell you how touching Lindemann was, how happy to see me. He had been in hiding during the Nazi years and they say that Gruendgens saved him.* I saw our old colleagues and friends; no one has changed much. They know a lot about us, just as we have known about them, but the most amazing thing is that the Hitler years have left no mark: it seems they have not existed. Only *we* know of the millions dead, murdered and martyred, of the unspeakable horrors. The people here pick up exactly where they left off in 1928. It's true that Gustav is shaken by Louise's death; she is constantly before his eyes. Nevertheless, he looks healthy, strong, and marvelously well preserved for his age.

The misery is unbelievable. And all those ruins! . . . and the people you see are ruins also, ruins of a nation which, in spite of all, goes on living and working harder than ever. However, the nationalism of the workers is quite different from the nationalism of the Nazis. Ah, well, in the end it is no different than everywhere else, only tougher, coarser and, therefore, more dangerous and just as loathsome.

Berlin is a witches' cauldron, the crucial place, and perhaps for this reason, in spite of its ruins, it is so alive. How much I would have liked to work at the *Deutsches Theater!* They wanted me so badly; they pleaded with me, but it is impossible with my American passport. They want me in West Berlin also and I have agreed to direct *The Glass Menagerie* at the *Hebbeltheater*, providing there is no war in autumn.

I saw our dear Luise Wenzel, and have spent as much time as I could with her. She lives in a tiny back room, emaciated, stooped with age but makes plans to

* Lindemann was a Jew.

reopen her Pension. The questions about you, the boys, Rose, Edward, Mama were pouring, your ears must have been burning . . . And what a wonderful, decent woman she has remained . . . Ah, Salka. . . .

It was now certain that having fulfilled his commitment in England, he would return to the German theater. His successes began in Zurich. Then he had several offers, from East and West Berlin, for guest performances, but he signed a longer contract with the Burgtheater in Vienna. This return to the city in which he was born, to the ambience of his youth, symbolically closed the cycle. . . .

The Austrian Government had entrusted the leadership of the State theaters, the Burgtheater and the Academie to my brother-in-law, Josef Gielen. Remembering only too well the transition from Viennese *Gemutlichkeit* to fierce Nazi brutality, Rose did not look forward to being *Frau Direktor*. Also it meant separation from her young daughter, who was married to the violinist Ljerko Spiller and lived in Buenos Aires. Rose's letters were mostly about her little grandson and about Michael, her son, who had inherited not only Edward's talent, but also his dedication to modern music. However, for Gielen it was essential to return to more challenging tasks than the staging of operas at the *Teatro Colon*.

Edward was not forgotten in old Europe either; his Viennese friends urged him to return. He refused, but accepted an invitation to teach in summer at the Salzburg *Mozarteum*.

"Hitler and the war destroyed our world," wrote Rose, "and for me art is not important enough to replace lost human values."

She promised that on her way to Vienna she would stop in the United States to visit Edward and Clara in New York, then spend a few weeks with us in Santa Monica.

As I could not afford to be choosy, I was taking all kinds of odd and badly paid assignments, some of them quite funny in retrospect. One was the rewriting of an already completed film, shot in Italy, with a cast which spoke every language except English. It had to be dubbed by American actors, but the producer, as he had to spend the money, insisted on changing the dialogue, but it had to match the lip movements of those on the screen. For many weeks, from nine in the morning until late at night, I sat in the dubbing or cutting room, writing and rewriting; and if it had not been for the patient help of two calm, efficient men, the cutter and the sound engineer, I would have lost my mind, while increasing my vocabulary extravagantly. The producer would telephone me from New York, often as early as six A.M., demanding new "A pic-

ture lines" for his B Picture, in which the beautiful shots of
Venice were tragically wasted. In the end he even stalled about
paying the balance of my salary.

After this experience it was heaven to work with Jean Renoir.
Previews of his film *The River* were unsatisfactory; the audiences
could not understand the story. Renoir invited me to one of the
screenings, and while I was watching the film it occurred to me
that if it were told in retrospect, and if there were more shots of
the Ganges, the lovely but loose scenes would gain clarity. When
Renoir asked for my impressions, I suggested a narration: something like a nostalgic recollection which would tie the story together. I went home and thought no more about it; but two days
later the producer, who had financed the film, called, saying that
Mr. Renoir intended to re-edit his film and would like me to write
the narration I had spoken of. In all my years in Hollywood this
was the first time that someone had not regarded all ideas as his
own.

The River had been made on a small budget and I was poorly
paid, but I had a wonderful time working with Renoir. Later, his
backer refused to have my name on the credit list. Renoir was in
France and could do nothing about it, nor could the Screen
Writers' Guild. The arbitrators admitted that my claim was justified but although a provision existed in the S.W.G. contract that
a writer might have credit for "additional dialogue," there was
none for a narration, even if it represented 25 percent of the
screenplay.

Money stays with people who love it, but much as I tried to
acquire this virtue, I was still poor. However my friends assured
me that I never looked better. I resigned myself to the haphazards
of freelancing, but the house, that dear old house which had sheltered so many, seen so much and served all kinds of good causes,
did not resist the years as well as I did. The roof leaked, the paint
peeled, the iron fence was rusty, the windows would not close, and
termites had invaded the basement. It was disastrous when a
major repair became unavoidable, and the mortgage persistently
reverted to its original amount. When he was working for a studio,
Peter came to the rescue, but he had a wife and child and was not
a Croesus. Edward contributed to the support of Mama, but
Hans's modest income and his passion for ancient Packards hardly
covered his own needs. He would buy his cars for seventy-five
dollars, sometimes even for fifty, and would drive them until they
fell apart, which happened sooner than he expected. He would
leave the wrecks on the road and the police towed them away,
presenting him with a bill and a summons. Even on the install-

ment plan this procedure became quite costly. I tried in vain to persuade my dear first-born that with the money he paid for his Packards, plus fines and repairs, he could get a decent Ford or Chevy. "Yes, but they don't compare in design," he would answer haughtily.

If it had not been for the generosity of my friends—the Chaplins and the Stewarts—foreclosure on the house could not have been averted. The sword of Damocles hung twice over my head. I thought of selling and moving into a smaller house, but as a "temporary recession" prevailed, it was easier to buy than to sell.

I began to give drama lessons—in Hollywood it is called coaching—because a few young actors suddenly "discovered" me. Had the rich been as talented as the poor, I could have embarked on a new and rewarding career; although I do not believe that acting can be taught, especially not in a hurry. I did my best to cure the mumbling and abominable diction, and tried to convince my pupils that the "mike" could not perform miracles. I induced a few to work seriously, and those few also discovered that Shakespeare was not a deadly bore. But the majority lacked dedication to their profession. The concern for a career was more absorbing than the passion for acting, and their days were spent chasing after talent scouts and producers. I was reluctant to accept payment for lessons for which they had no time to prepare. I spent more hours dissuading, comforting and advising those with mediocre talent, than working with the promising ones. They all tried hard to "develop a personality," but the young men imitated Marlon Brando or Tony Curtis, while the girls relied heavily on Vogue-model looks.

This may give a one-sided and perhaps unfair picture of Hollywood's young actors, but such was my experience. Of course, there were exceptions, and several of my pupils achieved a deserved success in films, on the stage, and in television.

As "entertainment," television is never as fascinating as when it is used as a political forum. I thought the Un-American Hearings were an unbeatable show, but I was told it had a disappointing rating—not to be compared with *Lassie*. An enterprising woman, Ilse Lahn of the Paul Kohner Agency, began to encourage me to write for T.V. I tried a few plays and to my great surprise she sold two of them. In the course of the years she stood by me staunchly not only as my agent but as a friend.

The summers in Santa Monica gave Edward a much needed rest and the leisure to compose, for which he never had enough time in New York. He would sit under the pithasporum tree, humming and scribbling on his score sheets, while Clara, stretched out on the grass, slowly turned into a dark brown Indian.

Again we were living in the nagging fear of another world war, around us intolerance and distrust. Those who sympathized with the legitimate urge of the Asiatic people to free themselves from age-old exploitation were denounced and suspected, while the United States supported their corrupt power cliques.

Arnold Schoenberg was getting old. He was emaciated and suffered from asthma; only his huge, burning eyes remained the same. Trude was exhausted by care and worry; the two boys strong, intelligent, enterprising, very American; the girl, Nuria, a beauty. Trude's brother, Rudolph Kolisch, and the philosopher and musician Dr. Theodor Adorno, Edward's friend of many years, came often to Mabery Road. There were excited discussions about the new Thomas Mann novel, *Dr. Faustus*. Without having read the book, Schoenberg objected that Mann had made his hero the inventor of the twelve-tone system. Dr. Adorno, who had been Thomas Mann's musical advisor, defended the author. There were impassioned arguments about "Geistiges Eigentum." * But everything was amicably settled when Thomas Mann, in a short note in his book, explained that despite all his respect and admiration for Schoenberg he had never intended to use him as a model for his hero.

Finally Rose arrived, her lovely face a little more lined and faded, more silver in her hair, but otherwise the same Ruzia, slim and graceful, her walk and movements unchanged. She told us about her life in the Third Reich, how courageous friends had helped her and the children to leave; then about Argentina under Peron. Young Michael participated in student demonstrations and would come home beaten-up and bleeding. Mama could not hear enough about Eva Peron—giving audiences to poor and frightened Jewish refugees, keeping them waiting from morning until ten or twelve at night, then trying to impress them by appearing in a Dior evening gown, a tiara on her head, and covered with jewels.

Driving along the coast or showing Rose the canyons and valleys, made me realize once more how much I loved California. In the back seat, his mane blown by the wind, one paw on my shoulder, Timmy seemed to agree with me.

Then Rose had to leave, and the farewell was sadder than any other. Would she ever see Mama again? Peter, Jigee and Vicky were also on the move. Peter was to write the screenplay to *Decision Before Dawn*, in Germany. They would visit the Gielens and Berthold, in Vienna.

* Spiritual ownership.

In the *Theatre Arts* of February 1950, Eric Bentley wrote: ". . . What [Berthold] Viertel's work preeminently shows is the quality left-wing directors have scorned or ignored: finer feeling, personal feeling . . . The revolutionary act is to go back and find the real thing, unhurriedly, without fanfare.

"There has been a lot of talk of Stanislavski of late among people who are worlds away from him temperamentally, humanly. Viertel's fresh, direct, and delicate humanity, his patient thoroughness in preparing his productions, his realism that can render all the transitions between sweet and bitter, is closer to the Russian master in spirit than anything else I have come across. . . ."

43

THE KOREAN WAR and the investigations influenced life in the United States, and many of my friends preferred to leave the country. Ella and Don went to London; Thomas Mann, disgusted by attacks on his anti-Cold War attitude, moved to his last exile: Switzerland. The Chaplins, who had planned a visit to England, were informed that the Immigration Board, disregarding Charlie's reentry permit, would not let him return unless he cleared himself of "charges of a political nature and of moral turpitude." He and Oona decided not to come back.

My agent Ilse Lahn firmly denied that I was blacklisted: "Everyone knows you are not a communist." And as usual the producers told her that if I had a good story and Garbo committed herself to appearing in it, I would be employed. "They know they are safe in their offer," I said, and she reproached me for my pessimism.

But with all our varied difficulties, life went on. Hans, Thomas and I were each having our share of trouble, although under the circumstances, mine was the lion's share. Nevertheless, people were still drawn to Mabery Road, especially the young. One of them was Norman Mailer, who seemed a mixture of ancient wisdom and astonishing naïveté, somehow thrown out of balance by his world fame; and much too young and complicated to be married. We were very fond of him. Then there was James Agee, critic and essayist, passionately addicted to films but essentially a poet. After a long day's work with John Huston, for whom he was writing a screenplay, he would come to Mabery Road and, if no other guests were present and no discussions and arguments going on, we would sit and listen to music: to Edward's when he was there, otherwise to radio concerts and records; or sometimes he, Agee, would sit down at the piano and play his favorite Schubert sonata, not ostentatiously and not very well. And very dear to me was the young poetess Naomi Replansky. She lived in Ocean Park, which was at that time a conglomeration of ghettos: poor, orthodox Jews, Negroes, beatniks, and white and black homosexuals, all living in peaceful coexistence.

I could not say that Mama had become an invalid, but her trembling had increased to such a degree that I had to bathe and dress her and on bad days, even feed her. The doctor thought that it was caused by the severe shocks during bombings in Poland and Moscow. As she was fastidious and independent, it depressed her to be attended at every physical function and she hated her disability and her old body. I assured her that I did not mind taking care of her and that she was still my lovely Mama. This was true: her skin was spotless and silky, her face finely wrinkled, her hands and legs slim and astonishingly unmarred by age. As long as I could remember, although rarely ill, she had been impatient with her doctors, convinced that she knew as much about remedies as they. But it was impossible to be angry with her because she was always gentle and considerate, and so grateful for everything I did that it brought tears to my eyes. She was happy to give Thomas his German lessons, and she read Proust, although she preferred Jane Austen. She was affected by the death of Heinrich Mann and asked me to take her to his funeral. She listened to the eulogies by Lion Feuchtwanger and the Reverend Fritschmann of the Unitarian Church; then said that although everything was very dignified, she found American funerals too cheerful.

A few months later Arnold Schoenberg died. To the last, Hollywood did not recognize his genius and only very few attended his funeral.

Peter had finished his film and he, Jigee and Vicky returned to Zuma. I could not help noticing that there was that certain tone of marital irritation between them, which makes the wife sound like a governess and the husband revert to adolescent rebellion. The war had left an indelible stigma on those who had participated in it, had seen horror and suffered incredible hardship; while their women, especially in America, lived in peacetime comfort and easily forgot what their men had gone through.

Restless, and running away from their problems, Peter and Jigee decided to sell the house they had built with such love, and go back to Europe to spend the winter in Klosters. Their predilection for the quiet mountain village also drew Peter's friends there as soon as the skiing season started. Irwin Shaw and Bob Parrish became enthusiastic Klosterites. Vicky was going to a Swiss school and sent me and Mama dear little notes in German. Jigee's delight in Europe sounded undiminished, at least as she expressed it in her letters. However, she and Peter did not get along and there were brief separations.

But in the autumn of 1951 I received the news: "You are going to be a grandmother." I was pleased because apparently the recurrent difficulties in their marriage were over. Outsiders never witness reconciliations.

It was La Rochefoucauld who said: "It is impossible to love a second time what one has truly ceased to love," and there is no explanation and no remedy for it. When it happens, hurt and pain are so overpowering that the heart does not forgive nor forget.

On April 30th, 1952, my granddaughter Christine was born in Paris and I received a cable from Peter saying that mother and child were well. A week later Jigee wrote me that she and Peter had parted. It was a long letter, very brave and decent, and it made me terrribly sad.

> Christine is a new joy and Vicky always is, but not having Peter anymore overshadows everything. He is in love with a French girl named Bettina . . . I sort of wish I could say or think otherwise, but actually she is nice, and beautiful in an extraordinary way, charming and thoroughly adorable. I can understand Peter's feelings; I only wish it had come at another time. . . .
>
> The baby came three weeks early. She is small but intact, and exactly you, to the tips of her fingers. It is as if I had no part in the making of her. Her eyes are blue, and she is clearly a Steuermann, only on a very small scale. . . .
>
> It is not a happy time for Peter either; he is thin and worried and sorry to have hurt me, but it's done and I told him it would be better if I did not see him at all for a while. Maybe later, on a friendly basis, but now I

am too hurt and too sick to be able to bear it . . . I know no one ever ruins anyone's life—and I cannot blame Peter alone.

I was heartbroken about Jigee's sorrow and I knew, only too well, what Peter was going through. He had been deeply attached to Jigee, but the accumulated bitterness had made it impossible for them to live together. "When love begins to sicken and decay. . . ."

"I wish you could live with us," wrote Jigee. "Life would somehow have a fuller meaning if we were together. You would be so much to Christine and she to you! I wish I could tell you how every expression and gesture of hers is absolutely you. It is a wonderful thing for me. . . ."

The photos she sent confirmed that Christine was an enchanting baby, but she was much more like Peter. I could not imagine myself having ever been so devastatingly charming.

> I congratulate you with all my heart on your, our, first grandchild [Berthold wrote]. That she was born on the anniversary of our wedding is an omen signifying the continuation of our love . . . I am terribly sorry for Peter and Jigee. I knew for some time that the marriage wouldn't last and it is difficult to say that one or the other was at fault. I am sad that I cannot be of any help either to her or Vicky of whom I think so often. Yes, we all grasp for some kind of happiness in this crumbling world. For us, the old ones, it will soon cease to exist . . . I have not been feeling well. The circulation disorder in my right leg has improved, but the bronchitis stays with me, an uninvited companion; and yesterday I had an attack of asthma, which could be regarded as a just punishment for a ruthless and selfish pursuit of happiness. Regardless, I am preparing Gerhardt Hauptmann's *Die Ratten*. But first I am taking a two months' vacation, of which I'll spend a couple of weeks in Bad Reichenhall, then at Liesel's house on the Grundelsee . . . And so we must go on . . . each of us according to the god in his heart. As long as we have this, no matter in what form, and as long as we are capable of love, what more is there to say . . . Our tiny Christine has just started. I hope and trust, Salka, she has inherited your lioness's strength.

But even lionesses become dead tired.

The Zinnemanns had sold their house and moved to a larger one; Freddie was now one of the most sought-after directors. It was lucky for us that a young physician and his family had acquired their home. Dr. Drenick was not only a very good doctor, but he spoke German, was patience and kindness itself, and Mama liked him because he "didn't make any fuss."

From day to day she was getting weaker and her trembling worse, but when Edward and Clara arrived in the summer she again recovered miraculously.

Jigee sent us new photos of Christine, now seven months old, sitting up and smiling and really adorable. She had decided to stay in Klosters, where Vicky was happy in her school and she herself liked living in the small community. She also had many American friends who were spending the winter in Klosters. "Christine has been inspected by everyone with interest and approval."

Christmas Eve that year was much "merrier" than I had expected. Lynn and Carlton, Wiesen, John Collier, Christopher Isherwood and a young painter, Don Bachardy, joined us for dinner. We had a tree, and Charlotte Dieterle had sent a huge turkey from their ranch. Mama came downstairs dressed in a light, gray silk dress, looking very lovely. She was delighted with her presents and stayed up until two in the morning, enjoying the party. Later, as I helped her upstairs, I noticed that she was short of breath and I made her rest after each step. I called Dr. Drenick, who came immediately, gave her a shot and prescribed digitalis. He said it was her heart. From that day, she did not leave her room. Sitting in her armchair, her breathing quick and shallow, she went on reading her novels. Our rooms were separated by a bathroom, the doors between her and my room were always open. She could see me typing at my desk and when I lifted my eyes I saw her in her armchair. Between us lay Timmy on the bathroom tiles, watching. He remained at a respectful distance from Mama, but he knew when she needed me and would come and put his paw on my knee.

She was pathetically undemanding. Gently and gradually she was withdrawing from life. She had no pain and complained only about the discomfort of her trembling. When I urged her to take some nourishment she obeyed with her usual friendliness, wondering: "Am I so clumsy or so weak that I cannot hold the spoon myself?"

On New Year's Eve Wiesen brought her sweets, then the three of us drank some champagne. Then on New Year's Day Gottfried and Silvia Reinhardt paid us a visit and Gottfried went upstairs to give Mama greetings from his mother, who was in Europe. When he returned to the living room he said that he had found her amazingly alert and in good spirits. Next morning she did not want to dress and I saw that she had a fever. Dr. Drenick came and diagnosed pneumonia. He ordered a hospital bed and oxygen, and showed me how to administer it, which was difficult because she refused to have the mask on her face. He gave her penicillin shots and in two days the fever went down and she felt better.

I had drawn my chair close to her bed. Her blue eyes, now very pale and lusterless, never left me. I tried to make her drink some orange juice and she took a sip politely, then thanked me with great tenderness for taking such good care of her, but she could not drink more. Her main worry was that I didn't get enough sleep, but she no longer knew whether it was morning or night. She did not hold onto life. She simply let it go. Now and then I heard her say: "Emil. . . ." It was the name of her young brother who had killed himself. I asked what she wanted to say. "He wanted fifty Gulden, but Papa would not give it to him. He was an incorrigible gambler—but had I sent the money he would not have killed himself." During the last days of her illness she had not mentioned Edward, most dear to her, nor Rose nor Dusko— but now, out of the depth of her being, came this heartbreaking whisper, this long suppressed guilt feeling.

Edward phoned asking if he should come, but I thought it would worry and frighten her. He insisted that I take a night nurse so that I could get some rest at night. When the nurse, a friendly, elderly woman, arrived she found Mama in a hospital bed, washed and in a fresh nightgown. "There is nothing for me to do," she said. The doctor, who had warned me that Mama might get bedsores, insisted that I turn her around frequently. It made her angry. "How stupid," she said, "it only makes me uncomfortable." Slipping my arm under her shoulders, I raised her on her pillow. As it seemed to soothe her I remained bent over the bed, holding her thin body until her eyes closed and she fell asleep. Then I withdrew my arm very gently. She was breathing so evenly and peacefully that Dr. Drenick said: "Perhaps—perhaps she'll pull through." He insisted I lie down, and the nurse promised to wake me as soon as Mama opened her eyes. It was midnight, the house unusually quiet, Thomas in his room, Hans downstairs reading. I remember that my calendar still showed the first day of 1953, and I corrected the date to January 6, and went to bed. I was sleeping when the nurse burst into my room and shook me, crying hysterically: "Come quickly, dear, your mother is gone."

I stumbled into Mama's room. She was lying there exactly as I had left her. I touched her and she was uncannily cold. She had died so softly and quietly that the nurse had not noticed that she had ceased breathing.

I did not want Edward to come to the funeral as it would have been a terrible strain on him and I knew Mama: she would have considered it an unnecessary expense and a gesture without meaning for her. I talked to him and Clara on the phone and cabled to the Gielens and Berthold. After the funeral I wrote a long letter to them.

She looked beautiful, but estranged, as she lay in her coffin. I had cut a few camelias from her favorite bush and put them into her folded hands. We buried her in the little non-sectarian Woodland cemetery in Santa Monica, under a large magnolia tree. As she disliked the mortuary atmosphere and organ music so much, the service took place at the graveside. A light rain was falling, when Hans, Thomas, Fred Zinnemann, Christopher Isherwood, Carlton and Hans's friend Edwin carried her to her grave. The Rabbi, new in Hollywood, said in simple words how courageous she had been and how loving, and how her life had been haunted by wars and sorrow. Then he asked us to say the Kaddish, and Hans, Thomas and I had to repeat after him the Hebraic words. Our voices were choked and only his was heard. At the horrible moment when one had to leave her in this foreign earth, we found ourselves surrounded by people and I became aware how many had come to say farewell to her. Not only those who were fond of her: the Renoirs, Feuchtwangers, Dieterles, Gottfried, Walter and Hedi, but many Negroes and German refugees and young Americans, some who had only met her once or twice, all sincerely moved and sharing our grief.

Now the house is empty and silent. The daily work continues. She had been so quiet in her last years—still she was there—and I miss her terribly. . . .

44

My SONS URGED ME to free myself from the house, the many chores and the worry connected with it. Thomas had moved to Hollywood, near where he worked; he did not drive a car and the bad bus connections from Santa Monica were too trying. He had his B.A. degree, but refused to go on with postgraduate work. At least for a while he preferred not to study. He was inspecting and cutting film for a small television outfit and liked his work. Hans had passed his exams at U.C.L.A. with honors, but, for "personal reasons," had decided to return to the University of London. He was working at the Lockheed plant in Burbank to earn the money for the trip.

John Houseman, who was producing films for MGM, and his French wife Joan, came to see me and said that they would like to rent the house for six months with an option for six more. As they did not mind Carlton and Lynn keeping the garage apartment, I was pleased to have them as tenants. It was April and as they wanted to move in on the first of May, I had to vacate the house in a hurry.

I drove around Santa Monica, stopping wherever there was a furnished room or an apartment for lease, but no one wanted me with my big, shaggy dog, and most landladies preferred single men. A pupil of Edward, Lucille Ostrow, took pity on me and invited me and Tim to stay with her until I found a place to live.

If Wiesen had not helped me with the packing I would never have finished. Joan Houseman let me keep some of my things in the house. Finally with Timmy and many suitcases, the largest and heaviest one filled to the brim with letters, notes and diaries, I left the house.

Then a friend of another friend asked me to move to her house near Ocean Park and take care of her fox terrier while she and her husband took a trip. I gratefully accepted for myself and Wiesen, my faithful helper, who was temporarily free, and loved dogs. She was the only one who really disapproved of my giving up Mabery Road. "It's foolish. You should stay in the house and rent single rooms." But I was set on going to Europe. I had sold a television script and was waiting to be paid, and Peter, affluent at the moment, offered to finance my trip. That summer Josef, my brother-in-law, was producing and staging plays for the Salzburg Festival, Edward had a commitment at the *Mozarteum*, Berthold and Liesel were spending the summer in Grundelsee, Peter was in Paris, Jigee in Switzerland, and the ideal place for a family reunion would have been Salzburg. Everyone wanted me to come.

Jigee urged me to live with her, Vicky and Christine. ". . . I do wish we were together now. Please know we think of you constantly . . . I love and need you. . . ."

In the spring Berthold had been ill. For several weeks he was in a hospital but Liesel assured me that he was recovering quickly. His handwriting, which had worried me, was again firm and clear: "Dearest Salka: My new and, I hope, permanent address will now be Zedlitzgasse 1. I am leaving the hospital a regenerated human being, not only looking but feeling as good as new, impatient to move into the new apartment, which Liesel miraculously acquired, and furnished with fantastic ingenuity."

How strange that Berthold would now live in the Zedlitzgasse, next to the house where, on the night we first met, he had said: "I am going to marry you. . . ."

After the serious warning I had received, I decided to take a long rest: a summer in Grundelsee, which I shall spend collecting poems and letters, also those from our time together which you offered to send me. I cannot cease regretting the loss of our correspondence during the First War, so important and treasured for all the love and ideals it contained . . . I feel the same today, as again and again I am reliving the past, trying to find coherence and unity in the manifold interwoven web. In the last years of our life we should say farewell and once more embrace, and bless and give thanks— even if we don't know to whom—but certainly to those we have loved and who have given us love, to those who have broken the bread of life with us, in happiness, but also in tears. While I was gasping for breath I was not able to think—it happened so quickly—in the last two years I had been in a bad condition. However, with the last of my strength, I rehearsed *Anthony and*

Cleopatra. Afterwards, in the hospital, when I began to come back to life, all the memories returned and I have thought of you often and lovingly. . . .

We are waiting impatiently for Edward and Clara, and hope they like the nations-devouring Salzburg. As it is close to Grundelsee I shall see them as soon as they arrive. If only you were with us. I know that you don't understand and perhaps cannot forgive me, that for the last five years I have "lived and died" for the Viennese *Burgtheater*. It is impossible to explain this to you, as no one chooses the road he has to take. We are all used and digested by life, which consumes us at will. If only I could talk to you, not about the theater, but about the things which tore us apart from each other and keep us apart. You see, Salka, if I had not recovered from this illness, which was quite serious (the doctors say that I am over the worst and the heart and lungs are not affected), we would have never seen each other again, nor Hans, Peter and Tommy. . . .

I read his letter and decided to apply for my passport at once. It was the first of June. After I had filled out the elaborate questionnaire, and confirmed that I was not a bigamist nor an anarchist, the gentleman at the desk assured me that it was only a matter of forty-eight hours to get a passport, as they no longer had to be issued in Washington, D.C., but by the State Department branch in San Francisco. I returned home and debated with Hans which would be cheaper, to go by plane or boat—he was always for boats—and which would be better for Timmy, whom, of course, I would take with me. The two days went by but my passport did not arrive. I waited two more, then telephoned the Passport Office and was informed that my application had been referred to Washington. I wrote a frantic letter and sent telegrams to Washington but weeks passed and they remained unanswered. My absent hosts were coming back and I could not stay in their house any longer. Wiesen took a new job, and again I tried to find a room, where I could keep Tim, who was melancholy and strangely subdued, obviously homesick for Mabery Road. A young actress offered me shelter. She had rented Wolfgang and Lally Reinhardt's house—they had returned to Germany—and had a lot of room. She was charming and liked Tim. After I was installed, I went to my lawyer and told him about the silence of the State Department. He dictated another telegram but it was August before I received a reply:

Department of State
Washington

In reply refer to
f130-Viertel, Salomea Sara   August 19, 1953

Mrs. Salomea Sara Viertel,
165 Mabery Road,
Santa Monica, California.

My dear Mrs. Viertel,

I regret to inform you that after careful consideration of your application for passport facilities, dated June 1, 1953, the Department of State is obliged to disapprove your application tentatively on the ground that the granting of such passport facilities is precluded under the provisions of Section 51.135 of Title 22 of the Code of Federal Regulations. A copy of the pertinent Regulations is enclosed for your information.

In cases coming within the purview of the Regulations above referred to it is the practice of the Department to inform the applicant of the reasons for the disapproval of the request for passport facilities insofar as the security regulations will permit.

In your case it has been alleged that you were a Communist. The Department has concluded that your case also falls within the scope of subsection (b) of Section 51.135 of that subsection as amplified by Section 51.141 (b) of the aforementioned regulations. The opinion of the Department is that the evidence indicates on your part a consistent and prolonged adherence to the Communist Party line on a variety of issues and through shifts and changes of that line during a period of many years. It is alleged that you have been associated with the Civil Rights Congress which has been listed by the Attorney General as Communistic or subversive.

It is also alleged that your connection with Hollywood Arts, Sciences, and Professions Council, has followed the Communist Party line. It is further alleged that you have been closely associated with known Communists.

Under Section 51.137 of the Regulations you may present your case and all relevant information informally to the Passport Office. If you desire to take advantage of this provision you may appear before a hearing officer of the Passport Office or you may take up the matter by mail. In either case you will be required to submit a sworn statement as to whether you are now or ever have been a Communist.

You are assured that any information or evidence which you may supply will receive most careful consideration and that every effort will be made to act upon your application promptly and justly. The Department desires to emphasize that the passport records are confidential government records and any information which you may submit or which may be received from other sources in connection with your application will not be made known to the public or to any unauthorized person unless you release it. The Department reserves the right to disclose factual information to supplement or correct any statement which a passport applicant may release for publication concerning the reasons why he was denied a passport or the Department's action in his case.

If a reply to this letter is not received within thirty days it will be assumed that you do not wish to have your case reconsidered at this time.

Sincerely yours,

For the Secretary of State:

R. B. Shipley
Director, Passport Office.

I showed the letter to Beilenson. As he had known me for so many years he did not doubt that I could refute the accusation. He made out an affidavit, which I was to sign under oath at a notary's. With good conscience I could swear that "I am not, nor have I ever been a communist, that I did not act, nor have I ever acted under the discipline of the Communist party, etc., etc." I was not going abroad "to engage in activities to advance knowingly, willingly or otherwise the communist movement." However, I insisted that: "the independence of thought and the expression of it, are essential in a democracy . . . and without trying to guess at what shades and changes the Department refers, I can only state that although I have often been on the opposite side of the so-called Communist Party line, on occasions my views coincided with it, because it supported the fight against fascism."

I denied that my membership in the Hollywood Arts, Sciences

and Professions, which had been accused of following the CP line, was the result of any "direction, domination or control" asserted over me by communists. And I admitted that "I have associated, because they were my friends, with persons who have subsequently been mentioned as alleged members of the Communist party or who have appeared before the Congressional committees . . . I assert that my desire to have a passport is entirely non-political. I want to visit with members of my family."

The State Department could not care less, and did not act "promptly and justly." Meanwhile Edward and Clara had been in Salzburg and Grundelsee, had seen Berthold and Liesel, and their letters reassured me about his health, although the enclosed snapshots showed him terribly thin and aged. They were all appalled that I had been refused a passport. I hoped that at least Thomas would be able to travel. But Thomas had lost his birth certificate, necessary for the passport. As he had been born in Vienna, Liesel promised to send him a copy. Hans's passport was issued in forty-eight hours.

My dog became ill. He would not eat, refused to go for walks, nor would he any longer jump into the car after me. The veterinary surgeon said that there was no alternative to save him but an operation, as he suspected an ulcer or a tumor in the stomach. When Timmy woke up from the anaesthetic he tried to put his paw on my shoulder but couldn't, and a few hours later he died. He had been my constant companion and my comfort for seven bad years. He understood everything and he truly loved me. Now no one seemed to need me any longer. The shackles of love were falling off.

In September Hans had to enroll at the University of London. As I was driving him to the station he suddenly remembered that a writer, Mr. Seff, wanted his station wagon driven from Los Angeles to New York, and he suggested that I should get in touch with him. "You must get out of the doldrums," Hans said. "You must go to New York where you have Edward and Clara, friends and theater and music. And when finally you get your passport, you will be three thousand miles closer to Europe."

When I get my passport! It sounded like a tale Hans was inventing so that I would not feel lost. But his advice sounded reasonable and I felt tempted.

I wrote Mr. Seff, who answered that he would appreciate having his station wagon in New York and gave me the address of a gasoline station where it was garaged. He advised me to get someone to share the driving, as he thought it would be a strenuous trip for a woman alone. Thomas, Lynn and Carlton also insisted I have a co-driver. I chose as my passenger—he could not drive—the writer Jay Leyda, a former pupil of Sergei Eisenstein.

Jay Leyda looked forty and had a pleasant American appearance, "clean cut" as they call it. He had written a book about Herman Melville, *The Melville Log,* and was at present working on a biography of Emily Dickinson. He intended to leave me somewhere near Colorado, because he had to look up an old lady who had letters from her.

It was hard to leave Thomas. I had wished so much for him to see his father and to get a glimpse of Europe, which he did not remember.

He came to see me off and we left Santa Monica in my old convertible to meet my traveling companion at the garage. The mechanic assured me that he had checked the oil and water and looked over the tires; the station wagon had been gone over thoroughly and would drive like a dream. Thomas transferred my suitcases and lifting the large one exclaimed: "For heaven's sake, Mother! What's in it?"

"Letters," I said, "nothing but letters . . ." and I embraced him with a heavy heart.

In Arizona an ominous noise in the engine made me slow down, and after a short, desperate choking and coughing the motor died. I let the car roll to the side of the road and Jay got out to signal for help. Cars whizzed by indifferent to our plight. Finally a small truck appeared and stopped. After a glance under the hood of our station wagon its driver said that all he could do was send a tow car from the next Automobile Association Garage.

It took more than an hour before the A.A.A. car appeared, to tow us to the garage in Williams. After much head-shaking and whistling the two mechanics who examined the engine diagnosed it as beyond repair! The bearings were burnt out because of a leak in the oil-pump. But they could order a new engine from the nearest Chevrolet plant. It would only take three days and three hundred dollars to make the car like new. I called Mr. Seff in New York. I must say he took it extremely gallantly and was more concerned about me, stranded in Williams, than about his damaged car. Could I bear to wait for the engine?

The mechanic drove us and our luggage to a motel. Not to desert me, Jay Leyda changed his original plan. Next morning he would take the bus to Colorado, and, as soon as I was able to leave, meet me in Albuquerque, so that we could continue the trip together.

The motel was a new place, quite a distance from the town, and we were the only guests. The manager, a friendly lady, complained that the only people who asked for rooms were Negroes and, much as she would like to, she could not accommodate them.

We sat in my room listening to the rain, and Jay asked why I was traveling with a trunk full of letters. I said that I was clinging to them as they contained so much of my life. I opened the trunk and right on top were the letters from Eisenstein, among them the long, desperate one from Mexico. I translated it for Jay, and he said that it was a very important letter.

I had met Jay Leyda and his Chinese wife Si-lan only once, at a party, and we were merely introduced to each other. The journey across the U.S. gave me and Jay the chance to become friends. At its outset I had been dispirited and discouraged, but his interest, his understanding and kindness inspired such confidence that I could talk to him as I had not talked to anyone for a long time. He listened attentively, then concluded that I should use my solitary confinement in Williams and begin writing my memoirs immediately. I thought that he overestimated my egocentricity.

Next day he left on his pursuit of Emily. I telephoned Edward, informed him about the unfortunate delay and that I was broke, because four days in Williams would exhaust my funds. He said he would wire me a hundred dollars, admonished me to drive carefully and call him every day to report my progress. I did not write my memoirs but listened instead to the life story of the motel manager. On the third day, as promised, the mechanic delivered the station wagon and I could proceed to my rendezvous with Jay. We continued along Route 66.

It was amazing how much we had to discuss. And he still insisted I should write my memoirs. After Missouri in the autumn coloring, which I had not imagined would be so lovely, we said good-bye to each other. In two more days I would be in New York.

Now came a long stretch of turnpike and straight road, across dreary country. I thought of Berthold back in Vienna, smoking his endless cigarettes and translating another Tennessee Williams play. I wanted to write to him that I was on my way, determined to get my passport. But there was no paper in the dismal motel at which I stayed overnight.

Edward and Clara were to meet me in a café in Somerville, New Jersey, so that Clara would guide me to New York. I was exhausted. The traffic had been heavy and made me late. After the numbing hours behind the wheel the sight of the dear faces revived me.

We sat down and had coffee and I told them about my plans: I wanted to stay with them for a few days, then go to Washington, because I was determined to get my passport. I *had* to go to Europe; I *had* to see Berthold. Clara remained silent, Edward had his eyes averted. Then he turned to me, took my hand and said almost brusquely: "Salomé, Berthold died last night."

I don't think I took this blow very bravely.

Then I thought of Thomas. Did he know? Yes, after the cable arrived Edward had called our friend Lucille and asked her to tell Thomas what had happened.

It was night when we arrived at the apartment and immediately I phoned Thomas. He sounded stricken but controlled. He had been worried about me, as I was still on the road when the obituaries appeared in the Los Angeles and New York papers. Carlton and Lynn had spent a lot of time with him. He did not want me to come back, but to stay in New York as I had planned.

Liesel, deeply grieved, but still brave, sent me Berthold's last letter, written the night before he died.

He was buried next to Karl Kraus, Peter Altenberg, Theodor Loos—whom he had admired and loved—greatly honored and eulogized by representatives of the Austrian government, the *Burgtheater* and the city of Vienna. He died before Hans and Peter could reach his bedside . . . They carried him to his grave.

45

IT HELPED ME, IN THOSE BITTER DAYS, to be with Edward and Clara; however, I could not stay with them indefinitely. I did not know what I was going to do, and when Etta Hardt, who was working for a publishing house, invited me to share her apartment, I gratefully accepted. The apartment was on East 73rd Street on the ground floor of an old brownstone house, and had a tiny garden with a single tree in the middle of it. Each of us had a separate entrance and we respected each other's privacy. Next door was an identical house, in which Eleonora Mendelssohn had lived, and had killed herself the year before. Francesco was in hospital suffering from deep depression, and not permitted to have visitors. I missed them and their friendship. But Greta was in New York—compassionate, unchanged, and very dear.

Unexpectedly, someone I had completely lost touch with called me. It was Ursula Blanke, whom I had known when she was the bride of Henry Blanke, a nineteen-year-old German girl, bewildered by Hollywood and the movies, and only at ease with my three-year-old Tommy. She had divorced Henry and was now married to James Reynolds, Under Secretary to the Department of Labor during the Truman Administration.

I don't remember how Ursula found out that I was in New York, but she appeared in my room at Etta's, still looking like a flapper of the twenties. Nostalgically she recalled Mabery Road. She and her husband lived in New Jersey, but she was sure that the next presidential election would get the Democrats and her Jim back to Washington, D.C. I had learned my lesson about "guilt by association," and felt I must tell Ursula that I had been refused a passport. She thought I was joking. This only happened to communists. Although affected by Trumanism and the mentality of the Cold War, she was appalled by the activities of Senator Joe McCarthy. The whole nation had watched on television the investigations of communism in the Army and the Defense Department. Ursula had been planning a trip to Germany and thought it would be nice if we could go to Europe together. "You *must* get your passport!" was the steady refrain of her persuasion that I take steps in Washington; but I remained apathetic. Once Edward said to me: "It is easier to be unhappy in a hellish place like New York than in a lovely countryside or on the shores of the Pacific," but this was not true for me.

We were a very scattered family: Peter was in Paris, Hans in London, Thomas in Los Angeles, Jigee with Vicky and Christine in Klosters. Ilse Lahn was assuring me that the money for my T.V. script would be mailed any day. The film had been shot with Hedy Lamarr and could not be released until everyone was paid. (Those who had seen it reported that it was ghastly.) The November days became shorter and darker.

Then Ursula rang me to say that she was in New York at the office of an attorney, Mr. Ernest C., to whom she had told my passport difficulties. I reminded her that she had promised not to tell anyone. "But you don't know Ernest C.; he is wonderful! Don't be foolish. Come and talk to him," and she mentioned casually that Mr. C. was the attorney of a famous gossip columnist. I was horrified; I stuck the State Department's letter and my affidavits in my coat pocket, ran out onto the street, hailed a taxi, and drove to a huge building on Times Square. Ursula was waiting for me on the top floor at the elevator door and quickly informed me that Mr. C. was brilliant, liberal and a great power in the Democratic Party. With that she dragged me into an office where a short, square man with a round head, who looked like a mixture of Peter Lorre and Fiorello La Guardia, greeted me. He was jovial and straightforward. I showed him the fatal letter, which was addressed with my full name. "Salomea Sara," he asked solemnly, "are you or are you not a communist?"

"I am not."

"Why not?"

I confined my answer to one sentence: "Because I am not able to accept or to follow any party discipline." This seemed to please him; he told me that he himself was a descendent of Italian anarchists. However, my affidavit would only irritate the authorities, because it did not say that I abhorred communism.

"I abhor cruelty, I abhor confessions made under torture, I abhor the Moscow Trials, war, dictatorship, arrogant nationalism, secret police, racial discrimination, militarism—but I have friends, wonderful people, who are communists, and I don't think this should deprive me of visiting my family."

"You are right, Salomea Sara," said Mr. C. "But I am afraid they will ask you precise questions in Washington."

"I have not asked for a hearing."

"I will ask for one for you," said Mr. C.

I did not want that. He was a famous lawyer, getting enormous fees for "keeping people out of trouble," as Ursula put it, and I could never afford to pay him.

"Don't talk rubbish, Salomea Sara!" he barked at me. "I like you. Ursula talks a lot about you, Salomea Sara."

"But I am a stranger to you."

"You are Ursula's friend, Salomea Sara, and when you have your passport you may give me a hug."

I was moved to tears, partly because he seemed so fond of my embarrassing first name; but I doubted that he would succeed. Days went by and I did not hear from Mr. C. until, on the evening of December 8, I received a call from Washington. Somebody said: "Just a minute." Then I heard Mr. C.'s voice: "Salomea Sara? Get on the first plane tomorrow morning, and meet me for breakfast at the. . . ." (It is irrelevant, but annoying, that I have forgotten the name of the hotel. The whole thing seems to lack authenticity!) However, next morning at nine A.M. I was in Washington sitting with Mr. C. in a sumptuous dining room with attentive waiters silently serving well-dressed, well-fed, well-shaven old men. Mr. C. and I had more than an hour for an elaborate breakfast and a full confession of my politics.

At ten-thirty we entered a large room in an office building which, I assume, was the State Department's Passport Division. It had a long table and a few chairs, but no other furniture. Two middle-aged gentlemen came in, one carrying a briefcase containing the list of my sins. It was as thick as the New York telephone book. I wanted to say, "What a waste of time and taxpayers' money," but I restrained myself.

The first thing I had to explain was my "association" with Hanns Eisler "in its political implication." The second: had I attended and sponsored the Civil Rights Congress in Chicago in November 1947? This was easy: at least fifty people could testify that I had not moved from Santa Monica. But I had signed an *amicus curiae* brief for the Hollywood Ten. Had any of them ever suggested my joining the Communist Party? No one ever had. Also I had signed "the so-called Stockholm Peace Petition," and the appeal for clemency for the Rosenbergs, what about that? Yes, I had signed it. Here Mr. C. emphatically stated that I was against the death penalty but that I had never acted under the direction and discipline of the Communist Party. There were many lies in my dossier, and the incredible distortions of "alleged" (I hate this word!) conversations which had taken place in my house made me indignant. The interrogator was matter-of-fact, polite, but extremely thorough. A remark I had supposedly (allegedly!) made was especially on his mind. Had I said that I'd prefer *any form of government* to the one in the United States?

"Any form?!" I repeated. "Do I give the impression of being a moron? And even had I said such a stupid thing, 'any form' could mean monarchy, feudalism or matriarchy, not necessarily communism!" He smiled and did not go further.

The hearing was over, and I was asked to wait. The interrogator left the room to discuss my case with the head of the department, I suppose the much-feared Mrs. Shipley. He returned looking somewhat embarrassed! The State Department could only give me a restricted passport for four months. Mr. C. was peeved, but as I was certain that if it had not been for him they would not have agreed even to that, I accepted the limited passport. After my return to the States I would insist upon a regular one.

I wish I could praise Mr. C.'s name to the whole world, but I am afraid it would only embarrass him. Once more, gratefully, I accepted the kindness of strangers, capricious like fate itself, and undeserved.

When my passport arrived, Edward, who had been full of misgivings, sighed with relief, and Clara took me immediately to Bloomingdale's, because my California wardrobe was inadequate for a European winter. My sons were overjoyed even by the limited victory. Peter took care of my airplane ticket, and I was to leave on December 26. And, as if the black spell had broken at last, even the television producer paid up.

Because of Christmas, changed plans and social commitments, Ursula had to postpone her trip. Also she intended to go by boat to Germany, while I was flying to meet Peter in Ireland.

I was alone on Christmas Eve. I tried to call Thomas, but it was three hours earlier in California and he was not home yet. Then I heard a knock at the door. It was Greta; she also was alone. I quickly improvised a supper and lit the candles on a tiny Christmas tree. It had been a bitter year, but its days were numbered. I poured Vodka into our glasses and we said "skol" to each other.

46

A TAILWIND MADE THE PLANE ARRIVE in Shannon an hour earlier than scheduled and, of course there was no Peter at the airport. It was seven in the morning. He had told me that John Huston's place was not far from Shannon but, as it turned out, it was near Dublin. When I finally got Peter on the phone he said he had not expected me so early. "Take a taxi," he advised, grandly. Obediently I did as he said and indeed I greatly enjoyed my ride; but it took more than three hours. How green the country was, even at this time of the year. It was raining and my driver, a talkative old man, happy to have a passenger who was a stranger in Ireland, enumerated all the members of his family who had emigrated to the United States. Most of them lived in New York but no money in the world would make him live in that city. Enchanted with the lilting cadence of his speech, the hard rr's and the clear vowels, I agreed with him.

The huge, gray mansion which John Huston had rented was crowded with guests. Peter embraced me, and introduced the very lovely Bettina, a lost soul among the hunters, writers, John's assistants and secretaries. The occasion for the gathering was Tim Durant's marriage to an American divorcée, which had been planned to take place during the meet, with everyone on horseback. It had to be postponed, because a few days before a woman had been killed riding to hounds and there were six weeks of mourning. Ricky, Huston's beautiful wife, was an emphatically gracious hostess, while he divided his day between horses and working on a screenplay with Peter. In spite of the mourning, everyone was very cheerful.

I liked Bettina: she was, as Jigee had written, "utterly adorable." She told me that she had been trying for weeks, with the help of a dictionary, to read Peter's novel, *The Canyon*. Peter looked well, his book *White Hunter, Black Heart*, had just appeared and although the fascinating hero was modeled on John Huston, it had not disturbed their friendship. He had arranged with Irwin Shaw, who was in Klosters, that I surprise Jigee on New Year's Eve at a party in the Chesa Grischuna. There was not enough time left to visit Hans in London, but he was expecting me later, on my way back to the States, when we would spend more time together. So, on December 30 I flew from Dublin to Paris to embrace the Achards and Pozners. Then, the next morning, I boarded the train to Klosters.

During the two days in Dublin I had hardly slept, and the brief hours in Paris were exhausting. The transition from America to Ireland had been too abrupt, too sudden. Dublin was as Joyce had described it—or did I imagine that? I promised myself to explore it the next time I went there. Meanwhile, the train was carrying me to Klosters, which I could hardly find on the map, and it seemed to take the longest time. My heart was pounding and I had a steady humming in my ears. The windows were covered with frost, the countryside invisible. All the compartments were packed with people in ski-pants and parkas, and from Basle on, the German sounded so foreign that I could not understand a word. It was like a traumatic recurrence of my *Gastspiel* in Zurich, when in the thick fog I could not find the theater.

It was dark when I changed into the Klosters/Davos train, which was so crowded that I had to stand between two broad-shouldered skiers, and every time the train took a curve I bumped into one of them. They did not seem to mind. Everyone was elated because it had been snowing for a week. The train stopped often, and at each station more skiers got on. One of the men I had been leaning on pointed to a just vacated seat, and I was starting toward it when a lady, who had overheard me mention that I was getting off at Klosters, said that Klosters was the next stop and the train would halt for only three minutes. I extricated myself from the embrace of the two skiers, who helped me to find my suitcases and I got off into the coldest, purest air, which cut my breath. Hundreds of people were on the platform but no porter in sight. Then I heard a scream: "Salka, Salka!" and Jigee in ski-pants and a black anorak pushed through the crowd and crying and laughing, we clung to each other. The next minute, Irwin Shaw, suntanned, bursting with vitality and more dear than ever, embraced me. He had told Jigee that some of his friends were arriving and suggested she go with him to the station. As she was utterly unaware of who was coming, the surprise worked even better than planned.

Of course, the first thing I wanted was to see Christine. But Jigee insisted that my first hours in Klosters belonged to her. "Once you have seen Christine we will all cease to exist." She refused to take me home. Vicky had gone to a party with school-friends and we could talk undisturbed at the Hotel Chesa Grischuna. We walked there in the starlit winter night, the snow crunching under our feet. I had not seen such a night and so much snow since my childhood.

Irwin left. We would see him and Marian later at the New Year's party in the Chesa. I realized that the Chesa was the center of Klosters's social activities. Jigee only permitted me to wash my face and hands, but would not let me change. We sat down in a corner of the empty restaurant. It was in the Swiss style, paneled with carved wood, elegant and comfortable. The owner, Mrs. Guler, a young, handsome woman, said that there was no room in the hotel, but invited me to spend the night in her own place. Peter had informed her about my coming and she had reserved a room for me in the Hotel Weisskreuz, only a few steps from the Chesa, but it would not be free until the next day.

She left us, and Jigee and I began our marathon talk, constantly interrupted by laughter and tears. Things we could not say in our letters poured out without restraint. I could not help noticing that she had made a certain image of herself, which was quite at odds with reality. She was full of contradictions but insisted upon her consistency. She had written me that she lived in Klosters because she loved skiing, but it came out that she hardly ever went on the slopes because she could not stand the cold. But this was unimportant. She could not accept that Peter, who had passionately loved her, had fallen in love with someone else. It was useless to remind her that she herself had not been immune from falling in love. She only felt her own suffering and refused to admit having ever inflicted it upon others. But Peter was very generous toward her and she wanted his friendship. She knew that the right solution for her was to go back to the States and start a new life, but she had no intention of doing so.

The restaurant had filled with people in evening clothes, and in our pullovers, and with our tearful eyes, we looked quite out of place. Marian and Irwin, Anatol Litvak, Robert Capa, Jigee's British friend Colette Harrison, embraced me. Chic people from Hollywood and New York greeted me, but everything was unreal and scrambled, like in a kaleidoscope. At midnight, the lights went off, then on again, and the old year was gone. Jigee and I were crying again. She lifted her glass: "To Vicky and Christine and to Peter, Hans and Tommy." Then Irwin and Marian clicked glasses with us, also Capa, with surprising tenderness. By then my reactions became more and more automatic and when Doris Guler finally came and offered to take me home, I clung to her like a drowning man to a lifebelt.

The white glare outside the window woke me. I was lying in a spotlessly white bed in a charming bedroom in a completely silent house. I looked out of the window; everything was covered with snow, huge mounds of snow, and not a soul to be seen. It was eight. I took a bath, dressed and went out. As I passed the Chesa Grischuna I saw that it was open and went in to get breakfast. I wanted to kill time until I could see Christine. Jigee had told me that she would be up at nine. The Chesa was spic and span and no one could have guessed that a large crowd had been dancing there until the early morning hours. Four sedate, pipe-smoking Swiss sat at a table, drinking red wine and playing cards. I had my cup of coffee and a croissant, then asked a pretty waitress in a Grisons costume if she knew how I could get to Frau Viertel's house. I had noticed that Jigee was very popular at the Chesa. The waitress described the way: I only had to cross the bridge over the river and walk to the last house at the end of the village, before the road turned uphill.

It was a perfect winter morning—almost too perfect, too much like a picture postcard. The sky incredibly clear and blue, the high mountains surrounding the valley not threatening at all, and everything white, white, dazzlingly white, the branches of the firs bending under the loads of snow. A river flowed through the valley which, to the east, was closed by the Silvretta glacier, transparent and glittering like a huge bluish crystal. Scattered on both sides of the river were chalets and farmhouses, neat and well-kept, many old ones weather-beaten but stately.

I passed the Hotel Weisskreuz, where my luggage was just being unloaded, then the Silvretta Hotel, from which American skiers were loudly emerging, and continued through the village street. From the stables on the ground floor of the old wooden houses came steaming warmth and the smell of cows; I heard their low mooing. Then I saw the house where Jigee lived. I could hardly breathe and felt like crying. "It's the altitude," I told myself.

The house was old, 1773 was engraved over its door, and Jigee's apartment, "Ferienwohnung" they called it, was on the ground floor. In front of the house was a child's sleigh with a blanket, ready to go for a ride. The door was open and I went in. I found myself in a dark hall. After a while I discerned a big tile stove in which a good fire was burning. I could hear whispering behind a door, which I approached on tiptoe and opened. In a spacious kitchen, warm and light, a beautiful young woman was sitting at a large table eating her breakfast, while a very small, delicate creature, in a dirndl dress and white apron, was pulling a toy wagon with a teddybear in it. She trod loudly on the floor with her sturdy shoes and the young woman was shooshing her. She stood still when she saw me. I called: "Christine!" She came toward me slowly, stopping now and then, smiling with her blue eyes, which had Berthold's dark lashes. Her hair was light blond, like Peter's when he was her age. I picked her up and held her while she looked me over very seriously, touched my white hair cautiously, then, with gleeful laughter, buried both hands in it. A tidal wave of tenderness and love engulfed my incorrigible heart.

AFTERWORD

SALKA VIERTEL CHOSE to end her memoir at a hopeful moment, on New Year's Day of 1954. With her habitual optimism she described a sunny morning in the Swiss resort town of Klosters, in which she first met her two-year-old granddaughter, Christine. Salka was then in her vigorous mid-sixties and ready to fall in love again. And fall she did, giving away her heart to the little girl who resembled both Salka's middle son, Peter, and Salka herself. She confessed in her diary several years later that "without Christine I don't know how I can live."

The following spring, unable to pay the mortgage on her beloved home in Santa Monica, Salka sold it to her old friend John Houseman. She never stopped regretting her surrender of the house, the "port of entry," as she described it, through which so many of Hitler's traumatized exiles had crossed to safety in America. Without a home Salka was as untethered as the thousands for whom she had cared. Her next seven years were given to itinerancy as she helped to raise her granddaughter, following Christine and Christine's mother, Jigee Viertel, back to California, then to Manhattan in 1956, then back to California again in 1958.

All the while Salka continued to hustle for television and screenwriting jobs in the States and abroad, venturing to Munich in early 1956 for story conferences. She earned credits on two more pictures, both European productions: *Loves of Three Queens* starring Hedy Lamarr (1954) and *Prisoner of the Volga* (1959).

The money Salka earned was not enough to remain solvent, much less to provide for others as she had done during her Metro-Goldwyn-Mayer heyday. In the end it was her dwindling finances, combined with a family tragedy, that propelled her out of Los Angeles and toward her final exile in the Swiss Alps.

The tragedy came on the heels of Peter's failed marriage to Jigee. He had fallen in love with the British actress Deborah Kerr and pressured Jigee into a divorce. Heartbroken, and unable to combat an addiction to alcohol and sleeping pills, Jigee lapsed into near incapacitation. Late one night in mid-December 1959, in the bathroom of her rented house in Pacific Palisades, while fumbling to light a cigarette Jigee set her nylon nightgown on fire. Suffering massive burns, she lingered in the hospital for five weeks and died on February 1, 1960, at age forty-four.

Immediately Peter arranged for eight-year-old Christine to join his and Kerr's household in Klosters. Salka went along reluctantly, too deeply invested in Christine's welfare to abandon her. She moved into a little apartment above a butcher shop, not far from the town center, and began to settle into a vastly new life. Almost as quickly, Christine was sent off to boarding school in England, returning only for brief holidays and dashing Salka's hopes of influencing her granddaughter's upbringing.

But even in Alpine exile, Salka's life over the next eighteen years was filled, as always, with visitors. Klosters came alive during the Christmas season, bringing old Hollywood friends and many movie stars who gathered at the town's most charming hotel, the Chesa Grischuna. In the late summers Greta Garbo came for weeks at a time, staying in a nearby apartment and walking with Salka through the hills and meadows. Salka herself traveled extensively throughout Europe and several times back to the States, where she was delighted to meet two more grandchildren: Valérie, born in 1952 to Salka's son Hans and his wife, Violette; and Andrew, born in 1973 to her son Tom and his wife, Ruth.

In these years Salka also devoted herself to writing, tackling draft after draft of her memoir, which after many rejections was published in April 1969 by a perspicacious young editor at Holt, Rinehart & Winston named Tom Wallace. She had hoped to produce a second volume and maybe even a novel, but over the next nine years her health declined as she bore the indignities of deafness and Parkinson's disease. She died in Klosters on October 26, 1978, and was buried in the small cemetery behind the Protestant church. For years thereafter, Garbo continued to vacation in Klosters during the summers as an homage to her closest friend.

In Salka's eighty-nine years, she left behind no monuments. That is the privilege of men. Instead she left this magnificent record of a grand and global life, lived with drama, *Zivilcourage*, and compassion.

—DONNA RIFKIND

OTHER NEW YORK REVIEW CLASSICS

For a complete list of titles, visit www.nyrb.com or write to:
Catalog Requests, NYRB, 435 Hudson Street, New York, NY 10014

Also available as an electronic book.